AA

COUNTRY WALKS
in Britain

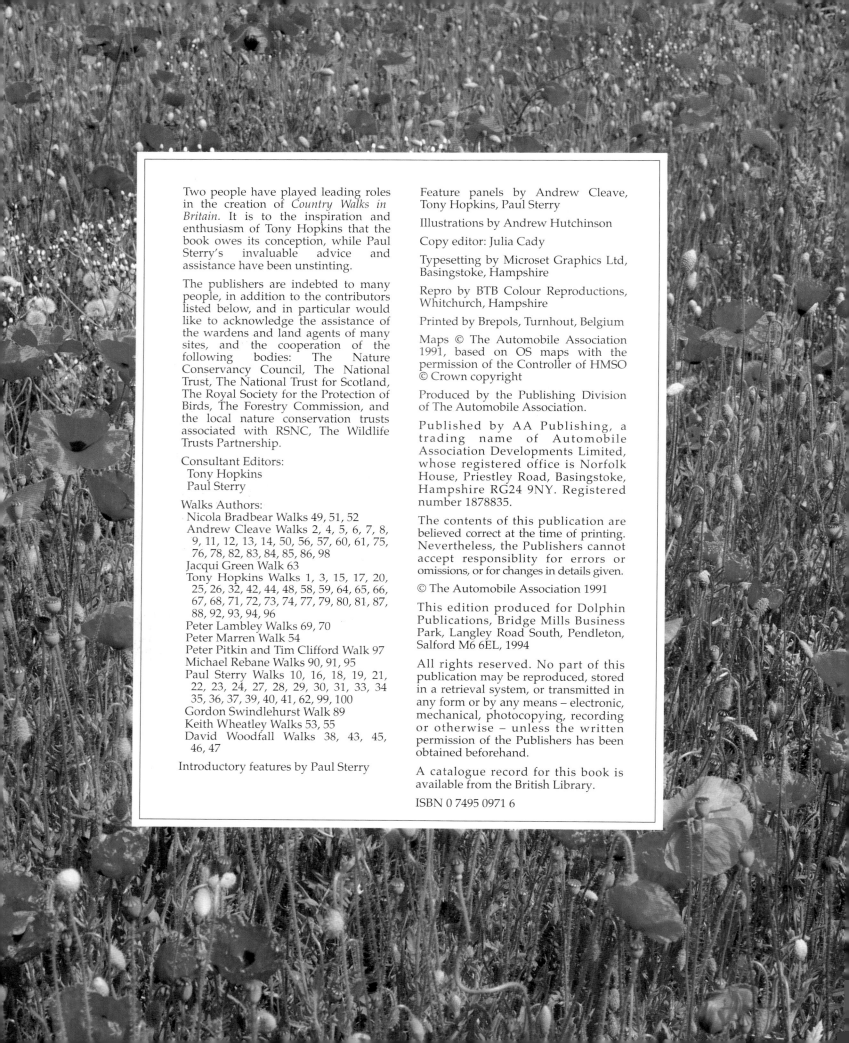

Two people have played leading roles in the creation of *Country Walks in Britain*. It is to the inspiration and enthusiasm of Tony Hopkins that the book owes its conception, while Paul Sterry's invaluable advice and assistance have been unstinting.

The publishers are indebted to many people, in addition to the contributors listed below, and in particular would like to acknowledge the assistance of the wardens and land agents of many sites, and the cooperation of the following bodies: The Nature Conservancy Council, The National Trust, The National Trust for Scotland, The Royal Society for the Protection of Birds, The Forestry Commission, and the local nature conservation trusts associated with RSNC, The Wildlife Trusts Partnership.

Consultant Editors:
 Tony Hopkins
 Paul Sterry

Walks Authors:
 Nicola Bradbear Walks 49, 51, 52
 Andrew Cleave Walks 2, 4, 5, 6, 7, 8, 9, 11, 12, 13, 14, 50, 56, 57, 60, 61, 75, 76, 78, 82, 83, 84, 85, 86, 98
 Jacqui Green Walk 63
 Tony Hopkins Walks 1, 3, 15, 17, 20, 25, 26, 32, 42, 44, 48, 58, 59, 64, 65, 66, 67, 68, 71, 72, 73, 74, 77, 79, 80, 81, 87, 88, 92, 93, 94, 96
 Peter Lambley Walks 69, 70
 Peter Marren Walk 54
 Peter Pitkin and Tim Clifford Walk 97
 Michael Rebane Walks 90, 91, 95
 Paul Sterry Walks 10, 16, 18, 19, 21, 22, 23, 24, 27, 28, 29, 30, 31, 33, 34, 35, 36, 37, 39, 40, 41, 62, 99, 100
 Gordon Swindlehurst Walk 89
 Keith Wheatley Walks 53, 55
 David Woodfall Walks 38, 43, 45, 46, 47

Introductory features by Paul Sterry

Feature panels by Andrew Cleave, Tony Hopkins, Paul Sterry

Illustrations by Andrew Hutchinson

Copy editor: Julia Cady

Typesetting by Microset Graphics Ltd, Basingstoke, Hampshire

Repro by BTB Colour Reproductions, Whitchurch, Hampshire

Printed by Brepols, Turnhout, Belgium

Maps © The Automobile Association 1991, based on OS maps with the permission of the Controller of HMSO © Crown copyright

Produced by the Publishing Division of The Automobile Association.

Published by AA Publishing, a trading name of Automobile Association Developments Limited, whose registered office is Norfolk House, Priestley Road, Basingstoke, Hampshire RG24 9NY. Registered number 1878835.

Contents

MAP AND LIST
OF WALKS

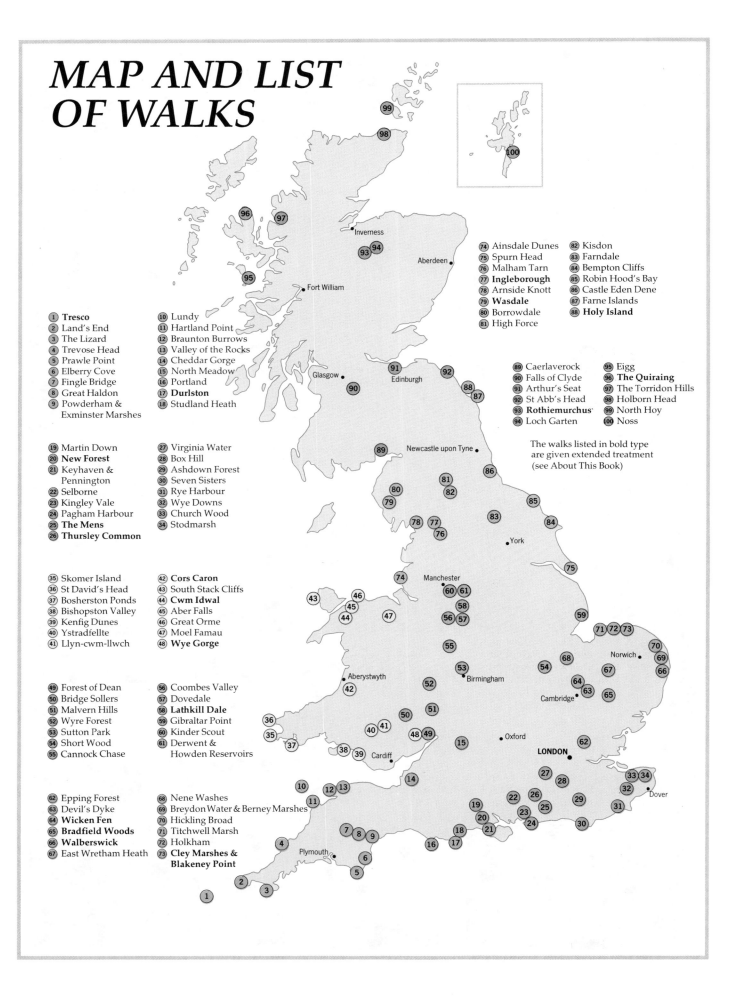

Inverness

Aberdeen

Fort William

Glasgow

Edinburgh

Newcastle upon Tyne

York

Manchester

Norwich

Birmingham

Aberystwyth

Cambridge

Oxford

LONDON

Cardiff

Dover

Plymouth

① **Tresco**
② Land's End
③ The Lizard
④ Trevose Head
⑤ Prawle Point
⑥ Elberry Cove
⑦ Fingle Bridge
⑧ Great Haldon
⑨ Powderham &
   Exminster Marshes

⑩ Lundy
⑪ Hartland Point
⑫ Braunton Burrows
⑬ Valley of the Rocks
⑭ Cheddar Gorge
⑮ North Meadow
⑯ Portland
⑰ **Durlston**
⑱ Studland Heath

⑲ Martin Down
⑳ **New Forest**
㉑ Keyhaven &
   Pennington
㉒ Selborne
㉓ Kingley Vale
㉔ Pagham Harbour
㉕ **The Mens**
㉖ **Thursley Common**

㉗ Virginia Water
㉘ Box Hill
㉙ Ashdown Forest
㉚ Seven Sisters
㉛ Rye Harbour
㉜ Wye Downs
㉝ Church Wood
㉞ Stodmarsh

㉟ Skomer Island
㊱ St David's Head
㊲ Bosherston Ponds
㊳ Bishopston Valley
㊴ Kenfig Dunes
㊵ Ystradfellte
㊶ Llyn-cwm-llwch

㊷ **Cors Caron**
㊸ South Stack Cliffs
㊹ **Cwm Idwal**
㊺ Aber Falls
㊻ Great Orme
㊼ Moel Famau
㊽ **Wye Gorge**

㊾ Forest of Dean
㊿ Bridge Sollers
51 Malvern Hills
52 Wyre Forest
53 Sutton Park
54 Short Wood
55 Cannock Chase

56 Coombes Valley
57 Dovedale
58 **Lathkill Dale**
59 Gibraltar Point
60 Kinder Scout
61 Derwent &
   Howden Reservoirs

62 Epping Forest
63 Devil's Dyke
64 **Wicken Fen**
65 **Bradfield Woods**
66 **Walberswick**
67 East Wretham Heath

68 Nene Washes
69 Breydon Water & Berney Marshes
70 Hickling Broad
71 Titchwell Marsh
72 Holkham
73 **Cley Marshes &
   Blakeney Point**

74 Ainsdale Dunes
75 Spurn Head
76 Malham Tarn
77 **Ingleborough**
78 Arnside Knott
79 **Wasdale**
80 Borrowdale
81 High Force

82 Kisdon
83 Farndale
84 Bempton Cliffs
85 Robin Hood's Bay
86 Castle Eden Dene
87 Farne Islands
88 **Holy Island**

89 Caerlaverock
90 Falls of Clyde
91 Arthur's Seat
92 St Abb's Head
93 **Rothiemurchus**
94 Loch Garten

95 Eigg
96 **The Quiraing**
97 The Torridon Hills
98 Holborn Head
99 North Hoy
100 Noss

The walks listed in bold type
are given extended treatment
(see About This Book)

ABOUT THIS BOOK

All the routes in this book have been carefully researched and written by experienced walks authors, and every effort has been taken to ensure accuracy. However, the landscape can change and features mentioned as landmarks may alter or disappear completely. The changing seasons also greatly affect the appearance of the walks, and paths may become overgrown during the summer months. It is of great importance to note also that some of the routes pass close to dangerous features in the landscape and need care, especially if children are in the party. For some walks, particular attention should be paid to weather conditions, especially where change can be sudden. Wherever possible, such hazards are highlighted in the text. See also Comfort and Safety, page 8.

HOW THE BOOK WORKS

The walks are numbered 1 to 100 and can be located by referring to the map on page 4. The walks listed on page 4 in bold type are, because they are for one reason or another very special sites, given extended treatment. Walks are arranged in the following regional order: South-west England, South-east England, Wales, Central England, East Anglia, the North of England, Scotland.

The ring-binder enables walkers to remove a particular page and carry it on the walk with them. A protective plastic cover is included for this purpose.

Each walk provides details of location and parking, site ownership or management where relevant, highlights to look out for, and other nearby sites of interest; there is an introduction to the site with a description of its habitat and specialities, a map of the route, walk directions and sometimes a short feature on a subject of particular interest.

PARKING

Individual parking details are given in the information section of each walk. If no distinct car park exists, walkers should park carefully and considerately where they can. Please remember that it is an offence to park in such a way that your car obstructs the highway, and a landowner can sue for damages if a car is parked on his land without permission. Remember, too, that whatever the time of day or year, farm vehicles must always have clear access to field entrances and tracks.

MAPPING

All maps are orientated north but are shown at different scales. Refer to the scale bar on each map.

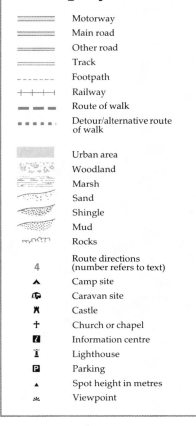

Map Symbols

═══════	Motorway
══════	Main road
──────	Other road
──────	Track
------	Footpath
+‑+‑+‑+	Railway
▬ ▬ ▬	Route of walk
▪ ▪ ▪ ▪	Detour/alternative route of walk
▨	Urban area
ᗺᗺᗺ	Woodland
≈≈≈	Marsh
⁀⁀⁀	Sand
⬮⬮⬮	Shingle
◠◠◠	Mud
ᘓᘓ	Rocks
4	Route directions (number refers to text)
⌂	Camp site
⊞	Caravan site
♜	Castle
†	Church or chapel
ℤ	Information centre
ᵎ	Lighthouse
℗	Parking
▲	Spot height in metres
⬩	Viewpoint

GRID REFERENCES

The National Grid references given in the information panel for each walk are for the car park (or, in the case of islands, the ferry landing point). The National Grid covers Britain with an imaginary network of 100km squares, each of which is identified by two letters eg, TR.

Each square is sub-divided into 10km squares, which in turn are sub-divided into 1km squares, as on the larger-scale Ordnance Survey maps (1:50,000 and 1:25,000) that walkers may like to use in addition to the maps in this book.

The first two figures of the initial group of three figures in the grid references in this book relate to the grid lines running from left to right across the Ordnance Survey 1:50,000 and 1:25,000 maps, numbered at the

bottom and top of each sheet. The third figure tells you the distance to move in tenths across the square to the right of each of these. Similarly, the first two figures of the second group of three figures refer to the numbered grid lines running from bottom to top of the map and the third figure indicates the distance to move in tenths above this line. The intersection is the location of the place in question.

USEFUL ADDRESSES

The majority of sites mentioned in this book come under the umbrella of the following bodies (acknowledged in the information panel for each walk). They may be contacted, at the addresses given, for any further information required.

Forestry Commission
231 Corstorphine Road
Edinburgh EH12 7AT

National Trust
36 Queen Anne's Gate
London SW1H 9AS

National Trust for Scotland
5 Charlotte Square
Edinburgh EH2 4DU

Nature Conservancy Council (NCC)
During the course of 1991 the Nature Conservancy Council ceased to exist. It has been replaced by three new agencies:

English Nature (The Nature Conservancy Council for England)
Northminster House
Peterborough
Cambridgeshire PE1 1UA

The Nature Conservancy Council for Scotland
12 Hope Terrace
Edinburgh EH9 2AS

The Countryside Council for Wales
Plas Penrhos
Ffordd Penrhos
Bangor
Gwynedd LL57 2LQ

RSNC, The Wildlife Trusts Partnership (incorporating the local Wildlife, Naturalists and Nature Conservation Trusts)
The Green
Witham Park
Waterside South
Lincoln LN5 7JR

Royal Society for the Protection of Birds (RSPB)
The Lodge
Sandy
Bedfordshire SG19 2DL

NATIONAL POWER AND WILDLIFE

Although the primary role of National Power is to generate electricity for the nation, it also has a commitment, as a major company and landowner, and as a neighbour in the local community, both to conserve areas of ecological interest wherever this is practicable and to create new habitats to replace those which may be lost during the development of power station sites. Numbered among its staff are environmental scientists who monitor and advise on this policy, the implementation of which is often carried out in collaboration with national and regional conservation bodies.

Throughout England and Wales, power stations are wildlife havens where plants and animals, some relatively rare, can, with little human disturbance, thrive in copses and plantations, ponds and marshes, meadows and pastures.

As a responsible industry and landowner, National Power uses the expertise of its environmental scientists to maintain the ecological value of these areas. Access to the sites is carefully controlled, not only for obvious reasons of safety, but also to keep the numbers of visitors to a level that causes minimum disturbance to the wildlife.

National Power's team of environmental scientists also fulfil another role; areas of wildlife interest have actually been created – ponds, meadows and woodlands – on areas of land previously disturbed, either during the building of the power station or by earlier activities. Despite these seemingly unpromising begin-

The Nature of National Power

On many of National Power's power station sites, nature reserves and nature trails have been developed to allow appreciation and study of the wildlife. Although these sites are not open to the general public, school parties and groups interested in natural history are welcome by prior arrangement.

For further information on National Power's environment programmes, please contact: The Manager, Environmental Information Services, National Power, Sudbury House, 15 Newgate Street, London EC1A 7AU

Roesel's bush cricket, seen at Tilbury

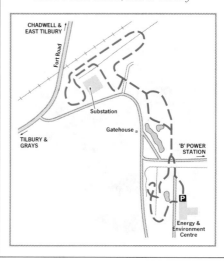

nings, considerable wildlife interest can develop within a few years, with plants and animals moving in from the surrounding countryside.

On some of the power station sites,

National Power has developed nature trails and information centres staffed by full-time wardens, where school parties and other organised groups with an interest in natural history (including the blind and disabled, on some sites) can come to study local wildlife. Four of the best locations are at Tilbury, Padiham, Thorpe Marsh and Rugeley.

TILBURY

Tilbury, the newest of National Power's wildlife and conservation projects, has an energy and environmental centre as well as a nature trail. The power station is sited at Grays in Essex on the northern shores of the Thames estuary and is flanked by coastal grazing marsh, a habitat much threatened by development. The site features freshwater marsh, reed-beds, drainage channels and a newly created lake, and is visited by parties of children from primary school age to sixth-form colleges as well as adult groups with an interest in natural history or energy.

The delicate, white star-like flowers of greater stitchwort appear in April

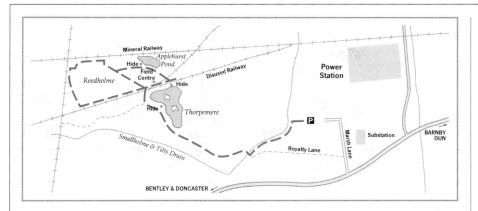

Above: *Hogweed at Padiham*
Left: *Field bindweed*

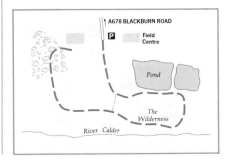

THORPE MARSH

The nature reserve at *Thorpe Marsh*, near Doncaster in South Yorkshire, developed in collaboration with the Yorkshire Wildlife Trust and Yorkshire County Council, is one of the longest-established of the National Power sites. It comprises a large area of unimproved pasture together with two large ponds – havens for wildfowl and other water birds – marshes and a disused railway embankment. The nature trail has six hides overlooking the ponds and some parts of the reserve are suitable for blind and disabled groups.

PADIHAM

Padiham power station lies close to the River Calder between Blackburn and Burnley in Lancashire. The land between the site and the river has been transformed into a wildlife area and nature trail and an information centre allows visiting groups from local schools to interpret and study the plants and animals which abound here.

RUGELEY

Rugeley power station lies between Rugeley and Lichfield in Staffordshire. Visiting parties of school children can follow a nature trail and explore wildflower meadows, a newly created wood and arboretum, and the borrowpit lake; the lake is stocked with fish and attracts large numbers of water birds. Over 5,000 visitors visited the centre in 1989 and activities included projects on mathematics, English, geography and art, as well as natural history and ecology.

Small Tortoiseshell butterfly

A Peak District walker reads up on what's ahead while taking a break for refreshment

COMFORT AND SAFETY

Careful planning is one of the keys to making the most of a walk in the countryside. If possible, read about the area before your visit, to get a 'feel' for the location, and consider carefully what you will need to ensure your comfort and safety.

Clothing

The right footwear is extremely important. For most of the walks in this book, tough, stout-soled shoes are essential for crossing rough terrain.

Try to dress in layers which can be taken off or put on according to the changing weather. You will soon warm up when walking but it is easy to become chilled when you stop. Lightweight, waterproof anoraks and overtrousers are a good idea since they can be packed away in rucksacks.

Safety and Peace of Mind

When walking one of the more challenging routes in this book, it is a good idea to take an Ordnance Survey map of the area with you, in addition to the route directions given in the book. Usually the most appropriate map will be one of the 1:50,000 series where 1¼ inches on the map corresponds to 1 mile on the walk (or 2cm corresponds to 1km). They can be used together with a compass to help get your bearings and are invaluable when walking in hills or mountains.

You should always carry food and drink to last a whole day; on the more demanding walks, a supply of glucose tablets as an energy supplement and a simple first-aid kit are advisable. A torch and a whistle should be carried when hill- or mountain-walking – the recognised emergency signal is six blasts repeated every minute. Before you set out, consider how long the walk may take, bearing in mind your own stamina and any breaks in the walk you may want to take. If possible, walk with a friend: this not only provides company but also means that there will be someone to raise the alarm in the event of an emergency.

Many of the walks in this book are around the coast. Although the routes are designed to ensure safety, a few points should be borne in mind.

Although exciting places to visit, cliffs are always potentially dangerous. Stay well away from the edge because the cliff-top soil is often loose and slippery, even though plants may be growing in profusion; there may also be an overhang.

Before venturing on to the seashore, it is essential to be aware of the state of the tide; this can be determined by consulting a local tide timetable. On shallow beaches, a rising tide can rush in at an alarming speed and there is always the danger of being cut off. When the seas are rough, always stay well away from the waves. Freak waves appear from time to time and could, under extreme circumstances, sweep you off your feet.

PHOTOGRAPHY

As 35mm cameras become increasingly popular, more and more people are recording what they see on their walks in the countryside. The following tips may be useful for beginners.

Films

Try a few different films and then, having found one that suits your needs, stick with it. A film speed of 64 ASA for slide film and 100 ASA for print film is usually adequate. As a general rule, the slower the film speed, the better its definition.

Lenses

35mm cameras are generally supplied with a standard lens (focal length 50mm) which records more or less the same field of view as the human eye. Smaller focal-length lenses are called *wide-angle* lenses and include a greater field of view; they are useful if you want to capture an expansive landscape, but will cause some distortion such as a curved horizon.

Lenses with a focal length greater than 50mm magnify a smaller area and lenses of 200mm or more are generally referred to as *telephoto* lenses. They are particularly useful for photographing birds and mammals where it is often difficult to get close to the subject. However, they suffer from the disadvantage of being rather heavy and can be almost impossible to hand-hold. A tripod then becomes useful, although some people compensate by using faster film.

Macro lenses allow close focusing and are particularly useful for subjects such as plants and insects. Before you buy a macro lens, check that it allows a magnification of 1:2 (image size on film: image size in real life) at minimum focus – not all lenses focus this close. As a cheaper alternative, extension rings can be fitted between an ordinary lens and the camera body. Although they allow a good image size to be achieved, the distance over which you can focus is restricted.

Taking the Picture

Composing a photograph is an extremely subjective matter but a few guidelines may help:
– make sure that your horizon is straight (this is not always as easy as it sounds)
– try to have an interesting feature in the foreground
– remember to use your depth of field preview to check how much of the view is in focus. If light conditions are poor and you have to use a slow shutter speed (less than 1/30th second) to get a good depth of field, you should consider using a tripod
– in general it is best to shoot with the sun behind you unless you are deliberately aiming for contrast and silhouettes.

BIRDWATCHING

A golden eagle and its young, spotted on their mountain ledge eyrie

Sooner or later everyone who walks in the countryside notices birds. While many people are happy for this interest to remain casual, some would like to develop a more serious interest in birdwatching.

Binoculars

These are *the* essential piece of equipment for the birdwatcher. They help in accurate identification and reveal plumage details which are invisible at a distance.

The range of sizes and prices can be bewildering. Each model has two specification numbers, such as 8x30 or 10x40. The first number refers to the magnification of the binoculars and the second to the diameter in millimetres of the binoculars' exit lens (the greater the number, the brighter the view).

For general use on country walks, binoculars must be light, compact and waterproof. For bird and wildlife spotting, image sharpness and portability are important factors.

– Look at compact models, such as 6x15, 8x23 and 10x25. Standard models, such as the 8x40 and 9x30, are also worth considering. If you need a very rugged or rainproof model, look at the rubber-armoured and waterproof designs.
– Make sure the lenses are glass, preferably coated on all surfaces to reduce flare and maximise the brightness of the image.
– Hold the binoculars about a foot (30cm) away from the eye and check that there is a bright, perfect circle of light in the centre of the eyepiece. If, instead, you see a square of light, the prism of the binoculars is of insufficient size, improper material or imperfect adjustment.

Books

Most birdwatchers use a field guide of one sort or another. Choose one to suit your level of proficiency – some cover only British birds, while others include birds from the whole of Europe.

Birdwatching in Practice

Since birds are often wary of man, one of the first problems faced by the bird-watcher is actually getting good views of them. Try using natural cover to disguise your outline; some of the sites in this book have specially designed hides and in reserves the birds may become accustomed to humans.

If you sit quietly and avoid sudden movements or sounds, birds will often come quite close, even though they are aware of your presence. A favoured feeding spot on a muddy lake margin, the edge of a salt-marsh or a quiet woodland ride may provide excellent opportunities for close observation. Seabird cliffs are also very rewarding, the birds often being surprisingly tolerant of people. However, remember never to venture too close – both for your own safety and to avoid distressing the birds – and try to look *along* the cliff at the birds rather than vertically downwards.

THE COUNTRY CODE

Ultimately, the continuing survival of our beautiful landscape and its varied wildlife depends on our attitude towards it. This applies both to land-owners and land-users, and to minimise conflict between the two the voluntary Country Code should be adhered to.
– Avoid damage to fences, gates and walls.
– Always close fences and gates to prevent livestock escaping.
– Keep to footpaths and other rights of way. Avoid causing damage to crops.
– Respect other people's property. Farm machinery must not be touched.
– Keep dogs under control and if necessary keep them on a lead. Rampaging dogs pose a serious threat to farm livestock, to deer, especially when they have young, and to other wild mammals, as well as ground-nesting and ground-feeding birds.
– Do not leave litter and especially do not discard lighted cigarettes, matches or anything else that could cause a fire.
– Drive slowly and safely in the country. Always assume that there might be a herd of cows or a stationary tractor round the next bend.
– When walking on country roads keep to the right, in single file.

WILDLIFE AND THE LAW

Wood anemones – don't pick them

In order to protect our wildlife and to help ensure its survival for future generations, the Wildlife and Country-side Act of 1981 protects by law some of our most endangered species. In general, the views of most responsible walkers and ramblers would be in accord with the legislation but a brief summary may be of interest.

Wild Flowers

It is illegal to uproot any wild plant without the permission of the land-owner and more than 60 species are further protected from picking, sale or collection of seed. These most vulnerable species include many of our orchids as well as other less showy flowers. The best policy for ramblers is not to pick any wild flowers.

Birds

It is illegal to kill, injure or take any wild bird as well as to take or destroy the nest or eggs of any species. There are certain exceptions to the Act which enable, for example, landowners to control certain 'pest' species, or permit bird ringers, under licence, to trap and ring birds for study. It is also illegal to disturb certain particularly vulnerable (Schedule 1) species whilst nest build-ing, brooding or caring for young. This applies even to photography of these species at the nest without a licence. For further details and a current list of Schedule 1 birds, consult a copy of the Act or contact the NCC (see page 5).

Other Wildlife

Many of our threatened mammals are protected from disturbance or injury and these include all species of bats and shrews as well as badgers and dormice. Invertebrates too are covered by the Act and several species of butterfly, moth, beetle, dragonfly and cricket have protection.

BRITAIN'S PRINCIPAL HABITATS

THE COAST

Puffins, both comical and colourful

Both for scenic beauty and for wildlife interest, the British coastline is outstanding. It has everything from towering cliffs to shallow estuaries, shingle beaches and sand dunes. The variety of richness in both habitat and wildlife is often stunning and, whatever the season, there is always something to see.

Cliffs

Sea cliffs never fail to be dramatic. The views are often exhilarating and spectacular and the full force of the sea can be truly appreciated. From April until July, some of our cliffs are home to vast numbers of breeding seabirds and several of the walks in this book visit excellent sites. Although these are

The chalk cliffs of the Seven Sisters

generally in the north and west of Britain, there are exceptions: Bempton Cliffs and St Abb's Head, on the east coast, for example.

Watch a seabird colony even for a short time and it soon becomes apparent that each species has its own special nesting requirements. Razorbills prefer crevices and boulders close to the sea; shags and fulmars nest on broad ledges; while kittiwakes and guillemots are often densely packed on narrow ledges overhanging sheer drops. Puffins dig burrows into the grassy slopes higher up the cliffs, while herring gulls and lesser black-backed gulls are found in loose colonies among the tussocks of vegetation.

Wildlife interest on the cliffs is not confined to birds by any means. Grey seals are found off the west and north coasts of Britain and porpoises may be seen off the Shetland Isles. During May and June in particular, slopes and rocky outcrops are often ablaze with colourful coastal flowers. Thrift or sea pink is especially prominent and grows alongside sea campion, scurvy-grass and English stonecrop. The underlying rock often has a profound influence on the flowers that grow inland from the cliff edge. At Land's End, the Lizard and St David's Head, where the rock is rather acidic, a maritime heath has developed, made up of several species of heather, gorse and dwarf gorse. Where the rock is base-rich (chalk or limestone), as at St Aldhelm's Head and the Seven Sisters, a rich chalk or limestone flora can be found.

Estuaries and Mudflats

Estuaries and mudflats, which are found all around our coast, provide wonderful opportunities for wildlife observation throughout the year. During the summer, the flora is colourful, and at other seasons both winter visitors and vast numbers of migrant birds – our estuaries are important staging posts – enjoy these rich feeding grounds. Common seals are an added attraction to some east coast estuaries.

One of the most conspicuous birds of the coast is the redshank. Often called 'the sentinels of the marsh', these red-legged waders are alert and quick to utter their loud alarm call. This brings potential danger to the attention of other wading birds such as dunlins, ringed plovers, grey plovers, knots, curlews and godwits. Shelducks are conspicuous mudflat inhabitants, together with teal and wigeon. In some areas, they feed alongside brent geese, which are winter visitors to south- and east-coast estuaries from their breeding grounds in the high Arctic. All these birds visit our estuaries to feed: huge concentrations of invertebrate life – molluscs and crustaceans in particular – live in the surface layers of the mud.

With time, mudflats become colonised by specialist plants that gradually consolidate the shifting substrata. Sea purslane, salt-marsh grasses and glasswort are among the first to appear, soon to be followed by seablite, sea-lavender, sea aster and golden samphire. In some south-coast estuaries, the last three species provide amazing displays of colour during July and August.

Beaches and Sand Dunes

One of the glories of these coastal habitats is the fascinating and superbly adapted flora found growing on them. Seemingly inhospitable to plant life, shingle beaches support yellow horned poppy, sea holly, sea sandwort and sea milkwort. The same species can sometimes be found above the tide-line on sandy beaches although the characteristic colonising plant of young sand dunes is marram grass.

Where they are protected, stabilised sand dunes develop a particularly rich flora with maritime species growing alongside wetland flowers such as marsh helleborine, marsh orchids, round-leaved wintergreen, marsh pennywort and creeping willow. The

insect life is often abundant: grasshoppers and butterflies such as grayling, small copper and dark green fritillary are characteristic.

Beaches and sand dunes, especially in southern Britain, suffer more than most habitats from human disturbance. This can lead to erosion of the soil and destruction of the flora. Nesting birds also suffer and it is only in certain protected areas in England that terns, oystercatchers, ringed plovers and black-headed gulls can breed in peace. Further north in Britain the beaches become less disturbed and you are more likely to encounter nesting birds. Always be on the look-out for signs of alarmed or distressed birds in these areas during the breeding season.

Threats to Coastal Wildlife

Seabirds and other marine creatures are superbly adapted to the rigours of a life at sea. However, they are coming under increasing pressure from man's activities: oil spillage, discharge of toxic waste and marine dumping all pose threats. More recently, our seabirds have faced a new and perhaps more insidious danger: over-fishing has begun to deny many species their food and breeding success has dropped dramatically, with young kittiwakes and arctic terns starving to death.

FRESH WATER

Great willowherb, common in wet places

Many of the walks in this book pass close to fresh water and whether it be a tumbling mountain stream or a lowland lake, wildlife will be much in evidence.

Streams, Rivers and Canals

Lowland streams and rivers in southern England are the haunt of kingfishers, which thrive on the rich supply of minnows and sticklebacks

Norfolk marshland flora in full bloom

they contain. The fish in turn feed on insect larvae. Those which are not eaten emerge in spring and summer as damselflies, mayflies and caddis flies. Little grebes, which make floating nests in the riverside vegetation, catch both the smaller fish and the insect larvae, while grey herons prefer larger quarry such as brown trout or eels.

The vegetation of streams and rivers becomes most evident by late summer. Yellow irises, tussock sedge, meadowsweet and meadow rue all grow profusely in suitable places on the river bank, while the white flowers of water crowfoot adorn the surface of the water itself. Moorhens, mute swans and other wildfowl are attracted to this rich bonanza of plant life.

Canals offer a similar habitat to slow-flowing lowland rivers. These arterial waterways need regular maintenance both to ensure their use for barges and to keep their wildlife interest. However, the work must be sympathetic to the needs of the plants and animals in order for them to survive. Sadly, in many sites, such as the Basingstoke Canal in Hampshire, commercial interests are at variance with those of wildlife and their future as havens for natural history is uncertain.

Marshes and Reed-beds

By late spring, marshland vegetation has burgeoned and a profusion of colourful flowers greets the eye. The yellow flower of marsh marigold is one of the first to appear, followed by early marsh orchids, southern marsh orchids, marsh birdsfoot trefoil and ragged robin.

In undisturbed areas of marshland, nesting birds flourish. Redshanks and snipe nest secretively among clumps of rushes, but occasionally perch on posts to survey their territories. Yellow wagtails (summer visitors to Britain) feed actively, and sedge warblers sing their scratchy song, often from the cover of the undergrowth.

Despite the uniformity of the habitat, reed-beds are rewarding places to visit. Although largely inaccessible, by the very nature of the terrain, some sites have hides and walkways to allow easy access. Reed warblers build their nests woven between the reed stems and are often parasitised by cuckoos. Reed buntings favour clumps of sallows and, in a few sites in southern England, visitors can find reed-bed specialities such as bearded tits, bitterns, marsh harriers and Cetti's warblers. Reed-beds are of year-round interest to the birdwatcher – some of the birds are resident and many other species arrive during the winter months. In particular, the population of water rails, which breed here in small numbers, is swollen by influxes from the Continent.

Open Water

Stretches of open water are home to great crested grebes which build floating nests around the margins. Wildfowl such as mallards, tufted ducks and pochards are often present throughout the year, but in the winter their numbers are augmented by species such as teal, goldeneyes, pintails and shovelers as well as by gulls.

Smaller ponds and lakes are often breeding grounds for amphibians. Frogs and common toads gather in large numbers in March and April, producing vast quantities of spawn. Newts – there are three species in Britain – are also often present but they are less conspicuous. Ponds and lakes are also havens for insect life; many species have aquatic stages in their life cycles. Among the most conspicuous are the dragonflies and damselflies, which hawk the surface of the water in search of insect prey. Their larvae are also carnivorous and some of the larger species will even tackle small fish and tadpoles.

Upland Lakes and Rivers

From the birdwatcher's point of view, upland lakes seldom harbour more than coots and tufted ducks, although common sandpipers are occasionally seen feeding around their margins, and whooper swans and goldeneyes may pay brief visits in the autumn and winter. However, upland streams and rivers usually have more to offer the visiting naturalist: the abundant insect life they contain, such as caddis flies, stoneflies and blackflies, supports dippers and grey wagtails, the latter species also being found on a few lowland rivers.

to the stump encourages the rapid growth of straight, thin shoots suitable for hurdles and posts. Trees such as hazel, ash and hornbeam are particularly suited to this practice and the resulting open woodland floor encourages an especially rich growth of woodland flowers, particularly the bluebell. Woodland insects also benefit from coppicing, where sunny rides are created and their larval food-plants can flourish; orange-tips, speckled woods and pearl-bordered fritillaries do particularly well.

Spring is also the best time for woodland birdwatching. Resident species and newly arrived migrants advertise their territories with songs, and willow warblers, chiffchaffs, blackcaps, garden warblers, robins, mistle thrushes and chaffinches are all widespread. Woodpeckers are also most easily seen and heard in spring.

During the autumn, broad-leaved woodlands are good for fungi, especially after periods of heavy rain. Seeds and fruits from the woodland shrubs and trees adorn the leaf litter and woodland mammals such as dormice, wood mice and grey squirrels cash in on the feast, along with birds such as jays. Fallow deer perform their annual rut in the autumn, and at this season roe deer are most easily seen.

Scrub, a general term embracing species such as willow, bramble, birch and herbaceous plants is characterised by its tangled undergrowth and is a haven for insects and nesting birds such as warblers.

Coniferous Woodland

Although many coniferous woodlands in England and Wales may appear natural, most are plantations created by man. The tree species used may not be native, and the age-structure of the woodland is generally uniform, with the result that wildlife interest is somewhat limited.

In the initial stages, the ground flora of conifer plantations often reflects the vegetation that would have been present prior to planting; for instance, heathers and bilberry or chalk flora. However, before long the leaf canopy becomes so dense that little plant life can survive on the woodland floor.

Young conifer plantations are often used by a surprising range of nesting birds. Short-eared owls, hen harriers and merlins breed in upland areas, while in lowland plantations wood-larks and nightjars may be found in heathland areas. Once the woodland is mature, however, its appeal to these

A woodland glade in Lathkill Dale

WOODLANDS

Male orange-tip butterfly

Broad-leaved Woodland

Although broad-leaved woodlands have much to offer the naturalist throughout the year, they are probably at their best in the spring. Before the leaves have appeared on the trees, a carpet of flowers often appears on the woodland floor. Wood-sorrel, wood anemone, wood spurge, violets and dog's mercury are widespread. On suitable soils, ramsons form large patches and, in undisturbed areas, early purple orchids, herb Paris and yellow star of Bethlehem can be found.

In many lowland broad-leaved woodlands, traditional woodland management practices can be observed. Chief among these is coppicing, where periodic cutting back

species is lost and the bird population changes accordingly to tits, sparrowhawks, redpolls and crossbills.

In upland areas of Scotland, a few areas of native Caledonian pine persist. Scottish crossbills, capercaillies and crested tits are resident and the specialised flora includes creeping lady's tresses, lesser twayblade, coralroot orchid, twinflower, serrated and chickweed wintergreen.

GRASSLAND

Speckled bush-cricket

Although grasslands are comparatively poor for birdlife – kestrels, skylarks and meadow pipits are the most widespread species – they are a haven for insects and flowers.

As their name implies, grasshoppers flourish in meadows and grasslands, but it is the butterflies that are more conspicuous. Meadow browns, ringlets, marbled whites and common blues are frequently seen and, on chalk soils, more unusual species such as chalkhill blue, Adonis blue and dark green fritillary may be found.

Among the tall grasses, a wide variety of herbaceous plants flourishes, especially where the underlying soil is chalk or limestone. Chalk downland, as it is known, is a fast-diminishing habitat, disappearing mainly because of changes in land-use and farming practices. At one time, sheep grazed these areas and the combination of the constant nibbling of the fast-growing grasses and the gradual impoverishment of the soil encouraged a wide diversity of less vigorous plants.

Some of the best areas of downland are now managed and protected to encourage their diversity and, from May to June, species such as greater knapweed, kidney vetch, carline thistle and stemless thistle thrive. Chief among the downland attractions, however, are the orchids: common spotted, bee, pyramidal and fragrant are widespread, with burnt, early spider and late spider orchids occurring more locally.

Breckland is a specialised type of habitat found in Norfolk and Suffolk. Short turf grows on the thin, sandy soil and many of the plants are unique to the area. Breckland has come increasingly under threat from farming in recent years and, sadly, only pockets of this fascinating habitat are left.

Limestone soils often support a similar range of plants to chalk downland. In some areas, however, the limestone bedrock is exposed at the surface. Weathering produces deep cracks in the rock and the resulting appearance resembles pavement; the grassland plants are confined to the limestone crevices and pot-holes, although ash woodland occasionally becomes established.

Farmland, Hedgerows and Roadside Verges

Much of lowland Britain now lies under the plough and many of the walks in this book will encounter arable fields. They may lack a tremendous amount of wildlife, but these wide open spaces are home to nesting lapwings as well as small parties of grey and red-legged partridges.

Of more wildlife interest, however, are the hedgerows which surround the fields. With woodlands declining in area, these now serve as refuges for many species of birds more usually associated with woodland edge. Yellowhammers, blackcaps, chaffinches, dunnocks and robins all nest and feed in hedges.

The age of a hedgerow can be roughly determined by the number of native species of shrub and tree found growing in it. Many date back several centuries. In addition to woody species such as hawthorn, privet, dogwood and blackthorn, climbing plants such as old man's beard, bramble and black bryony can also be found. In the autumn, many of the hedgerow plants provide berries and nuts for hungry birds and small mammals.

Except where repeatedly cut, roadside verges also provide a refuge for wildlife. Flowers such as red campion, rosebay willowherb, cow parsley, hogweed and tufted vetch do well and, in some places, small colonies of the more common species of orchid can survive. Small mammals such as voles and mice also thrive, providing prey for the kestrels now so frequently seen hovering beside roads.

Devil's Punchbowl, Wye Downs

HEATHLAND, MOORLAND AND MOUNTAINS

A majestic red deer stag

Heathland

Sandy and acid soils in southern Britain provide ideal conditions for one of our most vulnerable and threatened habitats – heathland. Characterised by plants such as gorse and heathers, they are home to many unique animals and plants but, sadly, they are increasingly under threat from land development and habitat destruction. The counties of Suffolk, Surrey, Hampshire, Dorset and Cornwall contain some of the best remaining examples of heathland and several of the walks in this book enable visitors to discover them.

During July and August, lowland heaths are a mass of colour. The subtle lilac and pink flowers of ling contrast with the deepers shades of bell heather. The two species often grow side by side with gorse on drier areas of heath, while boggy ground supports cross-leaved heath, along with specialised plants such as bog asphodel, bog myrtle, sundews and, in a few locations, the diminutive bog orchid.

Insect life flourishes on heathland. Grasshoppers and bush crickets are abundant but are often overlooked as they move among the vegetation. Dragonflies and damselflies are more conspicuous, and many areas of heathland are home to threatened and endangered species which breed in boggy pools. Bright red sympetrums are common and widespread, as is the large and showy golden-ringed dragonfly; many of the more unusual species require a close look at their markings to determine their identity.

Stonechats are perhaps the most characteristic of the heathland birds, males sitting boldly on sprays of gorse and uttering their loud alarm calls. Yellowhammers, tree pipits and meadow pipits are widespread and, in a few areas of heathland, Dartford warblers hold territories. All the small birds keep a wary eye open for hobbies – dashing birds of prey which catch small birds as well as insects on the wing. After dark, the heaths echo to the sound of a most curious bird – the nightjar. Cryptically marked, it is almost impossible to spot during the day, when it rests on the ground. At night, however, it takes to the wing to catch insects and its loud song, somewhat reminiscent of a sewing machine, fills the air.

Moorland

Moorlands often support many of the same species of plant found on lowland heaths – ling, bell heather and cross-leaved heath. However, the presence of purple moor-grass and rushes indicates a slightly more harsh environment.

In undisturbed areas, birds such as merlins, hen harriers, curlews, golden plovers and dunlins still breed, often being found near wet flushes or in areas recently burned to encourage a new growth of heather for red grouse. Grouse moors are characteristic of many upland areas of moorland, particularly in the North York Moors, the Yorkshire Dales and in parts of Scotland. A stroll across one of these areas will soon yield views of grouse as they take to the wing, uttering their loud 'go-back, go-back, go-back' call.

Mountains

Our mountains provide the walker with some of the most challenging routes and dramatic scenery in Britain. Although the weather often conspires to shroud the peaks in cloud, the rewards of finding some of our uplands' unique wildlife treasures more than makes up for the occasional dampened spirit.

Upland birds are generally spread rather thinly. On the lower slopes, visitors may find species more usually associated with the lowlands – chaffinches, dunnocks and wrens are all found at surprisingly high altitudes. However, once you encounter rocky outcrops and crags, look for ring ouzels – similar in size and shape to a blackbird, but with a conspicuous white crescent on the breast. Wheatears are often found nesting in similar habitats to ring ouzels.

It is only on a few of the highest peaks in Scotland that true mountain species are found. Ptarmigan – relatives of the red grouse – are characteristic and widespread, moulting their dappled brown and grey summer plumage for all-white feathers in the winter. Snow buntings and dotterels are also occasionally seen on a few of the Scottish mountains and that most majestic of birds, the golden eagle, is sometimes seen soaring high overhead in search of carrion or live prey such as ptarmigan and arctic hare.

Not surprisingly, mountain flowers are extremely hardy. Alpine lady's mantle, clubmosses, purple saxifrage, mossy saxifrage, moss campion and mountain everlasting are widespread but many of the more unusual species are confined to small areas, often where the underlying bedrock is base-rich.

Although hardy, mountain flowers have suffered greatly from overgrazing by sheep. As a result, many are confined to areas protected by their inaccessibility, such as rock ledges and overhangs, or where sheep are largely excluded. To visit one of these areas and see a profusion of alpine forget-me-nots, rock speedwell, yellow mountain saxifrage, gentians and mountain avens is a reminder of what many sites are now missing, but is a quite breathtaking experience.

Scottish Highlands in spring: the Five Sisters of Kintail seen across Loch Duich

Tresco

Scilly's largest stretch of fresh water, the Great Pool on Tresco is a magnet for water birds and wildfowl, including some rarities

Borough Farm, on the east side of the island

THE JOURNEY FROM PENZANCE TO THE ISLES OF SCILLY CAN TAKE HOURS OR MINUTES, DEPENDING ON WHETHER YOU GO BY BOAT OR AIR. THE *SCILLONIAN* TAKES UP TO THREE HOURS AND THE CROSSING CAN BE VERY ROUGH, BUT THE IDEA OF TYING YOURSELF TO THE MAST WHILST SOOTY SHEARWATERS AND SABINE'S GULLS SKIM PAST THROUGH A STORM-FORCE GALE APPEALS TO MORE ROBUST BIRDWATCHERS.

MAN AND PLANTS

Less than 30 miles (48 km) lie between Scilly's scatter of granite islands and the Cornish coast, but this is often sufficient for the islands to be free of mainland cloudbanks. Their climate is unique. Days of warm sunshine are relatively frequent, as are strong winds and high seas. This combination, together with Scilly's isolation and its long settlement by man, makes the islands a singular and attractive place, perfect for holidays.

Only six out of 100 islands in the group are inhabited, of which St Mary's is by far the biggest, with a town and a proper road system. To the north and north-west of it lie St Martin's, Tresco, Bryher and Samson and to the south-west lies St Agnes. The natural vegetation at the heart of these islands is a form of maritime heathland: heather and gorse buffeted flat by salt winds. Centuries of settlement by farmers and gardeners have changed this in most places. In particular, the frost-free winters have allowed a flourishing market-garden economy to develop, producing early vegetables and flowers of which the classic 'Soleil d'Or' daffodil is the most important. To protect their crops from the biting winds, landowners planted hedges and windbreaks, not of native trees but of shrubs from New Zealand, adapted to a similar oceanic climate. Since this is a seafaring community it is hardly surprising that other exotic plants should have found their way to

---

Tresco

Isles of Scilly
Grid ref. SV 894 142

Approx. 5¼ miles (8.5 km). Mostly level walking, but rocky in places.

The main island of St Mary's is accessible either by a daily boat service (the *Scillonian*) from Penzance or by a regular helicopter or air service. Tresco can be reached by boat from Hugh Town on St Mary's (the boats usually leave from 10am onwards, weather permitting) or direct from the mainland by helicopter – but this is not such a regular service as that for St Mary's. Boats from St Mary's to Tresco usually land at the quay below Carn Near, from where a metalled track leads to the Abbey Gardens, starting point of the walk. From the heliport, turn right (east) on to the track to reach the gardens.

The Isles of Scilly have a climate and wildlife all of their own. The breeding birds are interesting and the flora is unique, but most birdwatchers visit at migration time in spring and autumn.

Nearby sites: *St Mary's:* Holy Vale trail – woodland; Porth Hellick beach – waders, gulls; Porthloo beach – sheltered cove with nearby lake and hide; *St Agnes* – interesting flora and migrant birds.

The migratory painted lady

the islands too; sometimes it is difficult to know which are native and which are not, and the origins of some of the introductions may never be known. The result is a beautiful mosaic: islands with golden beaches where the dunes are colonised by sea holly and yellow horned poppy but are backed by tamarisk and fuchsia, and where fields of asparagus and daffodils are enclosed by 20ft (6m) hedges of pittosporum and coprosma. Monterey pines shelter farms tucked beneath granite tors of pink rock and purple heather.

ISLAND SPECIALITIES

Spring to early summer is probably the best time for a general visit to Scilly –

---

many interesting plants are in flower early in the year. In addition to widespread species such as thrift, sea campion and spring squill, the dwarf pansy grows on Bryher and nearby Tean, and orange birdsfoot occurs sparingly in patches of coastal heathland on a few islands. Least adder's tongue fern is only known from one small area of turf. None of these three species is known in mainland Britain. There are butterflies with unique island races or subspecies (speckled wood, meadow brown and common blue) and a mammal, the Scilly shrew, which occurs nowhere else in Britain – it is, in fact, a race of the lesser white-toothed shrew of northern France. Seabirds nest on many of the more remote islands. There are big colonies of Manx shearwater and storm petrel on Annet (close to St Agnes) although, because these only come ashore at night, they are seldom seen on land. Boat trips around the little islets are usually successful for puffins and the other auks, and for the roseate tern which is another of the Scilly Isles' specialities.

In October the whole tempo for enjoying Scilly's wildlife changes as the islands are invaded by several hundred 'twitchers'. Looking purposeful and carrying telescopes and short-wave radios, they are a daunting sight for anyone not taking life seriously enough. The reason for the sudden influx is the likelihood of westerly gales or easterly winds bearing migrant birds from America and Siberia respectively. Every year there is something quite unexpected – a nighthawk catching insects over St Agnes lighthouse, a dazed American purple gallinule sitting in a roadside gutter in Hugh Town, or a yellow-bellied sapsucker sucking sap from a group of elms on Tresco. Some of these vagrants may be 'firsts' – species never recorded before in Britain.

THE GARDEN ISLE

Anyone interested in wildlife and making a special trip from a far corner of Britain will probably want to spend time on at least three of the islands – St Mary's, St Agnes and Tresco. However, for a single day or as a broad introduction to the essential character of the Isles, Tresco is by far the best. In the north the island is quite unspoilt, windswept heathland broken only by a few ancient earthworks and Civil War ruins. In the south there are two lakes, a famous botanic garden, farmland, bulbfields, dunes and rocky headlands. The Tresco Ledges, off the southern shores of the island, are considered to be among the finest marine sites in Britain.

1 **The Abbey Gardens are the ideal place to start a walk round Tresco.** You will have passed a host of palms and other exotic trees by the time you reach the garden entrance. If time permits, explore the beautiful gardens (there is a fee). Migrant birds sometimes shelter among the bushes, which also harbour naturalised stick insects.

Follow the track eastwards from the gardens, with a pool visible through trees to the right, and turn right just after the Abbey building. Bear right off the concrete track and on to a broad path through bracken. There is a better view now of the pool to the right, and another sheet of water appears to the left. They are both worth exploring. The smaller Abbey Pool on the right, which is sometimes only half full of water and has a muddy shoreline, is good for migrant wading birds and has attracted some notable rarities. The other lake is called the Great Pool. A path off the main track allows a closer view across the reed-beds and the open water. Again this is a place for vagrant birds – a glossy ibis (from Asia) once took up residence on the shore and a Parula warbler (from America), a first for Britain, was discovered among the willow scrub. Even some of the ducks are not what they seem, being the descendants of an American black duck which came to stay and mated with a local mallard.

2 **Bear left, around the foot of the Great Pool, then turn right (eastwards) before turning left (northwards) past some greenhouses.** Alternatively detour to look at the beautiful white sands of Pentle Bay and the scatter of islands beyond. The dunes are attractive, backed by marram and with some patches of exotic garden escapes, notably agapanthus from South Africa.

The path continues northwards, past greenhouses and some tall hedges. These are planted to protect bulbfields from strong winds and did their job well until January 1987, when four days of heavy frost, unprecedented in the island's history, killed off many of the coprosmas and pittosporums. It will take many years to make good the damage. The Monterey pines proved to be more hardy and there are some fine gnarled

Gimble Porth's unspoilt white sands have helped earn Tresco its reputation as an island paradise. Off shore lies Northwethel, with Round Island lighthouse in the distance

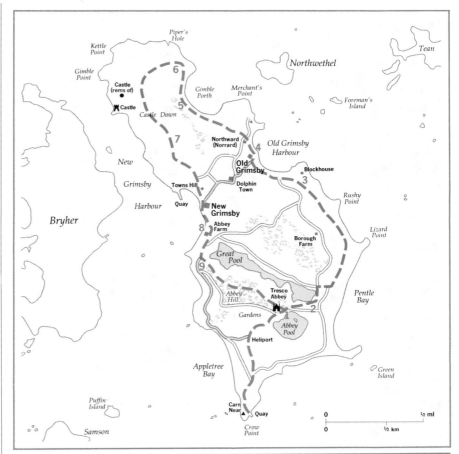

Small fields sheltered by trees and hedges – typical Scilly Isles farmland

specimens alongside the path as it passes little stone-walled fields and approaches Borough Farm. There are also some sycamores, often damned as an alien species but one of the bird-watcher's favourite trees because plagues of aphids usually cover the leaves, providing food for migrant warblers.

3 Continue along the path, with a 16th-century blockhouse (coastal defence) on a knoll or tor to the right. Passing this, the path descends to meet a concrete track, at which turn right, past a little terrace of cottages, and on into the little settlement of Old Grimsby (the word comes from the Norwegian *Grims ea* meaning inlet, not from any direct connection with the more famous fishing port). Turn right at a T-junction. A pretty section of coast lies to the right, backed by tamarisk (a Mediterranean shrub) and other exotics. The beach is private but the views, across to Tean and St Martin's, are excellent and free.

4 At another junction turn left (signed 'Footpath to Gimble Porth, Piper's Hole and Castles') up a path and over a stile, then past a knoll to the right and down to Gimble Porth. This is a pretty bay with sand, pebbles and rocks, ideal for beachcombing and a good place for finding shells. Again, there are fine views of the islands; in the foreground is Northwethel, then St Helen's, then Round Island with its lighthouse.

5 The path continues north-west, with pasture and woodland to the left and the bay to the right, then climbs steeply to another knoll or tor. This is a wonderful place to stop for a few minutes; the granite boulders make a good seat. On a September afternoon the colours can be dazzlingly pure – blue sea, blue sky, pink and dove-grey rocks, orange *Xanthoria* and *Caloplaca* lichens and mauve heather.

6 From this point there are several options available depending on the time. An exploration of the northern cliffs can be rewarding, as can be a visit to the castle ruins (one from the days of King Charles I, the other, more intact, from the days of Cromwell). However far you continue, the path back is down the central spine of the island. This provides an opportunity to take a closer look at the strange wind-battered heathland, composed of ling and bell heather.

7 Heading south-east, the broad sandy path begins to descend, past some low patches of western gorse, and is funnelled into a walled 'drovers' path' beside attractive little fields (with tall hedges again) and on to the road into New Grimsby. The route heads south with the road, past the quay and cobbled slipway. Bryher lies just across the water and this is the embarkation point. Boats from St Mary's sometimes have to put down their passengers here too, if conditions are difficult at Carn Near.

8 Just south of New Grimsby, pass Abbey Farm, then the north-western end of the Great Pool, which looks quite different from this side of the island.

9 Follow the track that runs around the south-western shore of the Great Pool from Abbey Farm to Tresco Abbey. At first, the waterside is lined by reeds and rushes. Scan the open water for wildfowl: blue-winged teal have been seen here among the commoner species. It is possible to walk along a track to a small hide on the shoreline. Towards the abbey, woodland begins to obscure views of the Great Pool. Abbey Wood is an excellent area for migrant warblers and flycatchers in autumn. If you fail to see a rarity don't feel too disappointed – only a handful arrive each year and if there have been no strong gales it will mean they may all have found their way to their proper wintering grounds.

From the Abbey Gardens, return to the quay at Carn Near or to the heliport.

THE MASSIVE GRANITE CLIFFS OF LAND'S END FORM AN IMPRESSIVE TURNING POINT ON THE SOUTH WEST PENINSULA COAST PATH. THE PATH IS WELL TRODDEN HERE, BUT THE MANY PATHS RUNNING INLAND ALONG LITTLE VALLEYS AND ACROSS THE COASTAL HEATH ARE FAR LESS WELL DEFINED. EVEN AT THE HEIGHT OF THE TOURIST SEASON THESE WILL BE QUIET.

COASTAL FLOWERS

The cliff-tops around Land's End support some very attractive areas of coastal heath. Dwarf gorse and bell heather flower in profusion in late summer and a colourful patchwork of betony, devilsbit scabious, sheepsbit scabious, rock sea spurrey and birds-foot trefoil grows among the gorse and heather. The gorse is sometimes smothered with the red, thread-like stems of the strange, parasitic dodder. In spring, bluebells and red campion fill the lanes, followed by early purple orchids, foxgloves and honeysuckle. The orange flower that blooms in late summer and early autumn is montbretia, an introduced species. It is more often seen in gardens, but has become successfully established here. Some of the stone walls alongside the lanes and fields are very old, and support a rich population of ferns and flowering plants. Lichens also thrive in the pure air, often making a colourful display. Look out for the orange *Xanthoria* and the pale green *Ramalina*.

MIGRANT BIRDS

The numerous tiny valleys running in from the coast are the first landfall for lost migrant birds newly arrived across the Atlantic; tiny warblers and thrushes which should really be in North America are found by keen birdwatchers searching every bush and hedgerow. In autumn, when small birds on both sides of the Atlantic are leaving their northern breeding grounds and heading south for the winter, a severe storm will sometimes blow them off course. If the birds find themselves far out to sea, they keep going until they reach land, and the Land's End peninsula is often the first land they reach. An impressive number of North American and Asian species have been found at Land's End and Porthgwarra.

RESIDENT BIRDS

Seabirds breed on the cliffs, although never in great numbers. Kittiwakes can be seen from several points on the

Meadow pipits favour open country

Land's End

Cornwall
Grid ref. SW 352 263

National Trust (part)
Approx. 8¼ miles (13.2 km) or 4 miles (6.4 km). Some steep sections and some close to cliff-edges. May be muddy after rain, and should not be attempted in stormy weather.

The walk starts at Sennen Cove, 8 miles (13 km) west of Penzance on an unclassified road off the A30. Park at the end of the road, on the seafront.

Land's End is the most popular tourist attraction in Cornwall, drawing thousands of visitors daily in summer, yet few of them stray far from the commercial area to see some of the finest cliff scenery in England. The cliff-tops are a blaze of colour in summer, when the coastal flowers bloom, and seabirds, seals, butterflies and marine life make this an area of exceptional interest for the naturalist.

Nearby sites: *Drift Reservoir* – migrant birds, including rarities; *Nanquidno Valley* – shrubs and dense cover attract migrant birds; *St Just Airport* – a good spot to look for migrant waders and larks.

---

walk, and shags and cormorants nest at the base of many of the steep cliffs. Fulmars have colonised the whole area, and there is such competition among them for good nesting ledges that they can be seen defending nest sites in mid-winter, long before the breeding season starts. Many more seabirds can be seen flying past in stormy weather.

Woodland birds are almost absent from this windswept and virtually treeless place but linnets, yellow-hammers, stonechats, robins and dunnocks can breed in the larger clumps of gorse. Wrens nest in the bracken and wheatears find plenty of secure nesting sites in the stone walls. Rock pipits usually find a safe nesting hole below the cliff-top, whereas meadow pipits nest on the ground in the open grassland beyond the cliff-edge.

BUTTERFLIES AND OTHER INSECTS

Butterflies abound, and many species may be encountered on a sunny day. Some will be residents, such as the wall brown and the small copper, while others, such as the red admiral and the painted lady, will be migrants. There are plenty of nectar-rich plants to encourage butterflies, some of their favourites being hemp agrimony, water mint and wild thyme. Sunny rocks and Cornish 'hedges' or walls encourage graylings and wall browns to sun themselves. Damselflies and dragonflies breed in the small streams and pools on the heaths and many species of beetle, including dor beetles and green tiger beetles, will be encountered.

The cliff-tops are good for sea-watching, but take care near the many sheer drops

WALK 2

THE *W*ALK

Coastal heath near Dr Syntax's Head

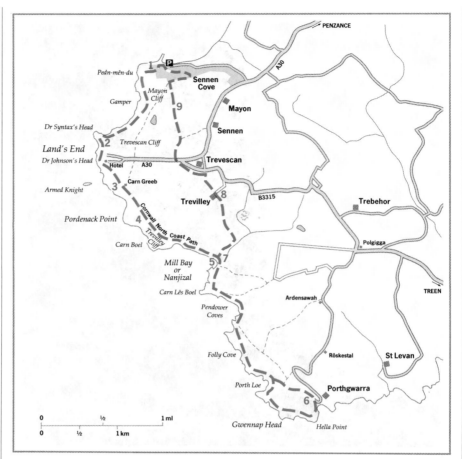

1 From the south-west end of the car park beyond the Round House at Sennen Cove, follow the waymarked coast path towards Land's End. (Look for posts with yellow acorn markers.) The area on the left of the path is a superb example of coastal heath, covered with bell heather and dwarf gorse. Cross-leaved heath, ling, sawwort, betony and hawkweeds add to the colour.

2 The path continues to Land's End, crossing a small suspension bridge. Dr Syntax's Head is actually the true 'Land's End', being slightly more westerly than Dr Johnson's Head, at the end of the road. Use binoculars to look for kittiwakes nesting on the cliffs below, and shags on the rocks. Grey seals haul out on the rocks out to sea around the Longships Lighthouse, and dolphins are sometimes seen passing further out to sea.

3 The coast path continues past the Land's End visitor complex and the little farm building of Carn Greeb. This former coastal smallholding has been restored and turned into a tourist attraction. Scavenging gulls and jackdaws wait here for scraps left by visitors.

4 Pordenack Point offers superb views both to Land's End and south-east along the coast to Carn Boel. There are more good examples of coastal heath here and wheatears, meadow pipits and rock pipits nest on the cliffs and in the stone walls.

5 Continue on the coast path to Mill Bay, or Nanjizal. The bay may have sand in it or it may be rocky, depending on winter storms. At low tide great forests of kelp and thongweed can be seen in the clear water. Shags fish in the bay. The derelict building by the little stream is a mill once used to grind corn and crush ore. Water mint and brookweed grow in the stream.

6 For a shorter walk, return to Sennen (see 7 below). Otherwise, follow the coast path past the coastguard post to Porthgwarra. The cliff scenery is superb, and the flowers make a spectacular display in summer. Porthgwarra is a very good spot for watching migrant seabirds, and many unusual species such as Cory's and sooty shearwaters are regularly seen here among the more usual migrants.

Return to Nanjizal.

7 To return to Sennen Cove from Nanjizal, take the narrow path which leads steeply uphill from the coast path a little way north of the derelict building and the stream. Follow this narrow, gorse-lined path, which runs north-east alongside a wall, to a T-junction. Turn left here to cross the wall by stone steps, then follow the path straight across the first field and on through more fields to Trevilley (the path is not very well defined). Many birds feed in these fields, and gulls, lapwings, curlews, starlings, rooks, jackdaws and smaller larks and pipits all form flocks here

from time to time. This is a good area for butterflies and several species may be seen on a sunny day; look for wall brown, meadow brown, gatekeeper, grayling, red admiral, small copper and common blue.

8 At Trevilley, follow the right of way over a series of stone-stepped stiles through the farmyards, leaving by stone steps beside a gate. Pass through two fields, keeping left of a wall and a stone cross, and at Trevescan go through a garden gate to reach the road. Turn left and walk for about 400yds (350m) to reach the A30. At the road junction, cross the A30 and take the signposted footpath opposite, heading due north. Yellowhammers breed in the bushes and buzzards soar overhead.

9 The path now leads back to Sennen Cove across the fields. Keep the coastguard cottages on your right and turn right along a narrow road with splendid views over Sennen Cove. In 200yds (180m) take the public footpath on the left and follow it down to the seafront.

View north-west as the coast path climbs towards wind-battered Rill Point. Jutting into the sea is the distinctive rock formation known as The Horse

---

SPECTACULAR SCENERY IS NOT ALWAYS A RECIPE FOR A GOOD WALK, BUT IT CERTAINLY HELPS. CORNWALL IS FORTUNATE IN ITS LOCATION: THE WILDLIFE ASSOCIATED WITH THE DRAMATIC SCENERY ADDS AN EXTRA DIMENSION TO A COUNTY ALREADY RICH IN NATURAL HISTORY INTEREST. FOR BOTH SCENERY AND WILDLIFE, THE LIZARD IS OUTSTANDING EVEN BY CORNISH STANDARDS.

WIND AND WEATHER

The Lizard peninsula has the warmest climate of mainland Britain, and in late summer it is difficult to believe it can also be very wet and windy. No other county in Britain is so affected by the elements as is Cornwall: an ocean batters it from the north, west and south, and gales buffet any trees or bushes into fugitive, crouching forms in clefts and hollows. A patchwork of fields has replaced the natural vegetation. Ancient woodland that once lined the small valleys of the low-lying 'killas' country (the sedimentary plateau) has gone without a trace, and the heathland of the granite moors has been fragmented. Nevertheless, the Lizard peninsula has retained

---

The Lizard

Cornwall
Grid ref. SW 671 180

Nature Conservancy Council/ National Trust
Approx. 9 miles (14.5 km). Steep in parts.

The Lizard is Cornwall's most southerly headland, lying south of Helston. Park near Mullion Cove, south-west of the village of Mullion along the B3296, either at the car park on the left at the top of the hill, or at the Porthmellin car park on the right.

The Lizard offers some of England's most dramatic coastal scenery, backed by unique heathland with unusual plants, birds and insects.

Nearby site: *Marazion Marsh* – wetland flora; unusual migrant birds in autumn.

Gorse – tolerant of sea winds

---

extensive tracts of heathland at such sites as Goonhilly Downs and Predannack Downs. Most of this is of very restricted access, but between Mullion and Lizard Point there is an excellent coast path.

FLORA AND FAUNA OF THE LIZARD

The combination of geology and climate makes the vegetation of West Lizard quite unique. This is the only place to find such obscure little plants as sand quillwort, large Lizard clover, twin-flowered clover and upright clover. It is also the only British locality for Cornish heath, a beautiful heather which is so abundant here that it is hard to appreciate that it is absent everywhere else. More widespread species include spring sandwort, thyme broomrape and the prostrate form of broom – all tolerant of poor, dry soil and salt-laden winds.

Birds of the Lizard include nightjar, grasshopper warbler and several birds of prey; butterflies include the internationally endangered marsh fritillary and the silver-studded blue. Migrants making their landfall above the rugged cliffs and coves may come from the Mediterranean or from America; one of the most regular transatlantic vagrants is the monarch butterfly, bigger and more colourful than many New World birds. It seems incredible that ocean winds, capable of driving towering waves with such force against the Lizard cliffs, can also bring butterflies safely to shore.

THE *W*ALK

1 Walk down the road from the car park, past hedgerows of tamarisk and tree mallow. Just before the road ends at the harbour, at a turning circle on the left and next to a building, turn left along the coast path (signed), then bear right. This takes you up a sharp climb, bearing left and providing excellent views of Mullion Cove. A few stops on the ascent will set the scene. The little harbour, owned by the National Trust, was built at the end of the 19th century to shelter the inshore fishing fleet, but the economy of the place is now dictated by tourism, and the hotel to the north is by far the most dominant feature. The large island, covered in tree mallows, is Mullion Island. Much closer to the shore is The Var, less imposing but a better bird island with nesting kittiwakes, razorbills and guillemots. Peregrines and ravens are usually about too. Choughs, often associated with Cornwall, vanished from the Lizard nearly 150 years ago.

The slope of the path eases as you continue south, levelling off at an excellent heath area. This introduces several of the botanic treasures of the area, notably Cornish heath. Common heather (*Calluna*) is relatively scarce here, but there is a mixture of three *Erica* species. Of these the cross-leaved heath is restricted to the wettest ground, while bell heather prefers the dry outcrops. Otherwise the rarest species dominates the flora here. Cornish heath looks remarkably robust and its flower spikes are impressively dense, but it is sensitive and has precise soil and climatic requirements. It may be abundant here, but you would have to go to south-west France to find another place where it grows so profusely. Other interesting plants of the Mullion cliffs include spring and autumn squill, chives and western gorse. Stonechats are usually in evidence somewhere among the gorse. If the wind is not too fierce they prefer to sit out on exposed branches, chatting loudly.

2 Continue along the coast path. The south-facing grassy bank here has recently been cleared of gorse to allow herbs to re-invade. The rock beneath the soil is the famous Cornish serpentine, but up the other side of the little valley it changes to hornblende schist and the vegetation changes again. Predannack Head is good scenically but not so interesting for plants, as the soil is very dry. The path arcs left at the headland following a 'hedge' (the local name for the earth and stone field boundaries). Thrift, sea campion and hoary plantain grow in profusion among the boulders of the hedge bank.

3 After the Predannack headland the path drops down below Wollas Farm to cross a little stream at Parc Bean Cove. After this you are back on serpentine, which can best be appreciated by looking at the steps of the first stile.

The path bears right to keep to the cliff-top. It does not go all the way to Vellan Head, but bears left to a stile and down across the valley of Soapy Bay. Vellan Head is flat and heavily grazed, with some extensive patches of gorse and Cornish heath. Again there is excellent cliff scenery on this stretch, with a view westwards to the Land's End peninsula.

4 From Soapy Bay the path rises steeply again and follows the cliff-top around Rill Point. From here Lizard Point can at last be seen, and it was also from here, in 1588, that the Spanish Armada was first sighted.

The path is now worn and dusty from much trampling. Kynance Cove lies ahead; Asparagus Island (on which grows wild asparagus) is off shore, separated at low tide by a sweep of golden sand and, at high tide, by a ribbon of turquoise sea.

5 The path bears right, downhill, then snakes its way left and into the cove at Kynance. (Take care not to be caught by the tide.) The beach is tiny but well worth exploring at low tide, with rock pools, caves, colourful faces of serpentine and patches of rock samphire. The buildings include an old mill and a curious assortment of stone huts with tamarisk around the doors.

The best route back to Mullion is to retrace your steps by the coast path, but there is an alternative, to avoid Rill Point, which follows an old walled track north towards Kynance Farm before turning left into the valley of Soapy Bay.

Cornish heath – rare everywhere but here

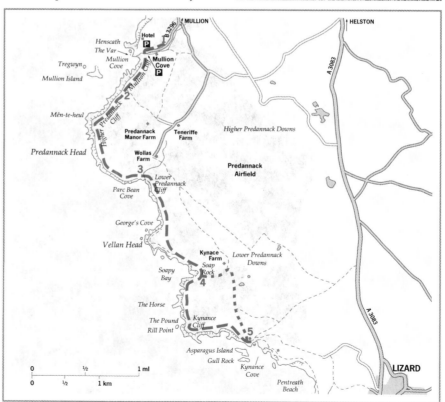

A PROMINENT LANDMARK ON THE NORTH CORNWALL COAST, TREVOSE HEAD IS SURROUNDED BY TYPICAL ATLANTIC BEACHES: GREAT EXPANSES OF SAND WITH SURF ROLLING IN AND BREAKING ON THE MANY JAGGED ROCKS RUNNING OUT FROM THE CLIFFS. WESTERLY GALES REGULARLY TEAR ACROSS THE COAST, CAUSING TREES TO LEAN AT CRAZY ANGLES AND CARRYING SALT SPRAY FAR INLAND.

CORNWALL'S ATLANTIC COAST

The windswept and exposed coast of north Cornwall is composed of a great variety of rock types and shows many fascinating geological features. The rocks vary in hardness, enabling the sea to carve out many bays, stacks and gullies. Deep caves sometimes form blow-holes as their roofs fall in, leaving sheer-sided holes in the cliff-top with the sea boiling at the bottom. Evidence of former sea-levels can be seen in the form of raised beaches above the present sea-level. Mining and quarrying have left their mark on the cliffs, and the quarries at Cataclews Point are still clearly visible.

PLANTS AND THE WIND

The salt-scorched leaves and stunted appearance of the wind-battered trees and shrubs gives a bleak appearance to the landscape around Trevose, yet the climate is relatively mild. The proximity of the sea means that prolonged frost and snow are rare, so

Grey seal – mostly found around rocky shores

Trevose Head

Cornwall
Grid ref. SW 879 754

Approx. 5¼ miles (6.4 km). Mostly easy walking, but with one section on sand dunes and other sections near cliff-edges which may be windswept.

Trevose Head is about 4 miles (6.4 km) west of Padstow. Park at the eastern end of Harlyn Bay.

Cliffs, dunes and sandy beaches capture the flavour of north Cornwall on this walk, much of which is along the coast path. The cliff-tops are covered with a mixture of coastal heath and sand dune flora, and are a landfall for migrant birds. They also provide a good vantage point to watch for seabirds, seals, porpoises and dolphins out at sea.

Nearby sites: *Camel Estuary* – good for wildfowl, waders and seabirds; *Pentire Point* – a rocky headland offering cliff walks and the chance of seeing migrant birds and coastal flowers.

Herb Robert, a common type of cranesbill

plants able to tolerate wind and spray can flower and set seed early in the season. A few sycamores grow where there is shelter, but the typical shrub of this headland is the tamarisk. Its feathery leaves offer little resistance to the wind, and the pliable stems are not damaged by the strongest gales; salt spray simply drips off the fine foliage.

A colourful coastal heath has grown up on the cliff-tops and a variety of dwarf forms of familiar plants grow here. Stunted bushes of European and western gorse shelter a carpet of bell heather and cross-leaved heath, and betony and devilsbit scabious grow among them with the occasional prostrate broom bush. Where shell sand blows on to the cliffs, lime-tolerant plants including kidney vetch, sometimes in its unusual red form, can grow. The rock faces are often clothed with rock samphire and small patches of the more colourful golden samphire, while the characteristic north Cornwall herringbone stone walls are draped with sea campion and rock sea spurrey.

SEA-WATCHING

The position of Trevose Head makes it a good vantage point for watching migrating seabirds and sea-mammals. Whatever direction the wind is coming from, it should be possible to find somewhere to shelter and scan the sea. Trawlers heading in and out of Padstow are followed by gulls, while shoals of mackerel coming close inshore in summer attract flocks of feeding gannets and sometimes dolphins. A strong north-westerly gale in autumn will drive flocks of migrating seabirds close to the shore as they move south from breeding colonies. Grey seals may be seen hauled out on rocks at low tide, and they sometimes bob up out of the water as they swim past. Dolphins and porpoises are often overlooked, but do pass Trevose Head quite frequently.

MARINE LIFE

The exposed nature of this coastline prevents all but the hardiest of marine creatures from living here, so the intertidal rocks have a very sparse covering of seaweeds. Barnacles and dogwhelks are common, but the brown seaweeds can grow well in only a few sheltered gullies and pools. Winter gales wash huge quantities of kelps and other seaweeds on to the beaches, and goose barnacles attached to pieces of driftwood are commonly found. Sanderlings run along the shore and gulls scavenge on the high-tide line; beachcombers will find plenty to interest them here.

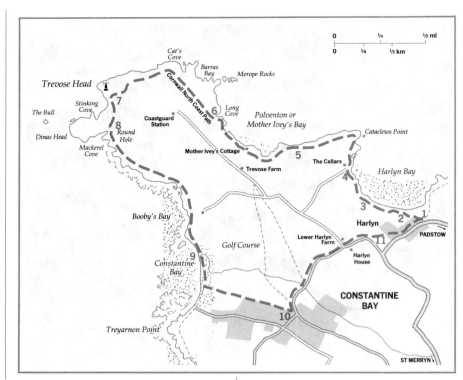

Typical north Cornwall coast scenery – though with an uncharacteristically calm sea. This sandy gully is near Mother Ivey's Bay

1 The stream and reed-bed south of the road at Harlyn Bay is a sheltered feeding area for warblers and wagtails. A few breed here, but spring and autumn bring large numbers of migrants. The willow trees behind the reed-bed are favourite feeding areas for willow warblers and tits.

2 **Walk west along the beach until some steps lead up on to the dunes. Follow the Cornwall North Coast Path along the cliff-top around Harlyn Bay.** Red valerian, known locally as 'Padstow pride', grows on the cliffs with rock samphire, sea plantain and kidney vetch.

3 **Cross the wall by the stone stile.** Note the herringbone style of building. The shrub with fine leaves is tamarisk, a species well suited to windswept conditions. In the wet hollows below the cliff-top, galingale and water mint grow, and birds like linnets and starlings often visit for a drink.

4 **Crossing several stiles, follow the path in front of the house and on towards Cataclews Point.** Wheatears and rock pipits are found here, and fulmars patrol the cliff-edge and the bay below. Stone quarries are carved into the cliff below the path; take great care near the edge. Two miles (3.2 km) off shore is wave-swept

Gulland Rock, a safe roosting place for seabirds.

5 **Continue through the kissing-gate.** The little stream has brookweed growing in it; its tiny white flowers attract small flies. Water mint, fleabane and hemlock water dropwort grow here as well, all attracting insects, especially butterflies.

6 **Follow the coast path past Mother Ivey's Bay, and at Long Cove cross the gully, then follow the path between the fences.** The walls are a little more sheltered here and are covered with English stonecrop, scurvy-grass, sea campion, rock sea spurrey, birdsfoot trefoil and a collection of lichens. The fleshy-leaved spinach-like plant growing at the base of the wall is sea beet.

7 **Continue to Trevose Head.** This windswept spot is an excellent vantage point for sea-watching. Throughout the breeding season the resident gulls, kittiwakes and fulmars fly by, and gannets from more distant breeding colonies often fly very close. Guillemots, razorbills and a few puffins also turn up here from breeding cliffs further up the coast. In autumn when north-westerly gales blow, especially early in the morning, large numbers of birds can be seen flying past on their way out to

sea for the winter. Bottle-nosed, white-sided and Risso's dolphins have also been seen from here.

8 **Follow the path past Round Hole with great care; the sides are very steep.** The rocks off shore look as if they have been painted black; this is the result of a complete covering of a black lichen, *Verrucaria maura*, which thrives in these spray-drenched conditions.

9 **Pass Booby's Bay and walk along the foot of the dunes at Constantine Bay. Mid-way along the beach, a small wooden hut marks the start of the path back across the dunes and the golf course.** Sea holly and sea bindweed grow among the marram grass in the dunes. Trampling has greatly damaged the dunes in places.

10 **Take the small road along the top of the golf course which runs to the left of the Clubhouse towards Harlyn.** The tamarisk bushes along the lane harbour migrant birds, while the golf course and the surrounding fields are important roosting and feeding areas for large flocks of gulls, pigeons and starlings.

11 **Pass Harlyn House, then take the footpath indicated across the field back to Harlyn Bay.**

The well camouflaged common blenny scours rock pools for barnacles, small molluscs and other tiny sea creatures to eat

PRAWLE POINT IS REACHED ALONG TYPICAL NARROW AND WINDING DEVON LANES WHICH RUN BETWEEN STEEP STONE BANKS THICK WITH HART'S TONGUE AND SOFT SHIELD FERNS. MUCH OF THE HEADLAND HAS BEEN CULTIVATED, SO THE STEEP BANKS AND CLIFF-EDGES THAT REMAIN FORM VALUABLE RESERVES FOR THE UNIQUE WILDLIFE OF THIS AREA.

WILD FLOWERS AND WEATHER

Outcrops of rock between the fields are clothed with gorse, blackthorn and bracken, and in the spring bluebells and red campion flower in abundance. Unusual flowers like balm-leaved figwort and bloody cranesbill flower alongside commoner coastal plants such as thrift and sea campion. Although strong winds are frequent for much of the year, the stone walls and patches of scrub provide shelter for delicate species. Ferns are abundant, springing from cracks and crevices in stone walls and enjoying the mild, damp climate.

Butterflies abound, and many of them are on the wing far earlier in the year than in other regions because of the exceptionally mild climate in this part of Devon. Both migrant species and residents benefit. Red admirals and painted ladies could well be visitors from Southern Europe or north Africa, while orange-tips and the various species of brown and skipper will be local butterflies.

Prawle Point

Devon
Grid ref. SX 775 355

National Trust (part)
Approx. 3 miles (4.8 km). Steep in places with some cliff-edge sections.

Prawle Point, the southernmost headland in Devon, lies some 7 miles (13km) south-east of Kingsbridge. Use the National Trust car park at Prawle Point, taking the unclassified road south from East Prawle.

Prawle Point is one of the most southerly areas of land in England. Dramatic cliffs and deep lanes provide contrasting landscapes on a walk which is rich in wild flowers, birds and insects.

Nearby sites: *Slapton Ley* – the largest natural freshwater lake in the south-west with a rich wildlife, including many rare birds and an interesting flora; *Start Point* – a dramatic headland, covered with wild flowers in the spring, and offering panoramic views along the coast from the lighthouse.

Thrift or sea-pink – widespread on cliffs

MIGRANTS AND SEABIRDS

One of our rarest breeding birds, the cirl bunting,, has its most important remaining British stronghold here, and many migratory birds make their first landfall on the Point after crossing the English Channel. Some even travel from as far away as North America, reaching land at Prawle after westerly gales have carried them across the Atlantic. Seabirds stream past the Point in the autumn, and there is a very good chance of spotting unusual species like the sooty shearwater among the more familiar gannets and kittiwakes. The Devon Birdwatching and Preservation Society has acquired a small nature reserve on the Point opposite the National Trust car park, and has encouraged wild flowers and shrubs which attract migrant birds in spring and autumn. Every little patch of scrub seems to hold small birds during migration times, as warblers and other insect-eating species stoke up with food before or after their arduous sea crossing.

THE SEASHORE

Down on the shore, a rich marine life inhabits the pools and gullies formed by the action of the sea on the unusual geological formations of the headland. Thousands of empty shells are washed up in tiny sheltered coves, and crabs, anemones, prawns and blennies shelter in rock pools.

Larger marine creatures are to be found off shore, and it is always worth keeping an eye out to sea, as you walk along the cliff-top, for grey seals or basking sharks. The latter – huge but toothless plankton-feeders – are summer visitors to British waters.

Take great care on the steep sections of the path and near cliff-edges, and please avoid disturbing nesting birds in the breeding season.

THE *W*ALK

Before setting off from the National Trust car park, study the view-board which gives a good idea of the layout of the headland. The bushes and hedgerows surrounding the car park are excellent feeding areas for small migrant birds and, with patience, several species of warbler could be seen here in spring and autumn.

1 From the car park, cross the stile and follow the path through the field to the left-hand edge, then join the cliff path and walk eastwards along it. Look back inland to the cliff by the car park; cirl buntings sometimes sing from the tops of bushes and yellowhammers also breed here. Linnets, meadow pipits and skylarks feed at the edge of the scrub patches. Look along the rocks on the shore below for oystercatchers.

2 Continue along the cliff path to a small rock outcrop with a tiny spring trickling out of it, known locally as Fish-in-the-Well Rock. The path divides here and the route continues up the hill to the left and alongside the rock outcrop. At the top of the rock, follow the old stone wall up the hill, keeping it on your right. English stonecrop, wall pennywort and sheepsbit scabious grow on the exposed rock, and foxgloves appear curiously stunted where the wind has dwarfed them. Wrens, robins and dunnocks feed below the gorse bushes, and male stonechats sit boldly on the branches. The wall brown butterfly often lives up to its name by basking

Start Point from Prawle Point. Uncultivated land in this mild area is rich in wildlife

on the rocks or the stone walls, and several other species of butterfly, such as skippers and the meadow brown, may be seen here.

3 On reaching the lane, turn right and walk as far as the corner, then turn left up the hill and take the left turn at the T-junction at the top of the lane. All along the lane the steep banks support a luxuriant growth of soft shield fern, an abundant plant in this area, but scarce elsewhere. The undivided fronds of hart's tongue fern can also be seen here. Black spleenwort and polypody are two more wall ferns which thrive here.

4 Continue along the lane. Search the small fields on the right for migrant birds and butterflies, and scan the horizon and the skies for birds of prey, especially buzzards, which soar effortlessly. Kestrels are more likely to be seen hovering over a

piece of rough ground searching for small mammals.

5 At the T-junction turn left and follow the lane down towards Elender Cove. Pause at the T-junction to look due west across to Bolt Head. The cliffs below the lane may have stonechats, meadow and rock pipits on them. Rock pipits have a parachuting song flight in which they propel themselves out from the cliff and parachute down, singing all the time.

6 The rocks here support many wild flowers such as the beautiful bloody cranesbill, a colourful relative of herb Robert, which blooms along more sheltered sections of the walk. Insects thrive on the sunny slopes: the green hairstreak butterfly and green tiger beetle both occur here. Look across the cove to Gammon Head, where herring gulls nest; you may also see fulmars gliding on stiffly held wings. A large black bird flying acrobatically over the cliffs is likely to be a raven; look for the distinctive, wedge-shaped tail. **Take the lower path along the cliff which skirts Elender Cove and leads around the Point past the coastguard station.** It should be possible to find a sheltered spot, whatever the wind direction, and look out to sea in search of seabirds. At any time of year shags and cormorants can be seen fishing, and herring and great black-backed gulls will be around, but in late summer and autumn, migrant seabirds will also be moving past, especially if the wind is blowing from the south. Look for wheatears and rock pipits on the rockier sections of the cliff.

7 The path now returns below the coastguard cottages to the National Trust car park.

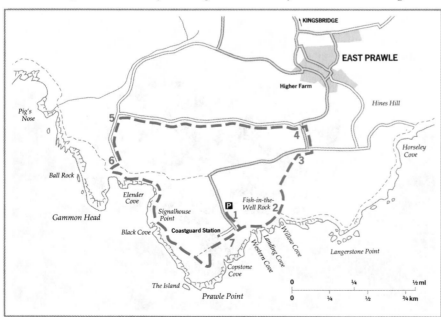

Elberry Cove remains surprisingly peaceful

TINY, PEBBLY COVES WITH TREE-COVERED CLIFFS SURROUNDING THEM; NATURAL ROCK GARDENS OF LIMESTONE COVERED IN WILD FLOWERS; DEEP, SHADY WOODS AND A PATCHWORK OF TINY FIELDS AND LANES – SURPRISINGLY, SUCH PLACES STILL EXIST BETWEEN THE BUSY HOLIDAY TOWNS OF PAIGNTON AND BRIXHAM. THIS SMALL STRETCH OF COASTLINE GIVES A GOOD IDEA OF WHAT THE WHOLE TORBAY AREA MUST ONCE HAVE BEEN LIKE.

COASTAL PLANT LIFE

The hard limestone rocks of the cliffs have weathered in places to form natural rock gardens on which a varied flora has developed. Small scabious, stonecrop, salad burnet, ploughman's spikenard, rock-rose, carline thistle and Portland spurge flower through the summer, and autumn squill makes a final show of colour in autumn.

Gentler slopes are clothed with thick scrub, colourful with fruits and berries in autumn: wayfaring tree, privet, spindle, blackthorn and butcher's broom are covered with a tangle of wild clematis and bryony. Woodland has developed on the cliff-tops and even some of the cliff-faces. Introduced sycamores grow to a great size here and among them are large, lichen-covered ash trees, with small groves of larch and the occasional oak. Hazel and holly make up the understorey and butcher's broom, stinking iris, tutsan, hart's tongue fern and soft shield fern form an almost complete ground cover. Ivy covers both trees and the soil in places, and the rare ivy broomrape, a curious parasitic plant, sends up its orchid-like flower-spikes through the ivy carpet in summer.

Elberry Cove
Devon
Grid ref. SX 898 573

Approx. 3½ miles (5.6 km). Mostly easy walking on waymarked paths, but with some steep ascents and some muddy sections after rain.

Elberry Cove is between Brixham and Paignton. There is parking at Broad Sands at the end of the unclassified road leading to Elberry Cove off the A379.

A few pockets of peaceful country-side and untouched coastline remain around busy Torbay. Here is a walk through coastal woodlands and along quiet lanes, where birds, butterflies and a good selection of wild flowers and ferns can be found.

Nearby sites: *Berry Head Country Park* – a dramatic limestone headland renowned for its wild flowers, seabird colonies and outstanding coastal scenery; *South Devon Coast Path* – the stretch between Berry Head and the Dart Estuary runs along an immensely varied stretch of coast, with much to interest the naturalist.

Red campion thrives in West Country lanes

INSECTS AND BIRDS

Butterflies are very common and in summer migrants like the red admiral and painted lady are easily found; migrant moths like the silver Y also arrive here in large numbers at times. Resident butterflies include the wall brown, which enjoys basking on sunny rocks. Common blues breed in open grassy areas, and speckled woods are common along the woodland paths.

Woodlands close to the sea attract migrant birds. In spring and autumn warblers abound, while resident songbirds find shelter here all year. Robins, blackbirds and song thrushes start breeding much earlier than those further inland.

CREATURES OF THE SHORE

The sheltered seashore is mostly rocky, and at low tide rock pools, weed-filled gullies and small patches of sand and shingle are uncovered. These are rich in marine life and a great variety of crabs, anemones, topshells, prawns and other seashore creatures can be found. Wrasse and blennies abound and in summer shoals of mackerel move in close to the shore.

In winter, Torbay can be very sheltered and many seabirds arrive to feed in the bay, including divers, grebes, sea ducks, auks and gulls. Purple sandpipers, turnstones and oystercatchers feed on the shore, and rock pipits and pied wagtails search for food along the strand line in the small coves. Kestrels hover over the cliff-top grassland and sometimes a peregrine wanders from further along the coast.

The limestone of Torbay is highly prized as a building material and was quarried extensively. Many abandoned quarries have been colonised by a great variety of plants. Old lime-kilns and derelict quays are other reminders of a once thriving industry.

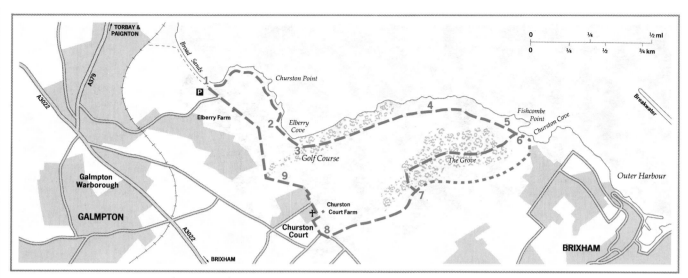

1 From Broad Sands car park follow the path along the edge of the bay towards Churston Point. Thrift grows on the low cliff-top and rock samphire grows just below the cliff-edge, flowering in late summer. In winter, purple sandpipers and oyster-catchers feed on the rocks uncovered by the tide, and gulls scavenge in the bay.

2 Follow the path down to the shore in Elberry Cove. At low tide, the exposed rocks are covered with barnacles and dogwhelks. Nearer the low-tide mark there are pools and gullies rich in marine life. The shingle above the high-water mark has a curious mixture of plants growing on it: ivy-leaved toadflax, red valerian and herb Robert are plants usually associated with walls, but they grow well here alongside more usual shingle plants like sea beet. Wood sage and woody nightshade also thrive on this beach. The ruined building at the far end of the cove is an old lime-kiln and loading quay.

3 Cross the beach and follow the steep path through the woods to the cliff-top. This woodland is made up of a mixture of native and introduced trees. Massive sycamores shelter an understorey of native hazel, butcher's broom and privet and a ground layer of tutsan and stinking iris. Many lichens grow on the bark of the trees here, especially that of ash and sycamore.

4 Follow the path along the cliff-top towards Fishcombe Point. (Several small side-tracks lead off the main path towards the cliff-edge, but these often end up at very steep slopes, so do not follow them.) The woods here are excellent for migrant birds in spring and autumn. Speckled wood butterflies are also common on this section of the path.

5 Follow the path down the steep slope towards Churston Cove. The small patches of open ground are interesting spots for lime-stone flora; small scabious, autumn squill, carline thistle and ploughman's spikenard are a few of the lime-loving plants that survive here where the scrub has not encroached. Strangely, bell heather, a plant of acid soils, also grows here. Butterflies are common on this sheltered slope.

6 At Churston Cove the path turns inland and can be followed either through the wood called The Grove or across some fields for a short distance. The Grove has a luxuriant ground layer of ferns, mostly hart's tongue and soft shield ferns, but wood spurge, enchanter's nightshade and the rare spurge laurel also grow here. Fungi are common in autumn and the showy dryad's saddle can be found on decaying stumps. Huge trailing stems of clematis hang down from the canopy and an abandoned lime-kiln is grad-ually disappearing under encroaching vegetation.

7 Where the path leaves the wood, cross the stile and turn right to follow the lane between the fields. House sparrows, linnets, gold-finches and chaffinches feed along the lane and in the fields, and yellow toadflax flowers at the base of the wall.

8 At the end of the lane, turn right on to the road and follow it round the church to Green Lane, which leads to the golf course. Pellitory-of-the-wall and Mexican flea-bane grow on the churchyard wall between large patches of the white lichen *Lecanora*.

9 Follow the path across the golf course between the yellow posts, taking care not to stray on to the course itself, then go down the lane between fields and houses to Elberry Farm and the car park. Teasels, mullein and bindweeds flower along the lane, and swallows and martins feed around the farm.

The old lime kiln and quay house

SET IN THE DEEP WOODED VALLEY OF THE RIVER TEIGN, OVERLOOKED BY CASTLE DROGO, FINGLE BRIDGE IS A WELL-KNOWN DARTMOOR BEAUTY SPOT. HOWEVER, AWAY FROM THE MAIN CAR PARK THE VALLEY IS QUIET, EVEN IN SUMMER. MANY MILES OF FOOTPATHS FOLLOW THE RIVER AND LEAD THROUGH THE WOODS TO THE HILLS ABOVE THE VALLEY.

PLANT LIFE IN THE VALLEY

The River Teign rises on Dartmoor and flows down off the moor through a dramatic valley lined with oakwoods and flanked by open moorland. At one time the whole of the valley would have been densely wooded, but now only remnants of semi-natural woodland remain. For centuries the oaks have been felled and allowed to regenerate, giving rise to a woodland in which oaks dominate, but other shrubs grow beneath them. Many of the present oaks have thin trunks and can be clearly seen to be growing out of stumps of trees cut down long ago. Hazel and holly grow well with the oaks on these steep slopes, and a ground flora of wood sage, cow-wheat, foxgloves, woodrush and golden-rod has developed. Bluebells, wood anemones and primroses make these woodland walks a delight in spring.

Sadly, in some parts of the valley the native oaks have been clear-felled and alien conifers have been planted, looking most out of place in this setting. Few of the oakwood species of insects and birds do well in conifer plantations.

The Teign valley from Sharp Tor. Castle Drogo is visible on the opposite hilltop

Fingle Bridge
Devon
Grid ref. SX 743 898

National Trust (part)
Approx. 4 miles (6.4 km). Steep in parts, but all on gravel or stony paths which are well defined and easy to follow.

The walk is along the Teign Valley, south of Drewsteignton. Park at Fingle Bridge, 1 mile (1.6 km) south-east of the village.

Climbing from Fingle Bridge out of the Teign valley, the walk first explores the moorland edge, rich in insects in summer and giving fine views of the woodland below and its birdlife. The return is along the wooded valley bottom, good for woodland birds and flowers as well as ferns, mosses and lichens.

Nearby sites: *Prestonbury Castle* and *Cranbrook Castle* – ancient hill-forts on either side of the Teign valley, with sweeping views, and reached by paths through interesting woodland and moorland.

Common dog violet – a welcome sign of spring

Mosses, ferns, liverworts and lichens grow well in the valley's pure, damp air. Rocks and tree-trunks are covered with a luxuriant growth, especially deep down in the humid atmosphere near the river, where every available surface is covered.

CREATURES OF THE RIVER

The River Teign flows into the sea at Teignmouth. Migrant sea trout and salmon lie in the estuary waiting for a spate, caused by heavy rain on Dartmoor, to rush down the river; they can then ascend the many weirs on their way up to the feeder streams on the moor. These streams have clear, well-oxygenated water and gravelly beds which make ideal spawning grounds. Fish ladders enable the fish to scale the weirs on their migration up the river. After periods of heavy rain, trout and perhaps salmon may be seen swimming and jumping up the rapids. The acidic water, coloured amber by the peat through which the feeder streams flow, does not suit many fish species apart from trout and salmon, but eels migrate upstream to moorland pools, and bullheads and stoneloaches live in sheltered stretches.

Stones in the river with white droppings on them are perches for dippers, which can run easily under water to catch their prey. Otters are now rare on Dartmoor, but from time to time their droppings (spraint), on boulders in the river, show that they sometimes pass through the valley.

WOODLAND BIRDS AND ANIMALS

Oak woodland with a thin understorey is typical habitat for wood warblers, redstarts and pied flycatchers – migrant birds which arrive in early summer to take up territories. The resident woodland birds, including great and blue tits, nuthatches, tree-creepers and great spotted wood-peckers, will already be nesting when the migrants arrive. From the upper levels of the valley it is possible to watch buzzards soaring and circling. The impatient cries of their young are heard in the valley in late summer as they wait for the parents to return to the nest with food. Jays feed on acorns in autumn and bury them in secret caches, so they are responsible for many of the seedling oaks.

Roe deer live in the woods but, despite the sparse shrub layer, are very difficult to see. The many small holly bushes show signs of their browsing, and their tracks and droppings are seen on the path. Fallow deer are also present, the result of escapes from deer parks.

Seldom active by day, the wood mouse has large eyes and ears to help it find its way at night

1 From the car park walk back along the road towards Drewsteignton until you see the sign indicating the Hunter's Path. Follow this path up the hillside. The woodland here is a mixture of oak and other broadleaved species, and the ground cover is very sparse. Purple hairstreak and holly blue butterflies are seen here in summer, and buzzards may be heard overhead. Grey squirrels are common in this wood and their untidy dreys are easily spotted in tall oaks.

2 At the top of the hill, the path leaves the woodland. Here is a small area of open moorland with European and western gorse, bell heather, wood sage and sheepsbit scabious. This whole section is excellent for butterflies in summer; several species of brown butterfly may be seen. Honey bees, bumble bees and hoverflies visit the heather flowers, and the occasional stonechat nests here.

3 The path leaves Drewston Common, passes above Sharp Tor and along the edge of Piddledown Common before beginning the long descent to the valley below Castle Drogo. There are various vantage points along the route where it is possible to look deep down into the valley and watch birds flying below. Swallows and martins pass through in summer, and woodpigeons can be watched giving their wing-clapping display. Sparrowhawks soar out over the tree-tops and the magnificent buzzard is nearly always present, looking very large when seen from this angle. Occasionally a raven flies ponderously through the valley. In spring a chorus of birdsong drifts up from the trees, but it will be necessary to descend to the valley to see the smaller woodland birds.

4 The path leaves the National Trust's Castle Drogo Estate through a hunting-gate. Turn back sharp left along a lane to join the Fisherman's Path alongside the river. Navelwort grows on the walls and the ferns, mosses and lichens become more luxuriant here. Robins, wrens and dunnocks, present all year, hunt for insects in crevices in the wall.

5 At the river, turn left and follow the wide path. (The narrow path close to the water's edge can be slippery in wet weather and is best avoided when the river level is high.) The weir has a fish ladder; when the river is in spate, trout and salmon may be watched jumping here. When the river is low in summer, the clear water makes it possible to watch trout poised in mid-current waiting for food to be swept downstream to them.

6 The path continues alongside the river all the way back to Fingle Bridge. In spring there is a good display of bluebells and other spring flowers here, and it should be possible to see wood warblers, redstarts, pied flycatchers, nuthatches and great spotted woodpeckers anywhere along this path. Later in the summer cow-wheat blooms; this semi-parasitic plant of old oakwoods obtains some of its food from the roots of grasses. Golden-rod grows where the soil is a little deeper and more fertile. Pink purslane is an introduced species which thrives in the damp soil close to the river, and lady fern and royal fern grow between large boulders on the river bank.

7 The path makes one or two detours up the bank to avoid landslips before reaching Fingle Bridge and the end of the walk. There are several sections where the river has eroded its banks and trees have fallen. Some of these are being left to provide habitats for fungi and beetles, and ultimately food for birds and mammals. In autumn they produce an interesting display of fungi and several species can be found on the oldest fallen tree-trunks. Although not often seen, woodmice are present here and if fungi are examined closely, toothmarks and droppings show where they have been feeding.

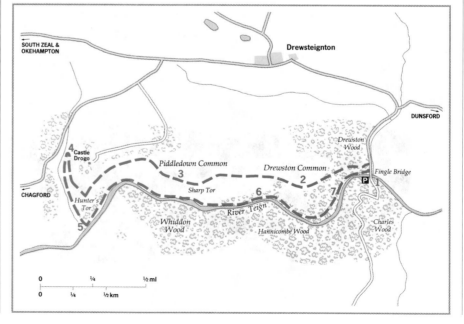

FROM THE HIGHEST POINTS OF HALDON FOREST MAGNIFICENT VIEWS STRETCH ACROSS THE DEVON COUNTRYSIDE, FROM THE GREAT SWEEP OF THE EXE ESTUARY TO THE DISTANT TORS OF DARTMOOR. CLOSER AT HAND, GREAT HALDON'S RICH MOSAIC OF HABITATS HAS ENCOURAGED MANY BIRDS AND INSECTS TO LIVE IN AN AREA WHICH WOULD OTHERWISE BE UNSUITABLE FOR THEM.

HEATH AND FOREST

The high ground of Great Haldon was once rough heathland with some natural woodland. Scraps of this remain in places, with patches of western gorse, bell heather and birch scrub serving as reminders of what the area once looked like. But large plantations of alien conifers, including Japanese larch, Douglas fir and Sitka spruce, have transformed the area into a vast forest and attracted many species of birds, insects and mammals which would normally not live here.

The common field grasshopper

BIRDS OF PREY

Haldon Forest is one of the best places in England to see birds of prey, and a 'raptor viewing station' has been created especially for birdwatchers. An extraordinary range of birds of prey can be seen from this high vantage point, including most of the resident species and some unusual summer visitors. Devon has a large population of buzzards, sparrowhawks and kestrels, and in summer hobbies and honey buzzards arrive to join them. Goshawks and peregrines are less common residents and other species like harriers and merlin are also seen here from time to time, so any bird-watcher who spends some time here could soon build up an impressive list of birds of prey.

WOODLAND BIRDS AND ANIMALS

The mature forest is home to many

Great Haldon

Devon
Grid ref. SX 882 847

Forestry Commission
Approx. 1¹/₂ miles (2.4 km), but the walk can easily be extended. Mostly easy walking, on waymarked forest trails, but with some steep sections. Parts of the tracks may be closed at times because of forestry operations, but alternative routes are always available and clearly marked.

Great Haldon is about 5 miles (8 km) south-west of Exeter. Park in the Forestry Commission car park, signed 'Forest Walks' off the A38.

Haldon Forest is a large area of planted conifers, many of them alien species in Britain, but small areas of natural vegetation have been retained and these, together with the forest rides and tracks, attract a wide variety of wildlife. The area is particularly noted for butterflies and birds of prey.

Nearby sites: *Yarner Wood National Nature Reserve* – a natural oakwood on the slopes of Dartmoor, with woodland walks; *Haytor Down* – open moorland, scrub, acid bogs and pools, good for moorland birds, insects and plants.

Hobby chasing house martins

---

woodland birds, including crossbills, attracted by the rich harvest of pine and spruce cones. Goldcrests and coal tits are quite at home in conifer forests, and jays, nuthatches and several other species of tit and finch all live here, some of them more dependent on the broadleaved species than the conifers.

Roe and fallow deer live in the mature forest, moving out into the growing plantations to feed on the rich growth of grasses, brambles and young trees. Their signs are every-where: tracks, droppings, browsing signs and bark frayed by antlers are all very obvious. The deer themselves take a little more finding.

INSECTS AND PLANT LIFE

An overhead power line cuts a swathe through the forest at one point and trees are cut back from beneath it, leaving an open, sunny area rich in butterflies. A remarkable total of 38 species live here, enjoying the protection of the surrounding forest and the freedom from agricultural sprays. In addition to the butterflies, grasshoppers and crickets abound and spiders and lizards prey on them.

Shadier parts of the forest are clothed with ferns, mosses and lichens, and in autumn fungi brighten the forest floor, but the wider, sunnier rides and tracks have a colourful display of wild flowers through the summer. Late summer brings the colours of bell heather and dwarf gorse, while in early autumn rowan (mountain ash) trees produce their crop of colourful red berries.

The Honey Buzzard

The honey buzzard is one of our rarest birds of prey and it has benefited from the creation of Haldon Forest. It is a migrant bird, arriving in the early summer after spending the winter in Africa. Although it will feed like a more conventional bird of prey on small birds, mammals and lizards, it has the unusual habit of robbing bees' and wasps' nests to take the grubs. It may sit on a prominent perch and watch wasps going back to their nest, then fly down to the entrance hole and scratch it open with its talons. It does not seem to have any special immunity to the stings of its prey because feeding birds are often seen to flinch as they are attacked by angry wasps or bees. Sadly, honey buzzards are heavily persecuted in the Mediterranean countries and many are shot before they cross to Africa.

THE *Walk*

1 Follow the blue markers on the track leading north out of the car park. Go through the wooden barrier on the left and follow the stony track down the hill. The slopes have been planted with larch and spruce but the banks show some of the original vegetation of this area: ling, bell heather, western gorse, hard fern and sphagnum moss are remnants of the former heathland vegetation. Meadowsweet and hemp agrimony have flourished in the shelter created by the surrounding trees. Orange- and buff-tailed bumble bees feed on the flowers, and several species of butterfly will be here on sunny days. Coal tits and goldcrests are common in this area of mature conifers.

2 At the bottom of the hill the damper conditions favour angelica, a favourite with insects. The small flowers of eyebright become conspicuous in summer and several species of grasshopper live here; the common field grasshopper has good camouflage and is only obvious when it jumps, but it can usually be heard 'singing' in sunny weather. Look in the damper patches for the tracks of deer and look for their paths crossing the main rides. Their droppings may be seen anywhere; they can be identified by the point at one end; rabbit droppings are more rounded.

3 The path continues up the hill, turning right by a beech tree (an unusual species in this area). Just below the summit is the raptor viewpoint, where seats and an information board are provided. This is an excellent area to pause for a while and scan the skies and tree-tops for birds of prey. At any time of day and throughout the year there will be something to see. Only the kestrel hovers, and only the buzzard soars for long periods on outstretched wings, but other birds of prey may soar or circle for shorter periods. In summer the rare honey buzzard may be seen here and a hobby may be seen high overhead chasing martins. Goshawks are more secretive forest birds, but they do display in the open earlier in the year. Woodpigeons, jays, magpies and crows all fly past, causing confusion when seen at a distance or in poor light.

4 The path now continues up the slope, crosses the road and leads down the other side of the hill. Broad buckler fern grows among the bracken and isolated bushes of holly and rhododendron grow on the old banks. Bees visit the many flowers on the banks, and spiders spin webs among the small gorse bushes. These sunny banks are good basking sites for lizards, but they are always very alert and difficult to approach. Wrens and robins scold in the dense bushes beside the track and there may be feeding flocks of finches overhead in winter.

5 The small track now joins a main forest ride at the bottom of the slope and leads back towards the road. Turn right at the bottom of the slope. Along the track are several viewpoints offering wonderful vistas of the Devon countryside, the city of Exeter and the Exe estuary. This is

Conifer plantations can be unattractive to wildlife, but Great Haldon's varied habitats support a range of animals, insects and birds

another good area to see birds of prey. They can often be watched from above as they hunt over the fields and hedgerows far below. This is a working forest, so along the track there may be felled timber awaiting removal; treetrunks lying in the sun make good basking sites for lizards and butterflies.

6 The track now joins the road; turn right through the gate and walk along the grassy verge back to the car park. Nuthatches and treecreepers both occur in this area of mature trees; both feed while holding on to tree-trunks. The nuthatch can run up as easily as it can run down, and may wedge nuts in bark crevices before pecking them open. The treecreeper runs up the trees like a little mouse, searching for insects in bark crevices before flying to the base of the next tree to repeat the process. The grassy verges are colourful with woodland flowers in summer, if the grasscutters spare them, and betony and rosebay willowherb are both visited by many insects.

7 From the car park, the walk can be extended to the south and west by following a further set of blue markers. This trail is steeper in places and more shaded, and many more ferns grow here, including scaly male fern, hard shield fern, soft shield fern and hart's tongue. The rare high brown fritillary butterfly is one of many species that may be seen, and in the early mornings and late evenings there is a chance of seeing roe deer. **This circular route also returns to the car park.**

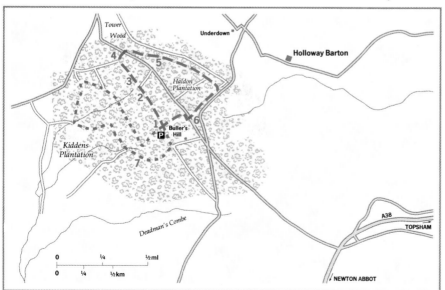

ALONG THE WHOLE OF ITS LENGTH THE EXE ESTUARY IS ENCLOSED BY ROADS, RAILWAY LINES, SEA WALLS AND FOOTPATHS, YET IT REMAINS A HAVEN FOR WILDLIFE AND OFFERS PEACEFUL WALKING AND SOLITUDE FOR THOSE WHO WANT IT.

BIRDWATCHING ON THE ESTUARY

The upper reaches of the Exe estuary are muddy and rich in burrowing worms, molluscs, shrimps and other marine life, so vast numbers of birds are attracted to feed here. For a time in mid-summer the bird numbers may seem low, as most of them will be away on their breeding grounds, but as the summer turns into autumn the populations build up until very impressive flocks are seen, turning the mudflats white as they feed ahead of the advancing tide. The rare and beautiful avocet is one of the star attractions here in winter, but many other species are always present. The calls of curlews and whimbrels, or the spectacle of a vast flock of dunlins wheeling and turning over the distant mudbanks, flashing white and then grey before they settle, makes any visit here worth while.

FISH – A PREY TO MAN AND BIRDS

Salmon migrate through the estuary on their way to the spawning grounds in the headwaters of the Exe far to the north on Exmoor. Traditional netting still takes place here in summer and occasionally a large fish breaks the surface with an energetic leap. Bass and mullet penetrate high up into the estuary from the sea, and in late summer the magnificent osprey may stop off and fish here for a short time on its migration south. It can sometimes be seen flying low over the water with a silvery fish held in its talons. Flounders are a favourite quarry for anglers, but cormorants seem to be better at catching them: one of these big, black birds can often be seen coping with a large fish which will only just fit into its beak. The many marker buoys and moored boats make good roosting places for the cormorants, which often sit in the characteristic position with wings held out to dry.

WILDLIFE ON THE MARSHES

The flat marshes on the landward side of the sea wall may seem rather barren at first, but they are a very important habitat for birds, insects and plant

Red-breasted merganser

Powderham & Exminster Marshes

Devon
Grid ref. SX 973 844

RSPB (part)
Approx. 5 miles (8 km). Almost completely level walking, but with some muddy sections in winter and some stiles to cross.

The walk is on the west side of the Exe estuary, 5 miles (8 km) south of Exeter. Park beside Powderham church.

The Exe estuary is one of the major estuaries in the south-west and is an important feeding ground for thousands of birds throughout the year. The adjoining marshes are rich grazing lands and support their own wildlife, even in winter.

Nearby sites: *Dawlish Warren* – an outstanding Local Nature Reserve with sand dunes, scrub, ponds and mudflats; *Powderham Castle Deer Park* (view from the road) – good views of the large herd of fallow deer as well as the many wildfowl, waders and birds of prey that feed in the park.

life. Cattle graze on the grasses and keep them low, providing suitable conditions for birds like wagtails, larks and pipits which nest here and feed on the insects attracted to the cow-pats. The marshes are criss-crossed by a network of drainage channels which are filled with marsh plants and insect life. Yellow iris, purple loosestrife, water plantain, flowering rush and water celery are just a few of the plants which thrive in these wet conditions and add colour to the flat landscape. Colourful damselflies and dragonflies hunt for smaller insects along the ditches and whirligig beetles gyrate on the surface, while in the clear water below sticklebacks hunt for water-fleas. Grey herons stalk the ditches in search of the abundant eels, and small groups of teal and mallards feed quietly at the edges. Winter brings flocks of waders like curlews, godwits and ruffs to feed on the fields and the elegant short-eared owl flies low over the fields in search of voles.

BRITAIN'S OLDEST CANAL

The Exeter Ship Canal is said to be the oldest working canal in Britain, built to bypass an obstructing weir at the head of the estuary at Countess Wear. Building started in 1564 and the first canal was opened to shipping in 1566. Its deep, clear water supports shoals of roach and bream, and large pike lurk in the weeds. Patches of yellow water-lily add colour to the margins of the canal and the extensive reed-beds on the estuary side are home for many warblers in summer and are used as a roost by starlings in winter.

Low tide on the upper Exe estuary. The mud teems with invertebrates of many kinds – food for a wide range of wading birds

THE *Walk*

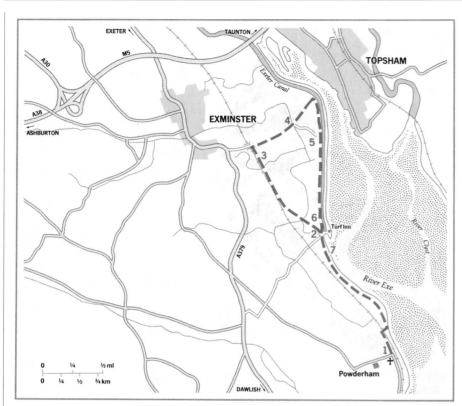

Flowering rush in bloom in high summer

1 Go through the gate at the bend in the road opposite Powderham church and take the rough track alongside the railway line. At the end of the track go through the gate and cross the railway line with care. The path now follows the sea wall. At low tide, the main channel of the River Exe can be seen and the surrounding mudflats will have many birds feeding on them. Black-headed gulls are always very numerous here, but in summer they are joined by Sandwich terns. Waders feed all along the shore in the rich mud, and cormorants fish in the deep channel. In winter they are joined by red-breasted mergansers.

2 At the Turf Inn cross the high stile and take the footpath which leads to the left across the fields away from the river and towards the railway line. The path is not very distinct here, so head for the gap in the hedge to the right of a distant clump of trees. At the clump of trees is a large drainage channel with well vegetated margins and, usually, a few ducks, so approach it quietly. Common blue damselflies and small red dragonflies hunt along these ditches in summer, but in winter they are the haunt of snipe and green sandpipers.

3 Follow the path alongside the main railway line, past the ruined signal box, and at the bridge turn right down the lane back towards the canal. The brambles along the lane are favourite feeding places for butterflies in summer, especially the wall brown, small tortoiseshell, peacock, red admiral and comma. When the fleabane, which grows all along the track, is in bloom its yellow flowers attract still more butterflies and insects, especially hover-flies and bees. The open fields are favourite feeding areas for swallows and martins, sometimes seen flying very low when rain threatens; swifts also feed here, but they are usually much higher up. In winter, scan the posts and isolated bushes for birds of prey and owls.

4 Pass the small factory on the left and continue to the bend in the lane. Cross the small drainage ditch here and take the signposted footpath straight across the fields towards the canal bank. Join the towpath here and head south towards Turf. In summer yellow wagtails may feed in these fields, but in winter the pied wagtail is more likely to be seen. Large numbers of starlings search for larvae in the short grass and gather in noisy flocks before going to roost in the reed-beds; an unwary bird is sometimes caught by a sparrowhawk before it gets there.

5 Follow the towpath south alongside the canal. In sunny weather it may be possible to see shoals of roach basking near the surface, and sometimes the sinister outline of a large pike as it hides in the weeds. Dragonflies hunt along the reedy margins of the canal, but in winter moorhens and little grebes are more usual inhabitants. Purple loosestrife and yellow water-lily grow in the sheltered margins, and reed buntings feed in the thick vegetation on the far towpath.

6 At the Turf Inn cross the lock and walk in front of the inn to the estuary bank. Turn left here and walk up the shore of the estuary for a few hundred yards (metres). This is a good vantage point for scanning the mudflats with binoculars in winter; many wading birds, including avocets, favour this area. The estuary is of international importance for brent geese and black-tailed godwit. The birds usually feed at the water's edge, so as the tide advances they come nearer to the shore, and can be seen more easily.

7 Return to the Turf Inn and cross the lock again, then retrace your steps back to the start of the walk. The lock basin and deep channel leading to it are good feeding areas for common sandpipers, regularly seen on migration. Mullet come nosing in with the tide and are often seen here on sunny afternoons. A flash of brilliant blue and orange is often the only view of a kingfisher; scan the banks carefully, however, as a sitting kingfisher is not conspicuous.
Take care when crossing the railway line before returning to the road at Powderham church.

LUNDY IS A DELIGHTFUL, WINDSWEPT ISLAND AT THE MOUTH OF THE BRISTOL CHANNEL. EASILY VISIBLE FROM THE MAINLAND, IT IS A LONG, FLAT-TOPPED, GRANITE PLATEAU FLANKED BY SHEER CLIFFS RISING 400FT (120M) FROM THE SEA. ITS AXIS LIES IN A NORTH-SOUTH DIRECTION, THE EAST SIDE BEING SHELTERED, WHILE THE WEST SIDE BEARS THE FULL FORCE OF THE ATLANTIC.

THE SEABIRD COLONIES

The name Lundy comes from the Norse word for puffin, reflecting the island's importance to breeding seabirds. Although the puffin population on Lundy has declined markedly over the last 20 years, a few pairs still breed here and may be seen from April to mid August. The cliffs support large colonies of guillemots and razorbills, also members of the auk family. Many of the island's important seabird colonies are inaccessible, but the North Light and Jenny's Cove are good places for birdwatchers. Kittiwakes, the most marine of our breeding gulls, have noisy and smelly colonies at the north end of the island, while herring, lesser black-backed and great black-backed gulls frequent the grassy slopes. Like the island's remaining puffins, Manx shearwaters breed in cliff-top burrows on Lundy, but they only return to land after dark. A nocturnal stroll is an eerie experience as dark shapes flutter overhead uttering strange, cater-wauling calls.

The seas around Lundy, now a Marine National Nature Reserve, are rich and productive. The accessible areas of shoreline reveal a wealth of intertidal life while, further off shore,

Lundy
Devon
Grid ref. SS 143 437

Landmark Trust/National Trust Approx. 7½ miles (12 km). For a shorter walk, see point 6 overleaf. Rough ground. Very steep in parts.

Lundy is an island in the Bristol Channel, 11 miles (18 km) off the north Devon coast. There are regular sailings (taking about 2 hours) from Bideford and some from Ilfracombe. There is a landing fee for non-members of the National Trust. A day trip to Lundy will allow a maximum of 4 hours ashore – long enough to complete the walk, but allowing little time to linger on the way, so keep an eye on the time.

Famed for its seabird colonies, Lundy also attracts a wide variety of migrant species. The coastal flora is outstanding in May and June and the island boasts an endemic species of plant found nowhere else in the world – Lundy cabbage.

Nearby sites: *Northam Burrows* – dune flora; *Instow beach* – shells

Guillemot in breeding plumage

Lundy's wild and frequently windswept coast takes on a less forbidding aspect on calm, sunny days. The mass of yellow flowers in the foreground here belongs to Lundy cabbage

numerous seabirds feed on the marine bonanza. In addition to the common breeding species, gannets (which no longer breed here) are easily seen off the west side or from the boat as it nears Lundy. During July and August basking sharks, immense but harmless plankton-feeders, sometimes come close inshore.

LUNDY'S PLANT LIFE

Lundy is also renowned for its flowers. Although the top of the island is heavily grazed, patches of heather moorland remain, especially in the northern quarter of the island. It is, however, Lundy's maritime plants that are especially spectacular: May and June see the slopes of the island's exposed west coast turn pink with thrift. White clumps of sea campion, patches of scurvy-grass and boulders covered in orange and grey lichens create the impression of a rock garden.

The rhododendrons, which so dominate the east side of the island, were introduced by a former owner. Although a beautiful sight in spring, they are a mixed blessing because their dense canopy eliminates most native plants.

The island is not without its botanical rarities. Balm-leaved figwort grows sparingly on the east side, sometimes in close proximity to clumps of Lundy cabbage. The cabbage favours outcrops of shale near the Landing Beach. Lundy is the only place in the world that it grows. The coastal turf on the south and west of the island harbours the best British colonies of dwarf adder's tongue fern.

1 Visitors first set foot on Lundy at the Landing Beach. After disembarking, begin the walk by following the path which winds its way up towards the village. Study the rock faces to your left for clumps of Lundy cabbage as well as balm-leaved figwort and sheepsbit scabious. Scan the water below for feeding seabirds such as razorbills, guillemots, kittiwakes and the occasional puffin, as well as grey seals.

2 Follow the path until you reach a small pond on your right. The trees to the left are good for warblers and flycatchers in spring and autumn, and the walled gardens beyond also harbour migrant birds and sometimes hummingbird hawk-moths.

Go through the gates, then turn right up a steep cliff path. Pass the 'Ugly' (a small shelter on your left).

3 Just after the path bends to the left, go through a gate on your right and follow the path through the rhododendrons. This climbs and eventually shadows a stone wall until you reach the ruined Quarter Wall Cottages. Scan the bracken and bushes for migrant birds (several extreme rarities have been found here in the past) and sika deer.

Carpets of thrift clothe the cliff-tops

4 From the Quarter Wall Cottages the path zig-zags past a small quarry pond and eventually descends to the terraces of the old quarries. This area is especially good for migrant birds; the Heligoland trap is used by visiting ornithologists to catch birds for ringing. The bare ground is good for butterflies such as grayling and small copper, while damp cliff-faces have clumps of royal fern.

5 The path climbs along the east side of the island and then forks. Ignore the path that continues near the coast and climb to meet the island's central road. Look for clumps of hay-scented fern.

If time allows, a detour can be made here by walking south-west towards Pondsbury, Lundy's main freshwater pool. Numerous gulls use it for bathing and preening, and it also attracts migrant waders and ducks. In spring, the boggy ground supports heath spotted orchids, bog pimpernel, round-leaved sundew and lesser skullcap.

6 Follow the main track northwards. (For a shorter walk, follow Halfway Wall to the west coast and rejoin the path at point 9 below.) You will pass Tibbett's Hill on your right, marked by a former coastguard lookout, now a holiday cottage. In this area you may see wheatears, meadow pipits, lapwings and Soay sheep.

7 At the north end of the island, steps descend to the North Lighthouse. Beware of the foghorn, which starts without warning in misty weather. Sizeable colonies of kittiwakes, guillemots and razorbills breed here. Puffins and gulls are seen in flight, and rock pipits forage among the boulders. Gannets and Manx shearwaters often pass close to the shore, and grey seals can be seen and heard.

8 Climb back up the steps and walk south, bearing right at the first opportunity. Cross the stone walls. The path here passes some of the most attractive coastal scenery in Britain, featuring landmarks such as St James's Stone and The Pyramid rock. Just beyond the latter is Jenny's Cove, the safest and most accessible spot to see puffins when they are on the island. Carefully pick your way down among the thrift, but sit well away from the cliff's edge. Before long, puffins will fly by. Search the thrift for

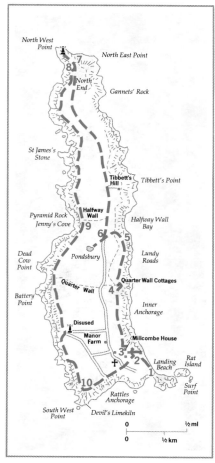

thrift clearwing moths and meadow grasshoppers.

9 Continue south along the cliff-top path. You will pass huge clefts in the ground known as the 'Earthquake', which are good for ferns. Energetic visitors may wish to descend the Battery steps for views of maritime flora, breeding seabirds and, occasionally, wild goats.

Climb back up to the top of the island and continue past the Old Light until you reach South-West Point and the Devil's Limekiln (take care). Look for ravens and distant seabirds, while beneath your feet will be patches of English stonecrop and sheepsbit scabious.

10 Continue along the south coast towards the church. Follow the path which descends past Millcombe House, checking the bushes and trees for migrant birds. The path eventually returns to the Landing Beach. If time and tides permit, look in the rock pools here for marine life.

THE SOUTH-WEST'S MILD CLIMATE MEANS WINTERS RELATIVELY FREE FROM FROST AND SNOW, BUT STRONG WINDS AND SEA FOGS ARE A FREQUENT HAZARD. THE WILD AND REMOTE STRETCH OF COASTLINE AROUND HARTLAND POINT HAS LONG BEEN NOTORIOUS FOR STORMY WEATHER, AND MANY A SHIP HAS MET ITS END HERE.

'A WATERY GRAVE'

The Hartland coastline was once the haunt of wreckers who lured ships on to the treacherous rocks below by lighting fires on the cliff-tops. Many rhymes have been made up about the dangers to shipping off Hartland, such as:

'Between Hartland Point and Lundy Light
Lies a watery grave by day or night.'

The stormy weather which sweeps in from the Atlantic was also recorded in rhymes, with many variations on:

'Lundy high, it will be dry,
Lundy low, expect a blow.'

Even with today's modern navigational aids there are still shipwrecks in this area, and their rusting remains are often exposed at low tide.

SEA-WATCHING FROM HARTLAND

Despite Hartland's stormy reputation, even on the windiest days there will be somewhere around the Point where wildlife-watchers can shelter from the prevailing winds. Strong gales in fact provide the best conditions for watching seabirds on migration, driving them near to the coast. From the Point itself it is possible to see

Blackberry or bramble

Hartland Point

Devon
Grid ref. SS 235 275

Approx. 6¼ miles (10 km). Some steep sections and some lengths near high cliffs, but mostly of only moderate difficulty. May be muddy in parts in winter.

Hartland Point is on the north coast of Devon, roughly mid-way between Bideford and Bude. Cars may be parked where the road ends at Hartland Point.

The Point forms a 'corner' on the map of Devon, flanked by dramatic cliffs and offering fine views out to sea. Wildlife highlights include porpoises and dolphins, as well as seabirds. The cliffs are good for maritime and woodland plants. Inland is an area of unspoilt farmland, tiny villages and deep lanes.

Nearby sites: *Brownsham Nature Reserve* – wooded valley near the sea, valuable for birds, insects and plant life; *Welcombe Mouth* – steep-sided valley with coastal grassland, scrub and woodland; *Tamar Lake* – reservoir and nature reserve attracting many bird species, dragonflies and damselflies and with an interesting flora.

migrating seabirds streaming past on their way to or from their more northerly breeding grounds. In summer the small number of resident seabirds can be seen flying to and from their nesting sites, while in winter numerous red-throated divers congregate in the sheltered waters of Barley Bay, to the east of the lighthouse. These fish-eating birds breed in the far north of Britain, but overwinter much further south. This is one of the best vantage points for watching porpoises and dolphins; they are present throughout the year, but are most abundant in late summer when the mackerel shoals arrive.

HIGH CLIFFS AND DEEP LANES

To the south of Hartland Point, dramatic cliffs stretch away to the coastline of north Cornwall, while to the east the cliffs lead to the wooded slopes above Clovelly and the great expanse of Barnstaple Bay. Both maritime and woodland flowers clothe the cliffs: maritime species can cope with salt spray and grow lower down on the cliffs, while woodland flowers appreciate the cool, damp conditions on north-facing cliffs, where they escape both grazing and trampling.

Many deep lanes, bordered with stone banks, criss-cross the area, providing welcome shelter from the wind. Tiny streams rush through the narrow valleys and end abruptly in cliff-edge waterfalls. Small songbirds are abundant here, nesting in the hedgerows and lanes. Many migrants join them in spring and autumn.

At any time of the year the walks and views can be exhilarating, and there is always a variety of wildlife.

Set high above the rocky shore that has claimed so many ships, Hartland's lighthouse emits one of the brightest beams in the country

The Porpoise

The common porpoise is the smallest whale, measuring no more than 6 feet (1.8m) in length. It is rounded and plump in appearance, lacking the beak and prominent dorsal fin seen in most dolphins. The body is black above and white below, with black flippers and a small, black dorsal fin. Porpoises are often seen close to shore and will even penetrate estuaries in pursuit of fish. They usually occur in small schools and do not engage in the acrobatic leaps and rapid swimming of the larger dolphins. Their local name of 'errin og' (Herring Hog) refers to their liking for larger shoaling fish such as herring and mackerel.

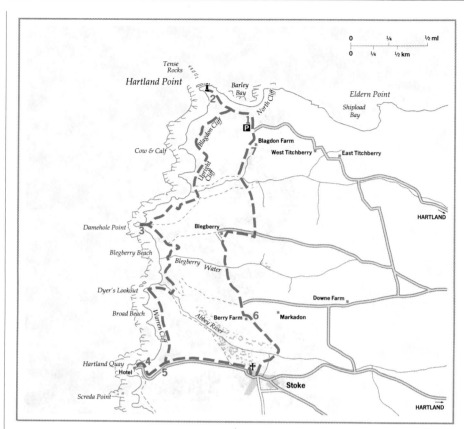

are sometimes the only creatures to be found on the most exposed rocks, but sheltered pools and gullies will have a rich marine life. Look for driftwood washed up with goose barnacles attached to it.

1 From the car park follow the road down to the lighthouse. (Do not approach it too closely if the foghorn is sounding – it could be literally deafening.) The steep cliffs on the right overlook Barley Bay; in winter there may be over 100 red-throated divers here. The resident cormorants and shags may be seen among them, and the occasional grey seal and common porpoise turns up at times. In summer fulmars, kittiwakes, guillemots and razorbills can also be seen in the bay as well as the resident herring gulls. The attractive, pale-flowered wood vetch grows in shady spots here in a most untypical habitat.

2 Return up the road towards the car park as far as the signpost marking the coast path; turn right here and follow the path, taking care near the cliff-edge. The strange concrete area on the slope was an emergency water-catchment area for the lighthouse. In summer many coastal flowers, including kidney vetch, thrift, sheepsbit scabious, English stonecrop and sea campion, bloom here. They are visited by butterflies and other insects. Green tiger beetles are very active in sunny weather and bumble bees are especially common in some places. Grayling butterflies are sometimes difficult to spot on the cliff-tops as they blend perfectly with the stony ground when their wings are closed.

3 At Damehole Point scan the sea below for feeding seabirds in summer and scavenging gulls in winter. Take great care here in very windy weather. Oystercatchers feed on the rocks at low tide. Ravens haunt the cliffs here and their acrobatic display flight in early spring is an exciting spectacle; in summer they are busy scavenging along the cliffs. Stonechats inhabit the cliff-top gorse and rock pipits nest on the stony slopes below.

4 Follow the path south to Hartland Quay. Check Blegberry Water and the Abbey River for dippers as you cross them. At Hartland Quay it is possible to walk down to the stony beach and look back at the extraordinarily contorted rock strata of the cliffs here, which are among the highest in the south-west. The rock ledges continue far out to sea, making ideal habitats for marine creatures, although only the hardiest among them can withstand the wave action on this stormy coast. Barnacles

5 From the Hartland Quay Hotel take the public footpath which runs parallel with the road as far as Stoke church and then take the narrow lane to Berry Farm. In late spring the lanes and hedgerows are a riot of red campion and bluebells, with early purple orchids growing among them. Honeysuckle twines through the other vegetation, and yellowhammers and linnets feed in the fields and along the hedges; in winter they are joined by migrant finches and larks, and flocks of lapwings build up in numbers as colder weather further north drives them to the milder south-west. Robins, wrens, dunnocks and song thrushes feed where they can find cover, whilst rooks and jackdaws patrol the small fields. Overhead, buzzards search for carrion or an unwary rabbit. Both common and pygmy shrews live in the lanes and hedges: their frantic, high-pitched squealings betray their presence.

6 From Berry Farm the lane meanders to Blegberry. Turn right here and then take the next left turn along the bridleway to Blagdon Farm. The lane leads down to a stream where both dippers and grey wagtails may be seen; it may be necessary to wait for a while by the little bridge before they appear. Marsh tits and reed buntings inhabit this section of the valley, and may be easier to see in winter. The damp conditions here have encouraged a luxuriant growth of ferns, including hard fern, prickly shield fern and polypody, and many mosses, liverworts and lichens thrive in the damp, pure air. The scrub-covered slopes leading back down to the sea on either side of the stream are excellent habitat for warblers, and many will be heard singing in spring. Look out also for cuckoos as they search for nests to parasitise, and kestrels hovering over open patches.

7 At Blagdon Farm follow the road to the left to return to the car park. Swallows and house martins feed and nest around the farm buildings, and collared doves compete with stock doves for grain. The old walls support good colonies of rock-loving lichens which testify to the purity of the air in this remote spot.

THE DUNES AT BRAUNTON BURROWS ARE BOUNDED ON THE NORTH BY THE HEADLAND OF SAUNTON DOWN AND ON THE SOUTH BY THE ESTUARY OF THE RIVERS TAW AND TORRIDGE. TO THE WEST LIES BIDEFORD OR BARNSTAPLE BAY, WHILE TO THE EAST LIES BRAUNTON GREAT FIELD. THE WHOLE AREA IS OF IMMENSE INTEREST TO THE NATURALIST AND OFFERS FASCINATING WALKS AT ANY TIME OF YEAR.

DUNE FORMATION

On a stormy day, with a gale blowing in from the Atlantic, it is easy to see how sand is blown off the vast beach to form dunes. Plants like marram grass bind the dunes with their extensive root systems, and eventually more delicate plants are able to grow as the sand consolidates. A series of ridges and slacks running parallel with the sea has built up, forming an area about 1 mile (1.6km) wide and nearly 3 miles (4.8km) long. Some of the dunes are 100ft (30m) high. If a storm, or damage by feet or vehicles, destroys the plant cover, a blow-out occurs and huge quantities of sand are moved; this stimulates the marram grass into vigorous growth and its new roots and stems help to bind the sand again. The sand is continually on the move through natural processes, but efforts are constantly being made by the NCC to combat unnatural erosion by excessive trampling. Visitors are asked to keep to paths and not climb the dunes.

The dune slacks, as the hollows between the dunes are known, are often very wet in winter and an interesting marsh flora has developed in them. Ponds have also been dug to help the resident frogs, newts and dragonflies.

BRAUNTON GREAT FIELD

This huge area of low-lying land is a fascinating survival of an ancient farming pattern. Once there were 100 farmers working the small plots of land that make up the field, but now there are only five. Dotted over the field are stone barns, or linhays, mostly derelict now, but originally intended as shelter for animals. The grazing marsh is drained by a series of ditches which are filled with purple loosestrife, yellow iris, fleabane, amphibious bistort and water parsnip. In summer the ditches come to life when brightly coloured dragonflies and damselflies emerge from them. Wildfowl, waders, larks and pipits feed on the marsh and swallows nest

Braunton Burrows

Devon
Grid ref. SS 463 351

Nature Conservancy Council
Approx. 5½ miles (8.8 km). Mostly on level ground, but with some steep scrambles up dune slopes and one stretch along a sandy beach. Part of the area is used for military training, so keep a look-out for the warning red flags.

The reserve is about 7 miles (11 km) west of Barnstaple. Park in the NCC car park adjacent to the unclassified road that leads to Braunton Burrows from Braunton.

Braunton Burrows is one of the largest sand dune systems in the British Isles and is internationally renowned for its flora and fauna. Two-thirds of the dune system are a National Nature Reserve, designated by UNESCO as an International Biosphere Reserve. The wild flowers make a spectacular display in summer and the dunes have a rich insect and bird population.

Nearby sites: *Northam Burrows Country Park* – a smaller dune system with rich and varied wildlife and an interesting shoreline bounded by a ridge of huge pebbles; *Taw-Torridge estuary* – extensive sandbanks and mudflats providing good feeding grounds for birds, especially in winter.

Burnet rose

in the linhays, feeding on the abundant insects in summer. Small clumps of stunted hawthorn, blackthorn and bramble provide cover for nesting birds and lookout posts for birds of prey in winter.

WILDLIFE OF THE ESTUARY

The mud and sandbanks of the estuary, exposed at low tide, are rich in

Lovely both to look at and to smell, the sea stock is closely related to garden stocks

burrowing marine life and flocks of gulls, waders and wildfowl come to feed on them. Early summer is the quietest time, when most birds are away on their breeding grounds, but for much of the year large flocks of feeding birds will be seen somewhere on the estuary.

Sea trout and salmon migrate through the estuary on their way upstream to spawning grounds on Exmoor or Dartmoor. Local fishermen net them, and other predators take their toll too. Eels, mullet, bass and flounders also feed in the deep channels, and herons and otters hunt them both in the estuary and in the shallow creeks running back into the salt-marsh. The deep-water channel near the mouth of the estuary has a sand bar marking its end; this can easily be spotted from the dunes by the waves which always break over it. Porpoises often play in the waters around the bar, sometimes penetrating into the estuary itself in pursuit of fish.

Sand Dunes

Wind-blown sand provides the building material for the extensive dune system at Braunton Burrows. Sand particles accumulate around pieces of driftwood and debris on the beach and pioneering plants such as sea rocket grow in these small piles of sand, beginning the stabilising process. Marram grass, with its extensive root system, can then grow in these sand piles and bind them together, gradually building a larger and larger dune; as more sand buries the stems, further growth is stimulated. Eventually other plants grow among the marram grass clumps and the dunes become more stable; a rich community of plants and animals thrives where once there was only a windy beach.

THE *WALK*

1 From the car park take the made-up track that leads through the trees towards the dunes. This area of dense vegetation illustrates the final stage in the colonisation of sand dunes. As you walk through the dunes towards the sea you will pass through earlier stages in the process. The trees provide food and shelter for birds, and are always worth searching for warblers in summer.

2 This flatter, open area is a large dune slack. Marsh plants thrive here, and there are excellent displays of marsh orchids and helleborines in summer. Water mint is also common, and its flowers attract bees and butterflies. The creeping willow which covers the ground in some wet slacks is the food-plant for the larvae of the poplar leaf beetle. The adults look like large, spotless ladybirds and produce a pungent smell to ward off predators.

3 The path climbs up on to the dunes. Conditions become drier and plants like rest-harrow, with its attractive pink flowers, become commoner. Viper's bugloss is common in drier places, and in late summer large areas of yellow ragwort provide splashes of colour as well as food for the black-and-orange striped caterpillars of the cinnabar moth.

From marram grass to tree cover, Braunton Burrows shows every stage of dune colonisation

4 The dunes nearest the sea are the most recently formed and conditions here suit plants able to withstand salt spray and drier, less stable sand. More sand is exposed and marram grass grows vigorously. The striking blue-grey, prickly leaves of sea holly help it to conserve water, while its blue flowers attract many butterflies, especially graylings. Sea bindweed twines around marram grass stems and the rare sea stock produces its beautiful scented flowers here.

5 On reaching the beach, turn left and walk south down the beach towards the estuary. On the beach itself grow a few hardy plants which can withstand the occasional covering by salt water. Prickly saltwort and sea rocket grow among the flotsam and jetsam thrown up by the tides. Many species of shell can be found here, including razor shells, striped venus, carpet shells, necklace shells and wedge shells. Gulls feed on the beach and in winter waders, including oystercatchers and sanderlings, feed near the water's edge.

6 Just beyond the end of a broken brick outfall pipe between Airy Point and The Neck is the start of a boardwalk which leads back across the dunes to the road. This has been provided to save the dunes from excessive trampling. The boardwalk passes through areas which

have a good ground covering of lichens and, growing among them, the diminutive sand toadflax, a tiny, snapdragon-like flower. Huge areas of rest-harrow cover the slopes, and butterflies and bees abound in summer.

7 At the road, it is possible to make a detour along the edge of Horsey Island by following the footpath along the sea wall. This gives excellent views of the Great Field and the brackish pools on the landward side of the wall. Teal, mallards, herons, migrant waders and flocks of smaller birds all use this area, and can be easily seen from the top of the wall. The deep-water channel of the Taw swings close to the end of Horsey Island and here it is possible to watch gulls, terns, grebes, cormorants and wildfowl, especially in winter. A small area of salt-marsh at the base of the wall is colourful in summer with sea spurrey and sea-lavender, and the silvery-grey, aromatic sea wormwood grows on the wall.

8 To return to the car park, turn left at the end of the board-walk and follow the rough road back north. The bushes and trees along the path hide many birds, and in winter flocks of fieldfares and redwings may roost in them. Check the Great Field from time to time for birds feeding in the grassland, and look at posts and isolated bushes for birds of prey.

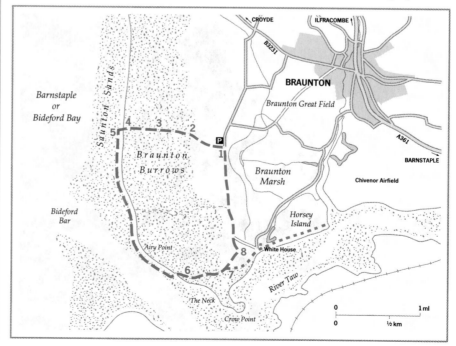

THE VALLEY OF THE ROCKS IS ALL THAT REMAINS OF WHAT MUST ONCE HAVE BEEN AN IMPRESSIVE RIVER VALLEY RUNNING PARALLEL WITH THE PRESENT COASTLINE. GRADUALLY THE SEA CUT INTO THE CLIFFS, SO THE MOORLAND RIVERS AND STREAMS COULD RUN STRAIGHT INTO THE SEA, RATHER THAN INTO THE LARGER RIVER ALONGSIDE IT. THE RIVER BED WAS LEFT DRY.

BETWEEN EXMOOR AND THE SEA

On the north side of the valley, steep cliffs provide a home for wild goats, which are sometimes bold enough to come down and scavenge among picnickers. The seaward side of the cliffs provides wonderful, safe nesting sites for seabirds; fulmars are especially fond of the updraughts created by the wind blowing against the cliffs. Down below, grey seals occasionally haul out to rest on almost inaccessible stony beaches, while maritime plants cling to rock ledges where they are safe from grazing sheep and goats. The famous 'White Lady' rock can be viewed from the road; it is formed from a hole in the rocks which, when viewed against the sky, looks like a lady wearing a long dress.

THE MOORLAND EDGE

Inland, on the south side of the valley, steep slopes lead up on to heather-clad Exmoor. Strong sea winds, and grazing pressure from sheep, have produced a characteristic stunted vegetation, but the colours in late summer, when the heather and gorse are in bloom, are a memorable sight. Ravens and buzzards soar over the hills, while wheatears and stonechats bob among the gorse bushes and drystone walls.

Valley of the Rocks

Devon
Grid ref. SS 706 498

Lynton and Lynmouth Borough Council (part)
Approx. 4¹/₂ miles (7.2 km). Very steep in places, but all paths have good surfaces and are well marked.

The valley lies west of Lynton, on the north coast of Devon. Park in the car park on the unclassified coastal road about ³/₄ mile (1.2 km) west of Lynton.

The Valley of the Rocks lies between the northern slopes of Exmoor and the Bristol Channel. It offers outstanding views inland across rolling moorland and wooded valleys, and out to sea as far as the coastline of South Wales. The variety of wildlife ranges from seabirds and maritime plants on the cliffs to woodland and riverside plants and birds in the sheltered valleys, where ferns and mosses are abundant.

Nearby sites: *Watersmeet* – deep wooded valley with excellent paths, offering good views of woodland birds and wild flowers; *Foreland Point* – Devon's northernmost point of land, with steep cliffs: seabirds, moorland birds and wild flowers are abundant, and there are dramatic views of the Exmoor coastline and across to Wales.

Above: *Common hair moss (Polytrichum commune)*
Top left: *A wren forages among brambles*

SHELTERED VALLEYS

Deep, wooded valleys provide a further contrast. Here the high humidity, and shelter from the strong winds, have encouraged an abundance of mosses and ferns which grow as luxuriantly on the trunks of oak trees as they do on the stream-side rocks. Woodland flowers grow among the moss-covered boulders and tree-trunks, and butterflies are common. Migrant birds such as redstarts and pied flycatchers nest in old trees and in the many specially erected nestboxes, and resident riverside birds like dippers and grey wagtails should be easily spotted along the many fast-flowing streams.

The strange 'moonscape' of the Valley of the Rocks, beloved of Victorian travellers

THE *W*ALK

1 From the car park, walk east along the road to the picnic site and take the waymarked path which leads steeply up the hill to the southeast. Stinking iris grows alongside the herringbone stone wall and in the scrub; its country name, roast beef plant, derives from the strange smell of the crushed leaves. Primroses and violets flower here in the spring, and in summer ivy-leaved toadflax blooms on the wall.

2 At the junction turn back sharply to the right and continue up the hill. Look carefully at the hedges and scrub and in the small fields; these are good feeding areas for migrant birds in spring and autumn, and excellent for butterflies in summer. Robins, wrens, dunnocks and song thrushes thrive in this area and are present all year.

3 At the top of the hill, pause to look down into the Valley of the Rocks; its origins as a river valley will be more obvious from this viewpoint. The stony slopes below are clothed with bracken and western gorse and make good feeding areas for meadow pipits, wheatears and stonechats. Buzzards are often seen here as they soar on outstretched wings.

4 The path continues along the top of the hill, passing the head of the South Cleave valley, and then zig-zags down to the start of the track through Six Acre Wood. Bilberry grows on the slopes; its sweet berries ripen in late summer. Large clumps of *Polytrichum* moss and hard fern show where tiny springs rise, and woodland plants like wood-sorrel indicate that this slope, like much of the surrounding land, must once have been woodland.

5 Follow the path into the wood and take the lower (right-hand) path at the fork. The mixed plantation of beech, larch and other species provides good cover and food for small woodland birds, and throughout the year several members of the tit family can be seen here; they are joined by migrant willow warblers and chiffchaffs in the spring. Hairy woodrush, violets and wood sage flourish in these damp, shady conditions, and the beautiful golden feather moss grows on fallen trees and boulders.

6 At the next junction, follow the path to the left along the hillside, cross the stream and continue into Caffyns Heanton Wood. This woodland has a more natural appearance, containing many more trees native to this area, but man's influence is still evident in the coppicing and replanting. Red campion, bluebells and wood-sorrel are native woodland flowers very much at home in this sort of habitat.

Violets here are food-plants for the scarce pearl-bordered fritillary butterfly, which may be seen on the wing on sunny days in early summer.

7 The path continues alongside the stream through the wood but becomes progressively narrower and more rocky. At Bonhill Bridge cross the stream (pausing to look for dippers and grey wagtails), and turn sharp right in front of Bonhill Cottage. The well made-up track now heads east towards Bonhill Wood. Scan the hillside opposite for buzzards and, in spring, the much smaller male sparrowhawk, which has a soaring display flight. Jays may be heard screeching, and are sometimes glimpsed as they dash across a clearing. The woodland on the left is being coppiced, resulting in a much more open type of woodland in which wild flowers, insects and birds thrive.

8 Where the main track turns back to the left, take the smaller path, signposted 'Lee Abbey', which leads down to the stream and then to the road. All along the stream grows a wealth of ferns including lady fern, male fern, broad buckler, hart's tongue and polypody. Beside the stream, and benefiting from the spray, is the attractive opposite-leaved golden saxifrage. The tiny flowers of moschatel can be found in drier spots. Brown trout live in the stream, and eels make their way up it from the sea.

9 Turn right on to the road and follow it back towards the Valley of the Rocks. The old walls are home to many interesting plants such as pellitory of the wall, ivy-leaved toadflax and English stonecrop; they are able to cope with quite dry conditions and a minimum of soil.

10 Where the road leaves the grounds of Lee Abbey and enters the valley, take the small track to the left, opposite the toll-gate cottage. Follow this down to the cliff, where there is a view of Wringcliff Bay. Fulmars and gulls nest on the cliffs and a few razorbills are usually present in summer. Sometimes a peregrine hunts over the cliffs, trying to catch an unwary feral pigeon or wild stock dove. Grey seals occasionally haul out on the beach below but are soon disturbed by people foolhardy enough to take the steep path down to the beach.

From this point it is an easy walk back through the valley to the car park.

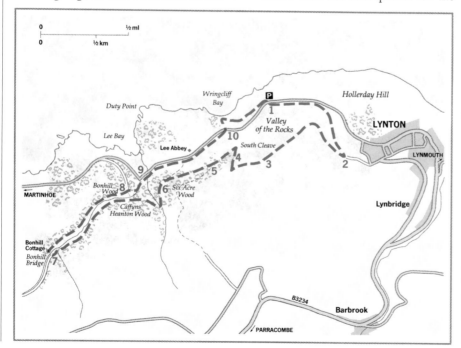

THE DRAMATIC CLIFFS AND VALLEYS AROUND CHEDDAR GORGE ARE CLOTHED WITH A FASCINATING VARIETY OF PLANTS. FOR A TIME IN SUMMER THE TINY PATCHES OF GRASSLAND ARE COLOURFUL WITH FLOWERS AND ALIVE WITH BUTTER-FLIES, WHILE THE WOODLAND FLOOR IN SPRING IS A DELIGHTFUL MASS OF BLUEBELLS.

BIRDS AND ANIMALS OF THE GORGE

Jackdaws are the most obvious birds of the gorge itself, but many smaller woodland birds abound and are seen by walkers who leave the gorge and explore the side-paths. The woods are home to many mammals, most notably the dormouse, a species which is becoming rare elsewhere in Britain. Its nocturnal habits and long hibernation make it difficult to see, and it is usually only the characteristically nibbled hazelnut shells that indicate its presence. Bats roost in trees and caves in the gorge, emerging to hunt for insects on summer evenings, and badgers and foxes are also present, but are not often seen by daytime visitors. Rabbits are common, and are very important for the effect they have on the plant life. Their constant grazing keeps the turf short, although they are not present in sufficient numbers to

Cheddar Gorge

Somerset

Grid ref. ST 482 545

National Trust/Somerset Trust for Nature Conservation (part)

Approx. 3½ miles (5.6 km). Some steep sections along stony tracks, but the walk is mostly of only moderate difficulty.

The gorge is east of Cheddar village, in the Mendip Hills. There is roadside parking off the B3135 at Blackrock Gate.

Cheddar Gorge is a well-known limestone gorge attracting large numbers of visitors, but few explore the surrounding woods and valleys, which support a very rich wildlife in attractive surroundings.

Nearby sites: *Blagdon Lake* and *Chew Valley Lake* – large reservoirs which attract great numbers of birds, including many rarities.

Honeysuckle or woodbine

prevent some scrub species encroaching on the grassland; lime-loving species like wayfaring tree are increasing in some spots.

LEAD MINING AND WILDLIFE

This part of the Mendips was used for mining and quarrying from pre-Roman times to the 1880s. Many spoil tips and abandoned mine shafts show where miners once worked. To the botanist there are other clues, for several plants grow here which are good indicators of the presence of lead; some of the early prospectors looked for these plants before sinking a new shaft. Spring sandwort and alpine pennycress both grow well on old spoil tips but are scarce elsewhere. Lower in the Velvet Bottom valley the levels of lead are still so high that the plants are contaminated and grazing could be dangerous to sheep; even the rabbits have high lead levels in their bodies.

PLANT LIFE AND BUTTERFLIES

The woodlands contain a variety of tree species. Ash is particularly common, but there is a rich under-storey of hazel, dogwood, privet, spindle and wayfaring tree and a ground flora of spring flowers including the unusual herb Paris. Scrub woodland in some areas gives way to a more sparse grassland in exposed sites where there is only a thin soil covering. Wild thyme, spring cinquefoil and rock-rose are among Cheddar's wealth of limestone-loving plants, as is the Cheddar pink, an attractive wild flower found nowhere else in Britain. Butterflies such as marbled whites and dark green fritillaries are abundant on the grassy, flower-studded slopes, and many commoner species are seen in great numbers through the summer.

The piles of rock left behind by the lead miners have gradually become colonised by lichens, mosses and ferns. Brittle bladder fern grows in sheltered crevices, and where soil has collected, a limestone scree flora has developed.

LIMESTONE CAVES

Exploration of the caves in the valley has revealed remains of hyena and woolly rhinoceros. The caves are still being explored and new chambers are discovered from time to time. The streams which run through the valley in winter disappear into caves in summer, emerging far below in Cheddar Gorge.

The gorge's own special plant, Cheddar pink, is protected by law and must not be picked

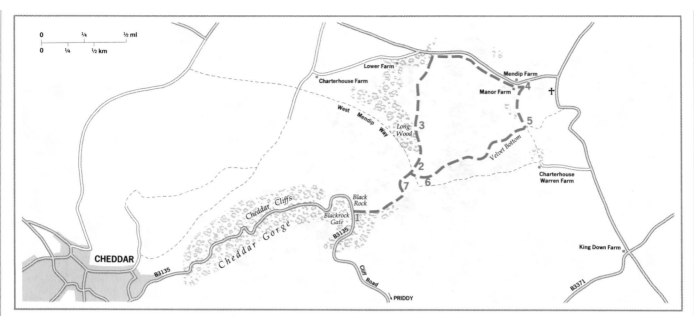

1 Go through the gateway east of the B3135 and follow the track through Black Rock Valley. Watch for jackdaws and jays flying overhead and, in the spring, the male sparrowhawk in its soaring display flight. Kestrels hunt here as well, but they hover rather than soar. Over 200 tree and wild flower species have been recorded here, many of them limestone-loving species. Butterflies are abundant; the common blue is noticeable in summer. Songbirds are common and an early morning visit in spring is well worth while for the dawn chorus.

2 Take the footpath through a gate to the right through Long Wood, where there is a nature reserve sign, and walk up the hill, keeping to the main path. (There are some detours around the rest of the wood along a nature trail laid out by the Somerset Trust for Nature Conservation.) Ash is a common species here, but lime-loving trees and shrubs abound and the ground flora is colourful in spring. Ash trees break into leaf comparatively late in the spring, allowing plenty of light to reach the woodland floor. In damper areas near the stream meadowsweet blooms and dragonflies such as the southern hawker hunt along the paths. Coppicing is taking place to ensure regeneration of the understorey; recently coppiced areas have a magnificent display of spring flowers.

3 Where the path leaves the wood, skirt the edge of the field and join the farm track, turning left and then right to reach the minor road. Woodpigeons and stock doves nest in the wood (the latter in tree holes) and feed on the open fields with larks and finches in winter. Badger tracks may be visible in muddy places on the path.

4 On the bend in the road just past Manor Farm, take the footpath to the right by the little pond – which may be dry by the end of summer. Follow this path down the field beside the wall as far as Velvet Bottom. The stone walls and banks have been colonised by a variety of mosses, lichens and ferns, and in some places the tiny fingered saxifrage can be found.

5 Cross the stile and walk round the hut to join the path through the valley of Velvet Bottom, turning right on to the path. The uneven ground is the result of mining activities; streams were diverted over spoil to wash away the lighter rocks, leaving the heavier ore-bearing rocks behind. Lead accumulated in the valley bottom and is still present. Spring sandwort, once called leadwort, grows on some spoil tips. The sides of the valley, above the level of lead contamination, have a rich limestone flora including lady's bedstraw, eyebright, rock-rose, centaury, thyme and quaking-grass.

6 Follow the path down the valley and cross the wall by the stile at the bottom. This brings you back to the path below Black Rock. An interesting collection of ferns grows here: wall rue, maidenhair spleenwort and black spleenwort are quite common. The coarse grasses are a result of a lack of grazing in this lead-contaminated area. Sunny rock surfaces in sheltered spots may be occupied by basking adders in spring and summer.

7 Turn left on the path to return to the road via Black Rock Reserve and Cheddar Gorge.

Scrub and coarse grasses soon gain a foothold in sheltered places – especially those too steep for grazing animals to reach easily

TRADITIONAL HAY MEADOWS ARE AT THEIR BEST IN JUNE. NORTH MEADOW HAS A WONDERFUL ARRAY OF SUMMER FLOWERS, BUT IT IS IN LATE APRIL THAT THE SITE ATTRACTS MOST ATTENTION. IT IS ONE OF THE FEW LOCALITIES FOR THE SNAKESHEAD FRITILLARY, A CLASSIC FLOWER OF SPRING. MORE THAN THREE-QUARTERS OF BRITAIN'S WILD FRITILLARIES ARE FOUND IN THIS REMARKABLE PLACE.

A LOST LANDSCAPE

Wiltshire has become a county of open roads and rolling cornfields. Mysterious mounds and hollows, stone circles and crop-marks hint at a long history of settlement, but links with the past have been broken and most farms lack any sense of evolution. There are few corners left for wildlife, which might otherwise have kept pace with the changes and brought variety and perspective to the landscape. The accidents by which parcels of old downland, forest and meadows have survived emphasises the scale of their removal (95 per cent of Britain's herb-rich meadows have vanished in the last 50 years), but also allows a glimmer of hope for the future.

TIME-HONOURED TRADITIONS

There is something reassuringly English in the way North Meadow has been bypassed by agricultural change. Not so much a field as a grassy plain, edged in the distance by trees lining the upper reaches of the Churn and the Isis (the infant Thames), this swathe of

---

North Meadow

Wiltshire
Grid ref. SU 078 960

Nature Conservancy Council
Approx. 4½ miles (7.4 km). Easy walking, but may be muddy or overgrown beside the old canal. The path around the meadow should be followed assiduously.

North Meadow is off the B4041 just north of Cricklade. This walk starts from the village of Cerney Wick, 2 miles (3.2 km) north-west of Cricklade. Park on the grassy roadside verge along the little side-road between the A419 and the Crown Inn in the middle of Cerney Wick. Alternatively, park in the village itself and walk back, over the bridge across the River Churn.

The National Nature Reserve of North Meadow is essentially a very large field (108 acres/44 hectares) which is managed as a traditional hay meadow. Although of consider-able beauty in June, when meadow flowers are out, North Meadow is especially famous and dramatic in late April and early May when the fritillaries are in flower.

Nearby sites: *Cotswold Water Park* – flooded gravel pits with wildfowl and other water birds, especially good in winter and spring; *Savernake Forest* – ancient woodland rich in butterflies and birds in spring and summer, fungi in autumn.

---

meadowland has been managed in the same way for at least a thousand years.

After the harvesting of the hay crop in June, commoners from Cricklade Borough and Hundred were allowed to graze their stock on the aftermath. In the early 19th century the meadow was separated into strips so that each of the original commoners was able to take his fair share of hay. Many of the stone boundary markers that defined the strips still survive, resembling weathered headstones. Because of the complex legal situation, the meadow could not easily be enclosed or improved, and when the site was declared a National Nature Reserve and bought piecemeal by the Nature Conservancy Council, the unique flora of North Meadow was still intact. Thus a fragment of a once widespread habitat – one that formed an essential part of many a lowland farm less than a century ago – has become one of Britain's most valuable remaining examples of an ancient meadow.

SPRING AND SUMMER FLOWERS

North Meadow is justifiably renowned for its fritillary population and estimates put the number of flowers in excess of a million in some years. They appear in April and May, but the meadow's botanical interest is not by any means confined to this species or this season. Following the fritillaries, a succession of colourful water-meadow flowers appears until the meadow is cut for hay in summer. One of the most attractive is the southern marsh orchid, which produces tall spikes of purple flowers. Meadow rue and yellow rattle add contrasting colour, and keen-eyed observers may also spot the curiously shaped adder's tongue fern.

Marsh marigolds are a cheering sight in spring

Meadow buttercups flourish in damp grassland

The Snakeshead Fritillary

A century ago, snakeshead fritillaries were a familiar sight in water meadows throughout central and south-east England. However, changes in land use as well as drainage have wiped them out from all but 24 of their original sites. Most of these now lie along the Thames valley. Fritillary flowers are generally purple in colour with chequered markings, although white specimens are not unusual. They appear in April and May and are pollinated by insects. The plant dies back above ground in the summer and can thus survive when the meadow is but for hay; an underground bulb persists throughout the seasons.

1 Close to the roadside sign for Cerney Wick, the minor road between the A419 and the village crosses the dry basin of the old canal. From here, take the little-used footpath (signed) that leads south-east along the derelict canal. In summer the old towpath and the basin of the canal disappear in tangles of balsam, reed and yellow flag. The going is much easier in the spring when the vegetation is still low; butterbur and marsh marigolds are two of the marsh plants to appear at this time of year. Celandines and violets are prolific on the wooded banks, and if it is a sunny day there may be butterflies on the wing, either woken from hibernation (small tortoiseshell, peacock, comma, brimstone) or fresh with the spring (orange-tip, green veined white).

Eventually the path crosses a stile after which the canal is only visible as a grass-covered earthwork grazed by cattle. Soon, even the earthwork disappears and the River Churn appears again on the right.

2 Go through a gate, then turn right along a track and over a bridge across the river. Turn right through a wide gateway, after which the track forks. Take the left-hand track; this leads towards a house. The house stands on the site of the old lock-keeper's cottage. Its garden is a fascinating piece of ingenuity, making use of the old basin and stonework.

3 Cross a stile to the left of the gate to the house and continue to the left of the house, crossing a little bridge then circling the grounds and regaining the line of the old canal on the far side. Cross a stile and continue into the deep shade of tall hawthorns. These were planted as the original hedge when the canal was built a century ago, but after a few decades of maintenance they were allowed to grow rank as the canal fell into disuse. Hawthorn was always the favourite tree for hedge-laying, 'quickset' and stockproof. Millions of hawthorns were planted in the English lowlands in the 18th and 19th centuries, and millions still survive despite the destruction of the 1970s.

Keep to the path, which crosses a bridge over a stream. There is an entrance to the nature reserve on the left, but continue along the path for about another 200yds (180m) towards another bridge, going through a gate and turning left over a stile before the bridge and down to the bank of the

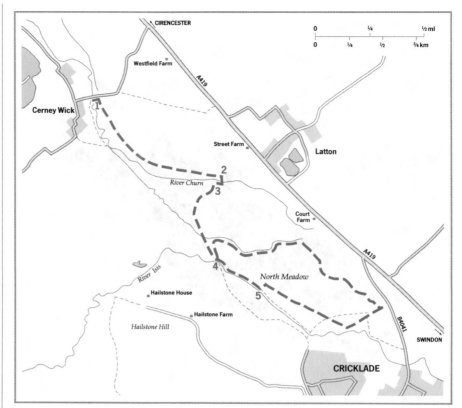

River Isis. A Nature Conservancy Council sign tells you that you are in North Meadow. If it is late April your eyes will be to the east where, in any normal year, the fritillaries will be in their full glory, scattered the length and breadth of the great flat meadow. Most of the fritillary flowers are purple (or a unique colour which is neither quite purple, pink, red or brown but a mixture of all of these), but there are some white ones, too, and dandelions and cowslips add other colours to the

North Meadow's display of fritillaries. They survive in the wild in very few other places

beautiful, tapestry-like picture.

4 Continue along the path beside the river. After haymaking there is no restriction about the route, but when the flowers are out it is important to keep to the edge of the field, on the marked path. One of the stone boundary markers, once used to separate the meadow into allotments, lies close to the river bank; others can be seen in the body of the meadow. The River Isis, which evolves into the Thames as it progresses eastwards, is here a beautiful little stream. During the summer it disappears amid bulrushes, bur-reed, marsh woundwort and yellow flags and is the resort of kingfishers, wagtails and water voles.

5 It is possible to keep with the river by crossing a stile into a field of rough pasture (grazed by cattle which like to wade in the shallows). However, when the fritillaries are out the main meadow is irresistible. Keep to the path; this is clear on the ground and follows a long anti-clockwise route all round the reserve and back to the Churn. From there retrace your route along the old canal to the start of the walk in Cerney Wick.

Cliffs and scree on the east coast

PORTLAND HAS A LONG HISTORY OF ASSOCIATION WITH MAN. IT WAS SETTLED BY THE CELTS, QUARRIED FOR ITS LIMESTONE OVER THE CENTURIES AND, IN MORE RECENT TIMES, IT HAS BECOME AN IMPORTANT NAVAL BASE AND POPULAR TOURIST SPOT. HOWEVER, PORTLAND ALSO HAS A RICH AND VARIED NATURAL HISTORY WHICH SOMEHOW STILL MANAGES TO SURVIVE SIDE BY SIDE WITH ITS HUMAN RESIDENTS.

MARITIME FLORA

First impressions of Portland are of a rather scruffy landscape with too many eyesores. Do not be put off by this, however, because behind this facade you will soon find a surprising variety of scenery and wildlife. The views are magnificent all year and attractive displays of maritime flowers greet the eye in spring and summer. Alexanders is the dominant plant around the coast, but on the cliff-edge look for thrift, sea campion and sea beet. In the summer, golden samphire and the rare Portland sea-lavender can be found.

A BIRDWATCHERS' PARADISE

Portland is good for birdwatching at any time of year. The cliffs on the west side support raucous colonies of breeding seabirds, and migrant birds are often numerous in spring and autumn.

Small passerine birds do not willingly choose to cross large expanses of water such as the English Channel, and many shorten the hazardous crossing by using Portland as a 'stepping stone'. Under certain

---

Portland

Dorset
Grid ref. SY 676 685

Approx. 4 miles (6.4 km). Easy walking, but take care near cliff-edges.

The Isle of Portland is about 3 miles (4.8 km) south of Weymouth. Portland Bill, where the walk starts, is at Portland's southern extremity. There is a public car park (charge).

Not quite an island, Portland is connected to the mainland by the long shingle spit of Chesil Beach. Its position makes it a fine site to observe seabirds and many kinds of migrants, and it is also a good place for cliff-top flowers.

Nearby sites: *The Fleet and Chesil Beach* – waders, shingle plants and scaly cricket; *Radipole RSPB Reserve* – reed-beds with bearded tits, water rails and Cetti's warblers.

Alexanders – a widespread coastal plant

---

conditions in early spring migrants such as swallows, martins, wagtails and flycatchers can be seen coming in from the sea while in autumn, when the winds are favourable, departing flocks take off from the cliffs, flying low overhead.

The best times of year to see birds on migration are from late March to late May and from August to October. Early morning is the best time of day – both to observe newly arrived migrant birds and to avoid the crowds of visitors which sometimes build up near Portland Bill in the afternoon. Search the bushes and gardens for warblers, firecrests, chats and flycatchers; the cliff-tops for wheatears; and the cultivated fields for tawny pipits and ortolan buntings. When the winds are from the south-east, Portland sometimes swarms with birdwatchers who are usually more than pleased to tell you 'what's around'. Portland has long been famous as a site for observing bird migration, and a bird observatory has been established in the Old Lighthouse on Portland Bill. In this vicinity rare birds are regularly found and there have been sightings of several species never before seen in Britain.

SEABIRDS OFF PORTLAND

Bird migration is not by any means confined to land birds: Portland juts out into the English Channel, so seabirds such as shearwaters, gannets, divers and sea ducks pass close by in large numbers, especially during south-westerly or southerly gales in spring and autumn. There is something to see here throughout the year, however. The tip of Portland Bill is the best vantage point, and people often use the Trinity House obelisk as a shelter.

1 From the car park walk past the lighthouse towards the tip of Portland Bill, marked by the Trinity House obelisk. Scan the sea for shags, fulmars, auks, skuas, gulls, divers and sea ducks. On the rocks below, three species of limpet plus barnacles, sea anemones and other marine creatures can be found. Take care when the seas are rough. In the winter, turnstones and purple sandpipers feed here.

2 Turn left and walk along the cliff-top path on the east side of Portland Bill. An old quarry winch is a reminder of the days when Portland stone was quarried and loaded directly on to ships here. It is now used for launching fishing boats.

3 Pass the Old Lighthouse on your left. This now houses the bird observatory. Search the bushes and bramble patches beside the path for migrants. Melodious warblers, bluethroats and wrynecks are annual visitors.

Beyond the beach huts, Alexanders and field pepperwort grow beside the footpath. On the cliffs look for golden samphire, sea beet and Portland sea-lavender. Scan the fields to your left for migrant wheatears, pipits and larks. A savannah sparrow from North America was found near here in April 1982 – the first record for Britain.

4 Continue along the coast, passing through some old quarries – part of a long stretch of workings that extends north-eastwards along the coast. Portland stone has been quarried on a large scale here since the 17th century, when Sir Christopher Wren chose it for his new London churches after the Great Fire. The durable and attractive limestone was loaded into barges and shipped to London. It has been highly prized as a fine building stone ever since.

Migrant birds shelter here in spring and autumn, and the lime-rich soils encourage a good chalk flora. Snails are abundant in wet weather. On warm days, look for sunbathing adders, slow-worms and common lizards.

5 Look out for Cave Hole, a vast cave in the cliffs, undercut by the sea. Here, follow the path which leads back to the main road. At the road, turn right and after $^1/_4$ mile (400m) turn left and follow the signposted public footpath which heads west. To the left you will see excellent examples of the Celtic field systems which would once have covered the island. Ploughed fields to the right can be good for migrant pipits, buntings and larks.

Cross a stile and carry on with the stone wall to your left.

6 After the next gate, turn right along the path which joins Sweet Hill Road. Continue down the hill and turn left into Sweet Hill Lane. This eventually becomes a footpath which continues to the west cliffs. In summer, listen for great green bush crickets singing in the bramble patches. At the cliff-edge, the view looks north towards Chesil Beach and, to the west of it, Golden Cap, Lyme Bay and the Devon coast.

7 Turn left and walk south-wards. The brambles and other bushes around here are good for

The ringlet is active even in cloudy weather

migrant birds. Look also for gatekeeper, meadow brown and ringlet butterflies.

8 Continue south, taking great care at the cliff-edge. Look for grey bush crickets and patches of chalk flora such as thyme, yellow-wort, carline thistle, pyramidal orchid and bee orchid. Clumps of Portland spurge can be found here in the early spring.

9 Pass a large MoD enclosure on your left, then an old lighthouse and a coastguard base. Shortly afterwards, the way is blocked by a fenced Admiralty enclosure; turn inland to walk round it. Before doing so, sit near the cliff-edge for a while and scan below for seabirds. They nest on ledges and in burrows below you, but can be seen well in flight. Puffins, razorbills, guillemots, kittiwakes and fulmars can easily be seen, and rock pipits forage in the turf and clumps of scurvy-grass.

Yellow vetchling grows in the rough ground to your left at the edge of the enclosure, and this area is good for butterflies including common blues, marbled whites and migrant painted ladies and clouded yellows.

10 Continue along the southern boundary of the fenced enclosure, returning to the cliffs near Pulpit Rock. At the cliffs, look north to see seabirds on the ledges below. Gulls, fulmars, kittiwakes and auks are resident from April until July.

Return to the car park.

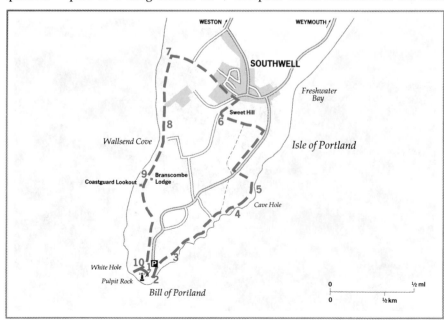

WESTON   WEYMOUTH

SOUTHWELL

Freshwater Bay

Sweet Hill

Wallsend Cove

Isle of Portland

Coastguard Lookout   Branscombe Lodge

Cave Hole

White Hole

Pulpit Rock

Bill of Portland

0   ½ ml

0   ½ km

Durlston

Sheltered, wooded valleys such as Winspit are a haven for tired migrant birds. The lynchets or terraces on the hillside above are a legacy of early farmers here

THE ISLE OF PURBECK IS NO ISLAND AT ALL, AND UNLESS YOU APPROACH FROM BOURNEMOUTH ON THE SANDBANKS FERRY, IT IS DIFFICULT TO PRETEND THAT IT IS. HOWEVER, PURBECK IS IN MANY WAYS A PLACE APART – A SELF-CONTAINED BLOCK OF COUNTRY, RINGED TO THE NORTH BY THE LOWLANDS OF THE HARBOUR, ARNE HEATH AND THE VALLEY OF THE RIVER FROME.

CASTLE AND CLIFFS

At the heart of Purbeck is a raised ridge of chalk, on top of which stands Corfe Castle. Further south there is a wide plateau of farmland before a steep slope of rough grassland and the famous combes and cliffs of the west Dorset coast. This narrow band of close-cropped turf, known locally as The Ware, may seem an inhospitable sort of place for wildlife. It is exposed to winter gales and summer droughts, and there are days when sea mists make it impossible to see more than a few yards (metres). Even so, it boasts an outstanding assortment of flowers and butterflies that makes it one of the most fascinating stretches of cliff-top in England. It is also an excellent place for migrant birds, fossils, bats, medieval history and sunshine.

The pale grey cliffs between Swanage and Durdle Door are all composed of limestone, mostly Portland stone, which was once quarried at such sites as the Tilly Whim Caves and Winspit. Both Corfe Castle and St Paul's Cathedral were built extensively of Portland stone, which was, and still is, in great demand. Its sediments were formed slowly in a tropical sea up to 160 million years ago. The rock contains some impressive fossils, particularly giant ammonites which can be found in several places on the tide-line, embedded in the shelves of darkened stone. Above the cliffs, and outcropping in places among the turf of The Ware, are beds of Purbeck limestone. These were laid down in swamp or lagoon conditions about 140 million years ago and also contain interesting fossils. By searching among piles of quarry debris (from shafts or 'quarrs') or along drystone walls it is possible to turn up pieces of turtle shell, crocodile teeth, shark teeth and fish bones. Dinosaur footprints have been found in several places and one set now resides in the British Museum.

WILDLIFE OF THE WARE

Because of the salty winds and the thin soils on the limestone there has been little attempt to till the slopes of The

The Lulworth skipper is exclusive to this area

Durlston

Dorset
Grid ref. SZ 033 773

Dorset County Council/National Trust
Approx. 9 miles (14.5 km), but the walk can be shortened by taking one of the obvious north-south public footpaths linking the outward and return routes. Generally gentle slopes, but some steeper.

Durlston lies less than a mile (1.6 km) south of Swanage. There is a large car park beside the excellent country park centre.

The Isle of Purbeck is an area of limestone and chalk with spectacular cliff scenery. Durlston Head and the adjacent section of the Purbeck coast is managed as a country park. Further west, much of the old grassland and the coast is owned by the National Trust. The limestone grassland is magnificent for flowers, butterflies and other summer insects, and the cliffs and sea are good for birds.

Nearby sites: *Purbeck heathlands* – a patchwork of heaths which are excellent for insects (especially dragonflies and grasshoppers), birds and flowers.

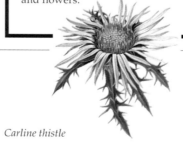

Carline thistle

Ware. Even the dramatic lynchets or cultivation terraces above Seacombe and Winspit may well have been grass-covered for 1000 years. The result has been a long, settled period of low-key agriculture; the grass was grazed by flocks of Dorset Down or Dorset Horn sheep, and by rabbits and cattle. Plants adapted to open, dry and sunny conditions established themselves and have maintained themselves ever since, most notably a wide assortment of orchids including pyramidal, green-winged, autumn lady's tresses, bee and early spider orchids. Sun-loving insects such as grasshoppers and solitary wasps appear along the cliff-top paths in abundance. Downland butterflies associated with short-turf food-plants and thriving on sunshine are well represented too. Marbled whites and Lulworth skippers are common, and chalkhill blue and Adonis blue butterflies are also found. Over 30 species of butterfly are recorded each year on this short stretch of coast, most of them in the sorts of numbers that must have brightened much of the English countryside a century ago. Flower-rich combes along the coast often prove to be a landing place for migrant insects arriving from the south: red admirals, painted ladies and clouded yellows cross the Channel every year and there is always the chance of seeing a hummingbird hawk-moth visiting a red valerian flower head.

MIGRANTS AND SEABIRDS

Because of its strategic position, Purbeck is also a landfall for migrant birds; the bushes growing in combes and flushes are a magnet for tired waifs and strays. Over the last few years there have been sightings of melodious warbler, woodchat shrike, bee-eater and hoopoe from the Mediterranean, and Pallas's warbler, yellow-browed warbler and Isabelline shrike from Siberia. Common migrant species include wheatears and swallows, which may appear as early as March, and warblers and flycatchers, which are seen during April and May. The return migration in autumn can be just as interesting.

Seabirds breed around Anvil Point and Durlston Head and, in places, there are excellent views of guillemots and razorbills. A few pairs of puffins breed further along the coast, and may occasionally be seen out to sea. Spring and autumn migration of seabirds from further afield can also be exciting during periods of onshore winds: gannets, shearwaters, terns, divers and skuas should all be looked for in April and May and again in September.

THE *W*ALK

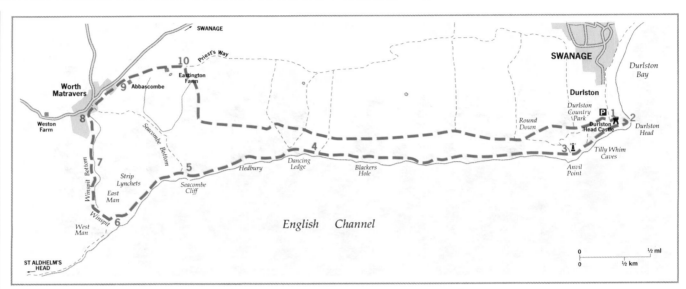

1 From Durlston Country Park car park, walk down the track signed Castle Café. This takes you past borders of exotic trees and shrubs, good for migrant birds, and past the castle and restaurant.

2 The track soon forks; the Great Globe, made of 15 pieces of Portland stone weighing about 40 tons (40 tonnes), may be worth a brief detour to the left but the route lies to the right, following the track downhill and then the cliff-top path round Durlston Head. At first there is a stone wall to the left, which provides a good leaning-post for watching the sea. There are usually a few kittiwakes, guillemots and razorbills about in the spring and early summer but these will have left the cliffs by late July. Scan the open water for seabirds on passage in spring and autumn. South-easterly winds offer the best

The limestone cliffs east of Seacombe

opportunities for good views. If the visibility is good there will be a clear view, to the east, of The Needles, the chalk stacks at the most westerly point of the Isle of Wight.

Beyond tamarisk and bramble scrub on the south side of Durlston Head, below a pair of nautical mile markers, the path passes the remains of the Tilly Whim Caves, worked nearly 200 years ago for Portland stone. It then drops down to a deep valley before climbing steeply and bearing to the left of the Anvil Point lighthouse. The cliff-top is more broken and rugged now, and there are some dense patches of rock samphire and sea aster growing among weathered debris and fissures. Other plants to look for along the cliff-top include sea campion, thrift, sea beet and buckshorn plantain.

3 Just after the lighthouse bear left, keeping to the cliff path. At first the path is constrained between a fence (a favourite perch for stonechats) and the cliff-top and leads through wind-cropped bushes of bramble and blackthorn. The shelter allows taller herbs such as nodding thistle and woolly thistle to make an appearance. These in turn attract some of the larger butterflies such as painted lady and dark green fritillary.

Further on, with the fence now on the left, the ground vegetation becomes shorter, with swathes of tor-grass and carline thistles, and by the time you have crossed a couple of stiles and passed a second pair of nautical mile markers you are on close-cropped downland, with quaking grass and dwarf thistle. The going is

not very easy as there are many humps and hollows, and wet flushes of ranker vegetation. It is here that you are likely, in late summer, to find the great green bush cricket, one of the most spectacular of British insects, as well as the smaller grey bush cricket. Purbeck is one of the best places in Britain for grasshoppers and bush crickets, and at least 10 species have been recorded for the Durlston area.

4 Across another stile, on the crest of a broad combe, there is an excellent view westwards. In the foreground is Dancing Ledge, a place where the cliff has been cut back by old quarrying to produce a broad shelf of limestone. In the distance is St Aldhelm's Head (St Aldhelm brought Christianity to this part of Dorset in the 8th century). It is possible to make a detour left, over a stile and down on to Dancing Ledge, to walk on ammonite beds or bathe in a little pool hollowed out of the rock, which is filled by the high tide.

The next dip in the rolling line of coastal hills contains another, smaller quarry in the cliff-face called Hedbury, though the working is so old that it looks like a natural feature. The marshy ground around is a favourite gathering place for downland butter-flies, including the marbled white, three species of skipper and at least four species of blue. The 'stars' are the chalkhill blue and the Adonis blue, the males of which are very brightly coloured (the former pale sky-blue, the latter an electric blue). The females are brown and spend rather more of their time on the dry hill slopes, laying their eggs on horseshoe vetch.

5 The cliff path continues towards St Aldhelm's Head, dropping down into Seacombe Bottom and bearing right at a fence (enclosing grown-over quarry spoil). It then turns left at the end of the fence, up through scrub and on to downland again, at which bear left again to pick up the cliff path. Beyond the field to the right, the slopes of the hill called the East Man bear 'strip lynchets' – terraces probably made by Saxon farmers over 1000 years ago. Towards the next major nick, called Winspit, there are views down on to an area of 'undercliff', a secluded and secret place where roe deer can sometimes be seen.

6 The path turns right and descends into the deep cleft of **Winspit.** The first impression is of a shrubby oasis after the downland, and this is probably how migrant birds see it too, for it is sometimes alive with small birds such as warblers and flycatchers. Winspit is yet another quarry site. Some of the main workings can be explored, while a few of the tunnels have been blocked off by iron grilles and are now the home of greater horseshoe bats.

7 Walk up the broad stony track at the bottom of the path, away from the sea. Bear right at a fork and head steeply uphill to the village of Worth Matravers.

8 Over a stile, bear right along the street, past Happy Cottage and into the centre of the pretty village. Pass the green, a pond and a tea-shop. Continue along the road until this forks at the Square and Compass pub, at which bear right along the road for several hundred yards (metres) until you are past a series of newer dwellings.

9 At a large barn turn right, over a stile (signed Eastington and Priest's Way). The path heads east, crossing a farm drive and pastureland, and with a steep slope to the right. This is Abbascombe; there are excellent views of the strip lynchets above Seacombe in the background.

10 The path heads for the left side of the farm ahead; keep the wall to your right and telegraph poles to the left and head towards a footpath sign. Cross a stile by a gate and continue past the farm to your right along a walled track – part of the Priest's Way, a medieval trackway between Worth and Swanage. After about 200yds (180m), by a National Trust signpost for Eastington, turn right, over a stile and along a track heading towards the sea. Past another stile the track drops down towards Seacombe but after only about 20yds (18m) turn left off this, along a narrow path signed Durlston. Continue, with the slope to the right and a wall to the left, until a gate and stile appear on the left.

11 Cross the stile and bear left with the wall. This marks the boundary between the improved farmland of the plateau and the rough grassland of The Ware.

The path is now easy to follow, keeping to the same contour and arcing high above Hedbury and Dancing Ledge. Eventually the path leads to a gate beside a tall marker post, then over a stile and through the National Trust's Belle Vue estate.

12 Past a Trust marker stone the route follows the same contour, not downhill but along a smaller path leading to a stile into Durlston Country Park. From here there are many alternatives, but the quickest is the path on the left. Keep parallel with the coast, over hummocky ground and with the lighthouse below to the right, until the lighthouse road is reached. At this turn left, back to the car park.

Summer flowers over, parched grassland rolls away towards St Aldhelm's Head

TO FIND LOWLAND HEATH IN A COASTAL SITUATION, AS AT STUDLAND HEATH, IS UNUSUAL. HERE VISITORS CAN WALK FROM SANDY BEACHES AND STABILISED DUNES TO HEATHLAND IN A MATTER OF A FEW YARDS, AND CAN FOLLOW THE PROGRESSION OF PLANT LIFE FROM ONE HABITAT TO ANOTHER.

A HAVEN FOR REPTILES

An important reason why Studland Heath was granted National Nature Reserve status was the presence of all six species of native British reptiles. A sunny day in early spring will provide the best opportunities to see these creatures as they warm up after winter hibernation. Without sunshine, they are comparatively inactive. Adders and common lizards are regularly seen, and lucky visitors may even spot a smooth snake or a sand lizard.

INSECTS GALORE

Studland Heath also harbours a wide variety of insects, many of which are scarce elsewhere in Britain. Freshwater habitats – lakes and pools – are home to dragonflies and damselflies in their aquatic stages. The nymphs are voracious predators. The adults make a similar impact on airborne insects and take a heavy toll – a welcome one, from the visitor's point of view – on the heathland's midges and biting flies. Look for emperor dragonflies, four-spot libellulas and common blue damselflies.

During the summer months, the heathlands are alive with grasshoppers and bush crickets. Damper areas, characterised by cross-leaved heath, are home to bog bush crickets while drier heath supports mottled and common field grasshoppers. The latter species is superficially similar to the nationally rare heath grasshopper, which also occurs here.

HEATHLAND AND COASTAL BIRDS

The walk around Studland Heath takes in several different habitats rich in birdlife. In winter the mudflats of Poole Harbour are home to thousands of waders including dunlins, black-tailed godwits and curlews as well as wigeon and brent geese. Black-headed gulls and shelducks remain throughout the year, breeding in quiet sanctuaries, and are joined by little terns and common terns. The Little Sea, in the heart of the reserve, attracts wildfowl and coots in winter and harbours a few ducks and little grebes

Studland Heath
Dorset
Grid ref. SZ 036 865

Nature Conservancy Council (part)

Approx. 4³/₄ miles (7.6 km). An easy walk on level ground.

Studland Heath lies on the southeast side of Poole Harbour, flanked on the west by the harbour's mudflats and to the east by Studland Bay and the open sea. Access is via the toll-gate by Knoll House Hotel, which is north of Studland village, or, from Poole or Bournemouth, by the Sandbanks ferry. The car park is situated near South Haven Point.

The whole area, and in particular the Shell Bay and Studland Bay beaches, is extremely popular with holiday-makers, so summer weekends are best avoided. On one section of Studland Bay, nude bathing is permitted and here cameras and binoculars should perhaps be used with discretion!

Fire, caused by carelessness or malice, is an almost annual problem. Please exercise the utmost caution, especially in dry spells.

The area comprises superb heathland and most of the key species associated with this threatened habitat can be seen. The Nature Conservancy Council leases and manages the best part as a National Nature Reserve.

Nearby sites: *Arne Heath RSPB Reserve* – excellent heathland with Dorset heath – a rare plant – and Dartford warblers; *Brownsea Island* – woodland (red squirrels), freshwater lagoon and nature reserve.

The Dartford warbler nests among gorse

in summer. The heathland itself is home to stonechats and linnets, as well as the bird most symbolic of southern heathlands, the Dartford warbler.

FLOWERS OF DUNES AND HEATHLAND

The reserve also has considerable botanical interest. The shifting sands of Studland Bay are stabilised by marram grass and soon colonised by sea lyme-grass and sea bindweed. Further inland, the heathland supports characteristic plants such as bell heather, ling, cross-leaved heath, round-leaved sundew and bog myrtle. The elegant royal fern grows in some of the shady, wooded areas.

Roe deer – Britain's smallest native deer

Grasshoppers and Bush Crickets

Grasshoppers and bush crickets belong to a group of insects called the Orthoptera. This literally means 'straight wing' and the name reflects the structure and shape of their wings.

Studland Heath is a wonderful site for Orthoptera: at least 10 species can be seen on or near the reserve. Of special note is the heath grasshopper, a rare species found nowhere in Britain other than the Dorset heathlands and a few sites in the New Forest.

THE *Walk*

1 Park in the South Haven car park and walk north towards the ferry. Scan Poole Harbour, to your left, for waders and wildfowl in winter. The waters of Shell Bay usually harbour divers and cormorants in winter; look for terns plunge-diving in spring and summer.

Walk along the tide-line of Shell Bay. Keep a look out here for shells. An extensive search should reveal over 20 species including thick-lipped dog-whelks, grooved razor shells, tusk shells and Pandora's shells.

2 At the point, follow the shore-line south along Studland Bay. Small flocks of sanderlings often feed at the edge of the water. The marram grass is stabilising the shifting sands above the high-tide line, but erosion by visitors has defeated this process in some areas.

3 At the National Nature Reserve sign, turn inland and follow the boardwalk and numbered posts. This is also the start of the Sand Dunes Nature Trail, for which a leaflet is available from the Nature Conservancy Council.

The path crosses several ridges and slacks before turning south and running parallel with the beach. Here excellent areas of both dry and wet heath can be seen. Ling and bell heather grow in the dry areas and cross-leaved heath in the wetter hollows. Look for sunbathing reptiles and grasshoppers, and for stonechats perched on sprays of gorse.

4 Follow the path towards the Knoll House Hotel. It passes close to the Little Sea, which is hidden from view by birches and willows. Listen for singing blackcaps in spring.

5 Continue towards the toll road. Visitors may wish to walk the NCC's woodland trail, which starts near the Knoll House car park and for which a leaflet is available.

At the toll road, turn right and walk north. This part of the walk is beside a road and is best completed quickly.

6 A detour to the right follows a track up to an observation hide and information centre. From the hide, look for bathing and preening gulls on the Little Sea during the summer, and wildfowl and coots in winter.

Return to the toll road. Wall brown butterflies and mottled grasshoppers can be seen beside the path, and it is worth looking for Dartford warblers.

A second possible detour from here is to follow the track down towards Poole Harbour. Here will be found some excellent areas of heathland, and good views of birds on the salt-marsh. Look for green tiger beetles and several species of grasshopper on the track, and day-flying emperor moths on the heath in April and May. Roe deer are occasionally seen browsing in this area. Keen-eyed observers may see a hobby dashing by during the summer months. In winter, scan the heath for hen harriers.

Return to the toll road.

7 Follow the heathland track which runs parallel to, and on the east side of, the toll road. Typical heathland birds and insects can be seen.

8 At the National Nature Reserve signpost, cross the road and walk back towards the car park along the shores of Poole Harbour. Alternatively, for a longer walk, take the track to the right which

Pressure for development has made the Dorset heaths one of our most threatened habitats

crosses the heathland to Studland Bay. The track goes through some areas of wet woodland and passes fine stands of royal fern.

To complete the longer walk, turn left at the beach and retrace your steps northwards around Studland Bay and Shell Bay.

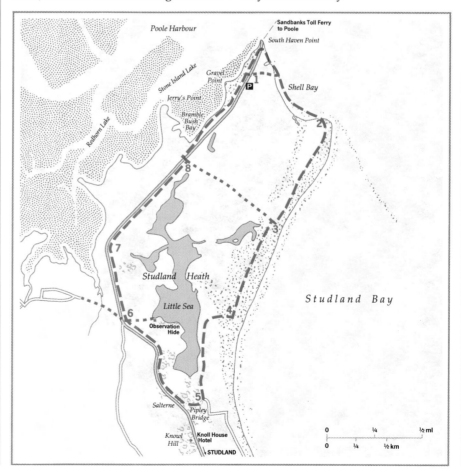

WITH THE SPREAD OF MODERN ARABLE FARMING ACROSS SOUTHERN ENGLAND IT IS EASY TO FORGET THAT, ON CHALKY SOILS AT LEAST, CEREAL MONOCULTURES ARE A COMPARATIVELY RECENT PHENOMENON. A CENTURY OR SO AGO, MUCH OF THIS SOIL WOULD HAVE BEEN DOWNLAND: SHEEP-GRAZED GRASSLAND CHARACTERISED BY A SHORT, HERB-RICH SWARD. MARTIN DOWN OFFERS THE VISITOR A CHANCE TO STUDY THIS THREATENED HABITAT ON A SCALE FEW OTHER SITES CAN RIVAL: THE NATIONAL NATURE RESERVE COVERS MORE THAN 800 ACRES (324 HECTARES).

THE ORIGINS OF CHALK DOWNLAND

Chalk downland owes the rich diversity of its plant life to man's intervention, or more accurately to the action of his grazing animals, especially sheep. Slow-growing herb species, including many orchids, were favoured as the sheep nibbled the coarser grasses and gradually impoverished the soils. The effect of centuries of grazing the slopes by day and sheltering the sheep in 'folds' in the valley bottom by night – a regular grazing procedure – was to gradually manure the valley bottom at the expense – in terms of nutrients – of the slopes.

Many of the best areas of downland left in Britain – including parts of Martin Down – have not been ploughed or sprayed, and have been almost continuously grazed on a seasonal basis for centuries. However, at Martin Down, a progression of ploughed and disturbed areas can be seen and their suitability to chalk flora assessed. Parts of the valley bottom in the northern part of the reserve were ploughed during World War II and have a rather limited diversity. Some parts of the reserve show signs of Celtic and medieval field patterns, untouched ever since, and the chalk flora is excellent. Bokerley Ditch – an extensive earthwork of Romano-British origin – has some of the finest patches of chalk-loving plants.

CHALK FLORA

For many naturalists, orchids are the highlight of a visit to chalk downland. At Martin Down, you are unlikely to be disappointed: pyramidal, fragrant and frog orchids are locally common and burnt-tip and early purple orchids are also occasionally found. However, the accompanying chalk flowers are

---

Martin Down

Hampshire
Grid ref. SU 057 192

Nature Conservancy Council/ Hampshire County Council
Approx. 4 miles (6.4 km). Easy walking, mostly on level ground, but with a gentle slope at the start.

Martin village is just off the A354 roughly 10 miles (16 km) south-west of Salisbury. The Nature Conservancy Council car park lies to the west of the village along Sillen Lane. There is an alternative car park just south of the A354 at SU 037 201.

Martin Down is one of the finest areas of chalk downland and scrub in southern England. It is especially rich in butterflies, harbouring all the species that could be expected in this habitat. Other insects are numerous and the variety of flowers is also outstanding.

Nearby sites: *Ibsley Water Meadows* (private: view from road) – Bewick's swans and other wildfowl in winter; *Blashford Gravel Pits* (view from roads) – water birds throughout the year.

Red-legged partridge – a bird of open country

also wonderful and not to be missed. The list is long but highlights include dropwort, chalk milkwort, field fleawort, bastard toadflax, horseshoe vetch and greater knapweed.

BUTTERFLIES

For the butterfly enthusiast, Martin Down is a paradise. Duke of Burgundy fritillaries and brimstones are on the wing early in the season, followed by small blues, common blues and Adonis blues. Later in the summer marbled whites emerge, accompanied by meadow browns, gatekeepers,

---

chalkhill blues and the second brood of Adonis blues. Dark green fritillaries are one of the summer highlights of the area; they are extremely active and fond of the flowers of greater knapweed. Silver-spotted skippers bring up the rear in August.

BIRDS OF SCRUB AND GRASSLAND

In common with many downland areas, the birdlife of the open grassland here is rather restricted. Skylarks are abundant and kestrels are occasionally seen hovering in search of unsuspecting small mammals. The scrub areas and hedgerows are more productive, however, and in May and June yellowhammers, whitethroats, lesser whitethroats, turtle doves and willow warblers can usually be found. There is even a chance of hearing that most renowned of songsters, the nightingale.

CHALK HEATH

Martin Down also has good examples of chalk heathland. At first this may seem rather a contradiction in terms: heaths are usually associated with acid soils whereas chalk provides just the opposite. However, under certain circumstances the soil conditions allow acid-loving plants such as gorse, dwarf gorse, heathers and sheep's sorrel to flourish on top of chalk.

Probably introduced from the Continent, sainfoin was traditionally cultivated as a fodder crop for cattle. Its pink flowers are now a familiar feature of chalk and limestone grassland in southern England

THE *W*ALK

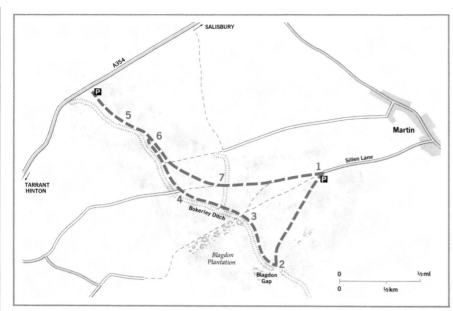

4 The path crosses another path. Continue walking beside the earthworks until the track eventually bends to the right following the line of the earthworks. You join another track from the right and bear left along the main path, keeping the banks of the earthworks on your left. The grassland is good for butterflies such as brown argus and chalkhill blue as well as a metallic green, day-flying moth called the cistus forester.

5 The path eventually becomes a gravel track with mown areas of grass to the left. It leads to an area of scrub and another Nature Conservancy Council car park. Butterflies are abundant, feeding between the bushes, and turtle doves, willow warblers and yellowhammers can be seen and heard here.

Retrace your steps back down the gravel path.

6 Ignore the path to the right – the one you arrived on – and continue down the main track. This gradually bears to the left and down into the valley bottom. The chalk flora and insect life beside the path are excellent: look for sainfoin, pyramidal orchids and dark green fritillaries.

7 Where the track meets a hedgerow at the corner of a field, bear to the left. Walk between the hedges for a short way. The bushes of privet, blackthorn and hawthorn shelter numerous hedgerow flowers. Butterflies are abundant here and include meadow browns, marbled whites, gatekeepers, holly blues and dark green fritillaries.

Continue along the track, keeping to the path with the hedge on your left, and return to the car park.

A poignant reminder of downland as it used to be, Martin Down is an oasis for wildlife among the vast arable lands that clothe much of Hampshire's chalk country today

1 From the Nature Conservancy Council car park, walk south for a short way on the track which runs parallel to the hedgerow, then follow the chalk path which runs diagonally across the valley bottom. This climbs gradually up the slope towards the earthworks. The grassland in the valley bottom is winter-grazed and comparatively lush. Six-spot burnet moths are abundant here: look for the yellowish, oval cocoons attached to grass stems, and for mating pairs which often sit on the cocoon following the female's emergence. In July, they feed abundantly on the flowers of greater knapweed, sometimes jostling for position with dark-green fritillaries and marbled whites. Other butterflies in the valley bottom include small and large skippers, meadow browns and common blues. The flowers include lady's bedstraw (food-plant for the larvae of the small elephant hawk-moth), harebell and dropwort. The air is full of the songs of skylarks, and yellowhammers sing from isolated hawthorns and patches of scrub. In winter, the valley is a good place to look for hen harriers and short-eared owls.

2 The chalk track climbs steeply as it approaches the long ridge of earthworks called Bokerley Ditch. Just before it reaches Blagdon Gap, turn right between the short wooden posts and follow the bridleway which runs beside the earthworks down the hill. The chalk turf is much shorter here. Look for plants such as salad burnet, pyramidal orchid, frog orchid, cowslip, squinancywort, wild thyme, rock-rose, kidney vetch, stemless thistle, carline thistle and fairy flax. In the summer months, grasshoppers are abundant and butterflies such as chalkhill blue and dark green fritillary may be seen. The slopes of the earthworks are colonised by patches of scrub comprising dogwood, elder, hawthorn and bramble. Areas of open grassland still have such flowers as yellow rattle, lady's bedstraw and wild carrot, however. Look for wild parsnip, a yellow umbellifer whose flowers are beloved of red soldier beetles. Whitethroats sing from the patches of scrub and green wood-peckers are occasionally seen feeding on the ant-hills that dot the grassland.

3 Continue on the path which runs beside the earthworks, ignoring another path which crosses it. On your left you pass a plantation woodland which harbours blackcaps while on the right is an area of scrub with extensive patches of gorse where linnets sing in spring and summer. The path then crosses an ancient ditch marked 'No Bridleway' on a Nature Conservancy Council signpost. The open grassland is extremely good for dark green fritillary butterflies as well as plants such as lady's bedstraw and rock-rose. Look for clumps of marjoram and listen for skylarks. The banks of the earthworks on your left are rather overgrown with elder, bramble, old man's beard and rosebay willowherb. Cuckoos are sometimes seen and heard here in spring.

New Forest

*One of the most important wildlife sites in Europe, the New Forest is a product of many
centuries of continuous woodland management*

A GRASSY PATH ALONG A WOODLAND RIDE; SHARDS OF SUNLIGHT ON BRAMBLE BLOSSOM, WHERE SILVER-WASHED FRITILLARY BUTTERFLIES JOSTLE FOR SPACE; DEER CROSSING YOUR PATH AND MELTING INTO THE SHADOWS; A NIGHTINGALE AMONG THE SALLOWS STARTLED INTO SONG BY THE CRASH OF A WOODPIGEON IN THE OAK CANOPY. THESE ARE JUST SOME OF THE MEMORIES YOU MAY TAKE WITH YOU FROM THE NEW FOREST.

MORE THAN A FOREST

Neither new nor just a forest, this lowland wilderness is a mix of woodland, heathland and mires. 'Forest' is more a social and historic term than a description. In ages past it denoted areas where kings and commoners both had rights, and uncultivated land was exploited but conserved. Trees were only part of the story. But while many English counties lost their ancient forests, Hampshire still possesses one of the jewels of the lowlands; a place where quaint laws, poor soils, warm summers and sheer size have ensured the survival of a remarkable assemblage of plants and animals.

WILDLIFE OF THE HEATHS

The dry heaths of the New Forest are a world in themselves, their white sand overlaid with seas of heather and gorse. Nightjars, Dartford warblers and stonechats feed on the abundant small insects. The bogs or valley mires usually grade into the heathland, mixing the range of habitats. The large marsh grasshopper and marsh fritillary butterfly are two of the special insects, but dragonflies are particularly numerous: 29 out of 39 British species are found here. This, combined with the mix of open woodland and heath, accounts for the relatively high population of the hobby, a handsome bird built to out-manoeuvre swifts and swallows.

THE WOODLANDS

A canopy of oak and beech covers much of the Forest, enveloping everything in its green shade. In most managed woods, trees are felled before they become over-mature, so there is little dead wood (for birds, beetles and wasps) and clearings are few. Thus rides and fire-breaks are of special importance in large blocks of managed woodland. The greater the variety of management, the more diverse the wildlife.

The New Forest has such a long and complex history and is so extensive that variety is guaranteed. When the Normans imposed the Forest Laws in the 11th century, the prime objective

New Forest

Hampshire
Grid ref. SU 308 079

Forestry Commission
Approx. 9 miles (14.5 km). Easy, level walking. However, it is remarkably easy to get lost in dense woodland, so a compass would be useful.

Park in Parc Pale car park on the open, north side of Beaulieu Road (the B3056), 1 mile (1.6 km) east of Lyndhurst.

The New Forest comprises a rich variety of habitats, but this walk concentrates on an area of old wood pasture and forested enclosures with brief glimpses of heathland, river and marsh. Butterflies, moths and other insects, such as the New Forest cicada, have always been a special feature of the Forest, but it is also excellent for birds. While some species (such as red-backed shrike and honey buzzard) have become rare or extinct, others (for example Dartford warbler and hobby) are more numerous than ever.

Nearby sites: *Hatchet Pond* – typical New Forest insects and marsh plants; *Old Winchester Hill* – chalk downland, scrub and woodland; good for butterflies, warblers and other woodland birds and, above all, superb chalk grassland flora. *Titchfield Haven* – marshes, freshwater lagoons, good for dabbling ducks, migrant waders and terns.

Male stonechat – easily recognised by its striking plumage and its call, like two stones clicking. Stonechats often perch on a twig or wire

Always a cheering sight on the Forest's heaths, gorse can be found in bloom almost all year round. Its golden flowers are very fragrant, smelling strongly of coconut

was to conserve the King's deer, but commoners' rights to pasture cattle and horses were protected, and over the centuries the system of 'wood pasture' has endured. When timber production became a third imperative, parts of the Forest were enclosed to allow oak regeneration; over the past few hundred years the balance between stock-browsed, unenclosed land and the special 'inclosures', set aside for coppice or timber production, has ensured both variety and continuity. Wildlife benefited tremendously.

After several attempts to replant much of the Forest with conifers, the Forestry Commission, which took over the management of the Crown Lands in 1923, has now become more actively involved in conservation. Some dead trees are left to rot and the 'ancient and ornamental' wood pastures and inclosures are no longer threatened with clear-felling.

A FRAGILE ENVIRONMENT

The New Forest's insect life was once much richer than it is today. Unfortunately, from the 1960s to the early 1980s the gates and fences around the inclosures were opened and many of the insects' food-plants were eliminated through over-grazing. Things may recover now that there are fresh attempts to exclude the livestock, but some of the rarities have probably gone for good. Of course, the oak trees provide a food source for a host of species, from the purple hairstreak butterfly to the black arches moth, and it is still possible to see – although depleted in numbers – white admiral and silver-washed fritillary butterflies.

Today, the 100 square miles (260 sq. km) of the New Forest is under pressure from more and more visitors, but even so it is possible to lose oneself on a sun-scorched heath or in an ancient inclosure of oaks, and imagine England as it was in the days of the Conqueror.

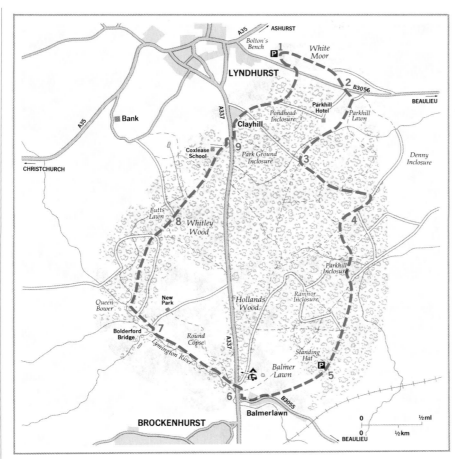

The large marsh grasshopper is one of the Forest's special insects, found only in boggy areas. It is the most spectacular grasshopper to be seen in Britain: the adult female, larger than the male, is as big as a locust. Here the grasshopper is seen perched on a spike of bog asphodel, which is also found in the Forest's acid bogs

1 From the flint-lined car park climb up the sandy hillside away from the road, reaching the highest point a little to the east at a triangulation column and wooden bench. This is a good vantage point, west to Bolton's Bench and Lyndhurst, south-east to the distant chimneys of the oil refineries at Fawley, and north across the heathland of White Moor.

About 50yds (45m) beyond the triangulation column, to the north, is a clear track, at which turn right. There are several paths through the gorse on the ridge, but they all link eventually with a wide sandy track. Continue along this. There are good views to the left (north) of drifts of gorse and heather, beyond which is a typical valley bog. Colonies of silver-studded blue butterflies may be found on the banks of heather, and this is also the place for several day-flying moths such as the clouded buff.

At a fork in the track bear right along the subsidiary track which leads over the brow of the ridge and down towards the road, heading for the Parkhill Hotel sign and a red post-box by the roadside. The track,

of silver sand, with heather and bell heather, leads out close to a Lyndhurst sign and opposite the Parkhill sign.

2 Cross the road and bear left down a metalled track (signed Park Dale Cottage) to the left of the post-box. Where the track forks, bear right and at the end of the track, continue straight on into the wood, along a narrow path through an area of hawthorn, crab apple and oak. This soon brings you out into a long clearing with a fence and trees to your right, screening the open fields of Parkhill. Head south-west, along the clearing, keeping the fence away to the right. The clearing narrows and the path leads over a little bridge. Keep to this path, through heavily browsed woodland. You will already have made the acquaintance of the ponies. To the right is the tall deer-proof fence encircling Pondhead Inclosure; the much denser shrub and ground cover within the inclosure demonstrates the effect the grazing has on the traditional wood pasture.

3 The clearing broadens again towards a gravel track. Turn left along the track, past some tall oaks and beeches. Continue straight on, past a turn to the right. To the left is a circular marsh, sometimes watery, sometimes baked dry. In most years it carries a good assortment of marsh plants such as bogbean, marsh penny-wort and marsh St John's wort, and attracts butterflies and moths. Look carefully at bumble bees visiting the bogbean flowers; the broad-bordered bee hawk-moth does an excellent imitation, but close inspection is just as likely to identify one of the Forest's wide range of 'genuine' bee species.

An entrance to Denny Inclosure soon leads off to the left, but continue straight on, until the gravel track ends at a junction. Turn right, along the subsidiary path, and go through a gate into Parkhill Inclosure. Foxes and fallow deer probably use the path as much as foresters, but in general the wildlife interest of this area is limited; the trees are mainly pine and the usual warblers are replaced by chaffinches and coal tits. Crossbills and siskins are possible in the taller plantations.

4 Continue along a gravel track, ignoring any grassy side-paths and another gravel track to the left. At a junction turn left (south) and follow the track, past another gravel track to the right, then past a triangular grassy clearing with a grassy path to the right. Soon after this the main track swings left, and another track bears right (signed 'No riding or vehicles'). Take this, but after only about 100yds (90m) turn left along a grassy track with some adolescent oaks. Go straight on where a grassy track crosses to right and left and continue until you meet a gravel track where five tracks meet. Go straight on, along the main track (the second exit) to follow a broad track edged with blackthorn and gorse. This leads through a gate to Standing Hat car park.

5 From Standing Hat bear right along the main track towards Brockenhurst. On the right is Balmer Lawn – an expanse of hummocky, close-cropped turf. The New Forest lawns are slightly richer than the heathland, gaining nutrients from the surrounding woodland. Balmer Lawn is the biggest, created by the drainage of a sweep of moor-grass in the middle of the 19th century and altered by grazing. Beyond the lawn is the big camp site at Hollands Wood.

Past some big-limbed oaks (a popular place for photographing ponies), bear right along a road (the B3055) on the outskirts of Brockenhurst. There is a little shop on the left.

6 At the main road (A337) turn right and cross the road. Continue until you are opposite the entrance to Hollands Wood camp site, then turn left to cross a stile and head along a woodland path, taking a left fork and keeping parallel with the river. The route continues either beside or close to the river for several hundred yards (metres). The mix of tall oaks and beeches, a good tangle of shrubs (holly, butcher's broom etc.) and the beautiful river make this a memorable part of the Forest. The bases of some of the trees may be wet with sap, having been damaged by the burrowing larva of the goat moth. The fermenting sap in turn attracts wasps and hornets – the latter recognisable by their yellow collar and huge size.

7 Eventually the path meets a track close to Bolderford Bridge. Turn right along the track then, before a gate, bear left along a path, still parallel with the river. This is a popular beauty spot, well trodden, but with some fine oaks and moss-laden beeches.

Continue to a bridge, but just before reaching this bear right along a path with an inclosure to the right. The path leads through oak woodland and bracken. Looking on the oak trunks may reveal one or two moths which spend the day camouflaged against the bark. The most notable of these are the light and dark crimson underwings, both of which are New Forest specialities.

The path meets gated tracks to the left and right. Continue straight ahead along the main, raised track. This winds and bears to the left of a small 'lawn' with birch trees.

8 Turn right, off the gravel track, on the bend and head along a grassy track, past more lawn areas. The woodland becomes denser as you head north-east. Eventually, houses come into view to the left and the path meets a gravel drive (to Coxlease School). At this, turn right to the road, then left along the road before crossing it, opposite the Lyndhurst sign, at a cottage and turning right down a track.

9 Turn left along the path behind the houses, with the dense woodland of Park Ground Inclosure to the right, then bear right, with a new housing estate to the left but still with very primeval-looking woodland to the right. Go through the gate and cross a gravel track. Pondhead Inclosure is now to the right, behind a good stock-proof fence which stands behind the much older wood-bank boundary.

When the track forks, bear left and keep on this track, through two gates, until Beaulieu Road is reached. At this turn left, back to the car park.

Some of the most interesting woodland in the whole Forest lies between Brockenhurst and Lyndhurst. Quiet walkers on paths like this one through the oakwoods near Butts Lawn have a good chance of seeing a fox or a deer

KEYHAVEN AND PENNINGTON MARSHES OFFER ONE OF THE RICHEST NATURAL HABITATS ON THE HAMPSHIRE COAST. FORTUNATELY THE AREA IS ACCESSIBLE WITHOUT CAUSING DISTURBANCE TO THE WILDLIFE, AND ALLOWS SOME WONDERFUL OPPORTUNITIES TO OBSERVE WETLAND BIRDS AND COASTAL FLORA.

PLANT LIFE ON THE SALT-MARSH

Behind the protection of Hurst Beach – a long shingle spit at the western end of the Solent – large areas of mudflat have formed, colonised in places by extensive patches of salt-marsh vegetation. Although, by their very nature, the mudflats are inaccessible in the main, excellent views over them can be had from the sea wall or from nearby Hurst Castle. Salt-marsh plants include glasswort, annual seablite, sea-lavender, sea aster and, in places, large patches of golden samphire. August and September are the months to see most of these plants at their best. The sea wall itself is of botanical interest, with rock samphire and sea plantain among the delights. On the seaward side, salt-tolerant lichens grow further down, in the splash zone, and below them different species of seaweed appear, each one adapted to different periods of exposure to air and immersion in sea water.

WADERS AND WILDFOWL

The salt-marsh is a haven for birds throughout the year. From late summer until spring, species such as grey plover, redshank, dunlin, ringed plover, turnstone, curlew, oyster-catcher, brent goose, mallard, shelduck, teal and wigeon are common, with smaller numbers of spotted redshanks and greenshanks usually present. High tide pushes these birds off their feeding grounds; some choose to roost on exposed shingle bars, but many fly over the sea wall to feed for a few hours on the pools and marshes on the landward side. The sight and sound of this daily high-tide 'fly-over' is truly memorable. Consult a tide table, and position yourself along the sea wall an hour or so before high tide. As the water covers the salt-marsh, the birds will take to the wing in flocks and circle overhead before settling.

OTHER BIRDLIFE

The freshwater pools on the coastal grazing marsh, which are carefully managed by Hampshire County

---

Keyhaven & Pennington Marshes

Hampshire
Grid ref. SZ 306 915

Hampshire County Council (part) Approx. 3 miles (4.8 km). Easy walking, on level ground, but wellington boots are usually essential.

Keyhaven, at the western end of the Solent, is reached by unclassified roads from Milford on Sea or from the A337 Lymington–Christchurch road. Park in the signposted car park (charge).

This straightforward walk explores the salt-marshes, grazing marshes and coastal pools of the western Solent. The area is good for coastal birds: the mudflats and marshes offer rich feeding grounds for wintering wildfowl and waders. Spring and autumn migration is also good, and terns and gulls remain to breed on shingle ridges. The salt-marsh flora is superb, and part of the area covered by the walk is managed as a Local Nature Reserve.

Nearby sites: *Hurst Beach and Hurst Castle* – good for migrating seabirds and salt-marsh flora; *Sturt Pond* – common water birds with the occasional unusual species.

With its striking crest, iridescent plumage and haunting cry, the lapwing is like no other bird. Large flocks gather on estuaries and coastal marshes in winter

Council, also attract species such as snipe and ruff and predators including short-eared owls, merlins and peregrines. Regular passage migrants include wood sandpipers and black terns, but occasionally something more unusual turns up: Eurasian rarities have included marsh sandpiper and

---

The cheerful daisy flowers of golden samphire bring bright splashes of colour to the salt-marsh in late summer

little egret while, in the autumn especially, transatlantic vagrants have included long-billed dowitcher, pectoral sandpiper and killdeer.

Although the winter months provide the greatest diversity for the birdwatcher, summer also has its highlights. Large numbers of black-headed gulls breed near by and feed on the mudflats, while tern colonies are carefully guarded against human disturbance. Sandwich, common and, occasionally, roseate terns can be seen, but the smallest species, the little tern, often provides the best views as it hovers and plunge-dives close to the sea wall.

SMALLER CREATURES

In addition to the birdwatching and botanical interest of the Keyhaven and Pennington area, the invertebrate life is also rich. The mudflats teem with molluscs and annelid worms while the brackish lagoons are often choked with gutweed and support an endangered species of shrimp and a burrowing anemone. Despite the rather unattractive appearance of the water, damselflies can be seen emerging in early summer while, later in the season, migrant hawker dragonflies (*Aeshna mixta*) dart over the surface. Lesser marsh grasshoppers abound on the grassy slopes of the sea wall and a careful inspection of clumps of rushes and grasses inland may reveal both short-winged and long-winged coneheads (species of bush cricket).

THE WALK

1 **Walk east along the road and stop just after the bridge.** Scan the harbour for waders and black-headed gulls at low tide. At high tide little grebes sometimes feed here. The brackish pool fringed with reeds, to the north of the bridge, sometimes has diving ducks and grey herons. In spring, reed warblers and reed buntings are occasionally heard.

2 **Turn right and follow the public footpath along the sea wall.** Pause at regular intervals to scan the salt-marsh and mudflats.

3 **Stop near an area of gorse and small pools (often indistinct).** Dartford warblers are occasionally seen among the gorse in winter, and the pools may harbour greenshanks and redshanks. Facing the sea, you will see a good range of salt-marsh plants which are at their best in the summer. Glasswort and annual seablite soon colonise the bare mud while, on more established ground, common and lax-flowered sea-lavender, sea aster and sea purslane can be seen. Look for the tiny laver spire shell (*Hydrobia ulvae*) and lugworm casts on the mud's surface.

4 **Continue along the sea wall until you reach a newly en-larged pool or 'scrape'.** Scan the pool's margins for waders such as ringed plovers, redshanks, curlews, godwits, dunlins and ruffs. This is an excellent spot to watch for waders pushed off the salt-marsh at high tide. Several rarities have turned up including a long-billed dowitcher in August 1989.

5 **Continue along the sea wall.** In areas where this supports lush grass, look for lesser marsh grasshoppers and short-winged cone-heads during the summer months. Sea plantain and rock samphire grow on the sea wall itself. At low tide, plant life on the seaward side shows very well how different species thrive in the different tidal zones (marine zonation).

6 **Continue to a right-angled bend in the sea wall.** The pools and marshes here are good for waders and ducks, and the long brackish channels attract little terns in summer and the occasional grey phalarope in autumn. This is also a traditional spot to scan the sea for passing seabirds. Common scoters, terns and skuas are all regularly seen in spring and autumn against a pleasant backdrop of Hurst Castle and the Isle of Wight.

7 **Continue along the sea wall as far as the long breakwater.** This marks the path of a sewage outfall out to sea: scan the open water for gulls attracted to this unappealing bonanza. Look also for waders, ducks and geese on the exposed mud.

Turn left and follow the track which leads inland (to an alternative car-parking spot). The fields on either side of the track often have waders and ducks, especially at high tide, and are a favourite hunting ground for short-eared owls and merlins in the winter. Clumps of gorse and brambles provide shelter for migrant birds in spring and autumn.

Old salt pans near Lymington. The numerous creeks and pools in the area support a host of tiny creatures which provide food for some of the coastal birds. The grassy areas in between make good roosting places at high tide

8 **Turn left at the car-parking area and follow the undulating track back to the start of the walk at Keyhaven. (After periods of heavy rain in winter this track may be impassable, in which case retrace your steps along the sea wall.)** Watch for hen harriers and short-eared owls quartering the fields in winter. Lap-wings and yellow wagtails may be seen in spring.

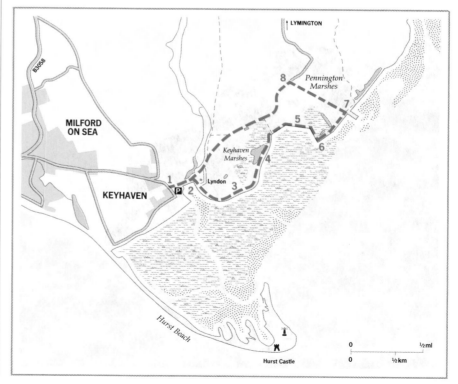

AS A NATURALIST, GILBERT WHITE – SELBORNE'S MOST FAMOUS FORMER INHABITANT – FOUND THE VILLAGE AND THE COUNTRYSIDE AROUND IT A CONSTANT SOURCE OF INSPIRATION FOR HIS WRITING. MUCH OF WHITE'S WORK IS STILL RELEVANT TODAY.

Fortunately for contemporary visitors to Selborne, the village's immediate surroundings have changed little over the centuries – especially when compared to other parts of Hampshire. The National Trust now protects some of the best areas, and the public can gain as much pleasure from this rural setting and its wildlife as Gilbert White did two centuries ago.

THE EFFECTS OF THE STORMS

The great beech trees of Selborne Hanger and Selborne Common have suffered badly from recent storm damage: giant specimens can be seen toppled, with their shallow root systems exposed. However, enough trees have survived for the woodland still to be impressive, and the occasional gap in Selborne Hanger, left by a fallen beech, allows magnificent views down over the village.

FLOWERS AND FUNGI

Clearings in the woodland encourage a wide variety of flowers to flourish. Wild arum, herb Bennet, sweet woodruff, ramsons, wood-sorrel, primroses, wood spurge, wood millet, sanicle and sweet violet are all widespread. In early spring, some of the beechwoods harbour green hellebores, which thrive in the shady conditions.

In autumn, Selborne would be well worth a visit just for the colours of the leaves. Beech leaves turn golden brown before they fall and are comple-

Selborne

Hampshire
Grid ref. SU 743 335

National Trust
Approx. 3¹/₂ miles (5.6 km). Steep in parts but generally easy. Mostly footpaths, but one short stretch of sometimes busy road.

Selborne is 4 miles (6.4 km) south of Alton on the B3006. There is a large, well signposted car park in the village, behind the Selborne Arms inn.

Selborne Hanger, a steep scarp slope cloaked in beech woodland, forms a stunning backdrop to Selborne village. The woods harbour interesting birds and flowers and are a renowned location for 'fungus forays' in the autumn.

Nearby sites: *Chawton Park Wood* – mature conifer plantation, good for fungi in autumn; *Alresford Pond* – water birds throughout the year.

Ramsons, a kind of wild garlic

The dainty flowers and distinctive leaves of wood-sorrel are a familiar sight in spring woodland. The plant can tolerate quite deep shade

mented here by the reds and yellows of other tree species. Autumn is also the best season for fungi. The rich leaf-mould of the woodland supports a wide variety of species such as death caps, blushers, wood mushrooms and wood blewits.

WOODLAND BIRDS

The birdlife of Selborne includes most of the usual woodland species such as woodpeckers, nuthatches, tits, tree-creepers and goldcrests. Several migrant warblers breed here including blackcaps, chiffchaffs and willow warblers; it was in fact Gilbert White who first distinguished the last two as being separate species. The more unusual wood warbler can also be heard.

Gilbert White

Gilbert White spent much of his life in Selborne. He was born in the vicarage in 1720 and, in 1793, died nearby in 'The Wakes'. The house has now been turned into a museum. He was educated in Farnham and Basingstoke and later at Oxford, returning to the area to become curate, first of Farringdon and then of Selborne itself.

White was a vigilant observer and recorder of all things natural in and around the parish of Selborne. He was also a keen correspondent. Letters to friends and colleagues about his sightings and speculations were eventually compiled and published as *The Natural History and Antiquities of Selborne* in 1788. The book has been widely read ever since.

THE *WALK*

Great spotted woodpeckers are quite common in woodland, parks and gardens, but a sighting of this handsome bird is always exciting. The bird pictured is a female: males have a red patch on the back of the head

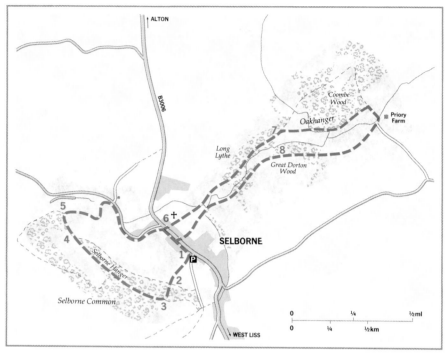

1 From the car park, follow the signposted footpath which climbs gradually to the foot of Selborne Hanger, with a field on your left and trees to the right.

2 Pass through a kissing-gate and, at the National Trust sign, turn left and follow the Zig-Zag Path up the Hanger. Ignore the Bostal Path to the right. As you climb, look beside the track for plants such as herb Robert, dog rose, herb Bennet, male fern (shaped like a shuttlecock) and hart's tongue fern. Speckled wood and meadow brown butterflies sunbathe on the vegetation.

At a bench, where the path forks, take either path.

3 At the top of the Zig-Zag Path, pause for breath at the seat and admire the view down over the village. Follow the signpost behind the seat to The Common, keeping to the right-hand track, nearest to the edge of the Hanger. The mature beech woodland is good for birds: wood warblers, nuthatches, great tits and blackcaps can be seen. Sweet woodruff, enchanter's nightshade, wood spurge and wood dock grow on the woodland floor.

4 Pause at another seat, at the junction with the Bostal Path, to admire the view of the village. For a short cut, take this path back towards the car park, otherwise continue along the path as it descends through excellent, mature woodland. Hart's tongue fern and wild arum grow on the ivy-covered banks, and wood warblers and goldcrests sing in the trees. Helleborines can be found in some of the less disturbed areas of woodland.

5 Where the path meets a well-worn track and a National Trust sign marked 'Selborne Common', turn right. This eventually leads into Gracious Street. Turn right and return to the village. (A possible short cut is to end the walk on reaching the B3006 and return to the car park.) Spotted flycatchers and swallows can be seen around some of the gardens.

6 Take the path through the churchyard signposted 'Short and Long Lythe'. Gilbert White is buried in a simple grave in the church-yard. Many of the older gravestones are covered in colourful lichens. Some of the churchyard's trees suffered badly in the recent storms.

At the far side of the churchyard, cross a stile and have a look at the Ramblers' Association map of the area. Cross the meadow, which contains some ancient oaks, and go over a small bridge by the National Trust sign marked 'Short Lythe'. Grey wagtails may be seen on the stream.

Follow the path through the woodland and over a stile to a National Trust sign marked 'Long Lythe' and then through more woodland. Ground elder and hedge woundwort grow beside the path, and blackcaps sing in the woodland. The woodland comprises beech, holly and ash on the left, with a poplar plantation on the right.

7 Go over a stile and cross the centre of Coombe Meadow, using plank bridges to avoid getting wet feet. Yellow iris, redshank and meadowsweet grow in the wetter parts.

Follow the footpath over a stile into Coombe Wood, taking the right-hand track. Emerge shortly from the wood and cross the field keeping left, heading for Priory Farm. Turn right on to the track at the farm. On the bend of the lane, follow the footpath straight ahead, signed Selborne.

8 Keep to the top of the field and go through a gate and on to the well-worn footpath through Great Dorton Wood. Many of the trees have suffered storm damage. Green hellebore grows on the steep slopes to the left, and the leaf litter is good for fungi such as death caps and fairy clubs. Scarlet elf cup sometimes grows beside the path, and oyster fungus can be seen on some of the beeches. The autumn colours near the end of Great Dorton Wood are especially stunning.

KINGLEY VALE IS WITHOUT DOUBT THE FINEST YEW FOREST IN BRITAIN AND AMONG THE BEST IN EUROPE. ELSEWHERE IN ENGLAND, YEWS OFTEN EITHER ARE SOLITARY OR FORM PART OF A MOSAIC OF WOODLAND SPECIES, BUT HERE THERE ARE STANDS OF PURE YEW. SOME OF THE OLDER TREES HAVE INCREDIBLY GNARLED AND TWISTED TRUNKS: GROVES OF ANCIENT TREES LIKE THIS ARE NOTHING SHORT OF ENCHANTING.

THE YEW WOODS

Yews are evergreen and form a dense and almost complete leaf canopy. Little light penetrates to the woodland floor, so the ground is comparatively poor in plant life. However, this does mean that visitors can walk with ease around some of the ancient specimens and marvel at their contorted shapes and shallow, spreading roots.

GRASSLAND, SCRUB AND MIXED WOODLAND

Elsewhere on the reserve, the Nature Conservancy Council is managing areas of chalk grassland by seasonal grazing by sheep. This encourages the characteristic short turf of downland country, which is rich in herbaceous plants including several species of orchid, round-headed rampion, salad

Kingley Vale

West Sussex
Grid ref. SU 824 088

Nature Conservancy Council
Approx. 4½ miles (7.2 km). Steep in parts but generally easy; mostly along a waymarked trail.

The car park for the reserve is at West Stoke, which is approximately 3¾ miles (6 km) north-west of Chichester.

Kingley Vale is a National Nature Reserve comprising some wonderful stretches of yew forest with many ancient trees. There are also areas of chalk downland and scrub which harbour interesting flowers, butterflies and other insects.

Nearby sites: *West Wittering* – sand dune flora and wintering waders and wildfowl, including brent geese; *Langstone Harbour* – vast area of mudflats (view from the northern shores); *Queen Elizabeth Country Park* – excellent chalk downland and scrub.

burnet, milkwort and thyme. Many species of insect also find this habitat to their liking: chalkhill blue and Adonis blue butterflies and stripe-winged grasshoppers can all be found at Kingley Vale.

Areas of scrub and mixed woodland have also been encouraged on the reserve. Oak, whitebeam, ash, elder, hawthorn, privet and blackthorn grow well and provide nesting sites for blackcaps, whitethroats, lesser white-throats and turtle doves.

A WORD OF WARNING

The start and finish of the walk are along a public right of way. However, most of it lies within the boundaries of a National Nature Reserve and follows the Nature Conservancy Council's waymarked nature trail. Please do not deviate from the trail or other designated public rights of way. Because sheep and deer may be encountered on the walk, keep dogs on a lead at all times or, better still, leave them at home.

Top: *Silver-washed fritillary. This beautifully patterned woodland butterfly is the largest British fritillary. Adults are on the wing during July and August*

Below: *Ancient giants in the forest. Yew trees like these may well be about 500 years old. Yew forests are very uncommon; there is nothing quite like that at Kingley Vale anywhere else in Europe*

1 From the car park, walk north along the public footpath. Yellowhammers sing from the elders, oaks, hawthorns and field maples which border the track. Look for goats-beard, pineapple mayweed, white campion and yarrow along the field margins. Where woodland borders the path, dogwood, traveller's joy, privet and blackthorn grow in profusion. Listen for singing blackcaps and turtle doves. Dog's mercury, hedge wound-wort and herb Bennet grow under the trees. The high-pitched squeak of shrews can sometimes be heard.

2 At the National Nature Reserve signpost, cross the stile, ignoring the footpath along the reserve's southern boundary. Pause, if you wish, at the field museum and buy a nature trail leaflet. Continue north along the trail, following the arrows and numbers. Listen for turtle doves, bullfinches and yellowhammers among the bushes and trees of ash, oak, hawthorn and privet. Speckled wood and silver-washed fritillary butterflies can be seen in summer. Where the path passes through yew groves, listen for nuthatches and goldcrests and look for grey squirrels.

3 At post 10 on the nature trail, bear right, keeping the fence and fields to your left and the woodland to your right. The path passes round the edge of a field and over a stile. Listen for skylarks overhead and look for green wood-peckers feeding on the ant-hills in the downland field. Lady's bedstraw is abundant. The pond, visible from the top of the field, attracts birds.

Wild daffodils are usually associated with meadows but they also grow in shady woods

4 The path bears sharply right at nature trail post 12 and passes through a dense stand of young yews. It then climbs steeply up the slope of the Downs amid chalk scrub and downland. Look for salad burnet, quaking-grass, milkwort and thyme in the open areas and listen for bullfinches. Small heath and meadow brown butterflies and speckled yellow moths can also be seen.

5 Cross a stile and turn left on to a well-worn track which climbs up the slope. The turf is rabbit-grazed and extremely close-cropped. Pause at the Tansley Stone (to the right of the path) and admire the magnificent view. Examine the downland for interesting flowers and butterflies.

6 Having passed the tumuli to the right of the track, fork left following the arrows and ignoring the bridleway signposts. The path descends through dogwood and hawthorn scrub and finally passes through a wonderful, dark yew grove. Common spotted orchids grow in small clearings and goldcrests sing from the yew trees. There is considerable evidence of recent storm damage to the yews.

7 From nature trail post 22 onwards, the path passes some fine areas of chalk downland. Keep to the obvious paths, and take great care where you walk. Listen for the rattling song of lesser whitethroats and that of the several species of grasshopper that

occur here. This is also a good spot for downland butterflies. The flora includes common spotted, pyramidal and frog orchids and rock-rose.

Continue down the well-worn track to the reserve entrance, from where you can return to the car park.

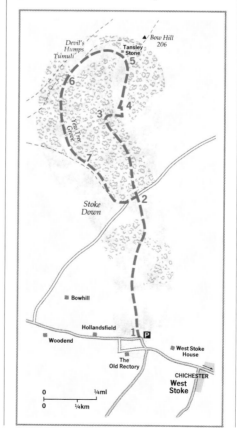

It is easy to see how the redshank got its name. This bird is widespread around the coast in autumn and winter, but usually goes inland to breed

PAGHAM HARBOUR IS ONE OF THE MOST UNSPOILT AREAS OF COAST IN SOUTH-EAST ENGLAND. AT LOW TIDE, THE HARBOUR EMPTIES TO REVEAL VAST AREAS OF MUDFLATS AND SALT-MARSH WHICH ARE A HAVEN FOR WILDFOWL AND WADERS AS WELL AS THE MARINE PLANTS AND ANIMALS WHICH SUPPORT THEM.

Since 1965, Pagham Harbour's status as a Local Nature Reserve has helped protect its wildlife. The sanctuary provided is reflected in the comparatively confiding nature of many of the area's birds.

SEASONS AND TIDES

Birdwatching on Pagham's mudflats can be rewarding at any time of year. In winter, large flocks of brent geese commute between the salt-marsh and the surrounding fields, sometimes accompanied by wigeon and teal. Shelducks remain in the harbour in the company of black-headed gulls and vast numbers of waders such as dunlins, oystercatchers, redshanks, grey plovers, ringed plovers, bar-tailed godwits, curlews and knots. The best views are had on a rising tide as the birds are gradually pushed closer to the shore. At high tide, large flocks take to the air in search of undisturbed roosting sites – a wonderful spectacle, which should not be missed. At low tide, grey herons stalk the creeks and channels in search of fish and crabs, while red-breasted mergansers, cormorants and Slavonian grebes keep to the open water. A telescope will come in useful for birdwatching at low tide, when many species will be visible only

Pagham Harbour

West Sussex
Grid ref. SZ 856 964

West Sussex County Council
Approx. 5¼ miles (8.5 km). Easy, level walking, but possibly muddy in places. One short stretch of sometimes busy road.

The car park is by the information centre at the signposted Pagham Harbour Nature Reserve at Sidlesham Ferry, 5 miles (8 km) south of Chichester on the B2145 between Sidlesham and Selsey.

The harbour – a Local Nature Reserve with a useful information centre – is a large area of mudflats and salt-marsh of special interest to birdwatchers. Large numbers of waders, ducks and geese can be seen in winter, while spring and autumn migration times bring a wide range of species to the reserve's various habitats. The flora includes many typical coastal plants associated with salt-marsh and shingle.

Nearby sites: *Selsey Bill* – good for sea-watching, especially during onshore winds; *Pagham Lagoon* – attracts smew in winter, and the surrounding shingle has an interesting flora; *Pagham village* – provides an alternative view of Pagham Harbour; *Chichester gravel pits* – attracts good numbers of pochards, tufted ducks, gadwalls and great crested grebes as well as more unusual species. Black terns appear during migration times.

Grey plovers are winter visitors to Britain, and are quite common on muddy shores

at some distance.

During the summer months, wildfowl such as brent geese and wigeon, and many of the waders, are absent. However, the shingle spit at

nearby Church Norton (partly closed during the breeding season) has colonies of ringed plovers and little terns: the latter can often be seen plunge-diving for small fish and shrimps. In winter, snow buntings are sometimes seen on the shingle.

A HAVEN FOR MIGRANTS

Birdwatching interest is by no means restricted to the mudflats. The fields bordering the harbour are the haunt of lapwings and golden plovers in winter, while the Ferry Pond attracts large numbers of waders and wildfowl, especially during spring and autumn migration.

The whole area is noted for sightings of rare or unusual migrants at these times, and the bushes and scrub at Church Norton are often extremely productive. Newly arrived warblers, flycatchers and other summer visitors find welcome food and shelter here in spring. These bushes are also a regular autumn and winter haunt of the firecrest, a tiny bird very similar to a goldcrest but distinguished by the black and white stripes around its eyes.

Migrants found at Pagham include butterflies as well as birds. Species attracted by the area's rich and varied flora include painted ladies, red admirals and clouded yellows. They join residents such as peacocks, gatekeepers and blues, making a wonderful display on warm, still summer days.

The variety of habitats that Pagham Harbour offers is reflected in the wide range of species encountered regularly at migration time. Each bird family has its own preferred habitat, so sea ducks, skuas and terns are largely confined to the sea, waders to the mudflats and marshes, and land birds to fields, hedgerows and woodland. This walk explores all of these habitats.

FLOWERS OF SALT-MARSH AND SHINGLE

Because of Pagham Harbour's proximity to the sea, it is not surprising that maritime plants flourish. On the salt-marsh, sea-lavender, glasswort, sea purslane, annual seablite and cord-grass can be found. These familiar estuary plants represent different stages in the colonisation of the seashore by plant life. Glasswort and, in recent years, the vigorous and often unwelcome cord-grass, are usually the first plants to stabilise the mud sufficiently for other plants to gain a foothold. On the shingle beach at Church Norton, yellow horned poppy, sea campion, sea kale and patches of the endangered childling pink occur.

THE *WALK*

1 Check the information centre notice-board for any recently reported sightings of interesting birds. Walk round the back of the information centre, taking the path across the reclaimed land to the old railway embankment. Look for goldfinches feeding on seed-heads and, in summer, for giant puffballs – fungi the size of a football.

2 At nature trail post 6, turn right. From here, scan the mudflats for waders and wildfowl. In addition to common winter birds such as brent geese, redshanks and grey plovers, more unusual species such as avocets may be seen. The first British record of a greater sandplover was at this spot.

3 Walk down the embankment to the ferry channel. Where the path comes to a T-junction at the bridge over the channel, turn right for a few yards (metres) to the hide which overlooks the Ferry Pond. Gulls, waders and ducks congregate here and allow excellent views. During autumn migration, ruffs, curlew sandpipers, wood sandpipers and little stints are regular, and both grey phalarope and Wilson's phalarope have occurred. The fields beyond are quartered by short-eared owls and hen harriers in winter.

4 Retrace your steps to cross the harbour channel and then follow the footpath along the harbour wall. During the summer months, look for dark bush crickets and gatekeeper butterflies among the brambles, and lesser marsh grasshoppers in the grass. Adders bask unobtrusively in the grass in early spring. Scan the mudflats for waders and wildfowl and to look at the summer-flowering sea-lavender and sea purslane.

Below Church Norton is a classic spot to sit and relax while watching ringed plovers, grey plovers, red-shanks, curlews, brent geese, wigeon and many others on the mudflats. The churchyard and surrounding hedges and bushes are good for migrant songbirds, and firecrests are regularly seen in winter.

5 Continue to the sea. As you walk, scan the fields and bushes to the right for linnets, lapwings and kestrels. Kingfishers are frequently seen on the small pools here, and unusual birds spotted in the area have included red-backed shrike and trumpeter finch.

When you reach the sea, scan the open water for Slavonian grebes, red-necked grebes, red-throated divers, eiders, gulls and skuas. During the breeding season, the shingle spit is closed to the public to protect nesting birds. Usually after the end of August, access is once again permitted and shingle plants can be seen in abundance. During the winter, flocks of waders often roost on the shingle, and greenfinches and the occasional snow bunting search for seeds.

6 Walk south along the shingle until you overlook some ponds known as The Severals. Reed buntings and moorhens are regular here, and unusual sightings have included bearded tit and purple heron.

For birds, mud is one of the main attractions at Pagham, packed with good things to eat

7 Follow the public footpath towards Greenlease Farm and turn right towards Church Norton. Check the bushes and hedges for buntings, finches and tree sparrows, and the fields for larks and pipits. Hoopoes are occasionally seen in spring.

8 At the road, turn left and immediately right to follow the public footpath across the fields back to Ferry House. In winter, check the fields for brent geese, lapwings, golden plovers and flocks of finches and buntings. Watch also for a short-eared owl, a merlin or a hen harrier.

9 When you reach the B2145, turn right and walk back to the Ferry Pond and information centre, taking great care because of the traffic.

The Mens

The great storms have left a few gaunt beech trees to frame the view from Bedham north to The Weald. Foxgloves thrive in the newly formed clearing, but will gradually be shaded out as the woodland regenerates

ON 16 OCTOBER 1987 – THE NIGHT OF THE GREAT STORM – WINDS OF OVER 100MPH (160KPH) TORE ACROSS SOUTHERN ENGLAND, SCATTERING MATURE TREES LIKE MATCHSTICKS. THE ANCIENT WOODLAND OF THE MENS WAS HARD HIT – BUT WHAT MIGHT HAVE BEEN AN UNMITIGATED DISASTER HERE IS NOW BEING SEEN AS A NATURAL NEW BEGINNING.

AN ANCIENT WOODLAND

The Mens is one of the most extensive blocks of ancient woodland in the South-East, a 400-acre (160-hectare) stretch of the old Wealden Forest. The heavy clay soil of this area made it unpopular with early farmers and it was only in Anglo-Saxon times that settlements began to appear in the wildwood. Since then a gradual process of clearance all around left The Mens, and nearby Ebernoe Common, as the only places where it is possible to lose sight of fields, roads and dwellings. The reason they survived was because of the rights of commoners to graze stock and cut underwood; the tall 'maiden' trees, grown separately from the under-wood, were the property of the landowner, usually the lord of the manor, but everything else was bound up in complex agreements with local people.

For hundreds of years The Mens (the unusual name comes from the Old English 'ge-mennes', meaning shared tenancy) was intensively exploited – trees were 'lopped and topped', saplings were cut or coppiced and any regrowth was browsed by farm stock – particularly by pigs, which also rooted out fruits and seeds.

In the 16th and 17th centuries many of the remaining trees were pollarded to provide firewood for local industries. By the middle of the 18th century, when The Mens became the property of the Mitford family, parts of the wood were almost parkland and it became necessary to enclose the commons to allow regeneration. This was not popular with the commoners, but it allowed The Mens to return to its former state of high forest, and apart from some felling early in the present century this is how it has been ever since. The wildlife is quite different from that of other types of woodland. There are few spreads of spring flowers, but fungi are exceptionally varied and several species of *Russula* toadstools found here are national rarities. Butterflies include all those species expected in a classic woodland community – white admiral, purple emperor, silver-washed fritillary and purple hairstreak. Where there are gaps or clearings in the woodland, orchids, bugle, violets and wild daffodils are found. Where the trees crowd in on all sides there are swathes

The Mens

West Sussex
Grid ref. TQ 024 237

Sussex Wildlife Trust
Approx. 4½ miles (7.2 km). Easy walking; care needed with route.

The wood is accessible from a side-road off the A272, south-west of Billingshurst and about 2 miles (3.2 km) south-west of Wisborough Green. A small car park lies on the south side of a side-road through the heart of the wood (signposted Hawkhurst Court).

This rare stretch of ancient woodland is good in spring for flowers, in summer for butterflies and beetles, and in autumn for fungi. An excellent comparison with more 'managed' forests, and with other traditional sylvicultural systems such as coppice, the Mens is an example of high woodland left to nature.

Nearby sites: *Arundel Wildfowl Refuge* – captive wildfowl on ponds and reed-beds are joined by a variety of wild birds including waders, ducks and swans in winter; *Amberley Wild Brooks* – wintering wildfowl and marshland plants.

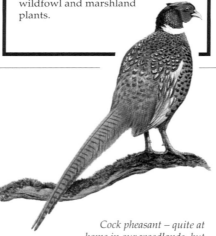

Cock pheasant – quite at home in our woodlands, but not native to Britain. Pheasants were probably introduced by the Romans

of mosses and lichens.

Most of The Mens lies on yellow Wealden Clay – waterlogged and cloying, the sort of place it is best to avoid after heavy rain. To the south the slopes of the Bedham escarpment are on Lower Greensand and are better

Primroses and bugle are among the flowers that flourish wherever enough light reaches the woodland floor in spring

drained. The trees of The Mens reflect the different soils, with oak dominating the clays and beech being the most common on the sand. The mix of other tree species testifies to the lineage of the wood; among the widespread yew, holly and hazel are Midland hawthorn, spindle, small-leaved lime and wild service tree – trees that are slow to spread and even slower to colonise new ground.

A NEW CHAPTER

It is hardly surprising that The Mens became a nature reserve in the early 1970s; by then it had been recognised as the finest single site for fungi in Britain and one of the best for lichens. Its woodland butterflies are exceptional – the purple emperor is the species that every naturalist wants to see. Mammals found here include dormouse and muntjac; birds include nightingale and all three species of woodpecker.

The storms of 1987 and 1990 caused havoc in The Mens. There are fallen trees everywhere, and it would take decades for things to be cleared up. However, the Sussex Wildlife Trust has opted for a commendable, and potentially very exciting, way of dealing with all the damage. The fallen trees will be left where they are and The Mens will be allowed to assume its place as the descendant of a primeval wilderness. Wood-boring beetles, longhorns and weevils, will become commoner, as for a time will flowers such as foxgloves and wood anemones.

The long-term effects are more difficult to predict. But by letting these natural disasters start a new chapter in The Mens' long history, the Trust has created a telling reminder that this is what most of Britain might be like without man. As most of the country replants for the future, this will be a fascinating experiment in leaving well alone.

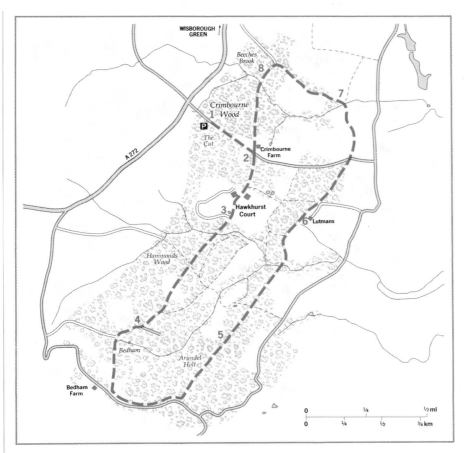

Tall oaks and beeches encircle the little parking area and there is only sufficient space for a few cars. If yours is one of them this is a definite advantage in that there is an immediate impression of being in the heart of the wood. As soon as you get out of your car you are part of its world; the ground is covered with wood spurge and yellow pimpernel. Above this there is a scrub layer of bramble, then hazel, hawthorn, holly and sallow, from where blackcaps, garden warblers and nightingales sing in spring. Finally there is the high canopy, a distant world of splintered sunlight and green shadows.

•••• **1** **From the car park turn right (south-east) along the road.** The oak tree on the corner of the car park has hefty outward-growing limbs and has obviously grown up with light all around it. Compare this with the oaks of similar age in the depth of the wood, which have tall straight trunks and limbs like

Sussex lacks good stone, so buildings are often timber-framed, weatherboarded or tile-hung. Crimbourne Farm shows all three

cathedral arches. The block of woodland on the south side of the road is called The Cut and is a mix of oak and beech with a ground cover of bluebells and sanicle. The earth banks are of medieval origin; they were used in The Mens to make parish boundaries or to separate 'assarts' or enclosures set aside for

cultivation. On the left is Crimbourne Wood, followed by Crimbourne Farm with its attractive group of barns and outbuildings.

•••• **2** **Turn right opposite Crimbourne Farm, along a metalled track towards Hawkhurst Court. Just before the buildings the track forks: bear right, past the old coach house and stables, then continue along the track between the old stables and the main house.** The grounds of the house contain some fine specimen trees – a cedar to the right of the track and a Wellingtonia to the left. Neither of these is particularly attractive to wildlife, though treecreepers find the warm spongy bark of the Wellingtonia irresistible on cold winter nights and smooth out little roosting nooks which look very cosy. Butterflies such as silver-washed fritillaries and brimstones visit the gardens for nectar.

•••• **3** **The metalled track leads past a pond on the right. After this, continue straight on (not right on a larger track, which leads to a private house). You are still on a metalled track, which descends into an attractive part of the wood with very tall beeches. Just after crossing a little stream, bear right off the track and on to a marked bridleway.** This leads through an area of high forest with some gaps in the canopy where goliaths have fallen in the storms. The old trunks take many years to rot away; one of the first signs is small holes made by beetle larvae. These attract hungry woodpeckers which enlarge any likely-looking cavity and let in the fungi which really do the damage.

5 The path levels and there are fields visible to the left. The path leads out to a track at a wooden squeeze-stile (to stop horse riders). Cross the track by another stile. The path becomes grassy and leads to the left of some paddocks. It crosses a small stream, then leads up past a house ('The Squirrels') and along a gravelled track. There is a hedge of blackthorn draped in honeysuckle, the latter being the food-plant of the white admiral butterfly which flies in the wood in midsummer and is the emblem of the Sussex Wildlife Trust.

6 Past the houses and after several hundred yards (metres), there is a footpath on the left as the road arcs right (just before the drive to 'Lutmans'). Take this footpath, at right angles to the road, but almost immediately turn right to go parallel to the road for a short distance and then keep to the left of a garden and chicken run. Eventually this leads out on to a road, at which turn right, then cross the road past a big bramble bush, then turn left on a path past a shed and into thickets again with a field to the left. This leads past a house and garden to the right, then bears left at a bridge. The stream here is very overgrown and rich in damp-loving flowering plants such as ragged robin and the very poisonous hemlock water dropwort. The mixed woodland further along the path is marshy too and is dominated by oaks, which can tolerate the 'gumboot' country of the Wealden Clay. The path can be very muddy after rain.

7 Continue past a house ('Freelands') and along a metalled road past West Cottage, then turn left off the road, back into the main body of the wood at a Sussex Trust sign. It is easy to stop looking at the trees by this stage of the walk, but this would be a mistake. About 100yds (90m) into the wood there is a wild service tree, one of the specialities of The Mens and an indicator of ancient woodland. It is related to rowan and whitebeam and has a leaf like a compressed sycamore.

8 Soon after this the path leads down through beech-leaf litter again and over a bridge across a stream. It then climbs again and leads through a last area of storm damage before crossing another footbridge and continuing south to Crimbourne Farm. The path leads out on to a road to the right of the farm, beside oak and field maple trees. Turn right at the road and make your way back to the car park.

The bridleway meets a crossroads of paths, at which continue straight on. (A detour along the bridleway to the right leads to an area of Hammonds Wood with a glade and a gipsy caravan.) The main path (still a bridleway) heads south-west, among tall oaks and beeches, with some sweet chestnut trees. It descends down a muddy bank to cross a little stream, after which continue on the bridleway, ignoring any side-paths. Soon the bridleway levels to pass a clearing on the right. This is the garden and orchard of a little cottage and is a wonderful place for orchids in the early summer.

4 The bridleway meets a metalled road, at which turn right past a barn and another pretty cottage, then a half-timbered house. The glades, clearings and old enclosures of this part of the wood, called Bedham, are rich in spring flowers such as wild daffodils.

Keep to the main track, which heads steeply uphill past some more cottages to meet a larger road, at which turn left. This area was completely devastated in the 1987 storm – people living in the cottages

Trees fell like dominoes during the 1987 storm, especially beeches on the light, sandy soils at the southern end of The Mens

thought a bomb had been dropped and described how the trees fell like dominoes. There is some replanting on the privately owned strip of woodland; otherwise the fallen trees have been left to their own devices. Beeches dominate because of the sandy soil on the steeper slope. They have particularly shallow roots forming a plate across the surface, and are quick to fall in a gale. Their absence on the steep ground to the left of the road allows a temporary view across The Weald towards the North Downs. It is a particularly fine view and quintessentially English.

Walk alongside the road, which follows the contour of the hillside, then bears right and begins to lose height. There is less wind-throw and storm damage here. As the road begins to head downhill turn sharp left down a steep footpath. Beyond the house and garden to the right, the overwhelming impression is of the cathedral of beeches and the deep shade and silence that they create.

Thursley Common

Heathland like this can seem like an almost limitless wilderness. In fact, Thursley is only a fragment of the great tracts of heather and gorse that once covered whole areas of southern England

BRITAIN HOLDS TWO-FIFTHS OF THE HEATHLANDS LEFT IN EUROPE, AND THEREFORE HAS AN IMPORTANT CONSERVATION ROLE. SOME OF THE BEST, INCLUDING THURSLEY COMMON, ARE ON LONDON'S DOORSTEP.

At one time the heaths of southern England were thought of as primeval wastes. Over the last few decades this attitude has changed dramatically. Firstly, we know that heathland only developed after woodland clearance, and was maintained almost by accident through the cropping of its meagre harvest of fuel and fodder. None of it is primeval. Secondly, heathland has acquired a value; it can be built on, or improved for agriculture. Because of this new-found value, the total area of British heathland has diminished to about 20 per cent of what it was at the turn of the century.

BRITAIN'S FINEST HEATH

Thursley Common lies a stone's throw from the A3, close to Godalming. Woodland crowds around it, softening its contours, but it is still a surprise to find a barren expanse so close to London. For its size it is certainly the finest heath in Britain. Most of it now lies within a National Nature Reserve. A network of paths, augmented by duckboarding over the bogs at the heart of the reserve, makes access easy.

By their nature, heaths are dry and dusty places. Thursley has about 26in (65cm) of rain a year, but this is lost through the sandy soil so quickly that the only plants able to survive are those specially adapted, like heather and gorse, to tolerate drought. Heather (*Calluna*) thrives on open ground where the soil is poor and acidic. Swathes of it grow on Thursley's bleached white sands, interlaced with valley mires or beds of black peat. Hill slopes may carry drifts of gorse or birch saplings. Where the mix is at its most complex the wildlife is most varied and exciting.

It might be expected that the dry, acid heathland is a poor wildlife habitat. This is certainly the case with wild flowers: for most of the year a walk across the reserve would be a dull affair if it were not for the mires. Even the flowering of dwarf gorse and heather, in the late summer, only sharpens the lack of variety. The heathland insect life is more abundant. A few very big caterpillars feed on the foliage; emperor and fox moth are both common and there is a chance of dark tussock and wood tiger. The silver-studded blue butterfly and the heather

beetle, a brown ladybird-shaped creature, also feed on the heather and sometimes have bumper years when they seem to be everywhere. Many predatory insects, as well as spiders, make an easy living from the visiting

---

Thursley Common
Surrey
Grid ref. SU 901 415

Nature Conservancy Council Approx. 2½ miles (4 km). Mostly level walking. Take waterproof.

Thursley is reached off the A3 southwest of Milford. The car park lies to the north of the village, on the east side of the unclassified road to Elstead, and next to The Moat Pond.

Heathland is a diminishing habitat throughout Europe, and Britain has some of the finest remaining examples. Of these, Thursley Common is one of the best. An excellent walkway allows people to cross the boggy ground at the heart of the reserve and complete a circuit along sandy paths through heather and gorse. Among the special birds are hobby and Dartford warbler, and there are very local insects such as the white-faced dragonfly.

Nearby sites: *Frensham Country Park* - heath, scrub and a lake; *Alice Holt Forest* - mixed woodland and a pond; *Devil's Punchbowl* - mixed woodland and heath.

Cross-leaved heath

---

hover-flies and frog-hoppers.

TRACKWAYS AND HOLLOWS

For most of the summer it is the trackways, hollows and pools of Thursley that attract attention. Not

The common lizard, Thursley's most numerous reptile

surprisingly, trackways and hollows often act as suntraps and their microclimate is almost Mediterranean. Solitary wasps and bees, which make individual nests in the hot sand, find these conditions ideal. Spider-hunting wasps (*Pompilidae*) are especially fascinating to watch.

THE POOLS

Most of Thursley's pools were created by peat-digging. However, when this practice stopped and the heather was no longer grazed or cropped, scrub encroached and the pools began to dry out. Several Surrey rarities disappeared, including the smooth snake and the natterjack toad - once called the Thursley toad because it had been so common here. Fortunately the trend has now been reversed and management of the site has included scrub clearance and the reinstatement of open heathland.

Today, the pools at Thursley are most famous for their dragonflies. Rarities include the white-faced dragonfly, the downy and brilliant emeralds and the small red damselfly. In all, 27 species have been recorded, making this the country's best single site.

BIRDS ON THE COMMON

Perhaps the classic specialist heathland bird is the Dartford warbler, which lives among gorse and is on the extreme edge of its world range here. Nevertheless, a few manage to survive even the worst winters. Thursley's Dartford warblers reached a record 20 pairs before the population crash of 1984. The scrub also attracts tree pipits and a host of warblers and chats.

The ideal time to visit Thursley is on a warm evening in early summer. The light is beginning to fade; sounds carry further in the still air. Hobbies have been chasing dragonflies and swifts in effortless spirals. Now there are noctule bats in the sky. Suddenly a nightjar begins to churr. It is hard to imagine a more perfect place to be.

Sandy trackways across the Common are worth a close look in summer for their insect life. Lizards or snakes may be basking in sunny spots on warm days, but are always ready to dart away if danger threatens

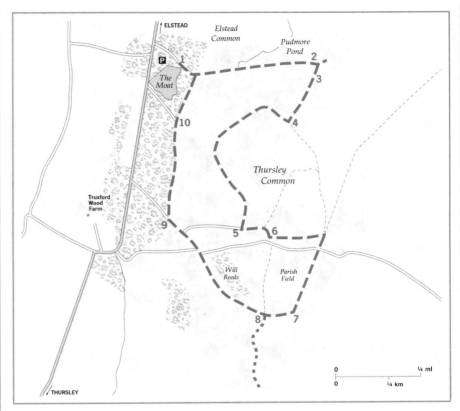

Next to the car park lies The Moat - a small lake, set among pine and birch trees and very popular with local families. The Moat always carries a few mallards, moorhens and little grebes and is a good place for dragonflies. Eighteen species breed here, including the emperor and the emerald, and the red-eyed damselfly.

1 From the car park a path leads left, clockwise around The Moat; take this for a few yards (metres), past a stiled right turn on The Moat bank. Where several paths meet, turn left. This path leads through an area of scrub pine and gorse and out to the main bridleway. Go straight across this, following a narrow tree-lined path. This leads out over the main valley mire and is duckboarded to protect both walkers and the bog vegetation. After about 100yds (90m) there is a pool on the right called Jill's Pond - a good place to look for raft spiders, and to count the different kinds of sphagnum moss (13 species are recorded).

2 Follow the raised path past several tall pines and peaty pools to a footbridge. The route turns right here, but a short detour onwards takes you to the heart of the mire and gives you an excellent all-round view. Distant silhouettes of birds are worth more than a passing glance. As well as wetland species such as curlew and snipe, there may be some good birds of prey about, most notably hobby. A pair usually nests near by in an old crows' nest in a tall pine, but there are several others in the area and they often hunt over the Common.

3 After crossing the bridge, the path heads south-west and rises to a pine-clad knoll. Summer migrants - redstarts, tree pipits and warblers - swell the bird population considerably in these scrubby areas. Sparrowhawks, which also like to nest in the pines, make the most of easy pickings by timing their breeding season to coincide with the appearance of fledgling songbirds in the middle of June.

The path descends to a boardwalk to skirt the main bog. There are several small ponds, suitable for raft spiders again and with classic plants. Among the sphagnum moss are asphodels and two species of sundew. There is also a chance at Thursley of the heath spotted orchid.

4 At a junction turn right, on to a sandy path. Continue through tall pines to a fork. It is possible to take a short cut back to The Moat car park by bearing right, but this would miss out most of the heathland and is only for those in a hurry. Instead bear left, along a wide track. The valley mire is left behind now as the track bears south. The ground is dry and sandy, and heather takes its place as the dominant plant. Until 1980 this area was covered with birch scrub, starting a process of plant succession that would have destroyed the heathland and soaked up most of the ground water, which fed the mire. The birches had to go, but the process has been gradual.

5 The track ends at a metal bar or fence with a gap to its left. Bear left after this and continue along a path through an area of pines until this leads out to open heathland and to a very wide sandy fire-break. In drought years the heath vegetation becomes tinder-dry and there is a risk of devastating fires. Under such circumstances, this wide swathe, stretching east and west right across the Common, would be its salvation.

6 Turn left along the side of the fire-break then, after about 300yds (270m), turn right along a marked path. Cross a track and continue south-west along a bridleway. The horizon to the left is now of rolling heath; a pine plantation and most of the birch scrub have been removed. The mound with its steep north-facing slope still shows the tracks of tanks and other military machinery from wartime exercises. On hot days the banks of heather shimmer in a heat haze and there is a buzz of activity as wasps and bees go about their work. After every few steps along the track you are likely to hear a flurry of noise as a lizard dives for cover. Although Thursley boasts all the British reptiles, only the common or viviparous lizard is really numerous. Adults measure up to 7in (18cm) long, but most of this is tail. Anything that looks bigger than this and is green might be the rarer sand lizard.

To the right of the bridleway is a group of oak trees within an ancient enclosure called the Parish Field. Now that grazing has been reintroduced, this is again used for stockholding, and the oblong enclosure is once more being used as a sheepfold.

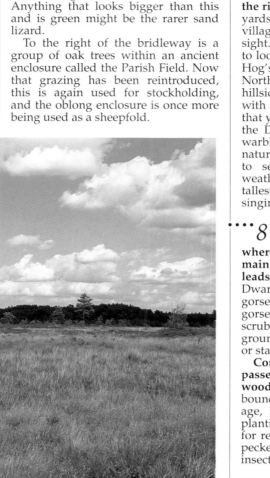

7 Bear right with the bank of the Parish Field until this bridleway meets a much broader track. The route crosses the track, but a detour left takes you to the top of the ridge. This lies only a few hundred yards (metres) north of Thursley village, though this remains out of sight. From the viewpoint it is possible to look across to the far horizon of the Hog's Back - an outlying spur of the North Downs. Closer at hand, the hillside on which you stand is covered with dense gorse scrub and it is here that you should listen for the `tchirr' of the Dartford warbler. Like other rare warblers, this bird is skulking by nature and therefore infuriating to try to see properly. However, in fine weather it sometimes sits out on the tallest gorse shoots, cocking its tail and singing a scratchy little song.

8 Back down the track, a path bears left opposite the point where the Parish Field path meets the main track. Follow this left path as it leads down through dry heathland. Dwarf gorse (*Ulex minor*) and common gorse (*Ulex europaeus*) are the abundant gorse species of Thursley. Beneath the scrub vegetation, on the surface of the ground, are several kinds of *Cladonia* or stag's horn lichens.

Continuing downhill, the path passes a fine fragment of ancient oak woodland to the right. An original boundary bank, possibly of medieval age, lies hidden among more recent plantings. These trees are now a haven for redstarts and lesser spotted woodpeckers, birds that enjoy searching for insects among the flaking bark.

9 The scrub melts away into open heather and the path meets a main trackway, at which turn right. Heather lies to the left, birchwoods to the right. The combination is ideal for nightjars, and this is a good place to sit at dusk to watch them as they flit like great moths over the heather, trawling insects into their gaping mouths. Their reptilian appearance is quite in keeping with the place and they certainly enhance the primeval atmosphere. Heathland may be a manmade habitat, but it owes nothing to civilisation.

10 Continue along the track until a path leads left, back to The Moat car park.

Careful management of the reserve has helped conserve Thursley's marshes and pools, which at one time had begun to dry out. On them depend numerous insects, including many species of dragonfly. Wetland birds such as curlews and snipe visit, and there is a range of fascinating bog plants

DESPITE ITS NATURAL APPEARANCE, VIRGINIA WATER IS A MAN-MADE LAKE, CREATED BY THE DUKE OF CUMBERLAND IN THE 18TH CENTURY BY DAMMING THE VIRGINIA RIVER. HOWEVER, TIME AND NATURE HAVE MASKED MOST TRACES OF ARTIFICIALITY AND NATIVE SPECIES BLEND IN PERFECTLY WITH INTRODUCED TREES AND SHRUBS AND ORNAMENTAL FEATURES. IN ADDITION TO ITS TRANQUIL BEAUTY, VIRGINIA WATER IS NOW A HAVEN FOR AQUATIC LIFE – FISH IN PARTICULAR – AND WATER BIRDS.

THE BIRDLIFE OF VIRGINIA WATER

Not surprisingly, wildfowl are the most important members of the water-bird community on Virginia Water. The winter months are best for variety: mallards, tufted ducks and pochards are regular but a careful search, especially during spells of cold weather, may reveal gadwalls, shovelers, goosanders, goldeneyes or even a smew.

Mandarin ducks are present throughout the year and the Virginia Water area is currently Britain's best breeding location for this exotic species. March and April herald the arrival of migrant birds, among them the garganey – an attractive duck that winters in Africa. However, the birdlife of Virginia Water is not restricted to wildfowl: grey herons and the occasional kingfisher can be seen around the margins and, in spring, great crested grebes perform their elaborate courtship displays on the water.

WINDSOR GREAT PARK

The Great Park was originally a deer enclosure within the larger Windsor Forest, which itself dates back to

Virginia Water

Berkshire
Grid ref. SU 980 691

Approx. 3½ miles (5.6 km). Easy walking on level ground.

Virginia Water is beside the A30, 1½ miles (2.4 km) south-west of Egham. The car park (charge) is off the A30.

Virginia Water is a pleasant, man-made lake surrounded by woodland. Water-loving birds are always an attraction, complemented by the forest wildlife of Windsor Great Park, in which the lake lies.

Nearby sites: *Staines Reservoir* – good for wildfowl in winter and waders in autumn, especially when one half of the reservoir has been drained; *Chobham Common* – excellent lowland heath. *Edgbarrow Woods* – mixed woodland, heath and bog, with a rich variety of species.

Meadowsweet, a well-known summer flower of damp meadows and woodland

Domesday Book and is named as a royal hunting forest. Some of the individual trees seen in the Great Park today share in its long history. Many of the gnarled and twisted oaks are thought to be over 500 years old. Their age and shape are due to a long tradition of pollarding. Older specimens have acquired a characteristic 'stags-horn' appearance, with dead branches emerging from a growth of leaves lower down. Their swollen trunks are often hollow inside.

In addition to the scenic attraction of Windsor Great Park, its open, park woodland also adds considerable wildlife interest to the walk. Many forest species of plants and animals are found away from the water.

WOODLAND HABITATS AND WILDLIFE

Ancient oaks are an important feature of Windsor Great Park and play a key role in the ecology of the area. They provide nest sites for woodpeckers (all three British species occur), redstarts, little owls, nuthatches, treecreepers and sparrowhawks, as well as refuge and food for hundreds of species of insects. However, many other habitats are found in the park: coppice, conifer plantation, mature beech woodland and mixed woodland, as well as open grassland, add to the variety.

During the summer months, the insect life of Windsor Great Park is prolific. Although some of the more unusual species of beetles and flies, for which the area is renowned, may be small or rather retiring, other groups are more conspicuous. Dark, oak and speckled bush crickets are common in areas of grassy scrub and over 30 species of butterfly have been seen. In particular, look for purple hairstreaks around the oaks, white admirals and commas feeding on bramble flowers, and skippers and 'browns' – for example, gatekeepers and meadow browns – in the grassland.

The Mandarin Duck

Although the exotic-looking mandarin duck is not native to Britain – it comes originally from the eastern USSR and from China – it is now established as an official breeding bird in this country, thanks to escapes from captivity. The female lacks the colourful plumage of the male, and both sexes are rather retiring, generally preferring to keep to the cover of waterside vegetation. Mandarins are hole-nesting ducks. Artificial nesting boxes are a perfect substitute for hollow trees.

THE *W*ALK

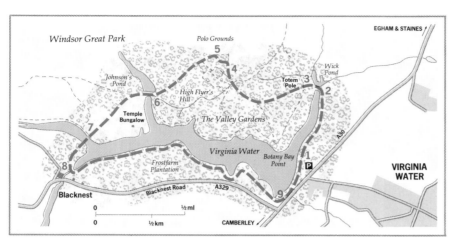
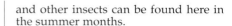

1 From the car park, walk to the lake-shore and turn right, following the margins of Virginia Water. The woodland between the car park and the lake comprises mature beech, sweet chestnut, oak, birch and pine. Look for holly blue butterflies in the car park and grey squirrels, magpies and woodland birds – including green and great spotted woodpeckers – under the trees. Scan the open water for tufted ducks, mallards and great crested grebes. Some of the shoreline is fringed with aquatic vegetation such as reeds, reedmace and yellow loosestrife. Listen for reed warblers in spring. As you continue along the edge of the lake, quiet, sheltered bays on the far side may harbour mandarin ducks and grey herons. Look for fungi under the trees in autumn.

2 Cross the bridge which bisects this narrow 'arm' of Virginia Water. Wick Pond, the small lake to the north of the bridge, has water lilies, moorhens and the occasional grey heron. The bridge is a favourite spot from which to feed the ducks. Black-

Native and introduced tree species harmonise to provide a fine backdrop to Virginia Water

headed gulls are attracted to the free meals in the winter.

3 Walk up the hill a short way to the Totem Pole and, at the signposts, follow directions to 'Valley and Heather Gardens'. The open, park woodland harbours native species of beech, birch and oak as well as introduced oaks, maples and many others. Look for signs of mole activity beside the path. When you reach an area of Wellingtonias and a splendid Monterey pine, look for heathland plants such as ling, bell heather and purple moor-grass. Goldcrests, coal tits and other woodland birds feed among the trees.

Explore some of the ornamental rides and then return to the main path.

4 Continue past the 'Valley Garden' notice-board until you reach the point where several paths radiate. The directions of the signposts are rather ambiguous, but take the third path on the left. This leads to the Heather Garden along a short path with wire fencing on both sides. Walk through the Heather Garden – the gates are unlocked during the daytime. Large numbers of butterflies

and other insects can be found here in the summer months.

5 Having left the Heather Garden through the gate, turn left on to the made-up track. Fork right at the 'Rhododendron Species Collection' notice-board and go down a steep hill. The path eventually joins a metalled road from the right. Continue down the valley. The path passes through beautiful areas of mixed ornamental woodland with native species interspersed. Look for woodland birds and butterflies.

6 Cross a causeway over an 'arm' of Virginia Water. Scan the open water and margins for water birds.

The path then passes through an area of open, park woodland with ancient oaks. There is mixed woodland on the right. Look for purple hairstreak butterflies around the oak canopy. Green woodpeckers occasionally feed on the lawns.

7 Cross the causeway over Virginia Water, then turn left and walk through the trees. Scan the open water for mandarin ducks and look for grey herons around the margins. In early summer, spawning carp, tench and rudd can sometimes be seen in the water.

8 Cross another causeway and turn left, following the path along the southern shore of Virginia Water. Look for mistletoe in the trees near the causeway. Mature beeches between the causeway and the Blacknest car park attract flocks of chaffinches, with the occasional brambling, in winter to feed on the mast. Mature hornbeams make this area one of the most reliable sites in southern England for hawfinches. They use their massive bills to crack the hard seeds and are best seen in late winter. In summer, the margins of the lake are fringed with yellow iris, yellow loosestrife, gipsywort and water mint, and are excellent for damselflies and dragonflies, including the impressive brown hawker. Great crested grebes and Canada geese are seen on the water, and swallows and martins hawk for insects above.

9 Continue past the ruins and the 'Frostfarm Plantation' sign until you reach the waterfall. The track continues around the waterfall, back to the lake-shore and thereafter back to the car park.

WALK FOR ONLY A FEW MINUTES AWAY FROM BOX HILL'S CROWDED CAR PARK AND YOU WILL BE IN A DIFFERENT WORLD. PEACE AND QUIET REIGN OVER THE WOODED SLOPES, AND THE BUTTERFLIES AND FLOWERS OF THE CHALK DOWNLAND GO LARGELY UNDISTURBED AND UN-NOTICED BY THE GENERAL PUBLIC.

BOX HILL'S VARIED WOODLAND

The woodland comprises a surprisingly wide range of tree species. Box – from which the area gets its name – can be seen along the wooded stretches of the walk. It grows best as an understorey tree because it is tolerant of shady conditions on well-drained soil. Beech and yew are also found and some wonderful, ancient specimens can be seen here and there. Also look for ash, oak and birch, especially near the car park.

Recent gales have felled many of the more impressive trees and in places the woodland looks rather devastated. However, this natural phenomenon is not without its benefits: new clearings are created which favour woodland flowers and butterflies. Fallen timber encourages a rich growth of fungi after a few years of decay, and broken tree limbs provide breeding sites for hole-nesting birds.

Scrub woodland is also much in evidence at Box Hill. It comprises species such as dogwood, hawthorn, wayfaring tree, spindle, privet, elder, sallow and hazel, with old man's beard or traveller's joy growing profusely in places. The flowers of privet and elder, in particular, are much favoured by insects in summer and the berries provide an autumn feast for the birds.

Box Hill

Surrey
Grid ref. TQ 179 513

National Trust
Approx. 3½ miles (5.6 km). Mostly easy walking but very steep in parts.

Box Hill Country Park lies approximately 3 miles (4.8 km) north-east of Dorking. The large car park (charge) is reached by turning off the A24 Dorking–Leatherhead road at Burford Bridge.

Box Hill lies on the steep scarp slopes of the North Downs. The chalk soil supports a range of habitats from open downland to mature woodland. A variety of downland and woodland plants, insects and birds can be seen.

Nearby sites: *Headley Heath* – a mixture of heathland and chalk downland with associated plants and animals; *Ranmore Common* – woodland and downland which is particularly good for butterflies.

RICH CHALK DOWNLAND

Chalk downland is a fast diminishing habitat but at Box Hill some fine areas are thankfully safeguarded. The history of the Downs is inextricably linked to man's activities: past generations of farmers cleared the wooded slopes to make way for sheep grazing, which produced the close-cropped turf so characteristic of this habitat. Because coarse grasses could never dominate, a rich community of herbaceous plants developed with associated insects and other invertebrates.

Walking over Box Hill's chalk downland can be a rather fragrant experience with thyme and marjoram growing underfoot. Other plant specialities include squinancywort, clustered bellflower and rock-rose with the occasional orchid spike to add extra interest.

Grasshoppers are among the most conspicuous of Box Hill's downland insects – several species can be heard 'singing' on sunny days – but pride of place must go to the butterflies. Meadow browns, marbled whites, fritillaries, blues and several species of skipper occur including the nationally rare silver-spotted skipper. This delightful butterfly appears rather late in the year – usually around the middle of August – and can be seen feeding on stemless thistles and other flowers. The bright, silvery spots on the underside of the hind wing give the species its name and help distinguish it from the large skipper.

Left: *The delicate, papery yellow flowers of rock-rose are often found on chalk grassland*

Below: *The scarp slope of Box Hill rises steeply from farmland. Despite weekend crowds, the country park is rich in wildlife*

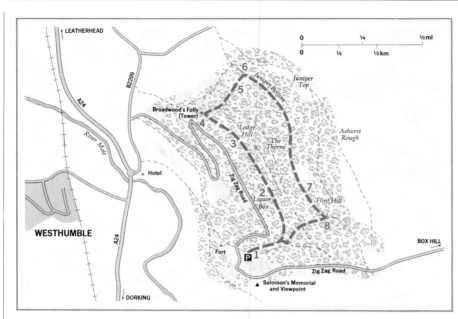

admirals and silver-washed fritillaries may feed on flowers closer to ground level. The horse-flies along this stretch of the walk can be extremely annoying and the hover-flies produce a continuous, loud buzzing. Green woodpeckers feed on the ant colonies and lesser whitethroats and garden warblers frequent the scrub.

7 **The path gradually moves into mature woodland with larger trees beside the path.** Look for beeches, yews and some good specimens of box. Areas of old coppice once provided straight shoots for stakes and hurdles.

8 **Turn right where the path crosses another, following the marked post, and continue walking through woodland until you rejoin the original path near the car park.** Look for fungi on the woodland floor in autumn, and listen for woodland birds in spring.

The Purple Emperor

This is one of our largest species of butterfly and also one of the most spectacular. The male has a beautiful purple sheen when seen from the correct angle, while the female is a more uniform brown. Purple emperors are found only in mature woodland – often oak – and only where sallow, the larval food-plant, is also common. Some areas of Box Hill provide just the right habitat, but adults can still be rather difficult to see since they only fly on sunny days and even then spend most of their time near the tree-tops. Occasionally they will visit the ground to feed on patches of moisture and dung. The curiously shaped caterpillars are difficult to spot on sallow leaves and the pupa is almost impossible to find: it is the same size, shape and colour as a leaf and even has markings which resemble the midrib and veins.

1 **From the National Trust car park and open space, follow the track that runs north-east, which is waymarked with grey posts.** The woodland comprises a mixture of trees: oak, birch and yew in some areas with mature beeches further on. There has been considerable storm damage and the fallen timber will, in future years, be good for fungi. Meadow brown, speckled wood and skipper butterflies can be seen along the path, and the brambles are good for hoverflies and speckled bush crickets.

2 **The path passes through an area of mixed woodland.** Here there has been extensive storm damage as well as recent tree planting. Wood sage, wood dock, male fern and bracken are common. Listen and look for great spotted woodpeckers and other woodland birds. Stinkhorns can often be smelt as you walk along the path; a careful look will reveal the 'head' of the fungus covered in flies. Look for box trees.

3 **To the left of the path, the habitat opens out into an area of good chalk grassland with fine views of the Zig-zag valley.** Plants of the short turf include rock-rose, rest-harrow, agrimony, marjoram, thyme, clustered bellflower and common St John's wort. Ant-hills indicate the undisturbed nature of the soil. Marbled whites, blues and skipper butterflies occur here and several species of snails can be found among the vegetation, especially after periods of wet weather in the spring.

4 **On reaching a tall tower, known as Broadwood's Folly, the path turns sharply to the right through an area of recently cleared woodland and scrub.** There is considerable evidence of recent storm damage and the newly disturbed soil has been colonised by common mullein, dark mullein, wild mignon-ette and nettles. Dark bush crickets thrive in this habitat. Dog's mercury and enchanter's nightshade – which are suffering as a result of the reduced shade – are reminders that the area was once densely wooded.

5 **The path descends steeply towards Juniper Bottom.** Open areas of chalk downland beside the path are good for plants such as pyramidal orchids and eyebright. The scrub to the left comprises dogwood, sallow and privet.

6 **At the bottom of the valley – Juniper Bottom – turn right on to the bridleway and follow this chalk track as it gradually ascends the valley.** The steep slope on the left of the path supports a mixture of open grassland and scrub woodland. In the grassland, look for chalk flowers including dropwort, salad burnet, wild thyme, greater knapweed – a butterfly favourite – and stemless thistle growing beside the path. Butterflies are common along this part of the walk, both in the grassland and along the woodland borders. Purple emperors are occasionally seen around the tops of the trees or investigating sallow bushes, while commas, white

ASHDOWN 'FOREST' IS SOMETHING OF A MISNOMER SINCE MUCH OF THE LAND COMPRISES THE MOST EXTENSIVE AREA OF HEATH IN THE SOUTH-EAST. HOWEVER, AREAS OF MATURE WOODLAND FRINGE THE HEATHLAND, ADDING TO THE DIVERSITY OF THE WILDLIFE.

A SPECTRUM OF HABITATS

Lying on a mixture of clays and sands, Ashdown Forest rises to 650ft (200m) above sea-level in places and is crossed by deep valleys. The result is a range of habitats from boggy mire through classic heath to terrain similar to heather moorland. The plant life and birds are typical of southern heathland, while the insects, in particular the butterflies and dragonflies, are outstanding.

THE HISTORY OF THE FOREST

The land that is now Ashdown Forest was once part of a Wealden royal hunting forest. Much of the Forest proper was gradually cleared of trees from the Middle Ages onwards, and land enclosures in 1693 reduced the area to the 6400 acres (2600 hectares) of commonland seen today. Much of the woodland had gone by the 18th century, the timber having been used to fuel blast-furnaces for iron smelting. However, because of the nature of the underlying soils, what replaced the woodland was open heathland, so from these rather destructive origins

Right: *Great grey shrike – an occasional, and elusive, winter visitor to the Forest*

Below: *The heathlands are at their best in late summer, with heather and gorse in bloom*

Ashdown Forest

East Sussex
Grid ref. TQ 456 289

East Sussex County Council.
Approx. 3 miles (4.8 km). Easy walking, but the ground is rough and steep in places and may be wet in autumn and winter.

Ashdown Forest extends roughly 5 miles (8 km) south-east of Forest Row towards Crowborough. Park in Friend's Clump car park, to the north of the minor road that runs west from the B2026.

Ashdown Forest is a superb area of heathland with bogs, woodland and scrub to add variety. Most of the species commonly associated with southern heathland habitat occur here, and the Forest is particularly good for insects.

Nearby sites: *Weir Wood Reservoir –* wildfowl, especially in winter; *Bewl Bridge Reservoir –* wildfowl in winter, waders in autumn; *Bedgebury Pinetum –* parkland trees, woodland birds.

---

was born the attractive, rolling landscape still known as Ashdown Forest.

Acts of Parliament in 1885, 1937 and 1949 put the management of the Forest in the hands of the Conservators of Ashdown Forest. However, preserving the essential character of the area is by no means straightforward. Grazing by cattle and pigs, formerly exercised under commoners' rights for all but five weeks in the year, has effectively ceased, so the open heathland is threatened by encroaching pine and birch. Bracken is no longer cut and collected, with the result that this hardy fern predominates in some areas. But perhaps most alarming of all is the increase in the incidence of fires caused by carelessness or malice.

BOGS AND HEATH

At first glance, the vegetation of Ashdown Forest's heathlands may look rather uniform. However, a closer look at the plants growing in different situations reveals considerable variation.

In the valley bottoms, wet bogs develop, dominated by sphagnum mosses. Round-leaved sundew, whose sticky leaves catch insects to supplement the plant's nutrient intake, cotton-grass, bog asphodel and marsh clubmoss can also be found in most bogs. Marsh gentians are a beautiful but rare autumn speciality; look carefully for its exquisite deep blue flowers. Cross-leaved heath borders the wetter areas and is home to bog bush crickets.

The open pools and mires support the nymphs of dragonflies and damselflies in abundance. While the male dragonflies may spend much of their time away from water, the females always return to the breeding pools to lay their eggs. The nymphs are entirely aquatic and it is sometimes possible to see them sitting among submerged weed. Some dragonfly species take several years to complete their life-cycle, but the adults usually live for only a few weeks.

The drier valley slopes are covered by different plants: ling, bell heather, sawwort and bracken predominate. The highest areas of Ashdown Forest harbour these species too, but gorse, dwarf gorse, petty whin and purple moor-grass can also be found. In these open areas the invertebrate life is prolific. Silver-studded blues, dark green fritillaries, graylings and emperor moths occur together with an abundance of spiders. These areas are also home to birds such as stonechats, meadow pipits and nightjars, the last most easily seen and heard at dusk on calm evenings in early summer.

THE *WALK*

A pair of silver-studded blue butterflies. This classic heathland species is on the wing during late summer. The male has characteristic silvery underwings

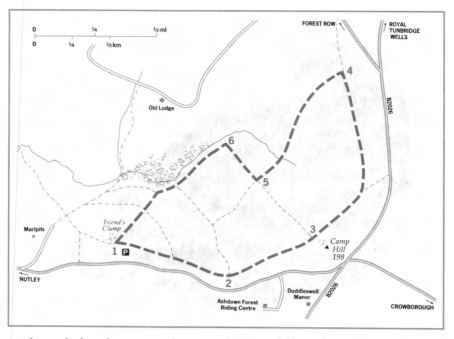

1 Walk east along the wide, sandy track which runs **between the car park and Friend's Clump.** Inspect the conifers growing in the Friend's Clump plantation for birds which may include the occasional redpoll or even a crossbill. As the track passes through an area of gorse, ling and bell heather, look for stonechats perched on sprays of gorse. Their loud, grating alarm call draws attention to their presence. Further along the track, the heathland becomes more open and patches of dwarf gorse appear. The heathland flowers are at their most attractive in July and August, which is also the best time of year for silver-studded blue butterflies, mottled grasshoppers and common field grasshoppers. Areas of bracken with stunted oak trees are followed by some superb, open stretches of ling. Look for common lizards sunbathing beside the track. Emperor moths may be seen here in the early spring.

2 The path bears left around a small pond on the right of the track. **Continue up the hill following the wide, sandy track.** The pond is full of emergent vegetation in the summer months and dragonflies are often abundant. In August, mating pairs of common sympetrums can be seen egg-laying at the water's surface. Willow warblers and reed buntings frequent the scrub woodland beside the pond. The hillside beyond is covered in open heathland – ling, bell heather, gorse and bracken grow here, with small patches of dwarf gorse and cross-leaved heath. Nightjars can be seen hawking insects over this area at dusk on warm June evenings.

3 Camp Hill is marked by a clump of pines. Ignore the **track to the left and continue straight on. The path soon bends sharply to the left, contouring around the valley hillside. Ignore the track that leads off to the right.** There is a sweeping vista of the heathland on the left, with rolling Sussex countryside in the distance. Look for sunbathing adders and grayling and gatekeeper butterflies along the track. In good years, painted lady butterflies can be seen feeding on the heather in summer. Silver-studded blues are common here, and stonechats perch on exposed gorse clumps.

4 At a small crossroads, take the track to the left which leads **down the hill, but fork left before you reach the valley bottom. Cross the stream – dry in summer but wet in winter – and take the right fork in the track which leads up the hillside, passing through an area of birch scrub.** In wetter areas, large numbers of bog asphodel spikes can be seen along with mat-grass and white beak sedge. The valley bottom hosts the occasional great grey shrike in some winters, and hen harriers are sometimes seen gliding over the valley slopes.
At a major crossroads, turn right and

5 follow the wide, sandy track **down towards a tree-lined hedgerow with fields beyond.**

6 Turn left at a T-junction with **another wide track.** A strip of woodland can be seen to the right of the track; here woodland birds such as woodpeckers and tits can be found.
The path crosses a tree-lined stream, which is dry in summer and wet in winter. Continue straight up the hill, ignoring paths to left and right, and head towards the pines of Friend's Clump on the horizon, back to the car park.

The Nightjar – A Master of Camouflage

This is one of our most curious birds. A summer visitor to Britain, the nightjar is largely nocturnal, catching insects on the wing in its large mouth. The bird is superbly camouflaged when resting on bare heathland – its preferred habitat – or among fallen branches on young plantations, and is almost impossible to see by day. At dusk, however, the strange, churring call is uttered from a song perch and the bird is sometimes seen silhouetted in flight. Nightjars do not make a nest as such. Two eggs are laid into a small scrape in the soil and incubated by the motionless parents.

FEW AREAS OF SOUTH-EAST ENGLAND CAN BOAST SUCH AN INSPIRING COMBINATION OF SCENIC BEAUTY, VARIETY IN HABITAT AND WILDLIFE APPEAL AS THE SEVEN SISTERS COUNTRY PARK. HERE, NATURE HAS CONSPIRED TO JUXTAPOSE CHALK DOWNLAND WITH SALT-MARSH, AND RIVER MEANDERS WITH CHALK CLIFFS.

The Seven Sisters – the imposing cliffs from which the park's name is derived – are undeniably dramatic and form part of the Sussex Heritage Coast. However, the bird, plant and insect life, associated with the park's other habitats, will also provide visiting naturalists with hours of fascination.

DOWNLAND AND MAN

Unlike many of our natural habitats, chalk downland – an important feature of the country park – is essentially man-made and owes a good deal of its richness to the activities of past generations. Woodland and scrub clearance followed by centuries of sheep grazing on the poor chalk soils have produced short turf, rich in herbaceous plants. Ungrazed areas soon become dominated by coarse grasses and lose their floral diversity.

Chalk downland is an endangered habitat in southern England, suffering from two major threats: neglect – leading to the invasion of scrub – and 'improvement', with the land often coming under the plough for cereal production or being fertilised for increased grass growth. It is ironic that man's intervention is also necessary for the long-term survival of downland. Without continued grazing by domesticated animals, it soon becomes the domain of hawthorn and bramble, which shade and crowd out the orchids and other exquisite plants still found on carefully managed chalk grassland.

Seven Sisters Country Park

East Sussex
Grid ref. TV 519 995

East Sussex County Council
Approx. 4 miles (6.4 km). Easy walking.

The car park is just to the south of the A259 between Eastbourne and Seaford at Exceat.

The country park comprises an unusual mixture of chalk downland, chalk cliffs, seashore, salt-marsh, lagoons and pools. Wildlife is good at any time of year, but the flowers and insects of Seven Sisters are at their best in spring and summer, while spring and autumn offer the best opportunities to see migrant birds. The downland harbours some unusual insect species and the flora includes a few national rarities.

Nearby sites: *Seaford Head Nature Reserve* – migrant birds, interesting chalk flora and excellent views of the Seven Sisters; *Friston Forest* – chalk downland and conifer plantation, forest walks and trails.

Horseshoe vetch, a plant of the Downs

The South Downs plunge abruptly to the sea at the Seven Sisters chalk cliffs

FLORA AND FAUNA OF THE CHALK

Thanks to careful management, Seven Sisters Country Park still retains some excellent chalk downland. 'Indicator' species such as thyme, stemless thistle, carline thistle, squinancywort and pyramidal orchid are locally common, and insects such as stripe-winged grasshoppers and chalkhill blue butterflies are welcome members of the park's fauna. In addition to the more widespread chalk species, keen-eyed observers may come across naturalised clumps of red star-thistle, dumpy centaury and wall germander, the last possibly in its only native British site.

BIRDLIFE THROUGH THE YEAR

For the birdwatcher, the country park's chalk downland offers little variety and few surprises: skylarks, meadow pipits, corn buntings, yellowhammers and kestrels are the most regularly seen resident species. However, the Seven Sisters' strategic position facing into the English Channel means that migrant birds are often evident in spring and autumn, when the valley bottom becomes the focal point for birds and birdwatchers alike. Early migrant wheatears are sometimes reported from late February onwards, often in the vicinity of the lagoon, and are followed later in the season by swallows, martins, whinchats and warblers, especially whitethroats. Terns and waders also pass through.

In addition to its breeding birds, the lagoon regularly attracts migrant waders including little stints and curlew sandpipers. Grey phalaropes have been recorded here after autumn gales, and black terns may pause to hawk insects either here or over the ditches and channels near the car park.

THE *Walk*

The Cuckmere River meanders to the sea, giving stunning views from the downland above

1 From the car park, walk south on the park trail which gradually climbs Exceat Hill. If you would prefer an alternative, level walk, follow the concrete track which runs south close to the river and associated ditches until you reach point 4 below. The chalk soil and the grazing of sheep on the hillside have produced the characteristic downland turf. See how many plant species you can recognise in a square yard (0.8 sq.m) – prime sites may harbour more than 30. Typical species include thyme, salad burnet, carline thistle, stemless thistle and fescue grasses. Listen for grasshopper 'songs' on warm, sunny days, and watch for downland snails after rain or at dusk.

2 Pass the site of Exceat church. The excavated foundations of the church are evidence of man's long association with the area. This was probably the focal point of a small farming community which dates back to early Norman times. Strip lynchets – earth banks – mark the boundaries of early fields. There are superb views of the Cuckmere valley and the former meandering course of the river.

3 The path continues towards the valley bottom. This is a good spot to search for migrant birds such as wheatears, pipits and yellow wagtails. During cold spells in winter, the patches of marshy ground and rushes are a favourite haunt of jack snipe. These small birds are rather difficult to spot, since they crouch low when alarmed and their plumage is usually well camouflaged. From the river embankment, scan the muddy margins for redshanks and common sandpipers during migration times.

4 At the junction of the paths, bear left up the hillside. The chalk grassland harbours interesting plants such as red bartsia, yellow rattle, weld and mignonette, as well as butterflies, grasshoppers and several species of snail. Patches of scrub can be seen in places, comprising plants such as bramble, hawthorn and privet. These harbour bush crickets in the summer months and provide cover and food for migrant warblers in the autumn.

5 Take great care when you reach the cliff-edge – the soil is extremely crumbly and cliff falls are regular. Turn west along the cliff path. The short turf harbours an interesting chalk flora, and the cliffs themselves are home to fulmars, herring gulls, jackdaws and feral pigeons. Migrating seabirds sometimes pass close to the shore during onshore winds.

6 Continue to the shingle beach. Some interesting but rather delicate plants grow here; please be careful not to damage them. Look for sea mayweed, yellow horned poppy, sea beet and sea kale. A small flock of gulls often collects just off shore or on the lagoon. Most will be black-headed gulls, but it is worth checking for the occasional little or Mediterranean gull. The shoreline here is part of the Seven Sisters Voluntary Marine Conservation Area. The man-made lagoon with nesting islands was constructed for the benefit of breeding terns and ringed plovers. In spring and autumn it can be extremely good for waders, including dunlins, curlew sandpipers, ruffs and spotted red-shanks. Numbers and species vary from year to year and even from day to day.

7 Walk back along the embank-ment of the Cuckmere River overlooking the adjacent strip of salt-marsh. Sea purslane, sea wormwood, glasswort and seablite are typical species. In the summer, look for the flowers of sea aster and sea spurrey. Waders feed along the tidal river margin.

8 Follow the path along the river embankment back towards Exceat Bridge. Grey herons, little grebes, shelducks and mute swans are often seen in the meander. Lapwings and redshanks occur in the fields.

9 At Exceat Bridge, follow the path which runs parallel to the road back to the car park. Kingfishers are regularly seen perched on over-hanging branches near the meander. Be sure to visit the Park Centre and the Living World exhibition, on the north side of the A259.

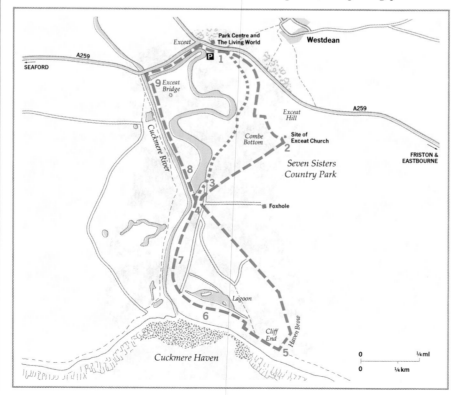

BIRDWATCHING AT RYE HARBOUR IS EXCELLENT: TERNS, GULLS AND WADERS BREED HERE AND A WIDE VARIETY OF MIGRANT AND WINTERING SPECIES APPEARS IN VARYING NUMBERS. IN ALL, 260 SPECIES OF BIRD HAVE BEEN RECORDED ON THE RESERVE.

THE ORIGINS OF RYE HARBOUR

Rye Harbour lies at the mouth of the River Rother; the canalised river forms the eastern boundary of the Local Nature Reserve. Much of the land area comprises shingle, stretches of which have been colonised by maritime plants and stabilised.

Less than 10 miles (16 km) to the west of Dungeness – the largest shingle beach in Britain – Rye Harbour is comparatively recent in origin. The shingle that now makes up much of Rye Harbour Local Nature Reserve would, at one time, have been carried along the Sussex coast to be deposited at Dungeness. However, a change in the River Rother's course in the Middle Ages interrupted the flow, causing some of the shingle to be deposited where we see it today at Rye.

Shingle is an important resource in the modern world and large quantities have been extracted from Rye Harbour over the years. However, many kinds of wildlife have benefited from this extraction: the resulting flooded gravel pits have become a haven for wetland plants and animals.

SHINGLE FLORA

At first glance, shingle appears to be so inhospitable that it is a wonder that any plant can grow on it. However, a wide range of species thrives in this habitat, many of them never found anywhere else. These are specialist plants – species that can cope with the shifting, well-drained pebbles and the salt-laden environment. On the walk, look for yellow horned poppy, sea kale, sea pea, sea mayweed, sea rocket, haresfoot clover and biting stonecrop beside the waymarked paths. Where the shingle grades into salt-marsh and grazing meadow, slender hare's-ear and least lettuce are occasionally found by keen-eyed botanists. Rye Harbour is the best British site for this latter species. It is rather unobtrusive and locating it is made more of a challenge by the fact that its yellow flowers open only in the mornings.

Disturbance and trampling are a major threat to shingle plants, and Rye Harbour is now one of the few areas in southern England where the whole

Shingle can look featureless and uninspiring from a distance, but a closer look is likely to reveal a great variety of specialised and interesting plants, some of them found in no other habitat

range of characteristic species can be seen. It goes without saying that flowers should never be picked on the reserve.

A WEALTH OF BREEDING BIRDS

Disturbance affects not only the shingle flowers but nesting birds as well – little terns, oystercatchers and ringed plovers lay their well-camouflaged eggs on the ground where they are vulnerable to trampling. Fortunately, sensitive areas are fenced off and visitors are asked to remain on the paths and keep dogs on leads. The Ternery Pool – a partly flooded gravel pit – is a focal point for nesting birds, which can be viewed from hides.

MIGRANTS AND WINTER VISITORS

Outside the breeding season, birds of many different species pass through Rye Harbour, some remaining in the area for the winter. The pools and gravel pits act as focal points for a wide range of birds, especially waders, gulls and terns. Exactly which species are present varies not only from year to year but also from day to day and hour to hour, but avocets, spotted redshanks, black-tailed godwits, little stints, curlew sandpipers and greenshanks are all regular. Black terns, sometimes in small flocks, are seen in spring and autumn, and Mediterranean and little gulls are sometimes found by careful searching among the black-headed gulls. In the summer of 1990, the term colony was joined by a least tern, a North American bird seen here for the first time in Britain.

Rye Harbour

East Sussex
Grid ref. TQ 942 187

East Sussex County Council
Approx. 4¾ miles (7.5 km). Easy walking on level ground. There is no shelter, so take windproof and waterproof clothing.

The car park (free) lies roughly 1½ miles (2.4 km) south-east of Rye, on the minor road signposted to Rye Harbour from the town.

Rye Harbour, adjoining the mouth of the River Rother, is a large area of stabilised shingle with a wide range of breeding birds and winter visitors, together with an interesting shingle flora. Salt-marsh, pools and grazing marsh add to the variety. The whole area, including parts of the Local Nature Reserve adjacent to the car park, can be crowded on sunny weekends in summer.

Nearby sites: *Pett Pools* – migrant waders in spring and autumn (view from the road using the car as a hide); *Dungeness RSPB reserve* – breeding birds plus migrants and good shingle flora.

Black-headed gull in summer plumage

THE *Walk*

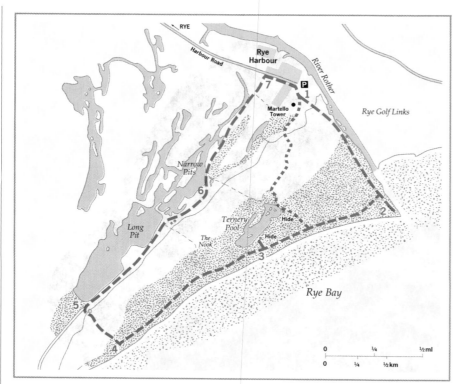

Rye Harbour

Harbour Road

River Rother

Martello Tower

Rye Golf Links

Narrow Pits

Long Pit

Ternery Pool

Hide

Hide

The Nook

Rye Bay

0   ¼   ½ ml
0   ¼   ½ km

The Little Tern

This is our smallest breeding species of tern, with a length of only 9in (23 cm). A summer visitor, the little tern arrives in April and departs for its wintering grounds on the African coast in September. Two or three eggs are laid in May on bare shingle or sand around the coast. Nests and incubating birds are vulnerable to attack by ground predators and disturbance by people. The best colonies of terns – known as terneries – are now found in protected areas where wardens prevent disturbance. Rye Harbour Local Nature Reserve holds one of the most important colonies in Britain.

1 From the car park walk south-east along the metalled track signposted 'No through road' which **runs parallel to the River Rother.** Between the river and the track is a stretch of salt-marsh comprising mainly sea purslane. Look for gulls and terns along the river. Viper's bugloss, mugwort, sea-beet and sea carrot grow beside the path, together with a few clumps of salsify. The fields to the right of the path should be scanned for yellow wagtails, buntings, larks and finches after any crops have been cut. Pause at the nature reserve sign-board and view the small pool on the right either from the path or from the small hide provided. Black-headed gulls and redshanks are invariably present and migrant waders can be seen in spring and autumn.

2 **Continue along the path until it reaches the seafront. Scan Rye Bay for birds.** At low tide, the exposed sand of Rye Bay will have gulls and waders. At high tide during the winter months, look for divers, grebes and the occasional eider duck on the water.

Retrace your steps and follow the path which heads south-west, parallel to the sea. Do not stray from the path, and keep dogs on leads. (Ignore the public footpath sign to the right unless you wish to take a short cut leading past a hide at the northern end of the Ternery Pool and back to the car park.) The shingle on either side of the track is covered with extensive patches of sea pea, sea kale, biting stonecrop, yellow horned poppy, birdsfoot trefoil, bittersweet and the shingle form of herb Robert. Look for small copper butterflies. Ringed plovers and wheatears are frequent nesters among the shingle, which is fenced off to the right of the path in order to protect them.

3 **Make a detour from the main path to the Guy Crittall hide, which overlooks the southern shore of the Ternery Pool.** Shelducks, black-headed gulls, cormorants, coots, Canada geese, common terns, little grebes and oystercatchers are common in the summer months. A wide variety of waders can be seen during spring and autumn migration times. This is a good spot for unusual species: a little egret spent several weeks here in the spring of 1990. Little terns can often be seen from the hide as they fly between fishing trips on the sea and their nests on the shingle.

4 **At the reserve sign-board and map, turn right.** The path is on shingle at first, but then follows a raised earth bank between two fields. Scan the fields for migrant birds and look for small skippers, gatekeepers and meadow brown butterflies and plants including black horehound, burdock and pineapple mayweed beside the path.

5 **At the footpath sign, turn right along a well-defined track and walk along the southern edge of the Long Pit.** Look for gulls, grebes, cormorants and wildfowl on the water. Flocks of sparrows feed in the field to the right of the path and a few reed warblers sing from the overgrown drainage ditches. Look and listen for the occasional marsh frog. This large frog was introduced to Britain from the Continent as recently as 1935 and is now found in wetland areas around Romney Marsh, where it was first released.

6 **Shortly after passing some farm buildings, the path runs around the margin of a reed-filled pool on the right of the track. Continue along the path, bearing left and keeping the edge of the Narrow Pits on your left.** Look and listen for marsh frogs, reed warblers and reed buntings. Swallows and martins are common over the water in late summer and autumn. Turtle doves are common in the fields and often perch in pairs on the overhead wires. The path passes through areas of recently disturbed ground where colonising plants flourish. Look for mignonette, dark mullein and poppies.

7 After passing through a cement works, the path meets **the road from Rye to Rye Harbour. Turn right and walk back to the car park.**

CLOSE YOUR EYES AND THINK OF THE NORTH DOWNS AND THE PICTURE IN YOUR MIND (WHETHER YOU HAVE BEEN THERE OR NOT) WILL PROBABLY BE OF A WARM GRASSY BANK BRIGHT WITH BUTTERFLIES AND FLOWERS. THE SOUND OF SHEEP AND SKYLARKS, AND THE SCENT OF THYME AND MARJORAM, MAY CROWD THE IMAGINATION TOO.

ENGLAND'S CHALK DOWNS

Downland is a particularly English phenomenon, but it has occupied a very brief moment in history. The steep slopes of chalk that form the classic sweeps of downland from Kent to Hampshire were once heavily wooded, but by the end of the 19th century they had been transformed into an almost treeless landscape of close-cropped grassland. Intensive sheep husbandry prevented scrub regeneration and encouraged a rich diversity of chalk-loving plants and animals.

When sheep grazing declined, scrub-woodland and patches of taller herbs began to flourish. Many of the open downland flowers were gradually excluded, unable to compete with the coarse grasses and shrubs. Some downland was maintained for a while by rabbits and reduced sheep-grazing; this was the golden age when some of the most engaging and memorable accounts of downland wildlife were written – WH Hudson's *Hampshire Days* (1903), *Afoot in England* (1909) and *Nature in Downland* (1923), for instance. By the early 1960s the rabbits had all but gone, their numbers drastically reduced by myxomatosis. Since then, most of the unique south-facing downland slopes

Wye Downs
Kent
Grid ref. TR 054 469

Nature Conservancy Council
Approx. 5¼ miles (8.3 km); uphill in parts.

Wye is 3½ miles (5.6 km) north-east of Ashford. The walk starts from the Church of St Gregory and St Martin, in the middle of the village. There is ample parking near by.

This National Nature Reserve is one of the few sections of the North Downs still managed as open grazing land. There is some woodland and scrub, but the rest is short-cropped turf on the steep, south-facing scarp slope – excellent for plants and insects.

Nearby site: *Yocklett's Bank* – good woodland flora including orchids. *Folkestone Warren* – chalk cliffs and undercliffs, grassland, noted for rich variety of its insect life, which includes many rare species of bugs and beetles.

Salad burnet, a typical plant of downland turf. Its edible leaves taste of cucumber

have been either covered by tangles of thorn bushes or turned over to more productive agriculture'.

A FORGOTTEN LANDSCAPE

Chalk grassland is still to be found in several southern counties, most especially Sussex and Hampshire, but it has almost vanished from the steep scarp slope of the North Downs. Almost, but not completely. There are several delightful walks along Kentish lanes which lead through old hazel and chestnut coppices and out on to forgotten fragments of downland overlooking The Weald. From Wrotham it is possible to walk along the Pilgrims' Way, beside ancient hedgerows of spindle, field maple, wild service and wayfaring tree, past clumps of knapweed dotted with marbled white and dark green fritillary butterflies, and turn up on to the Downs above Trottiscliffe. This is now a country park. Further east, the finest stretch of downland lies above the village of Wye, where a combe known as the Devil's Kneading Trough has become the centrepiece of a National Nature Reserve. The reserve boasts a list of 17 orchids (two of great rarity) and many notable insects. From the top of the steep green scarp you can have a picnic and look out over The Weald, listen to skylarks, smell thyme and marjoram, and perhaps watch chalkhill blue butterflies spiral together in playful dog-fights.

Nearly all the sheep-cropped grassland that once covered England's chalk downs has gone now, a victim either of neglect or of modern agriculture. Often the only scraps of downland to survive are on the steepest slopes, which would be difficult to plough – as in this photograph. Crops cover the higher and lower ground, with downland on the hillside between

THE *W*ALK

1 From Wye church, walk eastwards along the High Street, past Wye College and along the main road out of the village, called Coldharbour Lane. This is a section of the Pilgrims' Way, one of the most ancient trackways in Britain. Pretty gardens give way to tall hedges of hazel and poplar, with dogwood and old man's beard to hint at the alkaline nature of the soil.

2 Turn right along a side-road immediately before Withersdane Hall (part of Wye College), and follow this road as it bears left, with college grounds visible on the left. However, when the road bears right, continue straight ahead along a broad gravel track. The footpath crosses several stiles and tracks but keeps straight, in line with the edge of the tree-covered Downs. The fields on either side are farmed intensively, so there are few wild flowers along the way, but there are good views of the curtain of Downs to your left. Most of the scarp slope is now covered with woodland. The crown on the upper slopes is in the tradition of the Cerne Abbas Giant or the White Horse of Uffington, but of more recent origin, commemorating Edward VII's Jubilee.

3 Eventually the path leads out on to a road again - a more characteristic section of the Pilgrims' Way. The antiquity of the Way can be gauged by the composition of the hedge. Within a short section can be found hazel, wayfaring tree, dogwood, ash, dog rose and wild cherry.

Turn right along the road but almost immediately, and well before the house, turn left over a stile by a gate and a Nature Reserve sign. Climb some steps through the scrub, then another stile and a zig-zag path by fine field maple trees. Soon the view to the right opens out and you are walking on the close-cropped turf of Broad Downs. The path is steep, but there is suddenly so much to look at that there is plenty of time to catch your breath. Sitting down gives you an opportunity to look at the flora. Milkwort, birdsfoot trefoil, dwarf thistle, rock-rose and horseshoe vetch are a few of the common herbs. Of the orchids, the most likely to be seen here are fragrant and pyramidal orchid. The downland plants attract day-flying moths including speckled yellow, clouded buff, six-spot burnet and burnet companion, and butterflies such as chalkhill blue, brown argus and marbled white.

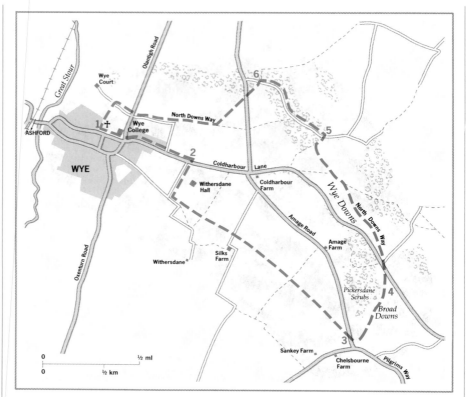

Continue up the slope to another section of zig-zag path and steps through the scrub to the left. Follow this until you reach a millstone with compass points marked on it. This makes an ideal viewpoint for a look southwards over the patchwork of countryside to Romney Marsh and the Channel. As the ground levels, there is an excellent view to the right of the Devil's Kneading Trough - a combe created by the thawing of ice after the Ice Age.

4 After the gate at the top you can bear right for a better view of the combe, but the main route turns left to cross a stile and meet the North Downs Way. Follow this through hazel coppice and scrub-woodland until you reach a road. Cross the road and go through a gate, then immediately turn left and go through another gate. Follow the fence, with downland to the left. Much of the grass here is too rank for flowers to flourish, but there are some interesting nooks and crannies on drier banks and in hollows.

5 At the beechwood turn right after a stile, then at a road turn left. The walk along this road captures the essence of a Kentish lane, and is delightful. To the right there are views

English downland at its breathtaking best – the Devil's Kneading Trough

of more downland, and the roadside verge has a host of flowers.

6 A footpath crosses the road; turn left along this, through a patch of woodland. This brings you out at a telecommunication mast. Head obliquely downhill to a stile to the left of the main gate, then cross the road. Cross a stile and follow the path through woodland again. This leads out on to arable fields; follow the path to a track, then turn right and go through the grounds of Wye College to meet a road. Cross the road and continue along a metalled side-road with college buildings and Wye church on the left. After about 200yds (180m), turn left through a gate, along a path to the churchyard.

VISITORS TO THIS POPULAR RSPB RESERVE CAN SEE A RICH VARIETY OF WOODLAND WILDLIFE. MOST OF THE BIRD SPECIES LIKELY TO BE FOUND IN AN ENGLISH OAKWOOD OCCUR HERE, ALONG WITH A WIDE RANGE OF MAMMALS, BUTTERFLIES AND PLANTS.

A WORKING WOOD

Part of a larger woodland mosaic – Blean Woods, which ring the north-west outskirts of Canterbury – Church Wood has probably always been a working wood. In addition to the trees grown to maturity for their timber, other trees would have been coppiced. This practice of cutting back to the stump encourages the growth of straight, thin shoots, ideal for stakes and poles. Sweet chestnut and hazel were particularly favoured species.

Nowadays, the 360-acre (145-hectare) reserve is carefully managed to encourage a diverse range of habitats. Areas of mature oak woodland, coppice of different ages and heathland can all be seen on the walk, together with woodland glades and rides, streams and ponds.

WOODLAND BIRDS

Birds have benefited greatly from the careful woodland management. Mature oak trees, many with dead branches, provide nesting sites for all three British species of woodpecker as

Church Wood

Kent
Grid ref. TR 123 593

Royal Society for the Protection of Birds
Approx. 3 miles (4.8 km). Easy walking, but muddy in places after wet weather.

Church Wood is roughly 3 miles (4.8 km) north-west of Canterbury. The car park is reached by following signs to Rough Common from the A290 Canterbury – Whitstable road.

The wood is an RSPB reserve which is managed to provide a diversity of habitats. Of particular interest are the coppiced areas, which favour migrant breeding birds, including nightingales, as well as interesting woodland insects.

Nearby site: *Elmley Marshes* – coastal grazing marsh and flooded scrapes with birdwatching hides. Excellent for waders, wildfowl, hen harriers and short-eared owls.

well as nuthatches, redstarts and several species of tit. Many smaller birds also benefit from the numerous nest boxes provided.

A few years after coppicing, hazel and other trees provide an ideal habitat for warblers and nightingales. Active woodland management is vital: neglected coppiced areas are soon abandoned by nightingales. Although this most renowned of songsters does sing at night, visitors to Church Wood in late April and May are just as likely to hear one during daylight hours – probably in an area of mature coppice.

COPPICE CLEARINGS

Insects benefit from the sunny glades formed in the coppice clearings. Wood ants, bees and a wide range of butterflies all flourish. Orange-tips and brimstones are frequent in April and May, and the pearl-bordered fritillary follows on in May and June. The heath fritillary, one of Britain's most threatened species, appears later.

Although Church Wood is not outstanding for woodland flowers, some fine displays of wood anemones and bluebells can be seen in spring. Along the rides look for common dog violet, cuckoo-flower, bugle and greater stitchwort. Later in the year, cow-wheat and lily of the valley appear.

Top: *Common cow-wheat, generally found in woodland on clay or acid soils*

Below: *A nightingale. This shy bird is seldom seen, but its song is unmistakable*

THE *W*ALK

1 Follow the waymarked path which starts behind the RSPB notice-board. This passes through birch scrub, with ling growing beside the path. Siskins and redpolls may be seen in the birches in winter.

2 After ¼ mile (400m) the path crosses a track and the trails diverge. Take the left fork, waymarked red, and continue through coppice woodland. Listen for chiffchaffs in spring, look for wood ants, and listen for the distinctive 'laughing' call of the green woodpecker.

The waymarked red trail crosses a track signposted 'short cut' to the right. A short detour can be made here to see spring flowers and butterflies. Although Church Wood's acid, London clay soils are not renowned for their flowers, careful woodland managemen ensures a good display early in the year.

Continue along the red trail. The path passes close to an area of devastated conifers, destroyed by the 1987 hurricane, then crosses heathland with ling, gorse, rushes and birch scrub. Look for grasshoppers and common lizards in summer, and parties of long-tailed tits in winter. In spring, listen for willow warblers and green woodpeckers.

3 At the junction of the red and green trails, fork left, following the red trail. The gravelled path passes through an area of mature oak woodland. Look for fungi on the woodland floor in autumn. In spring

The golden flowers of broom brighten Church Wood's nature trails in early summer. Walkers here on warm, still days later in the year may be startled by the sudden popping of the dry seed pods

you may see great, blue and coal tits, and perhaps a treecreeper, a nuthatch or a lesser spotted woodpecker.

The path crosses another track signposted 'short cut', to the right. This offers a second possible short detour to explore a grassy ride for woodland flowers and butterflies. The main path descends through mature oak woodland and sweet chestnut coppice. Look for butcher's broom and listen for chiffchaffs and great spotted woodpeckers. Some of the large trees were felled by the 1987 hurricane. The fallen dead wood will be good for fungi in future years. Look for wood ants on the woodland floor and purple hairstreak butterflies in the oak canopy.

Continue along the red trail, which soon crosses a third grassy ride signposted 'short cut' to the right.

Again, a detour along the ride is worth while for butterflies, spring flowers, blackcaps, cuckoos and green woodpeckers.

The red trail descends and passes an area of managed woodland on the left. Wood spurge, primroses, bluebells, brambles and wood anemones flourish here when the coppice growth is young, and nightingales regale passers-by in spring.

4 The path crosses a stream, after which the waymarked path bends sharply to the right. Continue along the track through mature oak woodland with coppiced chestnut and hazel. Listen for chiffchaffs and great spotted woodpeckers, and scan the trees for grey squirrels and perhaps a hawfinch. A clearing on the right has a good display of bluebells in spring as well as cuckoo-flower.

5 Ignore a small track to the right and continue along the red trail through an area of open woodland. Here mature oaks rise above an understorey of bramble and coppice. There may be nightingales in the denser areas of coppice.

6 The waymarked path meets two other paths at a reserve sign. Turn right, still following the red trail markers. Gorse, broom, common dog violets and wood ants can be seen beside the path, which passes through mature woodland.

7 The path bends sharply to the right and descends. Look carefully at the tree stumps for mosses. Just before the stream is an area of open oak woodland, on the left, where primroses and wood spurge flourish. Look for jays and treecreepers.

The path climbs and is soon joined on the right by the green waymarked trail. Nightingales and blackcaps can be seen and heard; common dog violet and bugle grow by the track.

8 At the next junction of waymarked tracks, keep left on the red trail. Wood anemone, yellow archangel and wood spurge flourish around the path junction. Mature holly trees can be seen and lily of the valley grows by the path.

9 The path bends sharply to the right. Scan for woodland birds and look for wood ant activity.

Continue along the path and return to the car park.

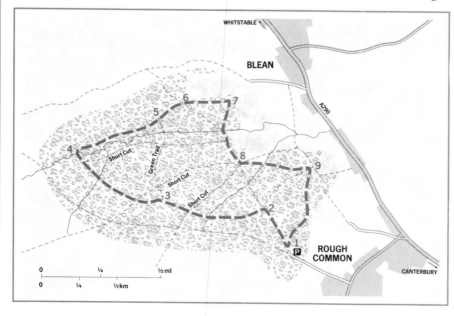

WHITSTABLE

BLEAN

A290

6
5
7
4
Short Cut
Green Trail
Short Cut
3
Short Cut
8
9
2

P
ROUGH
COMMON

CANTERBURY

0   ¼   ½ml
0   ¼   ½km

STODMARSH NATIONAL NATURE RESERVE IS ONE OF THE MOST EXTENSIVE AND ACCESSIBLE AREAS OF MARSH AND REED-BED LEFT IN SOUTHERN ENGLAND. THE HAUNT OF A RICH VARIETY OF WETLAND WILD-LIFE, STODMARSH IS EXCELLENT FOR BIRDWATCHING THROUGHOUT THE YEAR. IN SPRING AND SUMMER, MARSHLAND FLOWERS ADD A SPLASH OF COLOUR TO THE GREEN AND BROWN HUES OF THE REEDS.

GOOD WETLAND VIEWS

Reed-beds are, by the very nature of the wet terrain, usually inaccessible and most can be viewed only from the perimeter. Fortunately for the visiting naturalist, Stodmarsh is crossed by a raised embankment, the Lampen Wall, which affords excellent, elevated views across the wetland. In addition, a newly created nature trail, which cuts through wet woodland and an area of pollarding, offers an interesting contrast to the open marsh.

STODMARSH IN WINTER

During the winter months, when the birdwatching is often at its best, Stodmarsh can be rather inhospitable. Winds from the east whistle straight across the open fields and reed-beds, and the Lampen Wall can get extremely muddy. However, with appropriate clothing and footwear this is not a problem, and, as compensation, visitors often find that the birds are more obliging in harsh weather. Views of bearded tits and hen harriers will soon make up for any discomfort. Bearded tits and water rails sometimes feed on the open ground at the edge of the reeds, while hen harriers quarter the reed-beds, their numbers

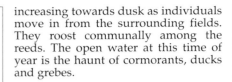

Stodmarsh
Kent
Grid ref. TR 229 601

Nature Conservancy Council
Approx. 3¾ miles (6 km). Easy walking on level ground. Extremely muddy in winter.

Stodmarsh village is roughly 6 miles (9.7 km) east of Canterbury. The Nature Conservancy Council car park lies along a rough track marked 'No through road' from the village.

This National Nature Reserve covers a superb area of reed-beds, open water, alder carr woodland and grazing meadows. It is good for birds throughout the year, and the marsh flora is also of interest.

Nearby site: *Sandwich Bay* – open fields, sand dunes and mudflats, with good maritime flora and migrant birds. *Reculver Marshes* – foreshore with good waders and wildfowl, grazing marsh, a haunt of raptors and wildfowl; sea lavender, yellow horned poppy.

increasing towards dusk as individuals move in from the surrounding fields. They roost communally among the reeds. The open water at this time of year is the haunt of cormorants, ducks and grebes.

SUMMER VISITORS

In spring and summer, Stodmarsh offers wonderful opportunities for the naturalist and especially the bird-watcher. As soon as you reach the open reeds, you will be greeted by the sound of birdsong. Sedge and reed warblers sing scratchy songs; their territories are dotted throughout the reserve, while Cetti's warblers generally frequent the few bushes and small trees that grow among the reeds. Stodmarsh is one of only a handful of British sites where Cetti's warblers are regularly seen. It is also home to one of our rarest migrant breeding species, the Savi's warbler. In most years, at least one can be heard singing its loud, reeling song from the reeds.

Swallows, martins and swifts are common in spring and summer, with countless thousands sometimes present at peak migration times. With all these numbers, there is always the chance of something unusual turning up: both red-rumped swallow and pallid swift have occurred in the past, and sand martins are common especially in the autumn.

Left: *Often hidden in dense vegetation where it searches for insects, the sedge warbler's presence is usually betrayed by its continuous chattering song, more varied than that of its relative the reed warbler*

Below left: *The reserve in May. Isolated trees and bushes like this may well shelter Cetti's warblers at this time of year. Listen for the loud, abrupt song of this skulking little bird – still quite a rarity in Britain*

Cetti's Warbler

The Cetti's warbler (pronounced *chetty's*) is a comparatively recent addition to the list of British birds: it was first recorded in 1961. Over the following decade more and more birds colonised from southern Europe – the species' stronghold – and the long-awaited first breeding record came in 1973. Although rather secretive and difficult to see, Cetti's warblers are easy to hear in the right habitats. The song is loud and explosive and Stodmarsh is one of the best areas in the country to find this species. There are more females than males, which means that males often have two or three mates.

THE *WALK*

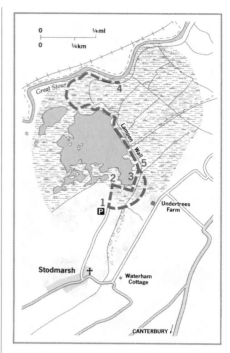

A member of the buttercup family, greater spearwort is taller than most of its relatives, reaching up to 4ft (1.2m) in the right conditions. It favours ditches and other marshy or wet places, but it is not very common in Britain

1 Before leaving the car park study the reserve signpost and map. Walk northwards along the track, ignoring the nature trail for the time being. Hedges on either side of the track sometimes attract warblers in spring. A marsh warbler sang here for a few days in May 1986. The remarkable song of this rare bird is seldom heard now, for the British population is fast dwindling.

2 Where the track is blocked by gates ahead and to the right, go through the kissing-gate on your right by the signpost. Scan the reed-beds to your left for sedge warblers and reed warblers in spring and summer. Reed buntings and Cetti's warblers are present here, as elsewhere on the reserve, throughout the year, and long-tailed tits sometimes feed in the bushes.

3 The path runs along a muddy embankment known as the Lampen Wall. After the path bends to the left, ignore a turning to the right. The copse on your right has orange-tip butterflies in spring; they lay their eggs on cuckoo-flower. In winter, small flocks of siskins and redpolls can

sometimes be found, and long-eared owls have been known to roost inconspicuously here as well. The ditches are usually covered with bright green duckweed.

Continue along the Lampen Wall, ignoring the nature trail turning on the right. The path bears to the left and passes a large area of open water on the left and an expanse of reeds on the right. In the winter, this is an excellent area to watch for hen harriers as dusk approaches. A penduline tit was once recorded here. In summer, reed warblers and the occasional Savi's warbler sing from the reeds; the latter species is especially vocal at dawn and dusk.

Pause half-way along the causeway and scan the open water. Cormorants roost on suitable perches and flocks of tufted ducks, pochards, teal and mallards are usually to be seen near the reed fringes in winter. In summer, look for grebes on the water and common terns, black terns, swallows, sand martins and swifts hawking insects overhead. To the east of the wall, the reeds harbour the occasional marsh harrier in summer, while bearded tits are present throughout the year. Listen for their high-pitched 'ping' calls as small flocks move among the reed heads in search of seeds. The ditches and channels are home to mute swans, moorhens and coots and in summer harbour frogbit, greater spearwort and flowering rush.

The path is soon flanked by bushes

and bramble patches in which robins and skulking Cetti's warblers are usually found. Listen for the Cetti's loud, explosive song, which can sometimes even be heard in winter. The patches of open, grassy marsh to the left sometimes have feeding snipe and water rails in winter. The water rail's call sounds like the squeal of a pig. Among the patches of reed and reedmace and occasionally on the banks, look for common meadow-rue, marsh cinquefoil and marsh stitch-wort.

4 The path turns east to run parallel to the River Stour. Just before you reach the boundary, marked by a reserve sign, areas of flooded fields and pools can be seen on the right. Outside the breeding season, flocks of lapwings and golden plovers are found here while in spring, yellow wagtails, garganey and snipe are seen. In winter, scan the open fields for hen harriers, merlins, short-eared owls and the occasional rough-legged buzzard.

Retrace your steps along the Lampen Wall until you reach the nature trail on your left.

5 Follow the boardwalk through the woodland. On the way, look for reed buntings and flocks of long-tailed tits.

The boardwalk continues through an area of pollarded trees and back to the car park.

MOST ISLANDS HAVE A ROMANTIC QUALITY ABOUT THEM. WITH ITS SENSE OF ISOLATION AND BEAUTIFUL MARITIME SCENERY, SKOMER IS NO EXCEPTION. COMBINE THIS NATURAL SCENIC BEAUTY WITH A RICH ARCHAEOLOGICAL HERITAGE AND EXTRAORDINARY NUMBERS OF BREEDING SEABIRDS, AND SKOMER CANNOT FAIL TO ENTHRAL.

OVER THE SEA

While crossing the narrow but treacherous waters that separate Skomer from the mainland, visitors will get their first views of the wildlife for which the island is famous. Groups of guillemots, razorbills and puffins are disturbed from the water and lesser black-backed gulls, kittiwakes and fulmars sometimes show a passing interest in the boat. Fortunate visitors may even see a grey seal bobbing among the waves, curious about the intruders into its territory.

MANX SHEARWATERS AND PUFFINS

Seabirds are superbly adapted to life at sea and none more so than the Manx shearwater. It is one of Skomer's most significant breeding birds, and one for which the island boasts an estimated 100,000 pairs. Although they are masters of wind and wave, on land these shearwaters are ungainly and vulnerable to attack. Consequently, they nest in burrows and only return to Skomer at night, thus avoiding gulls and other diurnal predators. The daytime visitor is only likely to see burrow entrances and the occasional injured bird. Stay overnight, however, and you will hear thousands of birds fluttering overhead, uttering strange wails and screeches in the darkness, and crash-landing near their burrows.

Without doubt, Skomer's most

Skomer Island

Dyfed

Grid ref. SM 734 095

Nature Conservancy Council/Dyfed Wildlife Trust

Approx. 3½ miles (5.6 km). Steep at the start, otherwise easy.

Skomer is a mile (1.6 km) or so off the Pembrokeshire coast at Wooltack Point. Park at Martin's Haven and catch the ferry. There is a charge for the ferry, and a modest landing fee. Visits can be made every day except Mondays, from March until September.

The island is well known for its archaeological interest and has some of the most important breeding seabird colonies in western Europe. Numbers of puffins, Manx shearwaters and lesser black-backed gulls are especially high. The island also harbours an endemic mammal – the Skomer vole.

Nearby sites: *Skokholm Island –* seabird colony; *Pembrokeshire Coast Path* – stunning coastal scenery.

Puffins – here from April to August

Skomer and the Pembrokeshire coastline. The sea here is relatively unpolluted and supports a rich marine life, which in turn makes this a fine feeding area for seabirds

endearing breeding seabird is the puffin. With brightly coloured beaks and black-and-white plumage, puffins look faintly comical as they laze about on the cliffs and rocks. Like the shearwaters, they too nest in holes, using abandoned rabbit burrows or sometimes excavating their own.

SKOMER'S OTHER BIRDS

Puffins share Skomer with their relatives – guillemots and razorbills. Guillemots breed on precipitous cliff ledges, relying on inaccessibility to protect them, while razorbills nest under boulders and in crevices – a site also chosen by a diminutive and seldom seen nocturnal visitor to the island, the storm petrel.

Other birds found on Skomer's cliffs include buzzards, choughs, kittiwakes, fulmars and shags, together with isolated pairs of great black-backed gulls and small colonies of herring gulls. The top of the island is the favoured haunt of lesser black-backed gulls, which form large colonies among the bluebells and bracken in spring. Short-eared owls also favour this habitat and can often be seen gliding overhead in search of Skomer voles, the main component of their diet.

PLANT LIFE

In May and June, the island provides a spectacular display of flowers. Among the bluebells covering the top of Skomer are tormentil, spring squill and heath pearlwort. On the cliffs, thrift or sea pinks grow in great drifts, with sea campion, buckshorn plantain and rock sea-spurrey providing contrasting colour.

WALK 35

i

1 The boat to Skomer lands at North Haven, where visitors are met by the warden or an assistant. Climb up the path from the beach. Puffins can sometimes be seen resting beside their burrow entrances. Many of the burrows are used by Manx shearwaters, nocturnal visitors to the island. Look for parties of choughs.

2 Continue past the old lime-kiln and the monolithic Harold Stone, then walk along the path heading west towards the farmhouse. The Harold Stone was probably erected by prehistoric man. Strip lynchets, marking the boundaries of ancient field systems, are further evidence of prehistoric human activity.

Skomer voles and slow-worms can sometimes be seen beside the old farm machinery. Look for lichens and wall pennywort on the old stone walls.

3 Walk north-west from the farmhouse to the Garland Stone. The vegetation comprises mainly bracken, lady fern, bluebells and wood sage – species more usually associated with tree cover. This suggests that parts of Skomer may have been wooded before man arrived. Large numbers of lesser black-backed gulls nest here, along with curlews and short-eared owls.

At the Garland Stone, scan the rocks below for basking grey seals. Groups of shearwaters – known as 'rafts' – can be seen out to sea, and basking sharks

The white flowers of sea campion make a fine show on Skomer's cliffs in summer

occasionally pass close to the shore during July and August.

4 Walk south-west along the coast path. At Pigstone Bay, look for grey seals and auks on the sea below. The display of sea campion is magnificent in late spring. Spring squill, allseed, chaffweed and heath pearlwort grow on the bare turf path.

5 Further along the path, a track on the left offers a possible short cut back to the farmhouse. The main walk continues south on the coast path to Skomer Head. Wheat-ears and the occasional little owl nest in old stone walls. At Skomer Head, scan the horizon for distant views of Grassholm, famous for its gannet colony. Seabirds, including a few gannets, often pass by the headland.

Thrift puts on an amazing display here in May and June.

6 Continue along the coast path, now heading east. Shearwaters nest in rabbit burrows among the thrift, heather and bracken. Pairs of great black-backed gulls nest near rocky outcrops, and wheatears scold intruders from nearby boulders.

At The Wick, pause to view the excellent colonies of seabirds. Puffins, which nest in the loose soil, often come to within a few feet of patient, quiet observers. Kittiwakes, guillemots and fulmars are also much in evidence.

7 Turn south, beyond The Wick, for a dramatic view of the Mew Stone. Look for great black-backed gulls, cormorants, ravens and the occasional buzzard and peregrine.

8 Follow the path north-east past High Cliff and South Haven. High Cliff supports good colonies of seabirds, and more are likely to be seen at the Welsh Way. In addition to the ever-present herring gulls, scan for kittiwakes, razorbills, guillemots and puffins. The South Stream valley harbours wetland flowers and the occasional sedge warbler in spring. The view across South Haven to The Neck is magnificent.

9 Continue back to North Haven.

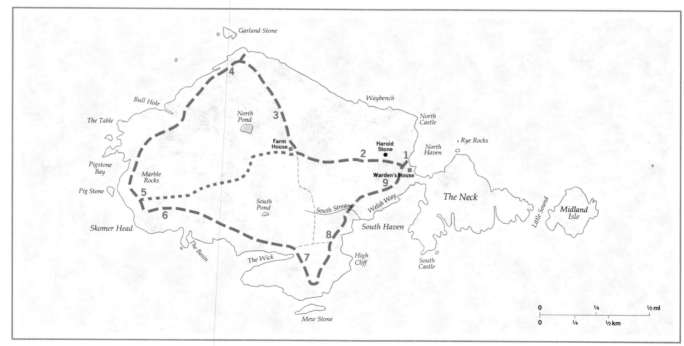

St David's Head from Whitesands Bay. Pembrokeshire has one of the loveliest and most unspoilt stretches of coastline in the whole of Britain. West-facing bays like this are especially memorable at sunset

BATTERED BY GALES IN THE IRISH SEA, THE CLIFFS AND SEASCAPE OF THIS WESTERNMOST POINT OF MAINLAND PEMBROKESHIRE ARE UNDENIABLY DRAMATIC. A MANTLE OF COLOURFUL COASTAL HEATHLAND – ONE OF THE FINEST BRITISH EXAMPLES OF THIS HABITAT – AND A WEALTH OF SEABIRDS OFF SHORE HELP TO MAKE THIS A REWARDING WALK BY ANY STANDARDS.

PREHISTORIC MAN AND ST DAVID'S HEAD

Man has a long history of association with this part of the Pembrokeshire coast: Stone Age people had settlements here and left widespread evidence of their activities. Arthur's Quoit, on the headland itself, is the remains of a burial chamber built some 5500 years ago, the great capstone still supported by one of its pillars. The outer defences of an Iron Age fortress are still visible near the tip of the headland. Careful observation will reveal many more relics and other evidence of man's influence on the landscape.

COASTAL HEATHLAND

Coastal heathland is one of the most attractive habitats in Britain but, sadly, also one of the most vulnerable. Many areas have disappeared through changes in land use; others have

A shag at its nest. Unlike the larger but similar cormorant, the shag's breeding plumage includes a crest. Shags outnumber cormorants in Britain, but seldom stray far from the sea

---

St David's Head

Dyfed
Grid ref. SM 733 271

National Trust
Approx. 3½ miles (5.6 km). One steep part, but not treacherous. Wear strong shoes.

The headland is about 2 miles (3.2 km) north-west of St David's. The car park (charge) lies at the end of a minor road signposted to Whitesands Bay.

Not only a beauty spot, St David's Head is also a superb area for the naturalist. The coastal flora is outstanding, seabirds stream past the headland during the summer and autumn, and land birds stop off on migration. General birdwatching is best in spring and autumn, while the flora of the maritime heath is at its most colourful in July and August.

Nearby sites: *Ramsey Island* – interesting geology and good colonies of choughs and grey seals (boats in summer from St Justinian); *Strumble Head* – excellent spot for sea-watching (migrating seabirds), best in autumn when a north-westerly gale is blowing.

---

simply been degraded. Even today, the remaining examples are not entirely secure even when managed by such a responsible body as the National Trust. These heaths are often in dramatic settings, as is the case with St David's Head, and they can attract large numbers of visitors. Accidental and deliberate fires are always a threat, as is erosion by trampling. However, if visitors keep strictly to well-worn and designated paths the adverse effects of this can be kept to a minimum.

July and August are the best months to visit for the flowers: deep purple clumps of bell heather contrast with paler sprays of ling and the bright yellow flowers of gorse. It is not only humans that find this display attractive: insects in abundance feed on the nectar, and bumble bees and butterflies are particularly in evidence. Birds likely to be seen among the heather and gorse include wheatears, stonechats and whitethroats.

WILDLIFE OF THE COAST AND OPEN SEA

The seas around the Pembrokeshire coast, including St David's Head, are rich in marine life. Although many of the creatures live in the open sea or in deep water, an abundance of life can be seen in rock pools. Crabs, starfish, anemones, winkles and many others flourish in the unpolluted waters.

This abundance of marine life supports a wide variety of seabirds. Many species are entirely dependent upon fish as a source of food, and the fish stocks in turn rely on a healthy marine environment. Gannets, Manx shearwaters, puffins, razorbills and cormorants can all be seen feeding off shore round St David's Head. Most of the gull species around the headland feed mainly by scavenging, although the kittiwake – our most maritime species and the only one that can really be called a 'sea gull' – fishes out at sea.

Seabirds are not the only creatures attracted to this coast by the good fishing grounds. Flat rocks and inaccessible little beaches make ideal basking places and, in some cases even breeding places, for grey seals.

THE *Walk*

1 From the car park, cross the stile and follow the path signposted 'Coastal Path' which heads north towards the headland. There is a second stile and then the path eventually crosses another stile, after which you should ignore the right fork. If the tide is out, scan the beach at Whitesands Bay for waders and gulls – black-headed, great black-backed, herring and sometimes common gulls. Look for kestrels hovering over the rough fields beside the track. The stone walls are covered with flowers which include sea beet, mallow and red campion. More exposed walls and banks harbour wind-pruned gorse, sea campion, thrift and sea carrot. Small flocks of linnets often sit on the wires and fence-posts, while rock pipits frequent the cliffs below.

2 The path descends as it passes round Porthmelgan. Cross a stream and continue to walk along the path towards St David's Head. If the tide is out, it is worth exploring the beach at Porthmelgan. The coastal heathland is superb in this area. Ling, bell heather and dwarf gorse put on an amazing show in the summer – a mosaic of purples and yellows. Western gorse can also be seen, low-growing and pruned by the wind, and patches of sea carrot, yarrow, rest-harrow and toadflax add to the variety. Look for wrens, dunnocks, white-throats, stonechats and wheatears among the gorse.

3 Reach St David's Head. Pause here and examine the rocks for lichens which are varied in both form and colour. Seabirds pass close to the cliffs, especially during periods of strong westerly or north-westerly winds. Look for Manx shearwaters, which breed on nearby Skomer and Skokholm, as well as gannets, kittiwakes, fulmars and auks. Migrant land birds, such as buntings, pipits and wheatears, also rest and feed here, especially in the autumn.

Continue along the coast path, now heading north-east. The paths diverge in many places: follow the main track nearest the cliff. From here on along the coastal stretch of the walk, the maritime heathland is outstanding. In addition to the dominant species – dwarf gorse, bell heather and ling – look for harebell, sawwort, thrift and tormentil. Pause at regular intervals to scan the sea and cliffs for seabirds. There is a chance of seeing buzzards, peregrines, choughs and ravens along

this part of the walk. Meadow pipits, stonechats and wheatears are often perched on gorse sprays.

4 When you can see some stone walls, take a right fork in the path, which first descends but then soon climbs towards the walls. The path bends to the right and heads up the hill with a stone wall on the left. Fork left and continue on the footpath as it climbs the hill, with a stone wall still on the left. The bracken-covered slope eventually gives way to some superb areas of heathland near the top of the hill. Pause to catch your breath and admire the view. Look and listen for ravens around the rocky summit to your right, and look for wood sage and fleabane among the gorse and heathers. The really energetic may not be able to resist a short detour to the summit – but if you see nesting birds in obvious distress at your presence, leave immediately.

5 The path descends from the hill with a stone wall on the left. Bell heather, foxgloves and brambles cover the wall.

At the base of the rocky outcrop the path bends to the right. Ignore the public footpath sign to the left and

The Grey Seal

Scan the seas around St David's Head for long enough and you should see a grey seal with its head bobbing in the water; this behaviour is called 'bottling'. Nearby Ramsey Island has a large colony of seals, but they also breed on some of the inaccessible beaches and coves around St David's Head, where their vulnerable young can be left without fear of disturbance. A bull grey seal may measure 9ft (almost 3m) in length, the females being smaller. Ungainly on land, seals are superb swimmers and divers.

continue contouring around the hillside. Turn left on to a track and follow the public footpath between the farm buildings and back to the road. In spring and summer the lanes are full of flowers such as herb Robert and navelwort or wall pennywort, which thrives in stone walls and rock crevices in western Britain, appreciating the damper climate.

6 Turn right and follow the road back to the car park.

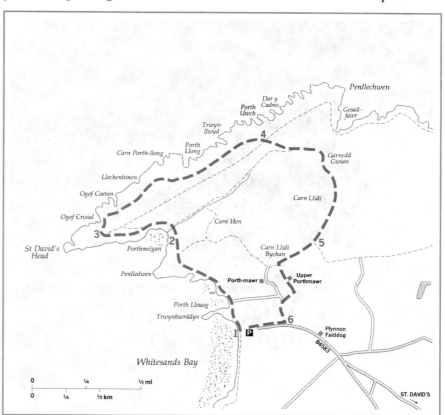

BOSHERSTON PONDS ARE PERHAPS MOST FAMOUS FOR THEIR WATER-LILIES, WHICH PUT ON A MARVEL-LOUS SHOW DURING JULY AND AUGUST. HOWEVER, BOSHERSTON ALSO HAS A RICH AND VARIED AQUATIC LIFE: FISH ARE NUMEROUS AND DRAGONFLIES AND DAMSEL-FLIES ABUNDANT IN SUMMER. BIRDWATCHING IS GOOD, AND UNUSUAL SPECIES ARE REGULARLY ENCOUNTERED.

THE MAKING OF BOSHERSTON PONDS

Despite their natural appearance, Bosherston Ponds are man-made. Between 1790 and 1840 work was carried out by the Cawdor family to block arms of the valley system, causing the stream to drown the valley bottom and creating a series of fish ponds. The first pond to be finished was the eastern arm – in 1795. Today, the 2000-acre (800-hectare) Stackpole Estate, which includes Bosherston Ponds, is owned by the National Trust. A quarter of this land is managed, in conjunction with the Nature Conservancy Council, to maintain its wildlife appeal.

AQUATIC PLANTS

Bosherston's water-lilies are undeni-ably attractive but there are many other species of water plant to see in the summer. Of these, the rarest – an alga called stonewort – is probably the least showy, growing submerged in long, trailing mats. By contrast, yellow

Bosherston's abundant water-lilies are only one of many attractions here. Woodland and scrub on the shores harbour songbirds, while other birds winter on the open water, or breed in the reed-beds

Bosherston Ponds

Dyfed
Grid ref. SM 976 938

National Trust/Nature Conservancy Council
Approx. 2½ miles (4 km). Easy walking on level ground.

Bosherston Ponds lie 4 miles (6.4 km) south of Pembroke. The walk starts from the National Trust car park at Broad Haven, 1 mile (1.6 km) south-east of Bosherston village.

Bosherston Ponds are set in attrac-tive, rolling countryside close to the sea. The walk is at its most colourful in July and August, when the water-lilies are at their best, but there is something to see throughout the year.

Nearby sites: *Stackpole Head* – breeding seabirds; *Elegug Stacks* – breeding seabirds (this is a military site and is closed when firing is taking place).

Comfrey – common in damp places

iris, fleabane, water mint and branched bur-reed are more conspicuous and attractive, while the common reeds of the reed-beds are important in stabi-lising the margins and providing a sanctuary for birds and insects.

FRESHWATER LIFE

The waters of Bosherston Ponds teem with life and this abundance is especially noticeable in the summer months. Fish are abundant, including tench, roach, perch and pike, and spawning shoals can sometimes be seen rolling and thrashing among the water-lilies. Among the invertebrates, the dragonflies and damselflies are perhaps the most conspicuous. The young of these active insects spend their lives in water before emerging in spring to fly over the pond surface, catching insects. The emperor dragonfly – our largest species, which has a bright blue abdomen – is the most dramatic of Bosherston's insects.

BOSHERSTON'S BIRDLIFE

Not surprisingly, the abundance of aquatic plants and animals in Bosherston's waters supports a wide variety of birds. Mute swans and coots graze the vegetation, while herons and kingfishers catch fish of different sizes. The ponds' position close to the coast means that migrants often pass through: waders are found around the margins and terns over the water's surface. Winter also has its highlights: in addition to widespread species such as tufted duck and pochard, more unusual wildfowl have turned up and there is even the chance of a vagrant such as a ring-necked duck from North America.

The Otter in Britain

Otters have suffered a dramatic reduction in numbers in Britain over the last few decades owing to persecution and loss of habitat. These threats are now recognised and combated where possible, and key sites are identified as sanctuaries or 'havens'. Although the Western Isles of Scotland and the Shetland Isles perhaps provide the best opportunities for seeing wild otters – there they live mainly on the seashore – a few of the estuaries and river systems of Pembrokeshire, and especially the Bosherston area, are also of national importance. Peace and quiet are essential when otter-watching, so try to visit early in the morning and move around with a degree of stealth.

THE *Walk*

1 From the Broad Haven car park, **walk down the path and steps to the beach.** The slopes are covered with old man's beard, bramble and bracken, and are the haunt of stonechats and of common blue and grayling butterflies. Pause on the beach to scan off shore for passing seabirds. Large numbers of Manx shearwaters pass by during the summer months, their numbers building up as dusk approaches.

Walk along the beach. Keep clear of the marram grass which is colonising the shifting sand, since foot erosion thwarts this plant's efforts to stabilise the sand.

2 When you reach the rocks at the far end of the beach, **turn left and follow the path which runs round the eastern side of the lake.** The rock faces and crevices are covered in rock samphire and sea plantain, together with the occasional clump of viper's bugloss. Goldfinches and linnets haunt the scrub. Black-headed gulls are usually present on the water and, if the levels are low, with muddy margins exposed, waders such as common sandpipers can be found in autumn. The reed-fringed margins host reed warblers, while cormorants can be seen on the open water. Look

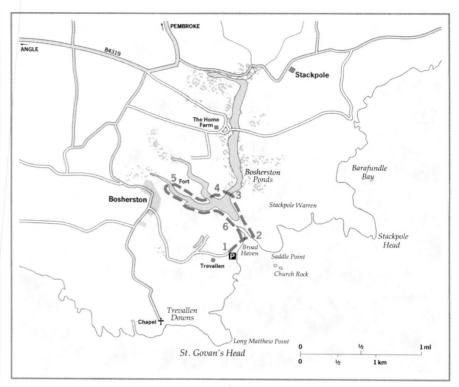

Birdwatchers must be very patient to get a good close-up view of a kingfisher. This small, shy bird is more often seen as a flash of unmistakable electric blue as it dashes past, usually low over the water

for water mint and greater water dock near the water's edge, and wall brown butterflies along the path.

3 Cross the bridge across the eastern arm of Bosherston Ponds. **Ignore the path to the right signposted 'Eastern Arm' and follow the track round to the left.** Pause on the bridge to scan the water for mute swans and other water birds. Grey herons can sometimes be seen sitting motionless on dead branches around the margin. As you continue along the path you pass through an area of scrub – dogwood, elder, old man's beard and hawthorn – which is good for warblers in autumn.

4 Fork left down to the water's edge and cross the causeway **bridge.** Black-headed gulls use the railings as a perch and the occasional kingfisher can also be seen here. On the right-hand side of the bridge, the water-lilies are particularly prolific. Look for mating pairs of damselflies among the emergent vegetation. On calm days in August, hundreds of pairs can be seen from this bridge. Mating shoals of fish also cause the calm surface of the water to ripple at this time of year.

Having crossed the bridge, continue up some steps. Here there is a vantage point from where you can

scan the lake with binoculars: swallows and martins hawk for insects over the water in late summer. Patches of bell heather and gorse can be seen here.

Continue along the northern shore of the lake. Look out for betony, gatekeeper and meadow brown butterflies, and thrushes' 'anvils' – stones surrounded by broken snail shells.

5 Cross the bridge and continue to follow the path round the **south-west side of Bosherston Ponds, following the signpost to Broad Haven.** The abundant water-lilies on the right of the bridge make an impressive show when in flower. Sycamores and ash trees along the lake edge are good for migrant warblers in the autumn. The ground layer is especially good for ferns here, with the undissected fronds of hart's tongue fern being most in evidence. Also look for maidenhair spleenwort and ivy-leaved toadflax.

6 Continue along the south-western shore of the lake, **passing over two lifting stiles, until you reach Broad Haven beach.** The grassland to the right harbours interesting plants such as centaury and sea spurge.

Return along the beach to the car park.

Early purple orchids particularly favour woodlands on limestone or chalk. Here they are growing with lesser celandines and dog's mercury, common plants of spring woodland

BISHOPSTON VALLEY IS A CLASSIC EXAMPLE OF A LIMESTONE VALLEY WITH A DISAPPEARING STREAM, RE-GENERATING WOODLAND FILLED WITH SPRING FLOWERS AND, AT ITS MOUTH, ONE OF GOWER'S QUIETEST AND MOST BEAUTIFUL BAYS, PWLLDU. A WALK DOWN THIS SECLUDED AND LOVELY VALLEY OFFERS FASCINATING INSIGHTS INTO GEOLOGY, LAND-FORMS AND ECOLOGY AND IS A RELAXING STROLL IN UNSPOILT COUNTRYSIDE.

RIVER AND WOODLAND

Bishopston Valley was formed by the action of the river on porous limestone rock along a dramatic fault line. For most of the year, the river runs underground for ³/₄ mile (1.2 km) before emerging as a crystal-clear, trout-filled stream. The unspoilt appearance of the valley belies its previous land uses, which have included the mining of silver and lead and extensive limestone quarrying, with a former village having once existed at Pwlldu Bay.

Since those times the natural vegetation of the lime-rich woods has re-established itself, so that the valley sides have open-canopied woodland of ash, elm and oak. On the western side of the valley, the National Trust has recently begun to coppice the hazel trees. This allows more light to reach the woodland floor, and the number of woodland wild flowers has increased dramatically. Among the most noticeable plants in spring are primrose, wild garlic, wood anemone and early purple orchid. Both the pearl-bordered and small pearl-bordered fritillary butterflies can be seen in the violet-filled glades. Early June is a good time to visit, for the adults of both these rapidly declining species will then be on the wing. This

---

Bishopston Valley

West Glamorgan
Grid ref. SS 577 894

National Trust
Approx. 4¹/₂ miles (7.2 km). Steep in places.

The valley is 6 miles (9.6 km) south-west of Swansea, just south of the B4436 Swansea-Pennard road. Park near Bishopston church.

Woodland, marsh, grassland, cliffs and beach make this a varied and attractive walk. Wildlife highlights include buzzards, ravens, green woodpeckers, wood warblers and stonechats. The outstanding wood-land and grassland flora attracts a wealth of butterflies.

Nearby sites: *Oxwich National Nature Reserve* – extensive reed-beds and sand dunes with associated birds and flora; *Gower Coast and Worms Head* – good coastal flora and shell beaches, plus small colonies of breeding seabirds; *Cefn Bryn and Burry estuary* – mudflats, wildfowl and waders.

Autumn hawkbit – found all over Britain

---

is also a good time for woodland birds: several species of migrant warbler, as well as the resident songbirds and woodpeckers, find food and nesting places in the valley. It is unusual not to see or hear buzzards and ravens circling overhead, either in the valley or over the cliffs.

PWLLDU BAY

Pwlldu (meaning 'black pool') is enclosed by gorse- and grass-covered limestone cliffs and is a safe place in which to swim. The bay is rich in the seaweed *Porphyra*, from which the delicious Welsh speciality laverbread is made locally. The 'black pool' within the bay is formed by the extensive pebble beach, which slows down the river before it flows into the sea. The bay contains many rock pools with an extremely good marine life. The headland to the east of the bay contains good examples of medieval strip fields, many of which still maintain their characteristic elongated shape and are bounded by hedges and hedgebanks full of flowers and ferns, among which hart's tongue fern, with its shiny green leaves, is most noticeable. Among the coastal grass-land are colonies of common rock-rose, betony, wild chives and wild carrot, all distinctive plants of limestone grassland.

New clearings in coppiced woodland are ideal for the pearl-bordered fritillary, whose caterpillars feed on violet leaves. This lovely butterfly, once common, has become much rarer as coppicing has declined

THE *W*ALK

1 From Bishopston church walk south down the river bed, which is dry in summer (or alongside the river when it is flowing). Pass Culver Pit, an amphitheatre-shaped abandoned quarry, and continue along the dry river bed to Guzzle Hole, on the right, where the stream can be heard flowing underground. Bracken-covered slopes at the start of the walk give way to dense hazel woodland rich in ferns. The ruined buildings just to the left near Guzzle Hole are the remains of a silver and lead mine, last worked in the 1850s.

2 Continue along the stream-bed until the stream emerges from the ground about 300yds (275m) further south at two separate points. On the valley's eastern side is a small scree slope; an open grassy area adjoins the river. The valley floor and slopes are carpeted with wood anemones and primroses in spring.

3 Pass a new wooden bridge and continue through two elongated meadows bisected by another bridge. Damp-loving plants including marsh marigolds and lady's smock grow among the grasses here. The National Trust has recently replanted the western side of the

valley with broadleaved trees which will eventually replace the existing grassland and gorse. This is a good area to watch circling buzzards.

4 Continue to follow the river on the right side, ignoring the track to the right leading to Widegate and Pennard church. Walk carefully on a steep path above the stream and pass another track to the right leading to Southgate. The woodland on this stretch is more open, with recently felled elm trees, killed by Dutch elm disease. Alongside the carefully re-routed path there is considerable regeneration of young trees, including elms. This is a good area for songbirds including chiffchaffs, wood and willow warblers.

5 Continue to follow the river down towards the bay, crossing a recent bridge over the stream. On the right the valley slopes sharply to the path and the river, with carpets of wild garlic, wood anemones and bluebells. On the east bank the character of the valley changes, with flat, marshy ground and extensive areas of willow, blackthorn and alder buckthorn scrub. Speckled wood and brimstone butterflies are common in this area. Green woodpeckers can

often be heard calling ('yaffling') from the gorse-covered valley slopes, and at one point the path overlooks an area of open marsh and a small reed-bed where sedge warblers and reed buntings nest. A small colony of the distinctive wood spurge, with its bright green flowers, grows close to the old stone and wrought iron bridge, before the stream comes into the open bay.

6 The path emerges into the bay, passing two houses before leading across the storm beach to the sandy and rocky beach of Pwlldu. The houses are all that remain of what was once a small village. The steep limestone cliffs on your right bear evidence of former quarrying – an industry which once employed over 100 people here. The stone was shipped across the Bristol Channel to Devon.

7 Cross the beach and take the cliff path or retrace your steps to the old bridge and walk up the less steep but stony track. The cliffs in spring smell of desiccated coconut – the tell-tale scent of gorse in full bloom. Stonechats and yellow-hammers are common on the coastal cliffs, as are adders, so tread carefully if you deviate from the path. The going is quite steep and you may have to rest, not forgetting to look back to the beautiful, secluded bay. Looking in the opposite direction, by contrast, brings one sharply back into the 20th century with distant views of industrial Port Talbot and Swansea.

8 At a small turning area for cars amid flat coastal grass-land, turn left up a narrow lane with high hedges on either side. Continue northwards for approximately ¾ mile (1.2 km) past fields and then houses on either side of the road. Where the lane turns sharply right, turn left down a narrow lane by a small thatched cottage. The hedgebanks contain many of the plants found in the valley, including wild strawberry and the pink herb Robert.

9 Bear right through a gate and past two cottages, across a stile and through a small field containing an old ruin known as the monk's cell. Cross the stone stile and follow the sloping track down the valley side to the new bridge which you passed at point 3 above. Cross the bridge, turn right and retrace your steps up the valley and back to Bishopston church.

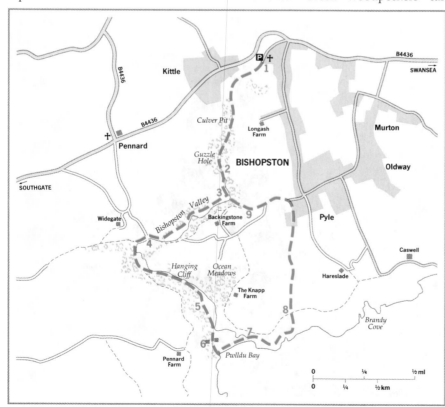

DESPITE ITS INDUSTRIAL BACKDROP – PORT TALBOT AND THE MARGAM STEELWORKS – KENFIG IS A WONDERFUL PLACE FOR THE NATURALIST. FROM THE SHIFTING SANDS AND MARRAM GRASS NEAR THE SEA TO THE STABILISED, FLOWER-RICH DUNES AND DUNE SLACKS INLAND, THERE IS A WEALTH OF INTERESTING WILDLIFE.

MAN AND KENFIG

Man has probably lived in the Kenfig area for over 4000 years. Flint arrowheads and scrapers found here may indicate that Stone Age and Bronze Age hunter-gatherers passed through, and settlements and burial mounds lie close by. After the Romans, a succession of settlers and inhabitants can be traced right up to the present day; there are detailed accounts in the information centre.

Today, the area is common land, held in trust by the Kenfig Corporation Property Trustees, although it took a controversial court case in 1971 to decide this. Mid Glamorgan County Council now leases and manages part of this land as a Local Nature Reserve, with the advice and assistance of both the Nature Conservancy Council and the Trustees. Kenfig is also designated a National Nature Reserve which, it is hoped, will further safeguard its future.

SAND DUNE FLORA

The whole of the Kenfig reserve lies on wind-blown sand, the more recently created dunes lying close to the sea with stabilised systems developing inland. Marram grass is the prime mover in this process of stabilisation and its efforts and effect can easily be seen as you trace your way back from the beach to the information centre. Plants such as sea holly, sea spurge and sea sandwort also tolerate this shifting, well-drained environment, but it is not until the dunes have become fully stabilised that the more colourful plants appear.

DUNE SLACKS

Possibly the most interesting and varied areas of the dune system are the 'slacks' – hollows between the dunes which are not only sheltered but also wet if their level is low enough. Here you will find the true delights of the dunes: drier areas support kidney vetch, burnet rose, thyme and viper's bugloss, while in damp hollows a carpet of creeping willow can be found. Among the willow grow other interesting plants: round-leaved

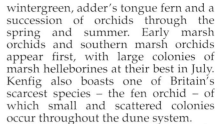

Kenfig Dunes
Mid Glamorgan
Grid ref. SS 802 813

Kenfig Corporation Property Trustees/Mid Glamorgan County Council
Approx. 3 miles (5 km). Easy walking on level ground. Parts of the walk can be wet underfoot after rainy weather.

Kenfig lies about 7 miles (11 km) south-east of Port Talbot. The walk starts from a car park just west of Kenfig, adjacent to the information centre.

Kenfig comprises a superb and extensive area of sand dunes which show all the stages of colonisation by plants. The flora is outstanding from May to September, and birdwatchers will always find something of interest on the pool.

Nearby sites: *Merthyr Mawr* – sand dunes and dune slacks with associated wildlife; *Ogmore River* – salt-marsh and mudflats, good for waders and wildfowl.

Teal – often seen on Kenfig Pool in winter

wintergreen, adder's tongue fern and a succession of orchids through the spring and summer. Early marsh orchids and southern marsh orchids appear first, with large colonies of marsh helleborines at their best in July. Kenfig also boasts one of Britain's scarcest species – the fen orchid – of which small and scattered colonies occur throughout the dune system.

All the plants of the dunes are easily damaged by foot erosion, so always keep to the obvious paths and tracks.

KENFIG POOL

Close to the information centre lies Kenfig Pool, a reed-fringed pool surrounded by marsh vegetation. This is the haunt of breeding visitors such as sedge and grasshopper warblers and reed buntings, and great crested grebes, tufted ducks, pochards and coots are usually present. In the winter months, the pool regularly attracts interesting species such as goldeneye, whooper swan and Bewick's swan, while more unusual visitors have included great northern diver and pied-billed grebe. Migration time is also good: waders such as wood sandpipers, greenshanks and whimbrels are regular, and secretive aquatic warblers turn up in some years in the reed-beds. A birdwatching hide makes observation easier, especially on windy days.

It is perhaps surprising that the free-draining, unstable ground of sand dunes can support much plant life at all, but parts of Kenfig Dunes are a carpet of colourful little flowers in summer. Thyme, eyebright, rest-harrow and others thrive happily in drier areas, and are among several hundred plant species recorded on this remarkable reserve

THE *WALK*

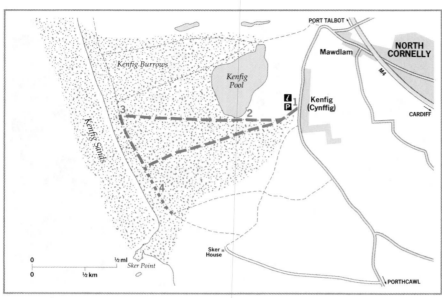

1 From the car park, follow the path that heads down the slope towards Kenfig Pool, passing close to the southern shore. Initially, the vegetation on the slope is grassy with dense patches of bramble, fleabane and horsetails. Here and there, areas of rest-harrow, lady's bedstraw and yellow rattle can be seen, the dry seed-heads of the rattle living up to their name in the autumn. Flocks of starlings and linnets roam this area in late summer.

At the edge of Kenfig Pool, pause to scan the water with binoculars. Coots, tufted ducks and pochards are almost always present. Migrant terns and waders pass through in spring and autumn, and a wide variety of wildfowl turn up in the winter months. A birdwatching hide at the far end of the pool provides good views of the water birds. During the summer months, dragonflies and damselflies are often abundant; mating pairs of ruddy sympetrums are a frequent sight in late summer. The reed-fringed margins harbour warblers and buntings and the willows, which form a dense scrub, are food to puss-moth larvae. During the early summer, damp flushes around the pool are full of yellow irises, great hairy willowherb, ragged robin, water mint, gipsywort and yellow loosestrife. Marsh orchids are present earlier in the year.

2 The path continues westwards through the dunes. It often diverges, but try to keep to the main path. If you stray on to one of the other tracks, continue heading in a westerly direction towards the sea.

Pause at frequent intervals to admire the flora. Harebell, thyme and ragwort – food to the orange, stripey caterpillars of the cinnabar moth – are common, and in the wet slacks look for round-leaved wintergreen, marsh pennywort, adder's tongue fern, marsh orchids and sheets of marsh helleborines. Other plants to look for include eyebright, autumn gentian, quaking-grass and sharp sea-rush. Common blue and dark green fritillary butterflies are often seen, and common field grasshoppers 'sing' from exposed patches of sand.

3 When you reach the gravel track near the beach, turn left and walk towards Sker Point. Sea holly, sea spurge, sea purslane and sea rocket grow in the bare sand. If the tide is out, scan the beach at frequent intervals for gulls and waders. Great black-backed, herring and common gulls are usually present and there is always the chance of something more unusual. Oystercatchers, curlews and other waders also frequent this area. It is worth scanning the sea, especially in autumn if the wind is blowing on shore. Gannets and Manx shearwaters pass surprisingly close, and sooty shearwaters are seen fairly regularly if conditions are right.

4 From the rocky shore at Sker Point retrace your steps along the gravel track and turn right, following the path in the direction of the information centre. Do not worry unduly if you miss the main path – several others wind through the dunes and all lead back to the car park eventually. Pause at frequent intervals to look at the flowers.

Smaller inhabitants of Kenfig Pool include the ruddy sympetrum, a handsome darter dragonfly seldom found elsewhere in Wales

WITH TREE-CLAD SLOPES, WATER-FALLS AND ATTRACTIVE RIVERS, THESE BEAUTIFUL WOODED VALLEYS STAND IN MARKED CONTRAST TO THE BARE UPLANDS OF OTHER PARTS OF THE BRECON BEACONS NATIONAL PARK. ALTHOUGH GOOD AT ANY TIME OF YEAR, YSTRADFELLTE OFFERS THE BEST BIRDWATCHING IN SPRING, BUT IS PERHAPS MOST BEAUTIFUL IN AUTUMN WHEN THE LEAF COLOURS ARE TRULY MEMORABLE.

Slopes clothed mainly with sessile oak rise to either side of the Afon Mellte

THE RIVERS

By walking along the banks of the Afon Mellte and Afon Hepste, visitors can see a wide range of geological features caused by water erosion on the underlying rocks. Some, such as the well-known cavern of Porth yr Ogof and the potholes near the car park, were formed where acid water flowing off the uplands gradually dissolved limestone. Others, such as the four waterfalls encountered along the route, were formed where rivers have eroded hard sandstone and softer shales at different rates. All the water-falls are impressive, but the fourth on the walk – Sgwd yr Eira – has formed in such a way that visitors following the footpath can actually walk behind the curtain of water.

THE HANGING OAK WOODLANDS

At one time, the Welsh valleys would have been covered in woodland, largely of sessile oak. Over the centuries, the forests gradually dwindled through felling for timber and changes in land use, with the result that only fragments remain today. The walk from Ystradfellte passes through one of the most extensive remaining areas of so-called hanging oak woodland, which

Ystradfellte
Powys
Grid ref. SN 928 124

Approx. 4¹/₂ miles (7.2 km). The walking is steep, rough and stony in places and can be muddy and very slippery underfoot in wet weather. Stout shoes are essential.

Ystradfellte is about 8 miles (13 km) north-west of Aberdare. From the A4059, take the unclassified road signed Ystradfellte. In 1¹/₂ miles (2.4 km) bear left, then in ¹/₂ mile (800m) bear left again. Go down the hill and turn right into Porth yr Ogof car park.

The walk is along the beautiful, wooded valleys of two rivers, with steep gorges, potholes and waterfalls – a wonderful setting for the waterside and woodland birds and flowers.

Nearby sites: *Craig Cerrig Gleisiad* – arctic-alpine flowers; *Llwyn-On Reservoir* – migrant waders, wintering wildfowl and woodland birds.

harbours a wide variety of species associated with this habitat.

WOODLAND BIRDS

Walking through a hanging oak woodland on a valley slope has one great advantage to the birdwatcher: birds that are usually seen, with difficulty, high in the treetops can often be seen at eye level by looking down the slope. In spring, the numbers of resident species such as blue tit, great tit, coal tit, nuthatch and treecreeper are swollen by summer visitors to the area. Willow warblers and chiffchaffs appear in April and May along with smaller numbers of wood warblers. This last species has a most charac-teristic song which has been likened to the sound of a silver sixpence spinning on a plate. Pied flycatchers and red-starts also arrive in spring. The males of both species are among the most handsome of our summer visitors. Mature oak woodland suits hole-nesting birds like these. The holes and cracks that appear on the older trees make good nesting places, while the rich insect life typical of oaks ensures an abundant food supply.

THE AUTUMN BONANZA

The changing colour of the leaves in autumn heralds the appearance of fruits and berries. Acorns are a major source of food for mice, jays and squirrels, while the bright red berries of mountain ash provide a feast for many species of birds, including migrant thrushes which appear from late September onwards. A careful search of the woodland floor will also reveal a range of fungi. Honey fungus grows on dead and dying trees while numerous species of *Russula* (usually with brightly coloured caps and white gills and stems) and species of *Amanita* – the caps are often spotted – adorn the leaf litter.

The Dipper – a Water-loving Bird

This curious bird is frequently seen along the Afon Mellte. Dippers feed under water by walking along the river bed in search of insects, the force of the current allowing them to stay submerged. The dipper often perches on exposed stones and boulders, continually bobbing its whole body. It is dark with a white belly, and flies low over the water. Dippers generally nest in holes under bridges or over-hanging or fallen trees.

Sorrel – a common plant of open spaces, once highly prized as a vegetable.

The Redstart – a Summer Visitor

This colourful relative of the robin is a summer visitor to Britain. Its name is appropriate since it has a conspicuous red tail which is noticeable in flight and which it wags up and down while perched. The male also has a white forehead, black throat, grey mantle and red underparts, and is indeed a most striking bird. Redstarts breed in open woodland, nesting in holes in trees and will readily take to nest boxes.

A path leads behind Sgwd yr Eira's dramatic curtain of water on the Afon Hepste. Farmers driving their livestock are reputed to have used this unusual and rather hazardous river crossing at one time

autumn, the changing colours of the trees are a wonderful sight, complemented by the golden bracken in the foreground. Buzzards are often seen soaring over the valley. Look for their broad wings and listen for the cat-like mewing call.

6 **Carefully climb down the steep path which winds its way to the fourth waterfall – Sgwd yr Eira. Although the path is carefully maintained, it can be extremely muddy and treacherous, so take great care.** The path leads under the waterfall itself and a profusion of ferns and mosses grows in the damp atmosphere. Dippers and grey wagtails perch on the stones and boulders in the river.

Climb back up the steep path and either retrace your steps or take the clearly marked footpath which leads across the wooded plateau and rejoins the original path north of Sgwd Clun-gwyn. Look for woodland birds, flowers and butterflies.

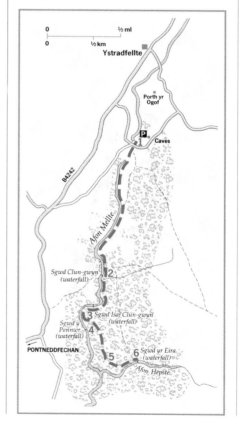

1 **From the car park, cross the lane and go through the gap in the fence, following the marked path.** Here there is a series of potholes scoured by the waters of the Afon Mellte. The river itself flows underground at this point, and can be seen and heard down the potholes. After the river emerges, its flow is fast over a wide, shallow bed. Blackfly larvae and mayfly and stonefly nymphs inhabit the waters and provide food for dippers, which perch conspicuously and fearlessly on boulders in the river. Grey wagtails are also a frequent sight. These elegant grey and yellow birds have a sharp and characteristic call, and pump their tails relentlessly up and down. Occasionally a common sandpiper can be seen feeding unobtrusively along the river's margin, while woodland birds are attracted to the ash, alder and oak trees of the wooded banks.

2 **Continue along the path to the first waterfall – Sgwd Clun-**

gwyn. Here the river drops 30ft (9m) over a sandstone ledge and the wooded margins make a superb setting for photography. Woodland birds, although present, are difficult to hear over the sound of the waterfall.

3 **Continue along the path beside the river to the next waterfall – Sgwd Isaf Clun-gwyn. Take a break to look at the view, then continue along the path through oak woodland.** Great spotted woodpeckers announce their presence with their loud alarm calls and 'drumming' in spring. Wood warblers trill from the high branches, and pied flycatchers and redstarts can sometimes be found.

4 **Pause above Sgwd y Pannwr waterfall to admire the view and then continue along the path, looking for woodland birds.**

5 The viewpoint offers a superb panorama across the valleys of the Afon Mellte and Afon Hepste. In

The Ring Ouzel

A relative of the blackbird, the ring ouzel is an upland species of thrush. The male is distinctive with its black plumage and white, crescent-shaped breast patch. The female is a sombre brown version of the male. Ring ouzels are summer visitors to Britain, arriving in March and April and departing in September. They nest among boulder scree and on rocky outcrops such as those found in this part of the Brecon Beacons. Loud, clacking calls often attract attention to their presence.

ALTHOUGH BLEAK AND FORBIDDING ON DULL, WET DAYS, THE MASSIVE PLATEAU OF THE BRECON BEACONS IS TRANSFORMED BY FINE WEATHER INTO A REGION OF INSPIRING BEAUTY. FROM THE VALLEY BOTTOMS, THE MOUNTAINS MAY LOOK MORE LIKE HILLS. DO NOT BE DECEIVED, HOWEVER, BECAUSE THEY CAN BE AS TESTING AS ANY IN BRITAIN.

THE BRECON BEACONS NATIONAL PARK

The Brecon Beacons National Park covers an area of 519 square miles (1344 sq. km), encompassing the Beacons themselves as well as many of the surrounding river valleys. Much of the main part of the range – including some of the land crossed by this walk – is owned by the National Trust. Together with the National Park Committee, the Trust safeguards the character of the region, keeping public access as a priority.

GEOLOGY AND GLACIAL FEATURES

Much of the Brecon Beacons range is composed of Old Red Sandstone. This sedimentary rock was laid down by slow-flowing rivers, then folded and raised by earth movements to form the plateau we see today. The limestone and coal-bearing measures which now border the mountains were originally formed on top of the sandstone, but erosion has stripped the plateau of all but the sandstone.

The last Ice Age, which, in geological terms, ended comparatively recently – 10,000 years ago – has left plenty of signs of its passing in the Brecon Beacons, several of which can be seen on this walk. Cwm-llwch is a glacial cirque – a natural amphitheatre carved by the erosion of ice and frozen snow, assisted by the shattering action of alternate freezing and thawing. A small glacier – long since gone – formed on its slopes and at what was once its base lies Llyn-cwm-llwch. Around the northern shores of the lake are small moraines – the remains of rock fragments carved by the glacier.

PLANT LIFE OF THE BEACONS

The sandstones which form the bedrock of the Brecon Beacons support rolling moorlands that give the region its feeling of wide, open space. The grasses that make up the moorland vegetation are mostly grazed and there is comparatively little variety in plant life. Rock ledges and outcrops of limestone are rather better, however, and may support moss campion (at its southernmost site in Britain), purple saxifrage, mossy saxifrage, globeflower and a variety of ferns. Although upland lakes and tarns are generally rather poor for flowers when compared to lowland ponds, there are still a few species to look for: shoreweed, which forms spiky rosettes of leaves on the lake bottom, lesser marshwort and lesser spearwort should all be looked for.

Equally at home on Welsh hillsides or suburban road verges, the meadow brown is one of Britain's most widespread butterflies. Its caterpillars feed on grasses

The Raven – Britain's Biggest Crow

The raven is the largest member of the crow family found in Britain. In flight it is distinctive, with its thick neck and wedge-shaped tail. The call, however, is often the feature that attracts attention: the loud 'cronk' carries a long distance. Ravens nest early in the year, generally favouring traditional sites on rock ledges. Three young are usually reared and are fed mainly on moorland carrion.

Llyn-cwm-llwch

Powys

Grid ref. SN 995 260

National Trust (part)
Approx. 6½ miles (10.5 km). Easy walking, but steep in parts. Stout, waterproof footwear is essential as well as sensible clothing.

Park in a lay-by on the west side of the A470, near the telephone box just north of Libanus, 4 miles (6.4 km) south-west of Brecon.

The walk climbs from the valley of the Afon Tarell to Llyn-cwm-llwch, an isolated glacial tarn at the foot of Cwm-llwch. The scenery is dramatic, making an imposing setting for the wildlife of the Brecon Beacons. Although the walk does not tackle the peaks, it encompasses a wide range of habitats and goes right into the heart of the Beacons.

Nearby sites: *Llandovery riverside walk* – waterside wildlife; *Talybont Reservoir* – wintering wildfowl.

One of nature's opportunists, the carrion crow adapts itself to many habitats

BIRDS OF THE VALLEYS AND UPLANDS

Although not renowned for its birdlife, the Brecon Beacons area nevertheless has a lot to offer the birdwatcher who is prepared to explore the different habitats. The rivers harbour dippers and grey wagtails, while in the winter months the reservoirs attract wildfowl including goosanders, tufted ducks and pochards. The wooded valleys are home to woodpeckers, nuthatches, treecreepers, tits and summer visitors such as redstarts and warblers. The open tops and rocky crags support yet another range of species: meadow pipits and skylarks haunt the grassland, while wheatears and ring ouzels prefer rocky boulder slopes and scree. Merlins hunt low over the moorland, while overhead, buzzards and pere-

THE *WALK*

1 Cross the A470 and go over a stile. Cross the field to another stile and turn left on to a minor road. At a T-junction, turn right and then left after a short distance. Ignore a turning to the left, and turn right and immediately left when you reach a junction. Along the narrow lanes look for ferns such as polypody, male fern and bracken as well as flowers including red campion and foxgloves growing in the hedgerow. In the spring, butterflies such as green-veined whites and small tortoiseshells visit the flowers to feed on nectar. Hedgerow shrubs include hawthorn and blackthorn, their berries providing food in the autumn for birds. Listen for the shrill squeaks of shrews in the undergrowth.

2 Go through a gate at Clwydwaunhir. Walk past the house, cross the stream on your left, using stepping stones, and go over a stile. Continue across the fields, crossing two more stiles, until you reach the buildings at Llwynbedw. Continue heading south over two further stiles, then keep the open woodland on your right. Examine the woodland on your right for woodland birds: chaffinches and several species of tit may be present throughout the year, joined by warblers in summer.

Bear to the right when you reach a river and continue through some woodland and over a footbridge. Streams in the Brecon Beacons provide a good habitat for brown trout, which generally remain small in size. The comparatively clean air in this part of the Beacons allows abundant mosses and pollution-sensitive lichens to grow on the trunks and branches of the trees.

3 When you reach Cwm-llwch, follow the signposted detour around the building. Beyond this, return to the main track, cross two stiles and continue up the hill. Cross the hill fence at the National Trust

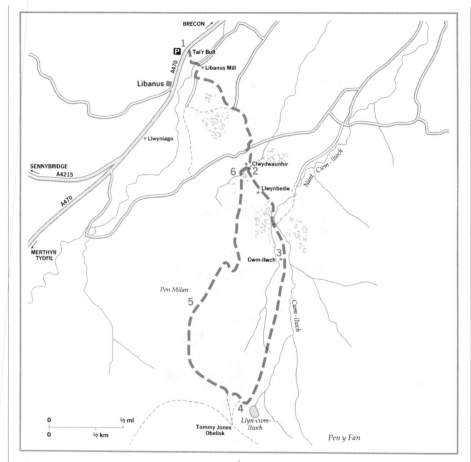

The dramatic slopes of Pen y Fan, beneath which lies the glacial tarn, Llyn-cwm-Llwch, are emphasised by a covering of snow

signpost, and pass two cairns. Ignore the left-hand fork in the track and continue heading towards Cwm-llwch. Look out for rowan or mountain ash trees. They produce bright red berries in the late summer and autumn – food for ring ouzels before they begin their migration south, and for redwings and fieldfares, which spend the winter in Britain.

4 At Llyn-cwm-llwch, pause to admire the glacial tarn set against the backdrop of Craig Cwm-llwch. The lake has a small population of palmate newts, and aquatic vegetation grows around its margins.

If time permits, a detour can be made to the Tommy Jones obelisk via a track to the left. This commemorates the death of a small boy in 1900.

Return to the original path and walk north-west around the head of the valley. The open, grassy moorland is home to meadow pipits. These rather nondescript brown birds have a thin call and a distinctive song-flight in the breeding season. They sometimes fall victim to merlins, which occasionally pass through the area.

Wheatears are summer visitors to the Brecon Beacons and scold humans intruding into their territories with loud, clacking calls. Look for buzzards soaring overhead. They have broad, rounded wings and utter a mewing call in flight. They can sometimes be seen being mobbed by ravens.

5 Just before you reach Pen Milan the path becomes broader and soon passes between two banks. The path bends sharply right then left as it descends. Continue down the hill, walking between the two banks. The vegetation in many parts of the Brecon Beacons has been reduced to acid grassland for sheep grazing, and mat-grass is a characteristic species. Listen for sky-larks singing in flight and look for fox droppings deposited in prominent places. Sensitive noses may also detect their pungent scent.

6 Go through a ford, then through a gate to the right at the bottom of the hill. Carry on to Clwydwaunhir, then retrace your steps to the start.

Cors Caron

*Britain's vast upland peat bogs took thousands of years to form. Most have been destroyed in the past few decades.
Cors Caron, seen here from Pont Einon, is one of the few remaining examples*

NOTE: **A written permit from the Nature Conservancy Council is necessary for this walk. Please write, well in advance, to the address on page 5.** Permits are rarely refused except when there is a shoot (organised by the Lisburne Estate, which still controls the shooting rights on some of the reserve), or during periods of high fire risk or flooding.

———————•———————

A SEA OF ICE-COLD MIST OFTEN COVERS THE FLOOD PLAIN OF THE AFON TEIFI NORTH OF TREGARON, LIKE A LAKE LAPPING AGAINST THE FOOTHILLS OF THE CAMBRIAN MOUNTAINS. NINE THOUSAND YEARS AGO THERE REALLY WAS A LAKE HERE, BUT IT BECAME CHOKED BY WEEDS, AND EVENTUALLY WILLOW AND BIRCH TREES TRANSFORMED THE SILTY GROUND INTO WOODLAND. INCREASED RAINFALL THEN CARRIED AWAY THE SOIL NUTRIENTS. PEAT BEGAN TO FORM AS BEDS OF SPHAGNUM MOSS CREATED THEIR OWN ACID CLIMATE.

———————•———————

A DISAPPEARING LANDSCAPE

In the right conditions, beds of sphagnum moss grow relentlessly upwards and outwards, acting like a giant sponge and trapping water. Only the outer layer is green and living; the rest is an accumulation of dead leaves and stems that have not properly decayed. To cut a section into a bog is to open a page in history; by identifying leaves and pollen grains at different levels it is possible to paint a picture of how the countryside has changed over thousands of years.

Not surprisingly, bogs are very special places to ecologists. However, anyone who has walked the Pennine moors will have a firm prejudice against bogs and may well imagine that the entire uplands are being swallowed up in recent decades. The truth is that most of the great expanses of blanket bog on the hill ranges of the north and west have themselves been swallowed up by farming and forestry, and that many of the smaller types of acidic mires, valley bogs and raised bogs which rely for any nutrients on rainwater have been drained or destroyed by peat-digging.

CORS CARON – THE 'RED BOG'

Cors Caron represents one of the best raised bog systems left in Britain. The National Nature Reserve covers an area of nearly 2000 acres (over 800 hectares) which includes a meandering stretch of the Teifi and its associated flood pools or flashes as well as a

---

Cors Caron

Dyfed

Grid ref. SN 696 631

Nature Conservancy Council (*permit required* – see page 5 for address) Approx. 5½ miles (8.8 km). Level walking, but stout footwear is essential and warm, waterproof clothing should be worn or carried because the weather here can change very quickly. Care is necessary on the banks of the river, which is deep and dangerous and subject to flooding. Do not deviate from the indicated route.

Cors Caron, or Tregaron Bog, lies in the valley of the Afon Teifi north of Tregaron. Park at the National Nature Reserve entrance, a walled lay-by area just north of Maesllyn on the B4343. A day permit (no charge) must be obtained before visiting the main part of the National Nature Reserve. The old railway line, however, is always open and is the best place to look for birds (kites, buzzards and other birds of prey are the speciality).

The walk around the reserve follows a prepared route, allowing visitors to look closely at one of the most fragile of habitats – a raised bog – without damaging it. Bogs can be beautiful, and the surface of the sphagnum is a tapestry of tiny flowers.

Nearby sites: *Devil's Bridge* – area of sessile oak woodland excellent for flowers and birds; *Llyn Fanod* – water plants and aquatic insects.

Trailing St John's wort

stretch of old railway line. There are three quite separate bogs within the reserve, each a lozenge of sphagnum resting on the old fen peats of the extinct lake and the boulder clay that lined its basin.

From a distance it is impossible to gain any proper impression of them. Indeed, bogs are the least prepossessing of wildlife habitats and, of course, very difficult to approach. The old railway line, raised above the flood plain, provides an excellent walkway for a view across Cors Caron. This is ideal in the winter when the chief interest lies in the wildfowl on the

---

flashes or the birds of prey – hen harriers and red kites – which can be seen soaring over the valley. In summer the picture is different.

A WORLD IN MINIATURE

Real appreciation of a bog means getting down on your hands and knees and studying it from a few inches away. Each hummock of sphagnum is a work of art, a tracery of beautiful little plants which might here include bog rosemary, cranberry or any of the three British sundews. Unfortunately, studying a bog on your hands and knees is likely to be an uncomfortable or even a dangerous business. Sinking into it also rips open the surface of the sphagnum carpet and establishes flows of water which break up the peat. It only takes a few people crossing a bog to cause irreparable damage. The answer is either to exclude visitors or to protect the bogs with duckboarding.

The Nature Conservancy Council has established a public path along the railway line, but is strict about any other access. The West Bog, the biggest and most impressive of the raised bogs, is out of bounds, but it is possible to obtain a permit and follow a route to skirt the North-East Bog, then turn south along the Teifi and so pass the West Bog and follow a duckboarded path into the heart of the South-East Bog. The walk described here is along this special route for permit holders.

FLORA AND FAUNA ALONG THE TEIFI

The Teifi has several backwaters and flashes, which may be full or empty according to the season. Wildfowl, wading birds and water rails make use of this marshland. The river also attracts occasional kingfishers and otters. Birds of prey hunt across the whole area. Buzzards and red kites (*bwncath* and *barcud*, in Welsh) nest in sessile oakwoods among the nearby hills and, while the buzzard is certainly the more common, there is always a good chance of a kite.

Willow and birch thickets and patches of rushes, meadowsweet and other marsh plants line the edge of the old railway, providing essential cover for wildlife. Some animals are hardly ever seen except among the shadows. Foxes, stoats and polecats will be lying up a few feet from the path, coming out at dawn and dusk when the watchers have gone. To see a polecat you need good fortune rather than skill or patience. Besides, few naturalists would sit in the cold, clammy twilight at Cors Caron.

THE WALK

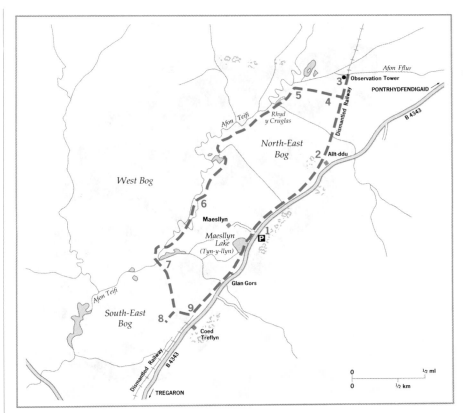

Valerian and foxgloves grow from the car park walls, and the hedgerow by the roadside is an attractive mix of ash, hazel, hawthorn and dog rose. Even before you have stretched your legs there are things to see. Large birds of prey will probably be wheeling overhead. Binoculars are likely to confirm them as buzzards, but look for the pale wing patches, buoyant flight and continually flexed, forked tail that will identify a red kite.

1 Go through the gate from the car park and turn right along a wide raised track. This is the embankment of the old railway that once carried holidaymakers and freight from Manchester to Milford Haven. The line opened in 1866 and closed in 1965. Hawthorn, blackthorn and hazel bushes, now unchecked by the occasional fires that were sparked from steam trains, have colonised the banks and are usually full of warblers and finches. Chaffinches gather wherever there is a car park and a chance of sharing someone's sandwiches. The Welsh word for chaffinch is *ji-binc*, a reference to the bird's call.

Further along the track there is a view to the right across the road to an oakwood, composed of sessile oaks which replace the pedunculate oak in

areas of the north and west of Britain. Special birds of this habitat include redstart, wood warbler and pied flycatcher, hard to see in the foliage.

Cinquefoils usually have yellow flowers, but those of the marsh cinquefoil, found in damp hollows at Cors Caron, are reddish-purple

2 The path continues past Alltddu Farm on the right. The view opens out now, with expanses of marshland and groves of birch and sallow in the rush-covered fields to the left. The wet hollows at the bottom of the embankment are full of reed canary-grass, meadowsweet and other tall herbs such as marsh cinquefoil – a close relative of the common yellow cinquefoils, but with large purple flowers. Grasshopper warblers and

sedge warblers nest in the denser patches of sallow. These skulking species are more easily heard than seen.

3 Keep following the path, which eventually leads to a tower hide. This is quite high and gives a commanding view over the north end of the reserve, but in summer the pools will hold only a few mallards and teal, so it may be better to spend your time closer to ground level.

4 (Note: from this point the walk is accessible to permit holders only.) From the hide retrace your steps for 100yds (90m) and turn right, off the railway line and through a gate on to a boardwalk. This crosses the edge of the North-East Bog, with some good patches of sphagnum, bogbean and marsh horsetail. There are also drifts of cotton-grass – food-plant of the large heath butterfly, which is on the southern edge of its British range here.

5 The boardwalk leads straight out over the bog. When it ends follow the posts, then bear left across a little bridge over a stream and continue to the Afon Teifi, at which bear left. Follow the river, crossing another little bridge over a side-stream, then continue either on the river bank or parallel with it by cutting across the meanders to link red-marked bridges. The route is not always clear; if in doubt simply keep to the riverside. Take great care: the river is deep and its level can rise rapidly after rain. The Teifi is full of aquatic plants such as water crowfoot, adapted to survive the currents by having strap- or hair-shaped leaves. Dredging operations in 1961 cleared the accumulated weed and removed a lot of silt and gravel from the river bed. This was dumped on the bank, establishing a flood barrier but making walking uncomfortable.

The side-channels and ox-bows are much prettier than the main river; their verges contain reeds and sedges and there are floating carpets of pond-weed and yellow water-lily. The river water contains more nutrients than that of the bog because of the mineral-rich gravels and the run-off of agricultural chemicals. Water voles are the only mammals likely to be seen, but there are also water shrews and otters. The latter are very rarely seen, but look for footprints in the mud.

After following the meandering

The Afon Teifi winds through the heart of Cors Caron, flooding large areas in winter. The main river can be deceptively deep and fast-flowing, while the side-channels are slower and support yellow water-lilies, shown here, and a range of other aquatic plants more often seen on ponds

river south-westward across rough grazing inhabited by a few sheep and horses, you become aware of a very different kind of country taking shape beyond the Teifi, as the dome rises into the remarkable West Bog.

6 Keep on the east side of the river, without crossing the first bridge over it, or the second, which appears soon after a wire fence. However, at the third bridge cross to the west side and turn left along the bank. The raised bog is now immediately to your right. Imagine it as a great lens-shaped sponge. The

base of the slope is called the rand and is dominated by purple moor-grass with some heather and bilberry. Above this is a zone of deer-grass, then comes the main central dome. Don't be tempted off the path to investigate!

7 After only a few yards cross back over another bridge (the diversion was to avoid the confluence of a side-stream). The path now continues along a boardwalk, away from the river and in the direction of a distant oak-lined hillside and a house. At first the vegetation is reed canary-grass, then rushes.

8 The boardwalk then bears right, up the dome of the South-East Bog. Ignore two side-routes going left and continue right up to the end of the boardwalk. You are now right on the top of the bog and

can at last get down on your hands and knees, in comfort, to look at the unique bog flora.

Retrace your steps and turn right along the side-route heading towards the hillside again. Along the path-side there is an area of peat digging, the face of the peat exposed to give a mahogany brown profile.

9 The path leads to a gate, after which turn sharp left and along the old railway. At first the green track seems more like a woodland ride than the ghost of a railway, with blackthorn and hazel, ash, oak and sallow lining the route.

The open track ends at a stile, after which there is a path through a thicket. Continue along the path, still the old railway, and past Maesllyn Lake, then along a wider track again, leading back to the start.

DRAMATIC CLIFF SCENERY, AND EASY ACCESS FROM HOLYHEAD, MAKE SOUTH STACK CLIFFS A GOOD PLACE FOR WALKING – WEATHER PERMITTING – AT ANY TIME OF YEAR. THOSE WHO COME HERE FOR THE WILDLIFE, HOWEVER, COME IN MAY AND JUNE, WHEN THE CLIFFS ARE THRONGED WITH NESTING SEABIRDS AND THE RESERVE'S RICH AND VARIED FLORA IS SEEN AT ITS BEST.

AN ABUNDANCE OF BIRDLIFE

Birdwatchers are unlikely to leave South Stack disappointed. The area is good for passage birds, including the occasional rarity, in both spring and autumn. It is always worth keeping an eye out to sea for gannets and Manx shearwaters; and in the breeding season three of Britain's species of auk – puffins, guillemots and razorbills – may be more easily seen flying and fishing off shore, rather than on the inaccessible cliff ledges. Guillemots are by far the most numerous, and can easily be distinguished from razorbills by their more slender, pointed bills. Both species are more agile in the water than in the air or on land. Better views of the nesting seabirds can be obtained in the information centre, Ellin's Tower, where a remote-control camera beams close-up pictures to a television. It is not unusual to have the opportunity to watch peregrines hunting rock doves and other birds – an unforgettable experience. Choughs, members of the crow family which were once much more common, are also resident on the reserve. Their distinctive, high-pitched calls easily distinguish them from crows, ravens and jackdaws, which are also present.

The Chough

Named after its 'chough'-like call, this elegant member of the crow family is regularly seen at South Stack. Groups of four or five birds often wheel through the air, riding the updraughts off the cliffs and calling loudly. Choughs are easily recognised in flight by the long, red bill and finger-like wing tips.

Choughs feed almost exclusively on insects which are found by probing and searching among the cliff-top turf. While feeding, they can be surprisingly confiding, providing excellent views of their bills and matching red legs. Choughs are fully protected by law. They nest in inaccessible caves and cliff crevices.

South Stack Cliffs

Gwynedd
Grid ref. SH 212 818

Royal Society for the Protection of Birds
Approx. 2 miles (3.2 km). Steep in places, with steps to climb.

The reserve is at Anglesey's most westerly extremity, 3 miles (4.8 km) west of Holyhead. Follow signs from the town, and park in the first signposted car park.

Sea cliffs, maritime heathland and grassland are the reserve's principal habitats. Wildlife highlights include breeding seabirds, peregrines, choughs; spotted rock-rose; marsh fritillary and silver-studded blue butterflies; and grey seals.

Nearby sites: *Menai Strait* – excellent intertidal marine life, seabirds including divers and grebes in winter; *Cemlyn Bay* – nesting terns and waders, interesting coastal flora; *Newborough Warren* – outstanding sand-dune system with nationally rare plants; *Bardsey Island* – migrant and breeding seabirds, including more than 8000 pairs of Manx shearwaters, grey seals in coves.

Adept at swimming and diving in search of food, the razorbill looks rather clumsy on land, moving with a shuffling or waddling gait. Several hundred pairs breed at South Stack Cliffs

GRASSLAND AND HEATH

The cliffs and their birdlife make up only a part of the natural history interest of the South Stack area. The sedimentary rocks of the cliffs is overlain by both basic and acid soils, ensuring a variety of plant life that is remarkable for such an exposed coast. Swathes of sea campion and thrift are intermingled with extensive areas of heather and dwarf gorse. Rarities such as spotted rock-rose and field fleawort are easily seen in the areas of fine maritime grassland, where spring squill and English stonecrop are also found. The heathland shelters some extensive patches of heath spotted orchid. Superficially this orchid is similar to the common spotted orchid, but is almost always found growing on acid soils.

Inhabitants of the heathlands include populations of both adder and common lizard and, rather surprisingly for such a well visited site, various nesting waders. Look out also for butterflies. Silver-studded blues may be seen among the dry grassland, while marsh fritillaries prefer the damper areas.

The exquisite little flowers of English stonecrop are often seen on Britain's western coasts. The plant's fleshy leaves help it to withstand sea breezes

THE *Walk*

1 **From the car park follow the signs for the cliff path along an old stone wall.** The walk leads through salt-pruned dwarf heath, with extensive patches of the diminutive spring squill and tormentil. Other plants in flower in late spring will include sea campion, thrift and the yellow-flowering field fleawort.

2 **Take care as the path approaches the cliff, which is very sudden and precipitous.** Immediately below you is a dramatic example of a sea-cliff stack, while to the left is Pen-las Rock where rock pipits – small brown birds – perch on rock ledges. The view south takes in less dramatic coastal scenery, while to the north is South Stack lighthouse and the stunning cliffs that many visitors come to see.

3 **Retrace your steps and then take the path north towards the lighthouse and cross the small wooden bridge over the culvert. Follow the coast path to the information centre at Ellin's Tower.** The maritime grassland in this area is worth a close look. There are cushions of the diminutive sheepsbit scabious, wild carrot and kidney vetch, while on the sheer cliffs unusually large numbers of ox-eye daisies can be seen. Wall brown and silver-studded blue butterflies are common, and are particularly noticeable on either side of the newly turfed path. The buckshorn plantain, a vigorous early coloniser, is

South Stack Cliffs rise to almost 400ft (120m), ensuring wonderful views on calm, clear days

there in abundance but will soon be replaced by plants of the sea-turf proper. To the left of the path grow plants typical of lime-rich grassland while to the right, swathes of heather, tormentil and bell heather show how a layer of peat changes the vegetation.

Ellin's Tower offers well-presented and up-to-date information on the wildlife and history of the area.

4 **Leaving Ellin's Tower, walk up the slate steps to the cliff-edge.** Puffins, razorbills, guillemots, fulmars and herring gulls can all be seen here. During the summer months

this is a good area in which to watch for hunting peregrines. On the cliffs around you are swathes of spring squill, and a few patches of the rare spotted rock-rose. This flowers in June, but you will only see it in bloom if you visit before midday, when it sheds its petals.

5 **Continue up the steep steps and then take the cliff path (rather than the road).** This is the most difficult stretch of walking, but rewarding for the pale green lichen called sea ivory. Several other lichen species festoon the granite rocks on either side of the path. Also worth exploring is the good maritime grass-land, where patches of the white-flowering scurvy-grass may be found in spring. Later in the spring, the yellow flowers of cat sear and hawkbit become more noticeable.

6 **Cross the low wall and walk to the picnic tables which overlook the lighthouse of South Stack, then follow the path up the gentle slope to the old World War II look-out post.** Two characteristic plants of the cliffs grow immediately in front of the building: the green, straggly sea beet, which has waxy leaves to reduce the effect of the salt-laden winds, and the more delicate scentless mayweed which minimises its water loss by having very finely serrated leaves. Walk through the extensive areas of dwarf heather; within this are patches of heath spotted orchids, which particularly like the acid soil.

7 **Follow the path around the wet hollow or pool, but you can leave the path for a short detour to look over Gogarth Bay where grey seals often haul out.** The cliffs between here and North Stack are important for nesting seabirds in May and June.

8 **Walk back to the path and pass the radar station to reach the opposite side of the pool.** The wet area is important for butterflies such as the marsh fritillary, a small, brightly coloured, chequered orange and fawn butterfly whose caterpillars feed on the devilsbit scabious leaves found in such areas.

9 **Continue through the heath-land back to the road, and follow it back to the car park.** As you go, watch for whitethroats on the telegraph wires.

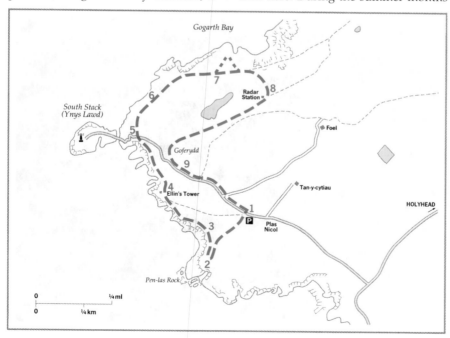

Gogarth Bay

South Stack
(Ynys Lawd)

Radar Station

Foel

Goferydd

Tan-y-cytiau

HOLYHEAD

Ellin's Tower

Plas Nicol

Pen-las Rock

0 ¼ ml
0 ¼ km

Cwm Idwal

Walkers who reach the foot of the 'Hanging Gardens' of Twll Du will be rewarded on a clear day by this unforgettable view of Llyn Idwal, with the Carneddau range rising beyond it

DRAMATIC VIEWS AND A SPIRIT OF ADVENTURE BRING HUNDREDS OF THOUSANDS OF VISITORS TO SNOWDONIA EACH YEAR, YET IN SPITE OF ITS POPULARITY IT REMAINS ONE OF THE GREATEST WILDERNESS AREAS IN BRITAIN. THE MOST INTERESTING WILDLIFE HERE IS THAT ASSOCIATED WITH HIGH MOUNTAINS, WHERE CLIFFS AND CHASMS IN OLD ROCK SYSTEMS LIE BEYOND THE REACH OF GRAZING SHEEP. IN SUCH WILD COUNTRY, CELTIC MYTHOLOGY AND THE BEAUTY OF THE WELSH LANGUAGE ADD A TOUCH OF ROMANCE EVEN ON DAYS OF MIST AND DRIZZLE.

THE BONES OF THE LANDSCAPE

Like all other mountain areas, Snowdonia is a study in earth forces: sediments were crushed and contorted and smothered by molten rock or magma, then worn away by water and ice. Classic studies in geology were carried out here during the 19th century and many students have made the trek to Cader Idris and Cwm Idwal. Even for the uninitiated, the signs of glaciation are so dramatic here that it really is worth spending a little while looking at the landscape and piecing together the clues. A walk from Ogwen provides a perfect opportunity.

Cwm Idwal is regarded as one of the finest examples of a cirque in Britain. It lies above the wide valley of Nant Ffrancon, where a great glacier once creaked and groaned its way north-west. Llyn Idwal now occupies the hollowed basin created by a smaller glacier which flowed north-eastwards into the main U-shaped valley.

THE DEVIL'S KITCHEN

From the shores of Llyn Idwal the arc of rock between the summits of Glyder Fawr and Y Garn looks impressive. At first glance it may seem to be a continuum – a single slab of volcanic bedrock engraved by ice. In fact the dip mid-way between the summits, where a lobe of the glacier once flowed, is marked by a lozenge-shaped wall of basalt. This fragment of the Snowdon syncline has a central chasm, Twll Du, sometimes nicknamed the Devil's Kitchen. It probably earned the name because a pall of cloud, like steam over a cauldron, often hangs in the air overhead. But on a sunny day the black shelves of basalt glow with a less satanic haze of bright green vegetation.

One of the first botanists to study Snowdonia's flowers was Edward Llwyd. In the late 17th century he discovered, among other things, a charming species now known as Snowdon lily; its Latin name, *Lloydia serotina*, honours his botanical achievements. Generations of Victorian botanists followed in his footsteps, and a favoured destination was the flower-rich ledges near Twll Du.

Over the last 12,000 years, the appearance of Snowdonia has changed markedly. Following the retreat of the glaciers, native forests colonised the lower slopes of much of the region. However, felling by man depleted the

---

Cwm Idwal

Gwynedd
Grid ref. SH 649 603

Nature Conservancy Council
Approx. 5 miles (8 km).
Challenging. Stout footwear, a good map, and a compass are essential. It is important to be prepared for bad weather even if the day looks warm and sunny from Llyn Ogwen. Conditions on the top of Y Garn can be very different.

The car park lies close to the Youth Hostel and National Park Warden Centre at the head of Llyn Ogwen, the lake north of the A5 (T) about 4 miles (6.4 km) south of Bethesda. The car park fills up quite quickly each day and it is a good idea to be there early.

The mountain tops of Snowdonia are best visited during mid-summer, the flowering time for most of Cwm Idwal's special flowers and a good time to see upland birds such as peregrines and ravens. The views, all the way from Llyn Idwal around the cwm and down from Y Garn, are quite exceptional, so try to choose a clear day.

Nearby sites: *The Miners' Track* – a comparatively easy route up Snowdon; *Gwydyr Forest*, near Betws-y-Coed – mature plantations, streams and lakes.

Heather or ling – widespread on acid soils

---

woodland and the subsequent action of introduced sheep and goats effectively prevented natural re-generation. Evidence for Cwm Idwal's forested past can be seen in the ancient roots and stumps found in the peat.

For the mountain flowers of Cwm Idwal's ledges and crevices, matters were rather different. The sheer rocky crags would never have been wooded and base-rich rocks encouraged a rich growth of arctic-alpine species. This created cascades of plant growth on these crags, which led to their becoming known to Victorian botanists as the 'Hanging Gardens'.

The precarious nature of their environment has been the key to the survival of many of Cwm Idwal's botanical treasures: they are all but inaccessible to grazing animals. Some have become rare while others remain quite common: Snowdon lily still persists, along with tufted saxifrage and arctic saxifrage. However, visitors would be extremely lucky to see these species. More usual are starry saxifrage, mossy saxifrage and moss campion. The presence of wood sorrel and wood anemone on the lower slopes is a further reminder of their once-forested nature.

FLOWERS AND BIRDS OF THE SUMMITS

A mountain summit provides one of the greatest challenges to plant life. Birds can move with the weather, but plants have to withstand snow and frost for much of the year, then cope with drought and scorching winds during the brief flowering season. For this reason most true alpine plants are compact and tussocky – robust yet delicate, and often small enough to be overlooked. Cwm Idwal's flowers are superbly adapted to this harsh upland climate and have also managed to survive the scrutiny and depredations of three centuries of naturalists.

Although Snowdonia lacks several high mountain bird species found else-where in Britain, there are still a few specialities. Peregrines and ravens are widespread and sometimes seen by keen-eyed observers. Other common upland species include ring ouzel, dipper and wheatear. Choughs are regular, and merlins visit the area occasionally in search of meadow pipits and other small birds.

Above all, Cwm Idwal is a place to appreciate the beauty and drama of mountains – a place where wildlife somehow survives in a hostile environment. For visitors, the going can sometimes be tough, but for most people, reaching the summit or seeing Cwm Idwal's rich variety of alpine flowers is reward enough.

THE *W*ALK

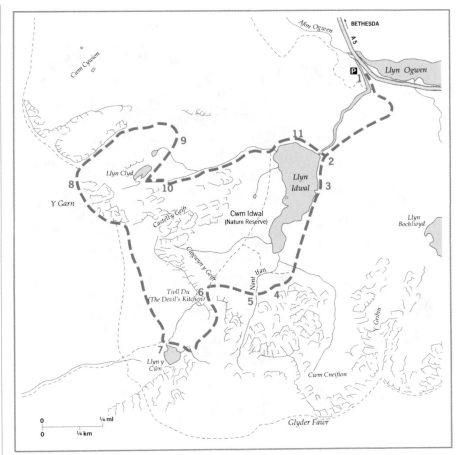

and climbs via some steps and past a right turn (the nature trail route around the lake). Keep to the main path. The view now is dominated by the curtain of rock forming the Idwal cirque; the route ahead can be seen angling westward to the base of the basalt wall below the Devil's Kitchen. This is a good place to appreciate the geological formation of the Snowdon syncline, to see the differences in the exposed faces of downfolded rhyolite – compressed volcanic ash – and the wall of pumice and basalt at the core of the syncline. Bands of slate make up some of the most dramatic rock faces. One of these, just to the left of the path as it begins to arc right to the headwall of the cirque, the Idwal Slabs, is popular with climbers.

4 Once past the foot of the climbing pitch, the path is clear up to the base of Twll Du. There is an excellent view to the right now of rocks and rowan bushes and the lake far below. Ravens and peregrines are sometimes seen using the updraught of air above the Devil's Kitchen; they compete for nest sites and have a mutual distrust which often results in spectacular battles. Ravens breed early and usually have well-grown young in the nest at the time peregrines are just getting down to egg-laying. However, territorial battles may begin in the late winter and go on for several months if nests are on adjacent crags.

5 The path fords a little cascade where the Nant Ifan, a mountain stream named after the reserve's first warden, takes a steep and direct course through volcanic tuffs. It is worth stopping here to look at the plants growing among the rocks. Purple and starry saxifrage, mountain sorrel and fir clubmoss are a few of the species to be found close by.

Moss campion, cosseted in alpine gardens, thrives happily in the wild at Cwm Idwal

1 From the car park, a path leads to the left of the toilet block/National Park Warden Centre and past the remains of a little slate quarry, then left up a track signed **Llyn Idwal.** Look for parsley fern in the crevices and mountain lichen on the rock surfaces. Reminders of the Ice Age lie all around as the ground rises: to the left of the path is a ridge of terminal moraine – rubble left by the retreating Idwal glacier – and to the right there are several erratics – blocks of rock that the ice carried downhill from the head of the glacier and dumped when the thaw came. Looking north across Llyn Ogwen, the ground rises over 3400ft (1040m) to Carnedd Dafydd, one of the highest peaks of the impressive Carneddau range.

2 The track leads to an iron gate marking the boundary of the National Nature Reserve. Once past the gate you are on the shore of **Llyn Idwal.** According to legend, no bird dare fly over this enchanted lake. Its water is pure and clear, and Llyn Idwal is not as deep as many other corrie lakes. There are some emergent plants such as water lobelia and water horsetail, and a few aquatic specialities such as pillwort and quillwort, but in general the lake-shore is bare and stony and the water looks uncomfortably cold. A few cormorants come to fish for minnows, and grey wagtails and common sandpipers are often to be seen bobbing among the boulders hunting for caddis flies and mayflies. Otherwise the legend may well be true and Llyn Idwal may indeed have been cursed by a Celtic daemon.

Directly across the lake to the west stands Y Garn; from its right shoulder a ridge angles north-eastwards, marking the descent route for the walk. It looks impossibly steep from here but is a relatively safe scramble in fine weather. If the clouds have begun to threaten, this is a good time to revise your plans and consider doing a circuit of the lake instead of completing the whole walk.

3 Take the path left (clockwise), and follow this southwards. Eventually the path leaves the lake

6 Soon after crossing the stream the path begins to zig-zag more steeply. Here the rock becomes more obviously volcanic, lumpy and dark, with tufts of vegetation growing in clefts and scars. You are now directly beneath Twll Du, at the foot of the Hanging Gardens. The great boulders were either ripped from the lip of the ridge or fell during an avalanche many thousands of years ago.

There are rare arctic-alpine flowers all around: pause for a few minutes here to look at the plants and enjoy the view northwards. Great care should be taken not to damage any plant or stray off the path, which winds among the boulders.

On the rock face it should be possible to spot roseroot and perhaps the rare Snowdon lily, while any shadowy crevice may contain green spleenwort, maidenhair spleenwort, Wilson's filmy fern or oak fern.

Follow the path south-eastwards, uphill again and over a scramble of fallen stones. The main face of the mountain should be on your right; the path keeps parallel with this and angles right (south-west), with an extensive area of scree on the left. A small lake appears ahead now and the path makes for its right (north) shore. The lake is Llyn y Cwn, shallow and edged in summer by a hazy circlet of bogbean and water lobelia.

7 North of the lake turn right, along a very clear and well-worn path leading uphill towards the summit of Y Garn. Just before a fence the path forks; take the right fork if the weather is fair (there are wonderful views) or the left for a more direct ascent. The vegetation of the mountain top is very different from that of its sheltered flanks. The exposed summit of Y Garn is covered by shattered plates of rock with a few tufts of woolly-hair moss. The only birds, even in the middle of summer, are meadow pipits, wheatears and ravens. But the views from the summit cairn are breathtaking, embracing Anglesey and much of the Gwynedd coast as well as 100 Cambrian peaks. Snowdon itself lies away to the left (south-west), across the Llanberis Pass.

8 From the summit, continue north-west on the path close to the mountain edge until, after about 200yds (180m), a path rises again to a lesser knoll or summit. Here, take the path that turns sharp right, then descends very steeply. This is the really testing part of the walk and should be taken with care. Jagged teeth of rock wait to trip your feet; your eyes should be down, even if ravens and choughs are flying around your head. A small pool or lake lies immediately below, cupped in a

A curtain of glacier-carved rock is the backdrop to Llyn Idwal's cold, clear waters. The immense wall of the cwm looks forbidding from a distance, but its rare and beautiful arctic-alpine flora is worth a closer look

hanging valley high above the main Idwal basin. In the distance you should be able to see Ogwen and the car park.

After a very steep section the path eases and the lake appears on your right across a sweep of marshland.

9 Turn right and make for the east bank of Llyn Clyd (avoiding marshy ground if possible), then turn sharp left at the head of the lake, below the face of the corrie, and follow a path downhill beside a stream.

10 At first the path keeps to the left of the stream but it soon crosses to the right. Keep to this path, descending quite steeply past waterfalls and deep chasms (where more flowers are to be found), all the way down to Llyn Idwal.

11 Avoid the boggy area on the lake-shore, if necessary, by picking up the main shoreline path a few yards (metres) away to the right, then turn left, back to the iron gate and the return route to the car park.

The valley's wildlife may be less exciting in winter, but Aber Falls can look stunning through leafless trees

ABER FALLS SPRAYS NOISILY OVER ANCIENT CAMBRIAN ROCKS AT THE HEAD OF THE AFON RHAEADR FAWR VALLEY. THE CURVED VALLEY LIES IN THE NORTH OF THE CARNEDDAU MOUNTAINS OVERLOOKING BOTH ANGLESEY AND THE IRISH SEA, AND THE PATH THROUGH IT TAKES IN AN EXTRAORDINARY RANGE OF WILDLIFE HABITATS. THIS IS A HAVEN FOR FAMILY PICNICS AND FOR NATURALISTS ALIKE.

WOODS AND GRASSLAND

The valley is steep-sided; on the eastern flank is a mixture of broad-leaved and coniferous woodland, while the western side is broadleaved woodland and grassland. The woodland is particularly rich in mosses and lichens, and contains both base-rich and acid-loving plant communities, with a particularly fine example of alder carr woodland with ground-water streams.

Woodland birds include pied flycatchers, which are common in the summer months. The striking black and white breeding plumage of the male makes him easy to identify. Other summer visitors to the woods include willow warblers and chiffchaffs – easily distinguished by their song, if not by their appearance. Redstarts and wood warblers also breed here. On the stream, look out for two species that are frequently attracted to fast-flowing upland rivers – the dipper and the grey wagtail.

Aber Falls
Gwynedd
Grid ref. SH 663 720

Nature Conservancy Council
Approx. 2½ miles (4 km) or 5 miles (8 km). Shorter route moderately easy but with some steps; longer route steeper and more difficult.

The walk starts at Bont Newydd, 1 mile (1.6 km) south-east of Abergwyngregyn off the A55 Conwy to Bangor road.

This is a scenically stunning walk through a mixture of oak, ash, wych elm, birch and alder woodland with waterfall, river, pasture and moorland blanket bog. Wildlife highlights include woodland birds, birds of prey, and exceptional mosses and other plants.

Nearby sites: *Carneddau mountains* – mountain flowers and birds; *Llyn Crafnant reservoir* – wintering wildfowl.

Lousewort – found in damp places in Wales

Much of the grassland is closely grazed, by Welsh mountain sheep and ponies, but there are still swathes of bluebells, and a meadow near the head of the valley contains orchids and bog asphodels.

THE HIGHER REACHES

Above the falls there are some areas of classic blanket bog, upland river scenery and a number of dramatic shattered granite pinnacles. In addition, the moorland birdlife is good. Ravens and buzzards, familiar birds of the Welsh hills, may be circling overhead, and there is always the possibility of glimpsing a merlin flashing by, chasing meadow pipits across the moor. This small falcon, like some of our other birds of prey, is threatened by habitat loss as areas of upland moor where it hunts are increasingly being turned over to forestry or sheep-grazing.

VISITORS AND MANAGEMENT

Because it is easily accessible, Aber Falls attracts large numbers of people, and an informative nature trail guide produced by the Nature Conservancy Council is usually available to visitors. Managing areas of countryside with wildlife, visitors and economic interests all in mind is a familiar conservation challenge, but this valley and the associated area are an extremely good example of integrated land-use management involving a number of organisations including the University College of Wales, Snowdonia National Park, the National Trust, the Forestry Commission and the Nature Conservancy Council.

THE *Walk*

1 Bont Newydd is a beautiful old and arched bridge; do not cross it, but walk through the gate by the Nature Conservancy Council NCC map and information sign. Follow the steps alongside the river among coppiced alder, hazel and elm trees. Then walk above the river. Keep a careful look out for dippers below you, either hunting or keeping territory. A good variety of woodland ferns in this area includes the common polypody growing on the oak branches above your head. This part of the woodland is much richer in plant life than higher up the valley. Particularly noticeable is the wild garlic, with its strong-smelling leaves and white flowers from early May to mid June. The rich flora is due to a greater amount of base-rich material in the soil and rocks in this part of the valley.

2 Cross a newish bridge, go through the gate and turn right. Follow the track on the old river terrace up the hill. This overlooks an old meander where the river once ran, which has been colonised by alder carr (trees growing on wetland). This area is good in the spring for marsh marigolds and opposite-leaved golden saxifrage. The woodland contains many species of moss and lichen, particularly on the mature ash trees. Compare the birdsong in the conifer plantation on the left – chaffinches, coal tits and goldcrests – with that of different species in the broadleaved woodland to the right – wood warblers, redstarts, blackcaps and the metallic tinkle of the pied flycatcher. Notice the mature sessile oak on your left (by number 3 marker post), which is covered with lichens and mosses.

Unlike many woodland birds, coal tits are quite at home among coniferous trees

3 Continue through the grass pasture. This is grazed by Welsh mountain sheep and ponies, so

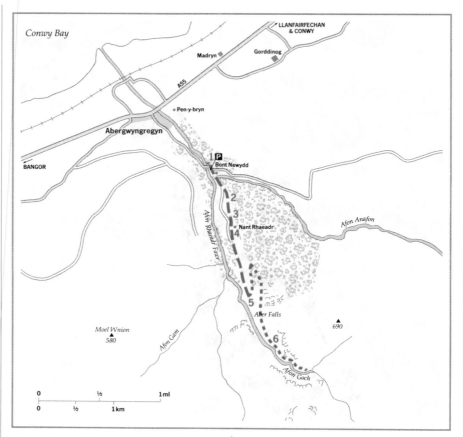

please keep dogs on a lead. On your left compare the flora of the fenced oak/alder carr, which contains a great variety of plants including the poisonous hemlock water dropwort, with that of the unfenced alder carr on your right. Here there is little sapling regeneration and the flora is poor because of over-grazing.

4 Walk past the cottage, Nant Rhaeadr, on your left, then through an extensive, more closely grazed pasture. Increasingly the woodland thins out, with occasional crab apple trees and a greater number of mountain ash. Recently the NCC has established a number of fenced enclosures to encourage the ash and mountain ash trees and their associated lichens. On your immediate right, amid oak woodland, is a good example of a wet meadow, with bog asphodels, orchids and ragged robin.

5 Walk up the steps. The sight of the falls dropping 200ft (60m) through lichen-filled woodland across smooth grey and white quartz-veined Cambrian rocks will not easily be forgotten. Ring ouzels can be seen and heard around the falls, and primroses

and anemones grow on all the inaccessible ledges.

At this point you can either retrace your steps to the car park or go on to higher pastures above the falls – a more difficult walk.

6 To continue the walk go back down the valley for about 100yds (90m), then turn right and walk up the twisting grassy track before a sharp right-hand turn which leads upwards over a granite scree slope (take care). Clamber carefully across a group of granite outcrops, slippery with interesting mosses and criss-crossed by streams, before reaching a more open area and a valley where the walking is easier. The character of the landscape changes immediately, with a wild mountain stream crashing through granite boulders and straggly heather. Steep slopes covered in deer-grass and mosses rise on either side. High to your right are frost-shattered granite pillars that stand out sharply in relief and offer excellent views – as far as the Isle of Man, on a good day.

At any point from here onwards you may retrace your steps to the starting point.

THE GREAT ORME IS A SUBSTANTIAL LIMESTONE HEADLAND WHICH WAS FORMED SOME 300 MILLION YEARS AGO, WHEN THE SEDIMENTS WHICH NOW FORM THE ROCK WERE FIRST LAID DOWN. THE NAME 'ORME' IS BELIEVED TO HAVE BEEN DERIVED FROM THE NORSE WORD FOR DRAGON OR SEA MONSTER – PROBABLY A REFERENCE TO THE UNUSUAL SHAPE OF THE HEADLAND.

VISITORS AND WILDLIFE

Jutting into the sea immediately north-west of the busy seaside resort of Llandudno, Great Orme is very popular with visitors, but careful management has helped to retain the features of natural history interest. These include maritime limestone grassland, a fine example of a limestone pavement, coastal heathland and sea cliffs. It is especially noted for its limestone plants.

The country park is managed from an informative visitor centre at the centre of the headland and there is a small wild flower garden showing many of the plants you are likely to encounter. Adjacent to the centre is a restaurant and café.

GRASSLAND, HEATH AND CLIFFS

Grazing by sheep and feral goats has modified the grassland, enabling many of the smaller plants to thrive in the comparatively short turf. These

Great Orme
Gwynedd
Grid ref. SH 765 835

Aberconwy Borough Council
Approx. 3½ miles (5.6 km). Mostly easy walking on a marked nature trail, but steep in some places.

Park at the visitor centre, 1 mile (1.6 km) north-west of Llandudno.

Great Orme is a fine limestone headland, managed as a country park and Local Nature Reserve. Habitats include limestone maritime grassland, coastal heathland, limestone pavement and sea cliffs. Highlights are breeding seabirds and specialised limestone flora.

Nearby sites: *Penmon Point and Puffin Island* – migrant and breeding seabirds, limestone flora; *Bodnant Garden* – magnificent gardens with rhododendrons and woodland birds; *Conwy Bay* – wildfowl and waders.

Spring squill

include the small, delicate blue spring squill, which flowers in late April and early May. Most of the characteristic plants of limestone can be found, including common and hoary rock-rose, bloody cranesbill, white horehound and wild thyme.

By contrast there are distinctive areas of coastal heathland with dwarf gorse, bell heather, ling and juniper. Amid this colourful mosaic, stonechats can often be seen. Unusual and interesting insects include the silver-studded blue and grayling butterflies, the silky wave moth and the horehound plume moth.

Occasionally glow-worms can be seen at dusk among clumps of bracken, brambles and gorse in the North Wales Wildlife Trust's reserve at Gogarth. Glow-worms are related to the fireflies – found in warmer climates – but only the male glow-worm can fly. The female, whose light is brighter, will often crawl up plant stems to enable her mate to find her more easily.

The cliffs provide nesting sites for a good range of seabirds including kittiwakes, guillemots, razorbills, fulmars and shags. Ravens are resident on the headland, while the commonest and most noticeable birds in the area are their much smaller relatives – jackdaws. Peregrines may also be seen on the cliffs.

Day trippers gone, it is almost possible to imagine Great Orme as it must have looked when St Tudno built his church here in the 7th century

THE *Walk*

1 From the visitor centre, follow the marked nature trail signs. The area of heathland here has formed on the glacial deposits overlying the limestone rock. In these more acid soils the bright bell heather, and paler ling, thrive amid patches of dwarf gorse and the larger common gorse. Stonechats often perch on taller sprays of gorse. These brightly coloured birds feed on the abundant insects of the heathlands. The small groups of noisy finches in the heathland are likely to be flocks of linnets, which often nest colonially.

Carry on down the slope to the corner of the wall, made from limestone quarried locally at Bishop's Quarry, and follow it round to the right. Continue along the side of the wall until you reach a direction post.

2 Walk down a steep slope. On the right are small rocky outcrops of limestone with groups of prickly juniper bushes. Soon you will notice that the limestone grassland has formed into small terraces – the effect of natural soil creep and of sheep walking across the steep slopes. Most of the limestone-loving plants here are short, with waxy leaves to help them withstand the dry conditions. Among the most abundant are rock-rose and wild thyme. This warm, south-west-facing slope is good for butterflies, including silver-studded and common blues. Meadow browns and graylings are also common. Wheatears can often be seen in this area, perching on the limestone boulders.

When you reach Marine Drive, cross the road to the small nature reserve at Gogarth. Here, amid clumps of bracken, bramble and gorse at dusk you may be lucky enough to see a glow-worm – actually a species of beetle.

3 Walk up the hill until you reach a small shelter and seats. Below you are areas of heathland. White feral goats graze amid the gorse here and in other similar places on the Orme.

The mountains on the other side of the bay are the Carneddau, part of Snowdonia National Park. The small island immediately to the west is Puffin Island, important for breeding seabirds. Beyond it is the low, flat island of Anglesey.

This is a good area to watch passage seabirds including gannets, skuas and Manx shearwaters. During the summer, grey seals, dolphins and pilot whales are occasionally seen swimming off shore.

4 Continue uphill, passing a gap in the wall, then a gate. Turn left at the second gap to waymarker number 4. You are now above a steep cliff and its colonies of breeding seabirds. The noisy gulls are the kittiwakes, with black-tipped wings. The dumpy, dark brown and white birds are guillemots and razorbills, which often fly several miles to obtain their fish. Large blackish-green birds with outstretched wings are likely to be shags, while grey and

Limestone Pavement

Limestone – composed mainly of calcium carbonate – is slightly soluble in rainwater which itself is slightly acidic. Weathering and erosion have produced dramatic landscapes in many parts of Britain – gorges, caves and scree slopes – but limestone pavements are perhaps the most fascinating and easily accessible. Here, flat limestone outcrops are scored and criss-crossed by deep gullies and crevices, the overall effect looking like neatly ordered paving slabs.

A dense scrub woodland, generally comprising ash, may develop where grazing and trampling of the pavement are limited. However, even on disturbed sites, there is plenty of botanical interest to be found growing in the sheltered crevices. Specialities of Great Orme include wild cotoneaster and dark red helleborine.

white birds, flying with stiff, outstretched wings, will be fulmars. Among the cliff flowers are sea-pinks or thrift, and straggly plants of wild cabbage.

5 Retrace your steps, walk up the road facing you and cross Marine Drive. When you reach the road sign, turn right and walk over to the fenced enclosure. The area of exposed rock here is a limestone pavement. The deep channels, known as grikes, have a distinctive flora including hart's tongue fern, herb Robert, and lords and ladies. In addition, hawthorn and blackthorn grow in extremely stunted forms, barely reaching above the rock surface. The plot has been fenced to see how the plants respond without the pressure of grazing.

Continue across the car park to the drystone wall and turn left (rather than right with the official nature trail). Continue until you reach the extensive areas of limestone pavement on your left. Notice the large limestone boulders, called erratics, which were deposited by glaciers around 12,000 years ago.

Turn south to rejoin the path a little beyond the point where you turned left, and continue to follow the wall back to the visitor centre and car park. On the way, near where the wall turns left, look for large patches of sky blue spring squill.

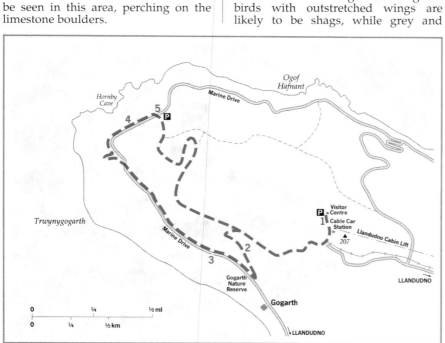

DISTANT VIEWS FROM MOEL FAMAU'S JUBILEE TOWER – OF SNOWDONIA, THE DEE ESTUARY AND MERSEYSIDE – ARE PERHAPS THE MOST MEMORABLE FEATURE OF THIS WALK, DEFINITELY ONE FOR A CLEAR DAY. CLOSER AT HAND IS THE VALE OF CLWYD, WITH ITS DISTINCTIVE PATTERN OF SMALL FIELDS AND VILLAGES. THE GLOWING COLOURS OF HEATHERS AND GORSE MAKE THIS FIRST PART OF THE WALK PARTICULARLY MEMORABLE DURING AUGUST.

THE CLWYDIAN HILLS

Moel Famau Country Park lies in the heart of the Clwydian Hills, designated an Area of Outstanding Natural Beauty. The opening stretch of the walk, as far as the Jubilee Tower, follows Offa's Dyke Path – though this section of the long-distance path does not coincide with the 8th-century earthwork from which it takes its name. The return is through planted coniferous woodland containing grassy rides and a pond with a healthy population of breeding frogs.

PLANTS AND INSECT LIFE

The acidic shale soils support large stretches of heather interspersed with bright green patches of bilberry, which produces small black berries in August. Among these areas are stands of bracken and shining yellow dwarf gorse, with mat-grass forming suitable areas for grazing sheep.

Despite the flocks of sheep and the many visitors, the area is still good for wildlife. Among the insects, look out in spring for the large, day-flying emperor moth, with characteristic 'eye'

The Black Grouse

Visitors who do this walk early in the morning, especially in the early spring, may be rewarded with a sighting of a black grouse. Despite their large size, these distinctive birds are seen comparatively rarely, partly because they spend most of the day under cover in the conifer woodland. At dawn, however, males congregate at traditional 'leks', where they display to attract a female. Male black grouse have elegant lyre-shaped tails and are essentially black. Females, on the other hand, are mottled brown and well camouflaged when sitting on their nest on the woodland floor.

Moel Famau Country Park

Clwyd
Grid ref. SJ 161 605

Clwyd County Council/Forestry Commission
Approx. 3½ miles (5.6 km). Hilly, but well signposted.

Moel Famau Country Park is 3 miles (4.8km) north-east of Ruthin, 1½ miles (2.4km) north-east of Llanbedr-Dyffryn-Clwyd on an unclassified road. The car park is on the north side of this road.

Setting out along Offa's Dyke Path, the walk crosses heather moor, heathland, coniferous woodland and grassland. Typical upland heath plants here include bell heather, ling and dwarf gorse. Emperor moths may be seen while, for birdwatchers, highlights may include red (and possibly also black) grouse, buzzards and kestrels.

Nearby sites: *Loggerheads Country Park* – mixed woodland with excellent ground flora and woodland birds; *Llyn Brenig* – open water, moorland and forest with a birdwatching hide and a nature trail; *Clocaenog Forest* – mature conifer plantation, notable for red squirrels, pine martens and crossbills, nature trail provided.

Poppies – fast colonisers of disturbed ground

---

markings on its wings. The orange-brown females attract the fast-flying males with a scent. Look out for groups of males gathered around females. Later in the year, their caterpillars can be found by carefully searching the heather on which they feed. Despite the fact that they are bright green, they are superbly camouflaged among the vegetation. Eggar moths are also a day-flying species and can be seen dashing across the moorland in July and August.

UPLAND BIRDLIFE

Most noticeable among the birds are kestrels and buzzards, which hunt along the scarp of the hills for small mammals and insects. Meadow pipits are the commonest of the ground-nesting moorland birds. This small, brown species can be recognised by its uniform plumage and high-pitched call. Less common but more noticeable are the moorland's red grouse whose sheep-like call, often described as 'go-back, go-back', is a familiar sound. Black grouse also occur, but are seldom seen. During the spring and summer, wheatears are quite common. Listen for their loud 'tchack' call and look for the white rump visible in flight.

Coniferous plantations are generally less productive for birds than deciduous woodlands. However, species such as song thrushes and mistle thrushes, great spotted woodpeckers, redpolls and sparrow-hawks should be present. During the winter months, mixed flocks of goldcrests, coal tits and blue tits roam the woods.

Looking north across upland heathland towards Moel Famau Country Park

---

WALK 47

i

THE *Walk*

1 From the car park, walk north-west up a gently sloping, twisting shale track. On your right notice how the path has exposed the thin, acid soils, leached of minerals, and overlying shale rocks. These poor soils determine the vegetation of the Clwydian Hills. A characteristic upland heath flora can be seen on your immediate left, with extensive patches of dwarf gorse, bilberry and bell heather overlooking the Vale of Clwyd with its 'enclosure' landscape of small fields and well-developed hedgerows. Look for whinchats perched on sprays of gorse. These distinctive summer visitors have cream and brown plumage and a conspicuous eye-stripe. Please keep to the footpath so as to avoid the areas of erosion which are being repaired, and also in order to prevent possible disturbance to nesting red grouse.

2 Continue on Offa's Dyke Path up the steep slope to the Jubilee Tower, built on the summit of Moel Famau, at 1820ft (554m). The tower was originally constructed in 1810 to celebrate George III's jubilee, and has subsequently been rebuilt. From it there are panoramic views, and directional points of interest are shown on a view indicator in the tower.

3 Leave Offa's Dyke Path and walk south-east on the marked path towards coniferous woodland. Go down a steeply sloping path parallel with the coniferous plantation, and past two twisted beech trees. On the right-hand side is a wide fire-break, created to prevent any moorland fires from spreading into the valuable timber crop. A beneficial side-effect of the fire-break is that it creates a different habitat for plants: both wavy hair-grass and the diminutive yellow tormentil are common in this shorter sward. To the right as you approach the plantation is a group of bird-sown rowan or mountain ash trees which have been able to grow because of the absence of grazing sheep. Their branches make ideal launching perches for the spiralling song-flight of tree pipits, characteristic birds of upland heath.

4 Cross a path/fire-break which runs at right angles to your path and continue with coniferous woodland on either side. The conifers on the right, with distinctive light green tips to the branches, are Sitka spruce. Plants growing along the grass

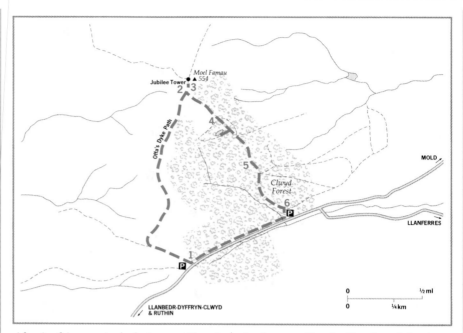

rides in this area include tormentil and white heath bedstraw, both of which prefer acid soils.

Turn right at the next path that crosses the ride and walk about 50yds (45m) before turning right again to reach a pond. In early spring this contains frogs and abundant spawn, while later in the season rushes and sedges are more noticeable – though in late summer the pond can dry up considerably.

Retrace your steps to the main path and continue downhill. Mistle thrushes, with their metallic songs, may be heard in early spring. Stones surrounded by fragments of broken shell show where the mistle thrush's smaller relative, the song thrush, has been at work, smashing snails on its 'anvil'. Noticeable on the right-hand side of the ride is a compact species of rush with a protruding stem – heath rush. A little further on are some European larches. This deciduous conifer is particularly striking in the autumn, when its needles turn bright yellow.

5 Continue down a particularly steep stretch of the path. Here the rides are frequented by wall brown and meadow brown butterflies, both of which feed on grasses in their caterpillar stage. Notice how the landscape is dominated by coniferous plantations on the surrounding slopes – an increasing reality on many of our moorland hills.

Cross a path at right angles to the ride and enter an area of more open

larch woodland. To the right is a mixed plantation of young broad-leaves and conifers – a particularly good place for willow warblers in spring and summer. Look for the small shale bank on the left; this rock is responsible for the acid nature of the soil. A little further, on the left, is a small indentation where shale has been removed. The resulting area is extremely good for wild flowers including self-heal, hawkweeds, marsh birdsfoot trefoil and rosebay willow-herb, which are attractive to a wide range of butterflies such as small tortoiseshells.

6 Ignore the path to the left and carry straight on, passing a fenced-in building on the right. Just after this, turn right down a worn pathway to a stream and a wooden bridge. On either side of the stream are extensive areas of both broad buckler fern and lady fern, thriving on the damp, acid soil alongside the stream. Look for grey wagtails beside the stream and brown trout in the water itself.

Follow the path downstream until you reach a car park. Walk through this and turn right on to the road. Continue up the hill towards the car park where the walk began. On the left-hand side of the road is a younger plantation, still light and open enough to be home to large numbers of small birds including tree pipits.

Cross a cattle grid at the brow of the hill to reach the car park, on the right.

Wye Gorge

*The Wye valley, seen from the justifiably popular viewpoint of Symonds Yat. The valley's steep sides have retained
their very special mixture of native trees, which support a wealth of other wildlife*

OLD FORESTS TELL INTERESTING STORIES; THE BIGGER AND MORE OUT-OF-THE-WAY THE FOREST THE BETTER THE STORY AND THE CLEARER THE CLUES. THE LOWER WYE VALLEY, BEYOND THE FOREST OF DEAN ON THE WELSH BORDER, IS A CLASSIC. HOWEVER, THERE IS MUCH MORE TO THE OLD MONTGOMERY BORDERLAND THAN ITS MAGNIFICENT TREES.

RIVER AND FOREST

The Wye is one of the cleanest and most beautiful rivers in Britain; it receives some effluent and nitrogen run-off on its way through Herefordshire, but compared with other major waterways this is insignificant. Long before the last Ice Age it probably meandered slowly through a lowland wilderness, but when the sea-level fell the river became more urgent and began to cut a deeper channel through Old Red Sandstone and Carboniferous Limestone, until a deep sinuous gorge had been established. Trees found a footing wherever they could on the steep limestone cliffs, and to the east of the river a tract of mixed woodland extended across to the Severn.

For the next hundred centuries farming eroded the plateau woodland but never even came close to removing it. The Forest of Dean became a valuable resource in its own right, though in later years the scale of exploitation changed and whole areas were felled. Today the Forest of Dean is a curious patchwork of conifer plantations, coal mines and delightful stands of oak and sweet chestnut. At its western boundary the valley woodland of the Wye fared much better: the timber was either left or was managed by traditional coppicing methods and so the original mix of trees was retained.

A NATURALIST'S HAVEN

Good fortune has blessed the Wye Gorge. It bears a marked resemblance to the Dordogne in its combination of limestone cliffs, woodland and water, yet it probably receives far fewer British tourists. Its fauna and flora are excellent without attracting particular attention. There is probably a great deal still to discover. The best-known wild inhabitants are a pair of peregrines which nest each year close to the public viewpoint of Symonds Yat, and some colonies of the rare greater horseshoe bat which roosts in caves among the limestone. However, anyone who walks along the woodland rides will be aware that there is an unusually varied mix of trees, birds, butterflies and fungi.

In Southern England the 'primary' tree cover only exists in fragments and any extensive blocks of ancient woodland are well known and are held in great esteem by naturalists. This is not necessarily the case elsewhere and it sometimes comes as a surprise to learn that there are equally important ancient forests in places such as the West Midlands and Wales.

The dominant trees of the Wye Gorge woodlands are oak, beech and ash, but this is also one of the very few British sites for the native large-leaved lime and for several rare whitebeams, as well as such ancient woodland indicator species as wild service tree and small-leaved lime. The latter tree is the food-plant of the scarce hook-tip moth, which occurs nowhere else in Britain. This and the silver cloud moth, plus a rich assortment of classic ancient woodland moth species (great prominent, black arches, lobster, green silver-lines, marbled brown) make Wye an important entomological site.

Between Ross and Chepstow the Wye rushes over limestone boulders and gravels and is therefore full of dissolved minerals. Thus even the twilight world below the surface is special and contains local species of aquatic pondweeds, mayflies and fish. Among the latter are the grayling and the Allis shad – both found only in unpolluted rivers.

LOCAL KNOWLEDGE

Like most other places, the Wye Gorge benefits from being taken at a gentle pace. The best walks, including the one described here, include steep ascents, river crossings and precarious viewpoints, so allow plenty of time. It is also worth allowing for stops along the way to talk to passers-by. Anglers are always worth talking to; not only can they tell you about fish, but they may also have stories about otters, kingfishers and other animals that use the river as a highway. Likewise foresters, who may know where white admiral butterflies are gathering on bramble blossom or where a fallow deer fawn is lying. The area is patrolled by countryside staff of the County Council and there are often people on hand at Symonds Yat to answer questions about peregrines and woodland management.

Despite the rich wildlife of summer, there is no doubt that the most memorable time to visit the Wye Gorge is in late October, when autumn frosts have touched the canopy and turned each tree's foliage a different colour: the variety of species is beautifully emphasised. This is also the time for fungi and autumn fruits – panther-caps and blushers beneath the beeches, and bryony berries draped among the hazel wands.

Wye Gorge

Gwent/Hereford and Worcester
Grid ref. SO 564 158

Gwent County Council/Gwent Wildlife Trust
Approx. 5½ miles (8.8 km). Steep in parts.

Symonds Yat lies about 4 miles (6.4 km) north-east of Monmouth. Park in the large car park close to the Symonds Yat viewpoint, accessible from the B4432 about 2 miles (3.2 km) north of Christchurch.

The Wye is one of the most beautiful of British rivers, threading its way through some of the most attractive and rich blocks of ancient woodland. This walk starts from the famous Symonds Yat viewpoint, from where, in spring and early summer, there is usually a view of nesting peregrines, and then takes a close look at the best of the woodland – good for birds in the spring, insects and flowers in the summer and fungi in the autumn. The tree community, including several rare species, is a particular feature.

Nearby site: *Avon Gorge, Bristol –* excellent woodland with unusual flowers, some unique in Britain.

Goldcrests are our smallest birds

THE *Walk*

1 Beyond the log cabin in the car park (an information point/café), a path to the right leads over a footbridge and left to Yat Rock. This is where most visitors will be heading: it is one of the most famous and most photographed views in Britain, and one of the best. Looking north (downstream – the river forms a sharp loop because of this ridge), Elliot's Wood lies on the left bank and Coppet Hill, a steep slope of heath and woodland, on the right. Beyond are the steeple of Goodrich church and the green fields of Herefordshire. Looking south-east, the river hairpins to the left through the deep wooded gorge. The cliff on the south side of the bend, to the right of the viewpoint, is called Coldwell Rocks and it is here that a pair of peregrines usually nests. This spot must be the best place to see peregrines in the whole country; looking down on to incoming birds is particularly exciting. The best time to see the peregrines (if they are here) is in early summer, when they have a family to feed.

From Yat Rock, return over the footbridge. **To the right as you look towards the log cabin is a path among the trees, signed 'Wye Valley Walk'. Take this path, which angles down-hill to a road, at which turn sharp left to follow a narrow path downhill, waymarked by yellow arrows, across a forest drive and so down the steep hillside.** The trees are typically varied: beech and ash, then wych elm and oak. Black bryony and clematis trail among the bushes, providing cover for some of the forest birds. Except in early spring, before the buds burst, the best chance of picking out different birds in the foliage is by their calls. The classic woodland species found here include redstart, pied flycatcher and wood warbler. Although they are surprisingly colourful, they still melt into the dappled canopy and it is only their songs that give them away.

2 **The path leads out at the Royal Hotel, at which bear right, down to the river, then left along the riverside track. There are two parallel routes; a broad track through the trees and a narrower fishermen's path along the bank. Alternating between the two allows good views of the river as well as a look at the tall herbs and shrubs of the open ride.** In autumn this is certainly a place to appreciate 'mellow fruitfulness' – there are seeds and berries everywhere: wild raspberries, guelder rose, bryony, hips, haws and

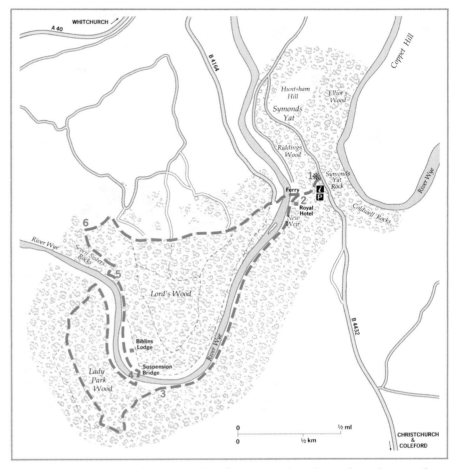

hogweed (crush a few of the seeds for a refreshing smell of orange-peel). There are also extensive patches of Himalayan balsam, an exotic-looking alien with large pink flowers which grows up to 6ft (1.8m) tall and produces 'touch-me-not' seeds which are irresistible to touch. There are some fine beeches on the high slopes to the left, and alongside the track there are very tall specimens of sessile oak, ash and birch.

The tempting-looking berries of guelder rose are inedible raw, but safe if cooked

At a junction of tracks, continue straight on along the riverside (the left turn is signed 'Bracelands') then past another left turn and on towards Biblins Bridge. Just before this suspension bridge, and before a Nature Conservancy Council sign, there is a path leading steeply uphill through Lady Park Wood. This National Nature Reserve is one of the most interesting woods in Britain. Most of it, however, is enclosed by a fence and is not open to the public for safety reasons. To the right, an area is being left unmanaged in order to observe the natural processes, while the area to the left is being managed so that the two areas can be compared.

3 It is possible to follow the path, and the fence, all the way round the wood; this brings you out further up the river and it will then be necessary to backtrack to the suspension bridge where the walk continues. Alternatively, a brief de-tour a few yards (metres) up the path will give a good impression of the place, and it is then possible to walk through the more open area of trees on the southern side of Lady Park, to the left as you climb the path. The small-leaved limes have obviously been coppiced in the past but are now quite tall trees. Sunlight filtering through the translucent foliage bathes the ground in a distinctive silver-green light.

4 Back on the river bank, cross the suspension bridge. This is an interesting experience, particularly as there is only wire mesh beneath your feet and you can see the Wye rushing some distance beneath you. On the far side turn left along a track, bearing half-left at Biblins Lodge to cross a field towards a riverside stile. The view of Lady Park Wood is breathtaking; tiers of trees (some draped in wild clematis) rise in a solid wall, mainly on the lower ground with some beech and oak growing on the higher slopes.

Continue along the riverside path past alders, field maple and a host more trees, then after several hundred yards (metres) turn sharp right, uphill on a waymarked path. The path is very steep and covered with limestone rubble. It leads to the foot of a limestone cliff, at which turn left. Anyone who has visited the Dordogne

may feel a sense of *déjà vu* and wonder if there are cave paintings on some of the rock faces. None has been discovered, though the two sites are very similar and there were certainly human settlements here in post-glacial times. Perhaps it was just too cold in the earlier Magdalenian period when cave art was at its zenith in France and Spain.

5 The path angles sharp right above the rock face, then uphill through woodland before turning left on level ground, following the marked route. The limestone flora is excellent, but the views to the left put everything else in the shade. The limestone outcrops on this side of the river are called the Seven Sisters and, for the moment, the path follows the summit ridge. The views are spectacular, perhaps even better than those from Symonds Yat.

6 The waymarked path bears to the right, then drops down over some rocks and bears right through high woodland of oak, ash and beech. Follow the yellow arrows, taking care at junctions, until the path meets a wide forest drive, at which turn right, then left on to the waymarked path again. The soil on

the top of the plateau changes and becomes more acidic and this is reflected in the vegetation which becomes dominated by heather and bilberry.

Eventually the path meets the wide drive again, at which turn left and follow the drive downhill, past some fine old beech trees. As the drive begins to rise again, a path leads downhill to the right. Take this path, which soon leads out on to a road. Turn down this road and follow it as it winds left to riverside cottages, then turn right between the cottages (signed to the ferry). A ferry (called 'Owld Butt') runs every 20 minutes across to the Saracen's Head. There may be time to stop and watch the Wye from the west bank; if not, it would be difficult to forgo a view of the river from the east bank, from the Saracen's Head or Rose Cottage tea-room.

There then remains a short walk along to the Royal Hotel and the steep ascent back to Symonds Yat and the car park.

The path beside the Wye near Symonds Yat. Himalayan balsam, nicknamed 'policeman's helmet' because of the shape of its flowers, blooms along this stretch of the walk long after the woodland spring flowers have faded

A Dean oakwood in early autumn. Bracken follows the spring flowers that thrive on an oak woodland floor

THIS FOREST IS ONE OF ENGLAND'S MOST ANCIENT. IT HAS PROVIDED MAN WITH VARIOUS RESOURCES SINCE PREHISTORIC TIMES. THE DIFFERENT ACTIVITIES THAT HAVE BEEN CARRIED OUT HERE GIVE THE FOREST A SPECIAL CHARACTER, AND REPLANTING OVER A LONG PERIOD HAS ENSURED THAT TREES OF VARIOUS AGES ARE GROWING THROUGHOUT THE FOREST. WALKING THROUGH THE FOREST OF DEAN TODAY IS A DELIGHTFUL AND RE-WARDING EXPERIENCE.

RICH RESOURCES

Iron ore has been mined in the Forest for nearly 3000 years: some of the underground tunnels and chambers of ancient iron mines can be seen at Clearwell Caves. Coal has been mined here for six centuries, the last pit being closed in 1965, and stone quarrying still continues near Coleford. William the Conqueror, Henry II and King John all hunted wild boar and deer in the Forest. Finally there are the trees. These have figured often as major, valuable resources in England's history, and are still managed for timber production.

Virgin woodland existed here until about the 12th century, when the Forest of Dean extended from Ross-on-Wye to Gloucester. The trees were harvested ruthlessly for iron smelting, charcoal burning, house and ship building, such that by the 14th century the Forest area was reduced by half,

Forest of Dean

Gloucestershire
Grid ref. SO 627 095

Forestry Commission
Approx. 4 miles (6.4 km). Easy walking.

The Forest lies south of Ross-on-Wye. New Fancy car park is 1½ miles (2.4 km) south of Speech House, on the minor road towards Blakeney.

The Forest of Dean comprises 28,000 acres (11,000 hectares) of deciduous and coniferous woodland between the Wye Gorge and the Severn plain. Highlights of the walk are beautiful, extensive woodlands of varying age, with abundant bird, mammal and insect life. The walk includes Speech House Lake and the Arboretum.

Nearby sites: *Nagshead RSPB Reserve* – oak woodland, good for pied flycatchers and redstarts; *Highnam Woods* – woodland birds and flowers.

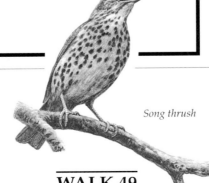

Song thrush

and by the 17th century few trees remained. Steps were then taken to prevent grazing and allow the Forest to regenerate. Some oaks standing today date from that period.

THE VERDERERS

The presence of such rich resources necessitated various legislation, and it is thought that the posts of 'Verderer', which still exist, were first instituted by King Canute in 1016. The Verderers' job was to administer the Forest laws. Speech House is the geographical and traditional centre of the Forest, and is still the meeting place of the Verderers' Court: the present building was completed in 1682.

THE FOREST TODAY

An Act of Parliament in 1808 resulted in the Forest as we now find it: four million English oak trees were planted at that time, and a further million ash, elm, sweet chestnut, Scots pine and Norway spruce. More replanting was necessary after the use of timber in the two World Wars. Today the Forest is made up of roughly equal numbers of coniferous and deciduous trees. The great oaks and beeches support a rich diversity of wildlife living on, in and beneath them, while in areas of coniferous forest, rides and abandoned railway lines provide a quite different type of habitat.

WALK 49

THE *Walk*

New Fancy was once a colliery: the spoil heap is now landscaped and planted with birch and hawthorn. Before setting off, visit the viewpoint. From here the Forest extends in all directions: the deciduous woodland of Nagshead RSPB Reserve can be seen to the west, with the town of Cinderford to the east.

1 From New Fancy car park follow the path marked 'Forest Trail' which leads down a slope to join an old tramway. Turn right. After the stile turn left on to a forest road. This (now incomplete) avenue of lime trees was planted in 1810. A mixture of tree species on both sides of the road includes beech, birch, holly, pine, oak and rowan. In spring, garden warblers, willow warblers, bullfinches, black-caps, chiffchaffs, whitethroats and cuckoos all sing here.

2 At a Y-junction overshadowed by a large lime tree, take the right-hand fork. After about 10yds (9m) turn left on to the old railway line. The railway was the Mineral Loop Line of the Severn and Wye Railway Company, opened in 1872. This grass-covered way shows the typical vegetation that regenerates in such open areas: bramble, rose, sloe, nettle, bracken, wild strawberry, stitchwort, vetch and rosebay willow-herb – an excellent flora to support bees, butterflies and moths. Look for the black and red wings of burnet moths, which are common here.

After the track crosses over a red-marked path it becomes more shaded, with plantations on each side. Birds to be seen and heard here are long-tailed tits, coal tits and goldcrests, joined in winter by redpolls and siskins. Look carefully for crossbills, which feed entirely on conifers, using their specialist bills to extract the seed from cones.

3 After the railway line bends to the right there is a cutting: take the steps leading down to the left. By the ivy-clad walls of the dismantled bridge flows the Blackpool Brook, and enjoying the shady and damp conditions here are coppiced alders, willow, large swathes of honeysuckle, foxgloves, ferns, woodruff, mosses and liverworts.

Go over the duckboards and back up to the railway track. After about 30yds (27m) there is another bridge. From here there is an excellent chance of viewing fallow deer as they browse in the forest rides.

On the far side of this bridge take the steps down to the right, then turn right and walk under the bridge. The route now follows a forest ride with plantations on both sides. Marsh thistles and foxgloves abound here.

4 Beyond a large oak tree, turn right on to a forest road, and then left before a small stand of young beech. On the left is a mixed plantation of pine and silver birch, on the right are spruce trees. Silverweed grows on the verges. After the path crosses a small brook it becomes more open with gorse, young pine and much honeysuckle.

5 Walk up a shallow bank to Speech House Lake, formed by damming Blackpool Brook. Reedmace grows around the lake margin, and the oval leaves of pondweed can be seen on the water surface. Tufted ducks, mallards and moorhens make their homes here, and damselflies and dragonflies abound in the late spring and summer.

6 Leaving the lake behind you on the left, cross a forest road on to a straight forest ride. Goldcrests sing in the larches on each side of the ride.

7 Turn left at the crossroads. On the left is an open area where, late on summer evenings, you may hear the 'churring' of a nightjar and even see it hunting for insects over the young trees. The Scots pines growing here may be native to the Forest. Bilberries grow by the side of the path.

8 Go through a five-bar gate and into the Arboretum. This is a collection of several hundred tree species. Most are named, and include both native and exotic species: wild service tree, Turkey oak, rhododendrons, azaleas, hemlock, Californian red fir. In spring there are bluebells, and wonderful colours in autumn.

Walk through the Arboretum towards the opposite gate: do not go through it, but turn left on to a path with blue markers. The path passes between two Corsican pines and on through stands of many different fir species.

9 Go through the gate near a very large oak. Speech House is on the right. In a clearing there is a sculpture 'Sliced Log Star' (Inside Out tree) by Andrew Darke: it is placed at the end of the Spruce Ride.

Walk along this ride to the cross-roads and turn right. There is an old beech tree on the left. Eventually join the main forest track and turn right.

10 Cross the stile, and then the road. The route now enters oak and beech woodland, with a few sweet chestnut trees. Woodland birds here include blue and great tits, green and great spotted woodpeckers, nuthatches and treecreepers, joined in summer by pied flycatchers, redstarts, wood warblers and other summer migrants. The woodland floor flowers with bluebells, foxgloves, wood anemones, wood sorrel, yellow pimpernel and wood spurge.

The path turns left by a plantation of young Scots pines. Join the road by two horse chestnuts and walk back to the car park – about 100yds (90m).

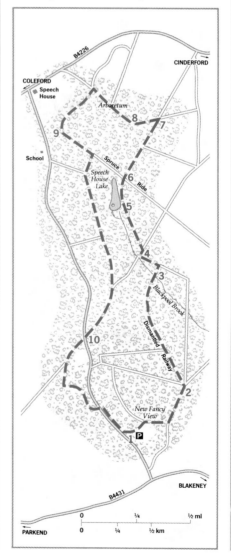

The semi-parasitic mistletoe is often 'planted' by birds who eat the berries, then clean their beaks by rubbing them on the bark

THE RIVER WYE IS WELL KNOWN IN ITS LOWER REACHES, WHERE IT FLOWS THROUGH A DEEP WOODED GORGE, BUT THE QUIETER UPPER RIVER IS LESS FAMILIAR AND OFFERS PEACEFUL WALKING THROUGH UNSPOILT COUNTRYSIDE. THE SOIL IS OFTEN DEEP RED, REMINISCENT OF MID-DEVON, AND IS VERY SUITABLE FOR DAIRY FARMING AND FRUIT-GROWING.

TREES AND WOODLANDS

Some of Herefordshire's woodlands are of ancient origin, containing oak, wild service tree and small-leaved lime, and an understorey of species such as herb Paris, spurge laurel and stinking iris – all indicators of continuous woodland cover. Badgers, dormice and roe deer all live in these old woods, and many butterflies, including silver-washed fritillary and white admiral, which are dependent on well-managed ancient woodland, are also present.

One reason for the survival of so much woodland can be seen in some of the village buildings. Many are half-timbered, and will have been constructed from local materials. Oaks were required for large-scale building,

but many other types of wood were needed for other jobs, so well-maintained woodland with a good mixture of species was essential.

Some fine examples of coppiced small-leaved lime can be seen here; this native species was used for turnery and carving, and the re-generating foliage growing out of cut stumps was a favourite food of grazing deer, sheep and cattle. The small-leaved lime has now become very localised in Britain.

The climate and soils of Herefordshire are very suitable for growing apples. Sadly, some of the smaller farm and village orchards have been neglected and are gradually disappearing. A large number of apple varieties were grown, many of them used to make the famous Herefordshire cider. Some of the older orchards are interesting conservation areas; the mature apple trees often support good growths of mistletoe and colonies of lichens on their bark.

THE RIVER WYE

The River Wye remains largely unspoilt along the whole of its length. There is little industrial development along the river's course, so the water is unpolluted in comparison with many of Britain's other major rivers. The Wye has healthy populations of aquatic plants, especially water crow-foots, and these support large numbers of invertebrates like caddis flies and mayflies. These, in turn, are the main food of many species of fish; the river is noted for its trout and 'coarse' fish like dace and chub. Salmon migrate up the river on their way to spawning grounds in the mid-Wales mountains. Wye salmon have long been much prized by fishermen; over-fishing during the 19th century nearly emptied the river of its salmon, and even today poaching is a serious problem. Other fish to be seen in the river include elvers, which enter the Wye by the thousand, returning years later as mature eels on their way to the Sargasso Sea to spawn.

Where the river has cut deep banks, the sandstone has been tunnelled by sand martins and kingfishers for nesting holes. Overhanging alders and willows provide perches for kingfishers, which can be surprisingly difficult to see among the foliage, despite their brilliant colours.

Public footpaths run along one or other of the banks for much of the river's course, but several sections are closed off, largely to protect salmon-fishing rights. A long-distance footpath is being created, so in time it will be possible to follow the Wye for most of its length.

Bridge Sollers

Hereford & Worcester
Grid ref. SO 414 426

Approx. 3 miles (4.8 km). Easy walking.

Bridge Sollers is just off the A438, some 6 miles (9.6 km) west of Hereford. Park near the church.

Setting out alongside the River Wye, this walk is a fine introduction to the Herefordshire countryside – an attractive blend of rich farmland, riverside flood-meadows, woodland, coppices and hedgerows and many tiny villages linked by twisting, high-banked lanes.

Nearby site: *Lugg Valley Meadows* – water meadows and unimproved grassland.

Common centaury – a plant of dry grassy areas

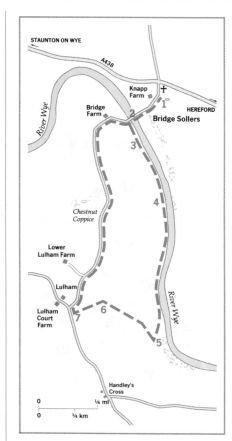

1 Follow the lane from the churchyard downhill to the river. The small Norman church is built on a prominent spot overlooking the river and with a fine view beyond to the Welsh border and Hay Bluff. Buzzards may be seen from here, and flocks of gulls, woodpigeons, rooks and jackdaws fly to and from feeding areas along the river valley. Old yews grow in the churchyard, and a few of the tombstones have fine patches of lichens on them. The churchyard has an uninterrupted view of the fields below because of the 'ha-ha', built to prevent any livestock from straying into it.

On the right as you go down the lane are some evergreen oaks which produce their acorns in hairy cups, unlike the native oaks. The hedge on the left provides good supplies of elder and hawthorn berries for birds in autumn and winter and usually has mistle thrushes or migrant redwings and fieldfares feeding in it in winter.

2 From the bridge it is possible to see how shallow the river is here. In dry summers, when the level is low, cattle can wade across; this is the site of an ancient ford. Long, waving tassels of water crowfoot can be seen in the river, and these will have aquatic insects living in them. Brown trout can usually be seen poised in the shallows upstream of the bridge.

3 Cross the bridge and climb the fence immediately after it on the left. Steps lead down to the river-bank path, which leads through the fields to the woods. Willows, alders and ash trees grow near the river, and mallards and moorhens nest among their roots. Kingfishers nest in holes deep in steeper banks, and may be seen perched on an overhanging branch or flying along the river at high speed.

4 The footpath runs along the river's flood plain, an area of rich farmland. The opposite bank is steeper and the river is cutting into it, making a cliff sometimes used as a nesting site by kingfishers. The sloping ground here cannot be cultivated, but it is rich grazing land and the traditional white-faced Herefordshire cattle may still be seen here.

Yellow iris and Himalayan balsam grow close to the water's edge. Several species of dragonfly and damselfly can be watched on sunny summer afternoons. In the deeper reaches of the river, chub and dace are sometimes seen. The stocky chub lurks under overhanging branches waiting for insects to drop into the water, while dace feed more actively in small, lively shoals.

Pass through a gate and then cross over a fence in the next hedge.

Native, but uncommon – a small-leaved lime

5 When the path reaches the wood, follow the yellow way-markers to the right and back along the hedge at the top of the field. The large tree in the field is a very old small-leaved lime which has been pollarded. Several fine hornbeams grow in the thick hedgerow; they are recognised by their winged seeds and serrated-edged leaves. Hawfinches are very fond of these seeds, so it is worth spending some time looking up into the canopy for feeding birds. The tangle of blackberry bushes below the hedge is full of insect life, and robins, wrens, dunnocks and warblers can usually be found here.

6 Turn left through a gap after the hornbeam trees at the end of the hedge line, still following the yellow markers, and pass a hop field on the left. At the next high hedge turn right, then after about 100yds (90m) follow the path to the left through a gap in the high hedge. The path then leads alongside a poplar hedge and past a small vineyard to the road. Look in the hedges and small fields for bullfinches, goldfinches and, in winter, bramblings, siskins and red-polls.

7 Turn right on to the road, then right again at the fork to pass through Lulham. At the fork, in front of Lulham Court Farm, is an old millstone, used to crush apples for cider.

Follow the road back to the start of the walk. Notice the old farm buildings, constructed of local timber, and check the fields for feeding flocks of finches and larks, especially after the crops have been harvested.

THE MALVERN HILLS RISE SPECTACU-LARLY FROM THE SURROUNDING FARMLAND AND ARE A DESIGNATED AREA OF OUTSTANDING NATURAL BEAUTY. A NARROW RIDGE RUNNING NORTH–SOUTH FOR 8 MILES (13KM), THEY ARE FORMED FROM SOME OF THE OLDEST ROCKS IN THE COUNTRY, OVER 500 MILLION YEARS OLD.

MANY LANDSCAPES IN ONE

The hills themselves are of granite, but on the western side are areas of limestone and on the eastern side is Triassic sandstone. These geological variations give the Malverns great diversity. Their surroundings are no less varied. On the Worcestershire (east) side is the flat Severn plain and the Vale of Evesham. To the south is the Cotswold plain of Gloucestershire and the Bristol Channel, to the west are the green fields and hedges of Herefordshire, with the Black Mountains in the far distance, while to the north lies Shropshire and the Wrekin. All this results in astonishing views in every direction from the Malvern summits.

The climb to British Camp is rewarded by this fine view north along the Malvern crests

---

Malvern Hills

Hereford & Worcester
Grid ref. SO 763 404

Approx. 4 miles (6.4 km). Easy, but steep in a few places.

The Malvern Hills are to the west of Great Malvern. Park in the British Camp car park (charge) at Little Malvern, on the A449 Malvern to Ledbury Road.

Highlights of the walk include a wide variety of wildlife habitats. From the summits there are views in all directions.

Added attractions are an Iron Age hill-fort and the Giant's Cave.

Nearby site: *The Knapp and Papermill* – wooded valley, meadows and stream.

WILDLIFE HABITATS

The ancient hilltops are bare, while others have open grassland with harebells, heather and bilberry. Lower areas are covered by bracken. The hills have in the past been quarried for granite, and here gorse, broom and stonecrop grow on the cliffs. In scrub areas there are gorse, bramble, wild rose, elder, hawthorn, willow and ash: home for many insects and small birds. Lower still, the slopes are thickly wooded with ash, birch, cherry, field maple, hazel, holly, oak, rowan and yew – home to woodland birds including robins, wrens, chaffinches and all three British species of woodpecker.

A number of areas of common lie at the foot of the Malverns and these provide yet more interesting habitats. On this walk Castlemorton Common is also visited. This very important area of wet heathland lies just to the east of the hills. The route described here is short, but spend time investigating the flora and fauna. Gorse and hawthorn predominate in dry areas, while in wetter regions there are rushes, sedges, orchids and other plants important for butterflies such as dog violet, birdsfoot trefoil and cinquefoil.

Birdsfoot trefoil – attractive to butterflies

WALK 51

i

THE *Walk*

1 From the car park take the path starting near the Warden's hut up to British Camp. The path rises steeply and it should take 10-15 minutes to reach the top. On a hot day watch out for lizards or slow-worms basking on the stone walls near the start of the walk. As you walk, the Severn plain becomes visible above the trees on the left.

British Camp is an Iron Age hill-fort hacked out of the hill known as the Herefordshire Beacon. Much later, the prehistoric earthworks were incorporated into the defences of a medieval castle.

2 From the summit walk along the ridge. There are several different paths to follow along the earthworks. On the right is the gentle countryside of Herefordshire. Ahead and to the right is an obelisk, Somers Monument, and to the right of that, in the trees, lies Eastnor Castle.

Skylarks and meadow pipits are abundant; look out, too, for wheatears and stonechats in spring. In the winter months watch for ravens and buzzards soaring high in the sky.

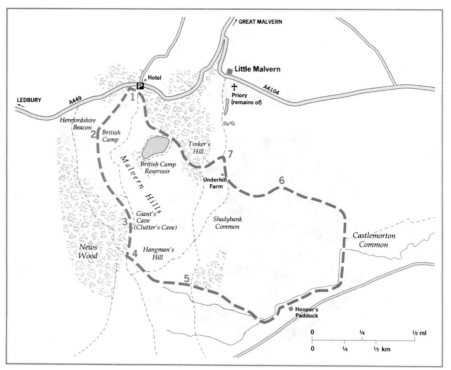

3 The route descends steeply to a circular stone waymarker where six paths converge. Take the one marked 'Giant's Cave'. Also known here as Clutter's Cave, this is a man-made cave of unknown history, although occupying Romans were often known as 'giants' by the British.

Below the path the steep hillside supports mixed vegetation: old and gnarled hawthorn, small oak and ash trees, with hazel, field maple, bramble, gorse and wild roses – an excellent habitat for insects and visiting warblers. A very common butterfly here is the small heath, on the wing from mid May to mid July. Watch out, too, for the grayling butterfly (mid July to mid September), which is conspicuous when feeding on bramble flowers, but is excellently camouflaged when it settles on the granite of the Malverns.

The route becomes gradually more shaded by large oak and ash trees. Throughout the walk, in such areas of dappled sunlight, speckled wood butterflies can be seen from April to October. This butterfly starts flying early – before 8am on warm mornings.

4 As the path drops down slightly, several paths intersect. Take the central, grassy path which leads to the other side of the hill, towards Castlemorton Common. The path narrows as it passes to the left of

a cottage. (The route may be muddy here in wet weather.) The route goes to the right of a double electricity pole, and opens out as it drops down into Castlemorton Common. This large area of wet heathland provides habitat for many wildlife species. Butterflies to be seen here (depending on the time of year) include common blue, gatekeeper, green-veined white, meadow brown, orange-tip, small copper, small skipper, and also the high brown fritillary, dark green fritillary and small pearl-bordered fritillary. Birdlife is abundant. Singing in spring are cuckoos, whitethroats, garden warblers, yellowhammers and, from the midst of dense cover, grasshopper warblers.

5 The route follows the track with trees on the left. After about 600yds (550m) bear left, following the path between the fence and a private house called Hooper's Paddock. The path opens out into a wide, damp area. Again, this is excellent habitat for insects and birdlife, with oak trees near by and bramble, gorse and many other flowers.

With the oak hedge on the left, turn a corner and walk to the end of the hedge. Little Malvern Priory can now be seen with the length of the Malverns behind it. Head across the Common in the direction of the

Priory, but if it has been wet you may need to make a detour along the path to the right.

6 Arriving at the top corner of the Common, the path narrows and is bordered by banks of brambles, and by oak, ash and willow. Listen for great spotted woodpeckers drumming here and for the 'yaffle' of green woodpeckers.

Go through the gate and, joining the main path on the right, walk around the edge of the fields and eventually in front of the black and white Underhill Farm.

7 Continue along the track as it goes uphill. At the large yew tree on the left, cross the stile and follow the path across the field, passing beneath a huge lime tree, and through a metal gate into the wood. On the right-hand side are oak saplings, on the left are mature alder, ash, oak and yew trees.

Follow the path of a small stream. It is always wet here, and ferns thrive in the moist and shady conditions.

Turn right at the T-junction and then go uphill towards the reservoir and the car park. A few mallards are usually present, and in late summer house martins and swallows gather here. Woodland birds are present in the many trees which overhang the path back to the car park.

Pools and streams in the Forest attract insect life, such as dragonflies, and provide drinking places for larger animals

Where conifers are naturally spaced (as are the Douglas firs on this walk) they too support an interesting variety of vegetation and associated bird, insect and mammal life on the ground beneath them. However, man-made forests of closely planted trees do not allow light to penetrate to the forest floor and, because all the trees are of the same age and are felled at the same time, there is no opportunity for the diversity provided by fallen trees. Associated plant, insect, bird and mammal life is therefore sparse.

MAMMALS AND REPTILES

Mammals living in Wyre Forest include badgers, fallow deer, foxes, grey squirrels, rabbits, shrews, voles and weasels. Throughout the Forest are clearings where the sunlight allows grass to flourish, and browsing animals can be seen: voles, rabbits, shrews and fallow deer. Evidence of the activity of these animals is visible all over the Forest: beech-mast gnawed by wood mice, shattered remains of acorns chewed by badgers, pine cones stripped by squirrels. Muddy areas are fine places for identifying the tracks of the many mammal species that inhabit the Forest. Keen-eyed observers may also spot some of Wyre Forest's reptiles: common lizard, slow-worm, grass snake and adder all make their home here.

INSECTS AND BIRDLIFE

The forest roads, rides and abandoned railway lines serve as 'glades' where the shrubs and flowers support an abundance of insect life, with an excellent range of bees, butterflies and moths.

The leaf litter shelters many kinds of creature from spiders to slugs, while dead timber supports insects such as beetles and wasps. The variety of habitats also supports numerous woodland birds, with different species exploiting the habitats at various times of year. In winter the small songbirds tend to congregate into mixed-species flocks, moving through the woods as feeding parties. In spring and summer, migratory species arrive to exploit the abundance of insect life. The visitors include chiffchaffs, pied flycatchers, redstarts, spotted flycatchers, willow warblers and wood warblers. By autumn these birds have departed and made way for species that feed on berries and seeds.

The siskin likes to feed on conifer seeds

WYRE FOREST IS A REMNANT OF THE WOODLAND ONCE PREDOMINANT IN THIS PART OF BRITAIN, WITH OLD OAKS AND OTHER DECIDUOUS TREES, NOW JOINED BY SOME CONIFER PLANTATIONS. ALTHOUGH THE PATHS NEAR THE VISITOR CENTRE ARE WELL TRODDEN, A WALK FURTHER INTO THE FOREST REVEALS MANY TRANQUIL AND DELIGHTFUL WOODLAND AREAS.

WOODLAND HABITATS

In many parts of Wyre Forest oak, beech and coniferous woodland are in close proximity, and it is interesting to compare the different habitats created by these species.

Oak woodland harbours a rich variety of other wildlife: birds, mammals, insects, fungi, ferns and flowering plants. In spring, the oakwood floor is a mass of bluebells, dog's mercury, primroses, wood anemones, wood-sorrel and yellow archangel. After they emerge, the oak leaves provide food for over 300 species of caterpillar and other plant-eating insects, and these insects in turn provide prey for others.

Beech trees cast a very dense shade and for this reason ground vegetation under beech is often sparser than under other deciduous species. In addition, beech leaves are relatively slow to break down, and form a dense carpeting layer beneath the trees.

Wyre Forest

Hereford & Worcester
Grid ref. SO 749 740

Forestry Commission/Nature Conservancy Council
Approx. 4½ miles (7.2 km). Easy walking.

The visitor centre is 2 miles (3.2 km) west of Bewdley on the A456. There is a large car park (charge).

Wyre Forest offers a great variety of habitats including excellent oak and beech woodlands. The woods are managed for timber, wildlife and public recreation, and some areas are designated Sites of Special Scientific Interest. Wildlife is abundant and includes many butterfly species.

Nearby sites: *Bittel reservoirs* – good for wildfowl; *Long Mynd* – extensive heather moorland.

1 Take the track that starts to the right of the visitor centre. Huge, dark green Douglas firs are to both sides of the path, together with larch, birch, oak, Corsican pine, willow and rowan. Such mixtures of tree species throughout Wyre Forest mean that many different birds can find a niche. Summer visitors to watch for are pied flycatchers, conspicuous by their black and white plumage and vigorous insect-catching behaviour, and redstarts, which attract attention by constant flicking of their red-brown tails.

Take the first turning to the left (marked by a red and green post), leading slightly uphill. Here the acidic soils of Wyre support bell heather, bilberry and gorse, and bright green wood spurge is abundant.

2 At the T-junction turn right, signposted 'Forest walks'. After about 20yds (18m) take the minor path to the right, signposted 'No horses'. On the left-hand side are the nests of wood ants, some piled up to 3ft (90cm) high. In early summer these ants can be seen capturing some of the many thousands of caterpillars in the oak trees above them. Armies of ants march up and down the oak trunks, sometimes carrying twigs and leaves for nest construction.

The most common caterpillars found on oak are those of the moth known as the green oak-roller, so called because the larvae curl the oak leaves around themselves as they feed and then pupate. In early June these provide an abundant food source for the young of blue tits and great tits.

In autumn, grey squirrels and jays are busy collecting and burying acorns. It is the jays that have ensured the survival of generations of oaks: acorns buried and forgotten by squirrels will not germinate, because squirrels nibble out the growing tip. Jays bury acorns undamaged, usually well away from the parent tree.

Look in the clay surrounding the bore hole on the left for the footprints of deer and other animals.

Follow the red markers as the path turns left, and then turn right when the track meets the main forest ride. The route passes through an area of managed deciduous woodland: 100-year-old oak and 50-year-old beech.

3 Continue downhill to Park House, a private house on the left. Turn right here on to the disused railway track. A rich flora has developed here: bees, butterflies and moths find habitat to their liking, on plants such as birdsfoot trefoil, bramble, dog violet, dogwood, gorse, heather, hemp agrimony, nettle, rose and willow. Wild columbine also grows here. Butterflies present will vary according to the time of year, but red admiral, small tortoiseshell, small heath, comma, gatekeeper and orange-

Spotted flycatchers breed here from May onwards

tip are all common. Two specialities of Wyre Forest can also be seen here: from mid June to mid July the small pearl-bordered fritillary, an orange-brown butterfly with dark spots; and from mid July to mid August the silver-washed fritillary, a very large and elegant orange-brown butterfly which feeds on bramble flowers.

4 After about 1 mile (1.6 km), at the end of the cutting, turn right (before a bridge). After about 20yds (18m) turn left on to a bridlepath. The route now passes through beautiful woodland: on the left are the oaks of Lord's Yard Coppice, on the right is younger beechwood. Saprophytic plants (those that live on decayed organic matter) are common under beech, and in damp autumns many fungi can be seen. Look for the white parasols of beech tuft, the large brown bracket fungus, shaggy ink cap, and the amazing forms of earth star.

Along the route are clearings in the trees where woodland flowers flourish, and on summer evenings the air is filled with the heady scent from honeysuckle.

5 The route follows the bridlepath as it winds to left and right through the forest, and eventually turns left where two paths cross. A forest pool is to the right of the path, and on sunny summer days dragonflies and damselflies can be seen here.

The route continues uphill and back to the car park. The path passes huge Douglas firs (originally from North America) planted in the 1920s, with seedling trees now becoming established. The final stretch is flanked by other evergreen species: young firs and pines, and yew.

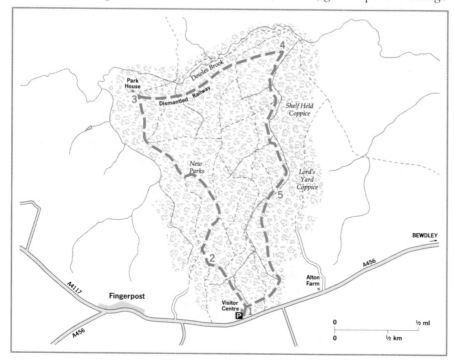

The elegant great crested grebe usually builds its floating nest in a secluded place

STANDING IN THE MIDDLE OF SUTTON PARK, IT IS DIFFICULT TO BELIEVE THAT THE CENTRE OF BIRMINGHAM IS ONLY 7 MILES (11 KM) AWAY, AND THAT THE PARK IS SURROUNDED ON ALL SIDES BY SURBURBAN SPRAWL. YET, IN SPRING, SKYLARKS AND WARBLERS SING AS IF THEY WERE IN THE HEART OF THE COUNTRYSIDE; BUTTERFLIES AND DRAGONFLIES EN-LIVEN THE AIR IN SUMMER; WHILE AUTUMN IS THE TIME TO SEARCH OUT THE VARIOUS FUNGI THAT GROW IN THE PARK'S DARK, DAMP WOODS.

A TRADITION OF CONSERVATION

Sutton Park has a long history, dating back to *Domesday Book*. In the reign of Henry VIII its upkeep was entrusted to a body called 'The Warden and Society' whose care has allowed it to remain a virtually unspoilt area. The park's 2400 acres (970 hectares) continue to provide a rich diversity of habitats. Extensive areas of dry heath, low-lying bog, mature mixed wood-land and several ponds are home to plants and animals of many kinds, although some species such as nightjar and adder have been lost.

WOODLAND WILDLIFE

The woodlands contain a variety of trees – mainly oak, beech, birch and rowan, with planted Scots pine and

Sutton Park

West Midlands
Grid ref. SP 113 962

City of Birmingham District Council Approx. 4¹/₂ miles (7.2 km). Generally easy walking, but muddy in places, especially in winter.

Sutton Park is about 7 miles (11 km) north of central Birmingham, just west of Sutton Coldfield. The main entrance, Town Gate, is signposted from the western section of Sutton Coldfield's one-way system. Go through Town Gate, take the left fork and after about 300 yds (275 m) park near the visitor centre, which is set back to the left of the road.

The most remarkable thing about Sutton Park is its location: seldom is such a large expanse of varied rural habitat found so close to the heart of a major city. Areas of mature woodland, heath, bog and several ponds attract a wide range of birds, and there is a good variety of summer flowers and insects. The park is likely to be crowded on summer weekends, but many paths criss-cross it and there is plenty of scope for exploring, including two nature trails.

Nearby sites: *Chasewater Reservoir* – good range of winter wildfowl, also waders on passage in spring and autumn; *Kingsbury Water Park* – nature trails and hides in extensive area of gravel workings providing excellent aquatic and waterside habitats with highlights including large numbers of winter wildfowl and several species of dragonfly.

Long-tailed tit – a restless little acrobat. Flocks may be seen flitting along woodland edges and hedgerows

larch. In many parts of the park, a dense understorey of large holly bushes greatly reduces the amount of light able to reach the woodland floor, so there is little ground vegetation. Only where a stream runs through the wood, creating a more open, boggy area, can a variety of low-growing plants become established. Birdlife, on the other hand, is more abundant. Nuthatches are common in the woods, and woodpeckers are also likely to be seen and heard. The heathland areas are dotted with birch clumps where willow warblers sing in spring. Winter brings fieldfares, redpolls and other thrushes and finches, to join the roaming flocks of tits.

THE OPEN SPACES

Skylarks, meadow pipits and yellow-hammers are typical birds of Sutton Park's open areas. The dry grassy heathland is interspersed with patches of gorse, flowering almost throughout the year. There is much bracken in places, and other plants of this habitat include heath bedstraw and zig-zag clover. Among the butterflies to be found are small heath, wall brown and small copper.

WETLAND AND WATER

The bogs have extensive areas of cotton-grass, and the insectivorous plants round-leaved sundew, bladder-wort and butterwort are present. Some wetland plants found here, such as cranberry and bog pimpernel, are very localised here in the Midlands. Dragonflies and damselflies hawk back and forth across the marshland, while the ponds harbour smooth, palmate and great crested newts. Among resident wildfowl on the ponds are Canada geese and great crested grebes, joined in winter by teal and wigeon.

The Water Rail

The water rail is a secretive bird which is more often heard than seen. Its loud, pig-like squeal shatters the peace in reed-beds, marshes and wet wood-lands throughout the country. Although water rails breed in Britain, their numbers increase dramatically during the winter months with influxes of migrant birds from the Continent. Water rails have blue-grey and chestnut plumage and a long, red bill. Their long toes enable them to walk with ease among wetland vegetation. They catch insects and small fish, and occasionally feed on carrion in cold weather.

THE *Walk*

Before setting off, it is worth calling in at Sutton Park's visitor centre, if it is open. Inside is a display on the wildlife and history of the park, and informative booklets can be obtained.

1 **From the car park near the visitor centre, continue along the road and, at a three-way fork, take the central path marked 'Pedestrians Banners Gate'.** After passing through an area of birch, gorse and close-cropped grass, the track enters dense woodland, dominated by holly, with little in the way of ground vegetation. Holly blue butterflies occur in late spring and again in later summer, but the wood offers little else of interest.

2 **The path emerges from the wood at a crossroads revealing open heath ahead. Continue straight on, taking care here as the road is used by vehicles. Better still, explore the tracks to the left which cross the heath.** The ground here slopes down into a valley. On sunny days a common lizard might be glimpsed darting among the two types of heather, ling and cross-leaved heath.

3 **Once into the valley bottom, turn right about 100yds (90m) before Longmoor Pool towards an isolated clump of trees, mainly Scots pine, known as Queen's Coppice.** The pool may hold a few ducks or grebes.

The path passes to the left of the coppice. On the left is an extensive low boggy area with a stream flowing through it. Here you may see and hear a snipe 'drumming' overhead. Ragged robin and southern marsh orchids provide a display of colour. Rowton's Well, beside the track, is a natural spring with supposed medicinal properties.

From here, bear right up to the crest of the hill, passing through more dry heathland which is dominated by bracken.

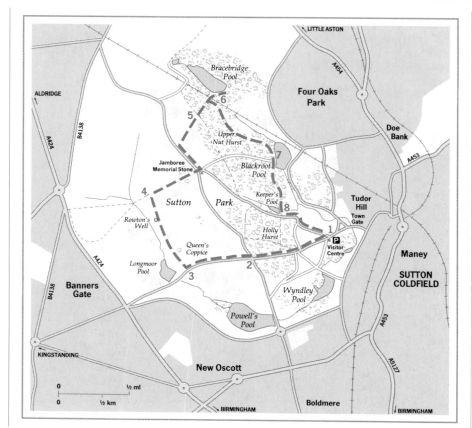

4 **Turn right at the top of the hill on to a gravel track, which** passes through a large patch of gorse and then open birch. **Turn left at the memorial commemorating the 1957 World Jubilee Jamboree of the Scout Movement. Walk down this tarmac road** with open grass on either side **and turn right after about 300yds (275m), just past a car park, down a path flanked by gorse bushes.** (This section contains nothing new of interest, and is quite busy, so you can hurry on through this part of the walk.)

5 **At the edge of a wood, continue straight on through the gate and cross a bridge over a railway, after which turn right.** On the left is Bracebridge Pool. In spring listen for a sedge or reed warbler singing from the poolside vegetation, while at migration time a common sandpiper might be spotted flying low over the water.

At the end of the causeway are a restaurant, a snack bar and toilets, making this a convenient point for a mid-walk break.

Keeper's Pool in autumn. A holly understorey makes the woodland here too dark for flowers

6 **Retrace your path back across the railway (alternatively, walk all the way around the pool) and turn left. Follow the path as it winds through woodland, and where the track forks, take the right-hand option, past a gate.** The large trees are mainly oak and beech with lots of holly, but woodland plants including wood-sorrel and wood anemones manage to find a place. At the point where larch predominates, look out for giant wood wasps (not true wasps, but a type of sawfly). Shortly, on the left, is a boggy patch flanked by sallows, where marsh marigolds grow.

After a while the path bears right by Blackroot Pool.

7 **Where a broad ride merges from the right, bear left. At the outflow of the pool continue straight on.** First stop to look for liverworts beside the stream. Another boggy area on the left has much the same species as the previous one.

8 **The next pond reached is Keeper's Pool. At the end of it turn left on to a main road. Follow this route through more woodland and you will soon be back at the car park.**

WITHIN THE TRIANGLE FORMED BY THE TOWNS OF STAMFORD, CORBY AND KETTERING LIES A HALF-FORGOTTEN SLICE OF OLD ENGLAND. ROCKINGHAM FOREST IS A DENSELY WOODED DISTRICT OF WINDING LANES, SMALL VILLAGES CLUSTERED AROUND THEIR CHURCHES IN THE CROOK OF A STREAM, OF GENTLY ROLLING HILLS AND LARGE COUNTRY HOUSES SET IN PARKLAND.

A HISTORIC FOREST

Rockingham Forest was a favourite place of relaxation for King John and his son, Henry III, when the area was administered by a small army of officials to maintain the woodland deer and their habitat. The name of the medieval forest, though not its system or purpose, lives on, and the boundaries of many of its woods have changed remarkably little since. Although most of the larger woods have been turned into conifer plantations since 1945, many of the smaller ones would still be recognisable to King John's huntsmen. One of the best of these is Short Wood.

CLUES TO THE PAST

Short Wood is mentioned in documents from Elizabethan England, but the wood is very much older than that; indeed most of it may lie on ground that has never been cleared of trees. Landscape features that give clues to

Short Wood

Northamptonshire
Grid ref. TL 024 913

Northamptonshire Wildlife Trust Approx. 4½ miles (7.2 km). Easy walking, but wellington boots are advisable in wet weather.

Short Wood lies 2 miles (3.2 km) north of Oundle between Glapthorn and Southwick. Park in the lay-by on the unclassified road between the two villages, where a signpost marks a bridleway. Keep dogs on leads.

This ancient wood contains old trees, a rich flora, ponds and earthworks.

Nearby sites: *Barnwell Country Park* – small country park near River Nene, with gravel pits which attract terns and dragonflies; *Rutland Water* – huge reservoir and surroundings with various habitats, excellent for winter wildfowl, good also for waders and passage migrants.

the wood's age include a deep, double-banked hollow way, a perimeter woodbank and a curved boundary typical of medieval woods. Some of the coppice stools – ash and maple up to 9ft (2.7m) across and with hollow centres – are several hundred years old, and the flora of Short Wood includes some 30 species that are virtually confined, in this part of England, to old woodland. They include yellow archangel, wood-sorrel, Midland hawthorn, spindle and wild service tree.

WOODLAND BIRDS

Its rich and varied plant life helps make Short Wood attractive to birds, and up to 300 songbirds are thought to nest here each year. Summer visitors include blackcaps and garden warblers; listen for their lovely, melodious songs, and for the familiar drumming sound made by great spotted woodpeckers.

The scrub habitat of Glapthorn Cow Pasture, further along the walk, is just as appealing to woodland birds. The most famous of songsters, the nightingale, breeds here regularly, and warblers include lesser and common whitethroats. Towards evening, listen too for the peculiar whistling song of a woodcock. Patient watchers may catch a glimpse of one of these well-camouflaged birds as it forages for grubs and insects in the leaf litter.

Top: *Great spotted woodpecker – resident here*
Below: *Old coppice being rejuvenated*

THE *Walk*

1 From the lay-by, walk along the bridleway to Short Wood. This section of the bridleway is a good vantage point from which to appreciate the layout of the land. The bridleway runs along a parish boundary which, typically, occupies the highest land and that furthest from the villages and therefore most likely to be woodland. What are now public footpaths were often wood lanes in the past, used by commoners to collect firewood and timber, to out-pasture cattle and pigs and, probably, to poach the king's deer.

2 Enter Short Wood over the stile at its south-eastern corner. This is a fine example of ancient woodland many hundreds of years old and consisting wholly of native trees.

3 Follow the path clockwise around the wood. If necessary you can cut corners by following one of the rides crossing the wood. These are signposted and have modern names: Keeper's Ride, Primrose Ride, Jackson's Ride. The main trees are oak, ash, maple and hazel. Notice that while most of the oaks are single-stemmed 'maiden' trees, virtually all the others, apart from saplings, are coppiced, with multiple stems rising from a common base or stool – the result of centuries of regular cutting. In its prime, Short Wood was managed as coppice-with-standards. The coppice, cut by rotation every dozen or so years, provided the small-bore wood for fencing, tool-making and firewood, while the standard oaks were felled at about 70 years old for timber. Regular cutting encourages flushes of spring wild flowers: Short Wood boasts the most spectacular carpet of bluebells in Northamptonshire.

4 At the south-western border of the wood is a fine hollow way with a deepened interior and banks on either side. Its original purpose is unknown, but it may well have been a trench to drag cut timber and logs from the wood – a difficult job in wet, sticky clay woods like this. Some of the biggest trees in the wood grow along the sides and bottom of the hollow, suggesting that it had fallen into disuse by about 200 years ago.

5 On the northern bank of the wood are several large pollards, trees cut at about 10ft (3m) high, which were useful as clear boundary markers. Cutting trees, either as pollards or as coppice, prolongs their life. Some of these pollards have been re-cut recently by the Trust. Some are hollow; their secret internal world of damp and decay is a vital breeding ground for many rare insects. Look out for the wood's solitary large wild service tree along this bank. When in flower in May, or again in autumn after its jagged leaves have turned a rich shade of red, it is a beautiful sight. Notable, too, are some huge maples, spreading like umbrellas in a vivid display of natural fan-vaulting. This is a wonderful place for the connoisseur of fine wild trees.

6 The eastern bank of the wood has a pond, recently cleaned out by conservation volunteers. Today woods are important refuges for pond life (so long as they are not over-shaded). Some woodland ponds seem to be natural, forming in deep, clay-bottomed dells. This one is probably artificial but old, a former drinking place for cattle. Look for damselflies and other flying insects in the summer.

7 Follow the bridleway further west, and in ³/₄ mile (1.2 km), turn left, passing downhill along the side of Glapthorn Cow Pasture. Follow the path along the pasture's eastern edge. The interior can be explored by means of the network of rides laid out by the Trust. This is another nature reserve belonging to the Northamptonshire Wildlife Trust, and is a good example of a common left to run wild. The northern and eastern parts are, like Short Wood, ancient woodland dominated by ash and maple. The rest used to be open cow pasture, as its name and the numerous open-grown oak trees imply. Scrub has spread over this area since 1914, and now it is well on its way to turning into a wood.

In late June look out for the speciality of the reserve, the black hairstreak butterfly, feeding on bramble and privet flowers along the sunny rides and glades. One of our rarest butterflies, this is virtually confined to the clay woods of Northamptonshire, Buckinghamshire and Oxfordshire, where its food-plant, blackthorn, grows in great abundance. It often prefers to walk rather than fly, and is active only at certain times of the day.

Return along the bridleway to the starting point.

The rare black hairstreak butterfly

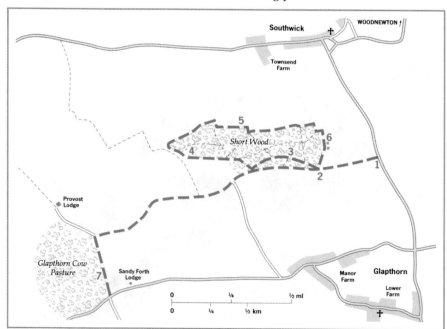

The combination of deciduous trees and water makes the Sherbrook Valley a good place for winter birdwatching. Deer may also be seen

THE HISTORY OF CANNOCK CHASE GOES BACK TO WILLIAM THE CONQUEROR, WHO USED THE AREA AS A HUNTING PRESERVE. THE PRESENT CHASE IS MUCH SMALLER THAN THIS ORIGINAL FOREST, BUT IT IS STILL AN IMPORTANT AREA FOR WILDLIFE AND RECREATION. IT IS A DESIGNATED AREA OF OUTSTANDING NATURAL BEAUTY – THE SMALLEST SUCH AREA ON THE BRITISH MAINLAND.

WOODLAND, HEATH AND BOG

Much of the Chase would once have been covered by native deciduous forest. Only small fragments of this remain, such as in Brocton Coppice. The presence in this coppice of certain species of beetle that are specifically associated with old oak woodland suggests that such trees have stood here for a very long time. With the felling of the forest, open heathland was created on the hillsides and then maintained by grazing. Reduction in grazing means that birch woodland has been able to invade in places, though of much greater significance is the large-scale commercial planting of pine. The other important habitat of the Chase occurs in the valley bottoms, where bogs are found alongside the streams.

SPECIALITIES OF THE CHASE

Cannock Chase holds the distinction of having a plant named after it: bilberry and cowberry both grow here, and hybridise to produce an intermediate form – the Cannock Chase berry – which is known from only two other

Cannock Chase

Staffordshire
Grid ref. SJ 980 190

Staffordshire County Council/ Forestry Commission
Approx. 4½ miles (7.2 km). A moderately hilly walk over some rough tracks.

Cannock Chase is about 5 miles (8 km) south-east of Stafford. The walk begins at Coppice Hill car park, close to the disued quarry 1 mile (1.6 km) south-east of Brocton off Chase Road.

Much of Cannock Chase is now covered by coniferous plantations, but a considerable amount of heathland still remains, along with much open birch woodland and remnants of the ancient oak forest that once stood here. The varied habitats hold a good variety of plants with their associated fauna, including deer.

Nearby sites: *Blithfield Reservoir* – large freshwater lake, good for water birds, especially in autumn and winter; *Tillington-Doxey Marshes* – riverside habitats.

Self-heal

counties and is nowhere as common as here. An important bird species here is the nightjar, whose Midlands stronghold is on the heathland of the Chase. To see these crepuscular birds, or hear their churring call, a visit at dusk is necessary. While waiting for them to start performing you may be lucky enough to see the peculiar display flight, or 'roding', of woodcock overhead.

The Chase is also well known for its deer population. Fallow deer are by far the commonest, but roe, red, sika and the diminutive muntjac are also present. By visiting in the early morning or late evening, it is possible, with stealth, to observe these timid animals as they emerge from the woods into a clearing or visit a stream to drink. A few red squirrels remain in the Chase, favouring coniferous areas.

Young adder – a much-feared yet timid reptile

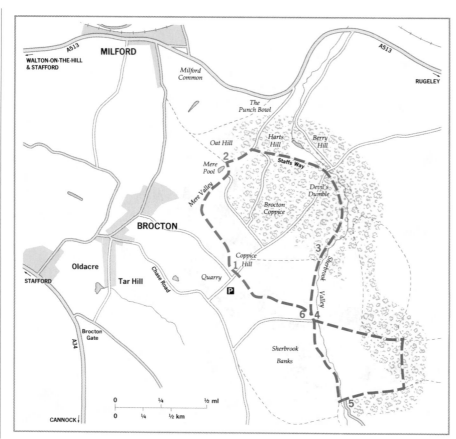

1 Just past the end of the disused quarry, take the track to the north signposted to Mere Pool (not the track immediately beside the quarry fence). The path descends and eventually bends to the right (at which point a gap in the trees gives good views to the left) and then slightly left. After a while reach Mere Pool, flanked by bulrushes in a hollow on the left. The dominant types of plant life of the Chase are quickly apparent on this first section of the walk: bracken carpets the ground, birch trees abound, while heather, gorse and bilberry grow in smaller patches.

2 Just past the pool, turn sharp right downhill (signposted to Punchbowl). After 300yds (275m), turn right on to the Staffs Way. Follow this path all the way round as it bears gently right for almost a mile (1.5km). The wooded hill on the right is Brocton Coppice, where the predominant birches are interspersed with gnarled and twisted oaks, some of which are 200 years old. In summer, the resident woodpeckers and nut-hatches are joined by migrant wood warblers and redstarts. Bracken again dominates the ground cover, but common cow-wheat can also be found.

Eventually a stream appears on the left, alongside which grow alders. These trees are favoured by siskins and redpolls in winter. Grey wagtails frequent the stream, while in summer hawker dragonflies patrol up and down.

3 Keep following the same path, with the stream on the left. The birchwood thins out and eventually gives way to open heath on the right, with a boggy area flanking the stream. This is Sherbrook Valley. The damp ground beside the stream has a rich plant life: among the purple moor-grass grow marsh cinquefoil, marsh bedstraw, marsh orchids, bog-bean, cross-leaved heath and other species. On the open heath, yellow-hammers, linnets, skylarks and meadow pipits are common, both stonechats and whinchats occur, and tree pipits can be found in the transitional zone between wood and heath.

4 At the point where the Staffs Way turns sharply right, turn left across the stream, through dense alder woodland dotted with small boggy pools. (Those wanting a shorter walk can turn right uphill just before the sign.) The track emerges from the trees, passes uphill across heathland and enters a coniferous plantation. At the end of the mature pines turn right and later right again, taking the track downhill with open heath on the right and pines to the left. Bell heather and cowberry (with bright red berries, as opposed to the dark purple ones of bilberry) grow among the bracken on the heath. There is little of interest in the pines, although the typical goldcrests and coal tits, which both seem to have a preference for coniferous trees, may occasionally be joined by crossbills; a rare two-barred crossbill from Siberia was seen at Cannock Chase a few years ago.

5 At the bottom of the hill, the path bears left. Towards the end of this bend, take the narrow path to the right which crosses the stream. Turn right on to a main track, with bracken-covered hillside on the left and flat bog on the opposite side. When the path veers sharp left, take the minor track to the right, which soon rejoins another main path. Look out for greater tussock sedge which, as its name suggests, grows in large clumps by the stream. In addition to the typical heathland butterflies, such as small heath, day-flying moths can be conspicuous. These include the oak eggar and the attractive emperor, though you may get only a glimpse as they dash past at high speed. The emperor – the only British moth with 'eye' markings on all four wings – flies in April and May, while the oak eggar is unlikely to be seen before July.

6 When you reach the Staffs Way, continue straight on up a valley (not along the Staffs Way). At the top of the hill, bear right through hawthorn scrub back to the car park. In this area the bracken gives way to masses of heather. On sunny days the 'songs' of field and mottled grass-hoppers are a frequent sound, and adders may be seen sunning them-selves among the heather, though these shy reptiles usually melt away at the first signs of approach. If you are lucky, a winter visit might be rewarded with a sighting of a great grey shrike. Though only the size of a blackbird, this striking winter visitor catches voles and small birds, sometimes impaling its prey on barbed wire or a thorn before eating it.

A special tree-top hide gives close-up views of woodpeckers, nuthatches and goldcrests

A VISIT TO COOMBES VALLEY IS RATHER LIKE STEPPING BACK IN TIME. SOMEHOW THE PATCHWORK OF TINY FIELDS, COPSES, BRACKEN-COVERED SLOPES AND HEDGEROWS – COMMON OVER A MUCH WIDER AREA UP TO THE MIDDLE OF THE 20TH CENTURY – HAS SURVIVED HERE, WHILE THE COUNTRYSIDE AROUND HAS SUCCUMBED TO THE PRESSURES OF MODERN FARMING AND THE ADVANCING URBAN SPRAWL FROM THE MIDLANDS.

TREES, SHRUBS AND WILD FLOWERS

The woodland on the reserve is pre-dominantly oak, but a good mixture of other native species such as holly, rowan, ash, birch and wych elm also grows, providing a valuable crop of seeds and berries for birds and small mammals. The shrub layer beneath the oaks consists of thickets of hazel, guelder rose, blackthorn and bird cherry and here and there, where the canopy is open enough to admit plenty of light, there are patches of gorse, wild rose and bramble. This great variety of trees and shrubs provides ample food for birds in the form of seeds, berries and insects, and there is an abundance of safe, natural nesting sites.

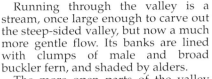

The Pied Flycatcher

Pied flycatchers are summer visitors to this country. Males have striking black and white plumage (females are brown and white), and the birds feed by catching flies and other insects. When alarmed, pied flycatchers flick their tails and utter a short 'whit' call.

The pied flycatcher usually nests in holes in trees, laying between five and eight eggs. The population of breeding birds in any given place is limited by the availability of nesting sites. In some areas nest boxes have been introduced most successfully.

Coombes Valley

Staffordshire

Grid ref. SK 009 534

Royal Society for the Protection of Birds

Approx. 1¾ miles (2.8 km). Mostly easy walking on gravelly paths, but some moderately steep ascents.

Set in the Staffordshire Moorlands, just south of the Peak District, Coombes Valley lies about 3 miles (4.8 km) south of Leek. There is a car park at the reserve entrance, on the minor road between Basford Green and the A523.

This deep wooded valley became a nature reserve in 1962 and has been sympathetically managed for wild-life since then in order to preserve its rich mixture of woodland, meadows and streamside habitats. It offers pleasant walking at any time of year, with ample opportunities to watch woodland birds and other wildlife.

Nearby sites: *The Staffordshire Moorlands Walk* – a network of way-marked footpaths crossing some of the unspoilt countryside around Leek; *Deep Hayes Country Park* – interesting flora and good bird-watching.

Willow tit

Running through the valley is a stream, once large enough to carve out the steep-sided valley, but now a much more gentle flow. Its banks are lined with clumps of male and broad buckler fern, and shaded by alders.

The more open parts of the valley are maintained as flower-rich meadows – a colourful reminder of what many meadows would have looked like before farmers began to use herbicides. Marsh marigolds flourish in wetter places near the stream while primroses, self-heal, betony, tormentil and birdsfoot trefoil grow on drier ground. Several species of orchid are found on the reserve, one of the most attractive being the greater butterfly orchid, but early purple and common spotted orchids also flower profusely in some years. Some parts of the reserve have more acid soils and have developed a heathland-type flora with bell heather, ling, cross-leaved heath, bilberry and purple moor-grass.

ANIMAL LIFE

The variety of habitats and plants encourages a rich and varied population of other creatures to live on the reserve. The valley's woodlands are noted for their abundance of beetles; over 1200 species have been identified so far, some of them extremely rare outside the reserve. Some 500 species of moth and 24 species of butterfly have been found; one of these – the high brown fritillary – has no other breeding site within 50 miles (80km) of here. Small mammals are abundant, and badgers and foxes also live on the reserve. The pond has been colonised by frogs, toads, smooth and great crested newts, and adders, grass snakes and common lizards are resident.

BIRDWATCHING

Coombes Valley is known mostly for its birdlife, and a good variety of woodland and river birds can be seen from the paths and observation hides. The chance to watch birds like dippers, kingfishers and grey wagtails from a hide is an attraction to many visitors, and there are also opportunities to look at tree-top species such as redstart, pied flycatcher, nuthatch, treecreeper and goldcrest from a hide built high up in a large oak. Many other woodland birds occur, and tawny and long-eared owls, sparrow-hawks, woodcocks, wood warblers and three species of woodpecker all breed in the valley. There is something of interest at any time of the year, and several visits will be necessary in order to appreciate the riches of this small but valuable area of countryside.

THE *W*ALK

1 From the car park by the information centre, follow the track down the hill between tiny fields. Before the valley became a reserve, some of these fields were farmed and treated with fertiliser, so they have less value for wildlife. They are gradually developing a natural flora as more sympathetic management takes place. The thick hedges contain useful berry- and seed-bearing shrubs like hawthorn and holly, which attract thrushes in winter.

2 At the Coombes Brook, cross the footbridge and turn left to follow the path up the slope to the tree hide. Check the stream for dippers and grey wagtails, and look for signs of foxes and badgers in muddy spots. The clear water is usually of good quality and rich in insect and invertebrate life, but it is susceptible to occasional contamination by agricultural chemicals from surrounding farms.

3 From the hide follow the path through Six Oaks Wood, keeping to the made-up track all the way. This is an excellent area to wander through slowly, looking for woodland birds; the old oaks and other trees provide insects and seeds, and a variety of species will be seen here. In summer, look for pied flycatchers

using the nesting boxes and redstarts, nuthatches and woodpeckers feeding in the mature trees. Dead timber is left to rot away naturally as it is of great value to wildlife. Many species of beetle spend part of their life-cycle in rotting wood, and are food for woodpeckers. The ground flora is impressive in spring, but by late summer the canopy will be too dense in places to allow many plants to flower beneath it.

4 At Cloughmeadow Cottage, follow the path to the left into the woodland and join the public footpath. Turn right on to the path and then right again before the bridge to reach the hide. A great variety of birds can be seen here, and it is worth spending some time sitting quietly. Dippers feed along the river, and kingfishers and grey wagtails visit the river and the pond. Moorhens nest beside the pond and frogs, toads and newts are all present in spring.

5 From the hide rejoin the path and turn right over the bridge, following the public footpath up the hill to Little Barn. Before leaving the stream, check the birches and alders

Badgers are unlikely to be seen before dusk, but daytime visitors may spot tracks, clawmarks and other signs of their activities

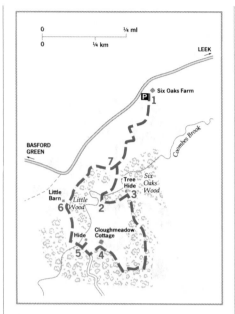

for feeding flocks of siskins and redpolls in winter. In autumn the woods are filled with a great variety of fungi, some living on rotten wood and dying trees, while others grow in the rich leaf-mould on the woodland floor. The most conspicuous is the red-and-white spotted fly agaric, but the yellow-orange sulphur tuft, growing in clumps out of stumps, is also easy to find.

6 Turn right in front of Little Barn, leaving the public footpath, and follow the path above Little Wood in the direction of the car park. In spring, sparrowhawks may be seen displaying over the woods, circling on outstretched wings. Normally they remain concealed, watching for a suitable victim and then dashing after it at the very last minute. At dusk in winter, flocks of birds arrive to roost in the woods, and these may be seen flying in from the surrounding farmland. Greenfinches, chaffinches, rooks, jackdaws and woodpigeons all use the wood, and in hard weather there may be flocks of redwings and fieldfares as well.

7 The path joins the outward route and returns up the slope to the car park. Some of the small fields are being planted with native tree species such as oak and alder in order to increase the woodland cover on the reserve and provide more food and shelter for the birds. These species have been chosen because they are thought to represent the valley's original tree cover.

FLANKED BY ANCIENT ASHWOODS AND FLOWER-STUDDED GRASSLAND, THE RIVER DOVE HAS CARVED FOR ITSELF A BEAUTIFUL LIMESTONE GORGE. IT IS HARDLY SURPRISING THAT DOVEDALE HAS BECOME ONE OF BRITAIN'S CLASSIC BEAUTY SPOTS, BUT MOST VISITORS DO NOT WALK FAR ALONG THE DALE OR STOP TO APPRECIATE ITS SPECIAL WILDLIFE.

A LIMESTONE LANDSCAPE

The limestone country of the White Peak is noted for its disappearing streams; the porous rock with its many faults allows water to disappear below ground and re-emerge many miles away. As it flows underground, the river continues to carve channels and caves. Occasionally the roof of a cave falls in, leaving a short section open to the sky; several such roof-falls along a stream eventually join to form a long gorge such as this one.

Some types of limestone are harder than others and remain as isolated pillars or hilltops when the surrounding softer rocks have been removed. The Twelve Apostles and Lover's Leap are examples of this, but even they are gradually being worn away. Rain works its way into crevices, enlarging them as it gradually dissolves the limestone. If it freezes, the ice expands, cracking the rock; fragments fall off to pile on the slopes below as a loose scree. Rock arches and pinnacles, and deep caves inhabited by bats, all add to the beauty and interest of the landscape.

DOVEDALE'S ASHWOODS

The tree-lined slopes of Dovedale are an indication of what much of the White Peak area would have been like before large-scale tree clearance took place. The slopes support an ash

---

Dovedale

Derbyshire/Staffordshire
Grid ref. SK 147 509

National Trust
Approx. 6 miles (9.6 km). Some steep climbs and some muddy sections, but mostly easy walking on way-marked paths with good surface.

Dovedale lies to the north-west of Ashbourne. The walk begins at a well-signposted car park north-east of the Izaak Walton Hotel, off minor roads 1 mile (1.6 km) east of Ilam. Dogs must be kept on leads.

Dovedale is a classic limestone gorge with outstanding scenery, mixed ash woodlands, herb-rich grassland and a crystal-clear river.

Nearby sites: *Ilam Country Park* and the *Manifold Valley* – walks in limestone country, with plenty of waymarked paths; *Wolfscote Dale* and *Biggin Dale* – also worth exploring and may be quieter than Dovedale.

Skylark – heard in open country all over Britain

Favouring limestone soils, the stately meadow cranesbill flowers in high summer

---

woodland which is thought to be a survivor of the original native forest. Hurt's Wood is a particularly fine example. Wych elm, hazel and hawthorn grow with the ash, and whitebeam, rock whitebeam, rowan and mountain currant also occur. The light shade cast by the ash foliage has allowed a rich ground flora to develop. Dog's mercury forms thick carpets, and wood anemones, ramsons, wood forget-me-not and moschatel are abundant. Not as common, but adding to the general richness of the flora, are species like wood goldilocks, meadow cranesbill, wood-sorrel, sanicle, yellow archangel, toothwort, giant bellflower and golden-rod. Ash regeneration from seed is commonplace, allowing self-perpetuation of the woodland to take place. In certain places, this is aided by fencing to keep grazing animals out.

GRASSLAND, ROCKS AND SCREES

Where the natural woodland cover has been removed an attractive limestone grassland has developed, rich in wild flowers and butterflies. Grazing helps prevent scrub encroaching and maintains the variety in the flora. The rare green spleenwort, normally associated with mountains, is one of the more unusual ferns of Dovedale but many other species grow here, including rusty-backed fern, once endangered by collectors, and brittle bladder fern. Wall rue and maidenhair spleenwort are much more common rock-dwelling ferns found on walls and cliffs. Herb Robert is a typical plant of screes, sometimes turning a rich red colour in the autumn, while bright yellow hawkweeds flower in summer on inaccessible ledges.

RIVER LIFE

The clear waters of the River Dove were made famous by the 17th-century angler and writer Izaak Walton, who fished here for grayling and brown trout. Both species can still be seen rising to flies in summer or lying head-on to the current waiting for food. Gently waving tassels of water crowfoot grow in the river, bursting into bloom in the spring. Procumbent marshwort grows completely submerged in the shallows. Caddis flies, stoneflies and mayflies abound, providing food for the trout and the typical birds of clear streams, dippers and grey wagtails. Kingfishers also live on the river, catching bullheads and minnows. The curious lamprey, with its sucker-like mouth, can be seen spawning in gravelly shallows in spring.

THE WALK

Although popular, Dovedale is a peaceful place for those who time their visit carefully

1 From the car park cross the lane and take the path across the fields behind the Izaak Walton Hotel. Go through the gap-stile, bear diagonally right after the next one and continue over two more stiles to reach the open hillside. The path then goes left over the shoulder of the hill. The fields are less rich in limestone flora and butterflies than the open hillside, but can still be colourful with meadow flowers in spring. Swallows, martins and swifts feed overhead in summer.

2 Follow the contouring path, past a rocky section, across the flanks of Bunster Hill. As the ground becomes less steep, cross the next stile and follow the path to the right of the Moor Plantation and over the wall by the stone steps. Head across the field to the trees at the far end of the plantation and turn left through a squeeze-stile into the lane. Skylarks, meadow pipits and lapwings are typical birds of these hills in spring, with perhaps a passing wheatear or pied wagtail perched on a wall. A weasel is sometimes seen weaving its way in and out of the crevices in a wall, hunting mice.

3 Follow the lane northwards for about ¾ mile (1.2km), then turn right on to a walled track, following it past a building and then left at the end by a wall. Rooks and jackdaws feed in the fields, the jackdaws nesting on the crags of the nearby dale. Woodpigeons and stock doves fly over from the valley woods to feed in large flocks. Mistle thrushes often nest in isolated trees here and also feed out in the open fields.

4 Follow the ridgetop path northwards for about ⅓ mile (500m), then turn right at the head of Hall Dale and follow the path down Hall Dale for about ¾ mile (1.2km) to join the riverside path. Hurt's Wood, on the south side of the valley, is a superb natural woodland and full of birdsong in spring. Willow warblers and chaffinches are both very common, but blackcaps and garden warblers, with their confusingly similar songs, are also present in shrubby areas. Spotted and pied flycatchers, redstarts and wood warblers may all be found here, but never in large numbers.

5 Cross the footbridge by Ilam Rock and turn left again along the path to make a detour to look at Dove Holes. One of the Peak District's more popular visitor attractions, Dove Holes are the remains of an enormous cave system.

Return to the riverside path by the bridge and follow it downstream through Dovedale. Look for stones in the river with white droppings on them; these are perches used by dippers. Pied and grey wagtails feed on insects by the waterside and kingfishers may also be seen. Wet flushes and patches of meadow by the river are filled with wild flowers and insects in summer. The cliffs are home to jackdaws, and sometimes small colonies of swifts and house martins nest high up on limestone crags. The surrounding woodlands have a fascinating ground flora.

6 Cross the river by the stepping-stones, then turn left to reach the car park along the lane. If the stepping stones are difficult to cross, the path continuing along the left bank arrives at a footbridge just before the car park. The hawthorn and blackthorn scrub has breeding warblers, tree pipits and linnets in summer, and for a time in autumn hungry flocks of redwings and fieldfares feed on the berries before dispersing to lower altitudes. Resident kestrels can be seen hovering here. In winter months, look out for siskins feeding on alder trees.

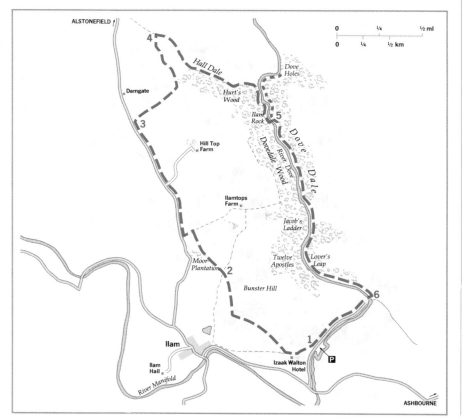

Lathkill Dale

*Limestone grassland, crags and scree – three classic habitats of the White Peak dales,
each with its own very special plant life*

THE CLEARANCE OF BROADLEAF WOODLAND MAY CAUSE AN OUTCRY TODAY, BUT 4000 YEARS AGO THERE WAS LITTLE ALTERNATIVE: NEOLITHIC FARMERS EITHER CUT DOWN THE TREES OR STARVED. SEVERAL NEW HABITATS WERE CREATED WHEN PRIMEVAL FOREST LOST ITS HOLD ON THE LAND, BUT THE MOST ENDURING CHANGE WAS THE DEVELOPMENT OF GRASSLAND FOR SHEEP GRAZING.

DARK PEAK AND WHITE PEAK

Much of north Derbyshire is dominated by Millstone Grit – a hard, rough sandstone, acidic and infertile, laid down as sediment from the great Palaeozoic delta which stretched over northern England. Amid this 'Dark Peak' lies a plateau of mountain limestone, a fragment of the sea deposits that the gritstone covered, stretching from Thorpe to Castleton. The contrast is immediately apparent: the drystone walls turn from dark sienna to dove grey and the fields lose their sullen look and become studded with flowers.

The White Peak, as this area is called, contains a number of classic dales – often dry or containing diminutive rivers – tucked away in the tableland. Dovedale is probably the most famous, but Lathkill, to its north-east and closer to the heart of the county, is less visited and is richer in both atmosphere and limestone wildlife. Its size is not apparent from any of the approach roads; the countryside seems cobwebbed by drystone walls enclosing rough pasture and hay meadows, with few trees or grassy banks. This makes the discovery of the Lathkill gorge a far more dramatic affair, and the walk from Monyash uncovers an impressive variety of habitats in what, at first, appeared to be an agricultural landscape.

CRAG, SCREE AND GRASSLAND

Individually, the most exciting habitat is probably the crag and scree, high on the shoulders of the dale and covered with unusual flowers. Below this, where the scree has consolidated, north- and south-facing grassland provide contrasting conditions – dry and base-rich at one extreme and wet and acidic at the other. Sheep grazing is not so widespread now, and there is a danger that much of the herb-rich grassland will gradually disappear. Rabbits coped with the encroaching thorn for a while, but myxomatosis dealt a heavy blow. Despite this, the area retains the essence of its history; thorn scrub gives way to ash wood-

Male robins sing nearly all year

Lathkill Dale

Derbyshire
Grid ref. SK 157 665

Nature Conservancy Council
Approx. 7½ miles (11.8 km). Easy walking.

The dale lies between Monyash and Over Haddon, south-west of Bakewell in the Peak National Park. Park the car in the lay-by on the B5055, ½ mile (800m) east of Monyash village.

Lathkill Dale is managed as part of the Derbyshire Dales National Nature Reserve. The main habitats are ash woodland and limestone grassland, with rocky outcrops, scree and riverside to vary the scene. The walk also includes some attractive farming country on the White Peak plateau.

Nearby sites: Other dales to visit include *Cressbrookdale*, *Monk's Dale* and *Miller's Dale*. The first two have particularly good ashwoods; the others are grassland sites. Other interesting habitats in the area include the heather moorland at *Big Moor* and *Beeley* (near Chatsworth), and the sessile oakwoods at *Grindleford*.

---

land, which looks as if it has stood here for thousands of years.

WOODLAND LOST AND REGAINED

In fact the story of the Dale is very complex. Neolithic settlers cleared the original woodland completely, but the picture altered over the centuries. There was a period of scrub or heath regeneration in the late Bronze Age followed by the establishment of oak/ash/lime woodland in Roman and Saxon times. However, sheep husbandry returned after the Norman Conquest and has survived here ever since.

The interaction between woodland and grassland, created by the pastoralists, was temporarily marred by lead

---

mining at the turn of the 19th century, when the dale was almost completely cleared. Thus none of the trees here are more than 200 years old, though the ash communities are of great beauty and significance. However, the singularity of the place is not to be found just in its origins but in the intricate combination of plants and animals from the north and south. The walk shows how attractive a man-made habitat can become.

Thin, dry soils on the slopes of the dale support short turf and grassland flowers, in contrast to the taller, lush growth in the damper valley bottom

The Ash Tree

The leaves of ash burst from sooty-black buds very late in the spring, and are the first to fall in the autumn. In woodland habitats this short growing season, and the open canopy, allow spring flowers such as primroses to thrive.

Ash wood is dense and can be steamed and bent into curves and angles; traditionally it was used for tool-handles and hoops, and trees were pollarded or coppiced so that they would grow a plentiful crop of straight stems for this purpose.

The great height and beauty of mature ash trees have given them a special place in country lore.

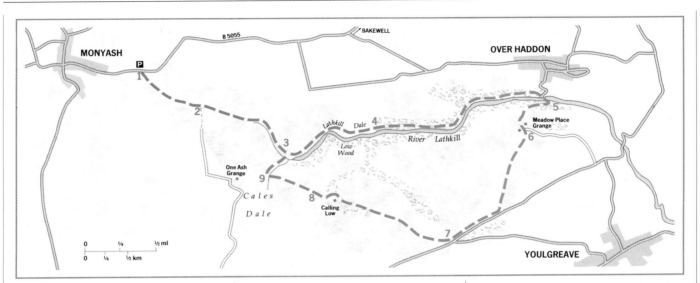

1 Across the road from the parking place, at the start of the walk, stands a group of signs and waymarks. From the stile there is little to suggest the way ahead leads anywhere unusual: the shallow dry valley could be one of a hundred in the area, terraced on the right by a shallow face of limestone and rising gently to an upland meadow on the left. Ash trees by the roadside are the first of many, the descendants of those that invaded the area in Mesolithic times.

Cross the field, keeping the rock terrace to your right. Early purple orchids grow on the northern slope, and rue-leaved saxifrage on the limestone terrace. The most obvious flowers later in the summer are meadow buttercup and spear thistle.

2 After crossing two stiles between meadows the valley becomes a gorge. To the south (right) a path leads obliquely up to One Ash Grange while the main route follows the dale. The sides of the dale become steeper now, lightly wooded to the south (with families of redstarts usually in evidence in summer), grassy to the north, and strewn with limestone boulders. These boulders increase in size as Ricklow Dale is approached, and the debris from the old quarry has been colonised by a variety of herbs such as water avens and herb Robert. The bare patches of scree are edged with a tide-line of red: the leaves of shining cranesbill.

The path leads between two small trees rooted among the boulders. One is a sycamore, the other a purging buckthorn. One of our most attractive butterflies, the brimstone, lays its eggs on this food-plant. The butterfly emerges in August and hibernates through to the following spring. Thus it survives in the adult stage for 10 or 11 months and is the longest-lived species in Britain.

A stile crosses the path, marking the entrance to the Derbyshire Dales National Nature Reserve. The scrubby woodland abruptly ends. The soil is deeper here than on the surrounding slopes and retains more moisture, supporting one of Lathkill's most important plants – Jacob's ladder, an impressive species about 3ft (90cm) tall, with a thin fretwork of leaves and a fine head of blue flowers. It is restricted to shady limestone valleys and has decreased throughout the country, making Lathkill Dale one of its few strongholds. Pink-tailed bumble bees (*Bombus pratorum*) visit the flowers, and so do *Volucella* hover-flies, which mimic the bees so well that it is difficult to tell which is which.

On through a scattered stone wall the herbage gives way to hawthorn scrub and the River Lathkill makes its appearance as a narrow trickle (often obscured by vegetation) from a cave to the right. To the north stands a wide amphitheatre of limestone with crags at each side, pebbledashed with rock-rose and thyme and ringing with jackdaws. This is a good place to stop and look at how the shelf and scree have been colonised by short, tufted plants. The grassland on which you walk is silver-green; the soil is thin and the water runs through quickly, taking away any humus with it.

3 The route continues down the main dale. Passing a foot-bridge, with Cales Dale opening to the south, the path winds north-east, snaking its way along the Lathkill. As the river broadens it develops a rich semi-aquatic flora; water parsnip is the

Lathkill Dale's fine ashwoods are not as old as they appear, for the dale was cleared of its trees by 18th-century lead miners

most obvious to the eye, but it is the smell of water mint that is most memorable. A large leaf beetle creates holes in its leaves; look for an iridescent green jewel plodding slowly among the foliage.

Another interesting habitat is the south-facing limestone grassland of the open slope below the crags and scree on the north side of the river. Steep and heavy with summer flowers, it is best approached at eye level. Rock-rose, kidney vetch and quaking-grass are a few of the common components. On a sunny day, butterflies on the wing here might include the northern brown argus, the common blue and the small heath.

The most interesting section of the dale lies ahead. The woodland on the far bank, which started as hawthorn, is now dominated by ash with occasional wych elm and bird cherry, and with a scrub layer of hazel. When the whole dale was cleared by the London Lead Company at the end of the 18th century it is possible that only a few patches of scrub remained, from which the present ashwoods evolved. Ash seeds germinate slowly – often not at all – but every few years drifts of saplings become established, covering bare slopes with green mists of foliage. The short leaf season and open canopy of the ash encourage insect-eating birds. Along this section in spring and summer, spotted flycatchers and redstarts are as numerous as robins.

Seen from the pathway, the river resembles a chalk-pond, deeper and slow-running because of a hidden weir downstream. Mallards and moorhens nest among the pondweed and crowfoot, and water voles are usually in evidence, paddling to and fro or sitting to nibble willow leaves.

4 Along the path a walled stile leads into Palmerston Wood. Ash is again the dominant tree here, but with wych elm and the invasive sycamore as welcome and unwelcome additions. The field layer is dog's mercury, wood avens, wood sage and wood melick grass (the rarer mountain melick also occurs here).

The path moves away from the river, which progresses by a series of artificial weirs. This is the least enjoyable section of the walk; the track becomes straight and wide, and the river loses its sparkle. Twin Dales, with caves and mysterious (early industrial) monoliths among the trees, provide a diversion, particularly with an abundant assortment of tall herbs on the wider margins. Dippers and grey wagtails hold territories all along the Lathkill, and are often seen through the trees as they fly from one weir to the next. Be prepared to sit and wait

The upper dale in winter – inhospitable to wildlife, but quiet and beautiful

and you may see a dipper as it plunges without hesitation into fast-flowing water to search for stonefly and caddis-fly larvae among the pebbles.

Rock outcrops appear to the left of the track with spleenwort, wallpepper and a host of rock-garden plants rooted in the fissures. Most of the open grassland has now disappeared and the whole gorge is heavily wooded. A stile alongside a derelict house marks the road to Over Haddon, which zig-zags steeply to the left. The stone-slabbed roof of the building is carpeted with wallpepper, or biting stonecrop, a plant credited with the colloquial name of welcome-home-husband-though-never-so-drunk. The old kitchen garden has been taken over by comfrey and butterbur.

5 Across the stone footbridge the path runs left (east) up through mixed woodland, then hair-pins west and rises to the rim of the gorge. The whole walk changes dramatically now. Through a five-bar gate the enclosed, heavily wooded scenery is gone and ahead rises the undulating meadowland of the White Peak plateau.

The footpath bears left (south) to Meadow Place Grange, through the middle of the stone-cobbled court-yard. In late spring and summer, swallows and house martins will be feeding families in the outbuildings and hawking flies in the cattle-yards. The steading can have changed little since it was built in the early 19th century, though the fields are 'improved' and the flora is less varied.

6 After the farmyard the path forks; turn right for Middleton and Moor Lane. After three fields the path joins a minor road. Turn right along this. Several uncommon plants grow along the roadside in this area, including fly orchid.

7 At the junction where an acute road to the south leads to Youlgreave, a footpath on the right (north) leads back to the dales. Take this path (signed Monyash 2 miles) and walk through a few fields to Calling Low Farm. The footpath detours to the right to avoid the yard. Calling Low is much like Meadow Place Grange – a dip into another century. The view downhill from here is graceful and typical of the White Peak. It encompasses the wide hills and upper dales, drystone walls, alder-lined valleys and farmsteads.

8 The footpath leads over buttercup meadows to the edge of Cales Dale and then plunges down into its wooded gorge, crossing the southern spur of the National Nature Reserve. Lady's mantle and several species of the smaller cranesbills may be seen growing alongside the path.

9 Turn right with the path to follow Cales Dale down to its junction with Lathkill Dale. Cross a footbridge and turn left to retrace your steps past the Jacob's ladder and out to the Monyash lay-by.

THE SKY ALWAYS SETS THE MOOD ON THE EAST COAST; LEADEN CLOUDS OPPRESS WHILE BRIGHT SUNNY DAYS QUICKEN THE SENSES. THE SLIPPERY GREY MUDFLATS CAN SPARKLE, AND DRIFTS OF SEA-LAVENDER BATHE THE CREEKS AND POOLS OF THE SALT-MARSHES IN A HAZE OF PURPLE. HOWEVER, TO A NATURALIST THIS IS SECONDARY TO THE EFFECTS OF WINDS AND SEASONS, WHICH BRING HOSTS OF BIRDS OF MANY DIFFERENT SPECIES TO BREED, FEED OR OVER-WINTER HERE.

DUNES, MARSH AND SHINGLE

Seaside towns do not usually rank high on the naturalist's list of places to visit. Even so, a stone's throw south of Skegness lies one of the most interesting sweeps of salt-marsh, sand and shingle in the country, worth a visit at almost any time of the year and with footpaths that link together into an adequate walking circuit. Gibraltar Point makes mud exciting!

The North Sea can be immensely destructive, but it can also create land. Gibraltar Point owes its existence to storm beaches thrown up in the 18th and 19th centuries, and to the gradual accumulation of mudflats and a shingle spit which now extend southwards to form an obvious promontory at the entrance to The Wash beside the outfall of the River Steeping.

The two storm beaches or dune ridges have been colonised by shrubs and some of the more recent, seaward ridges, in particular, are covered in

Male brambling

Gibraltar Point

Lincolnshire
Grid ref. TF 556 581

Lincolnshire and South Humberside Trust for Nature Conservation
Approx. 3 miles (4.8 km). Easy walking over level ground.

The Point is situated about 3 miles (4.8 km) south of Skegness, at the entrance to The Wash. The car park is reached off the unclassified road running due south from Skegness. It is just beyond a sharp kink in the road and before the Field Centre.

Gibraltar Point is a combination of sand dunes and salt-marshes and has been managed as a nature reserve for many years. It is most famous as a migration station, but is also good for winter birds and salt-marsh flowers.

Nearby sites: *Saltfleetby National Nature Reserve* – coastal dunes, mudflats and marshes; *The Wash,* to the south, is accessible from several points such as *Holbeach* – a wintering and migration location of international importance for wildfowl and waders.

very extensive patches of sea buckthorn. Between the dune ridges lies mature marshland, separated by Bulldog Bank into the Old Salt-marsh and the Freshwater Marsh. At the southern spur of the West Dunes lies an old coastguard station which has long served as a bird observatory and field study centre and has permanent displays about the nature reserve, managed by the Lincolnshire and South Humberside Trust for Nature Conservation.

PLANTS AND BIRDS

The mudflats, creeks, dunes and salt-marshes of Gibraltar Point have been colonised by all the classic coastal plants, including sea holly, shrubby seablite, sea milkwort, sea aster, glasswort, and two species of sea-lavender. But it is for its wealth of birds that 'Gib' is best known. It has never been a place for outstanding rarities. What is impressive is the variety and number of birds. During migration time in May, and again in September/October, the sea buckthorn on the dune ridges can be alive with whatever small land birds are on the move, while Gibraltar Point's strategic position on the lip of The Wash often brings seabirds close inshore. Hundreds of thousands of waders feed on the mudflats of The Wash, and in the middle of winter there are also snow buntings, shore larks and twites, short-eared owls and hen harriers.

The salt-marsh at high tide. Marshes like this form where tidal mud is anchored by plants that can withstand immersion in sea water

THE *Walk*

If the Field Centre is open it is certainly worth a visit – if only to look on the notice board at what birds have been seen recently.

1 From the car park walk north-east (in the opposite direction to the Field Centre), through a gap beside a gate and on to a metalled track which bears right, over a bridge. The creek is typical of east-coast salt-marshes; oozing mud flanked by sea purslane. To begin with most of the marsh vegetation is sea couch-grass but as you walk eastwards, towards the ridge of the East Dunes, there are wetter patches with lots of sea-lavender. The piping calls of redshanks are bound to be heard somewhere along the track; this sound is the essence of the marshes. Other waders such as green sandpipers and green-shanks come and go, but the redshank is always here.

2 At the end of the marsh, and before the wooden sleeper track over the dunes, turn right and go along the chalk track to the 'Ringing Laboratory'. This is a grand title for a stone hut. Near by is a Heligoland trap which has been used for decades to trap migrant birds for ringing and research purposes. The birds are driven into the mouth of the trap and are funnelled into a catching box.

3 Turn left just beyond the Ringing Laboratory and climb the steps beside the hut then continue along the path towards another hut. To the right is an area called the New Marsh – salt-marshes still at the mercy of the North Sea – and a shingle spit which, in summer, provides a nesting area for ringed plovers and little terns.

4 Just after the hut, on shingle with marshland beyond, turn left and walk northwards along the high-tide mark. The scrub area to the left may be ablaze with the bright orange of sea buckthorn berries. The bushes are very thorny and provide good cover for birds, but the berries are not very nutritious and so are usually left until all the elders and hawthorns are bare.

Continue along the tide-line, between the dunes and the salt-marsh, passing the wooden sleeper path (which provides a short cut back to the car park if the weather has deteriorated). North Sea flotsam cast up on the shore is always interesting. Among the inevitable detritus of the

The ringed plover nests on sand and shingle, laying its eggs in a specially scraped hollow

consumer society (plastic bottles, blobs of oil, old shoes, light bulbs etc.) there may be skate egg-cases, skulls and feathers of all shapes and sizes.

5 Eventually a crossroads of paths is reached; the clearest path, marked by posts, goes to the left and leads to a railed viewpoint. This is the main route to follow, but it is possible to turn right for a better look at the beach, then turn left and go north for several hundred yards (metres) until an area of muddy inlets

begins – a good place for waders and waterfowl. Turn left here and cross the low dunes and dry salt-marsh to meet a path below the main ridge of sea buckthorn. The path is then followed back to the crossroads, just beyond an old pill-box. Turn right. The railed viewpoint of Mill Hill provides the best panorama for miles and is a good place for birds of prey.

From Mill Hill head westwards along a wooden walkway until this meets a track, at which turn left along a clear gravel track with Bulldog Bank to your left. The bank separates salt-marsh from freshwater marshland, so the pools beside the track are particularly interesting. Pig-like squeals from the reed-beds indicate a good population of water rails.

6 Past the ponds there is a brick-built hide on the right, for views of the Mere. Opposite this is a grassy path off the metalled track. Take this path, which rises to detour to the right of a new mere or lagoon area, then continue southwards between the West Dunes and the Old Marsh, back to the car park. If time permits, and particularly if there is an incoming tide to bring waders close inshore, an excellent view of The Wash can be obtained by walking past the Field Centre and riverside moorings to Lill's Hut – converted from a gun emplacement into a boat-house and now known as The Wash Viewpoint.

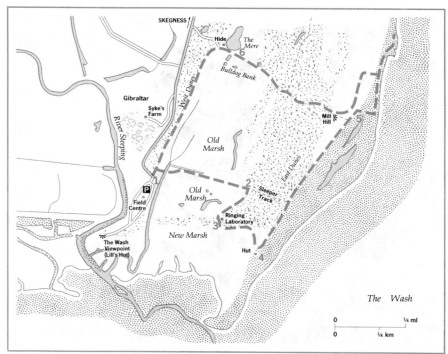

Moorland rises to gritstone crags on Kinder Scout. Bad weather can quickly turn this into one of the most desolate places in England

ONE OF ENGLAND'S CLASSIC WILDERNESS AREAS, KINDER SCOUT IS THE HIGHEST POINT OF THE DARK PEAK. THE PLATEAU AROUND IT IS A VAST AREA OF PEAT – THE HAUNT OF RED GROUSE, GOLDEN PLOVERS AND MOUNTAIN HARES.

THE PEAT PLATEAU

The great mass of peat absorbs rain like a sponge, then allows the water to trickle out slowly by way of the innumerable small streams which eventually join forces to form the River Sett and other rivers which drain the western edge of the High Peak.

The depth of peat is quite surprising, and walking across this sort of terrain is very difficult; in poor visibility it should be attempted only by those who have a compass and can navigate by it. Despite the difficult conditions, high rainfall and unpredictable weather, the area is extremely popular with walkers. This does contribute to the conservation problems. Erosion by walkers' boots and a series of disastrous fires have depleted the peat cover in some areas, leading to poor water retention and further erosion.

A KEY SITE FOR WALKERS

Present-day walkers in the Peak District and throughout Britain owe a

---

Kinder Scout

Derbyshire
Grid ref. SK 048 869

Approx. 7½ miles (12 km). Some steep sections on open moorland and hillside. Very exposed in places, and should not be attempted without proper equipment or in bad weather.

Kinder Scout lies in the heart of the wilderness of north Derbyshire's High Peak, between Manchester and Sheffield. The walk begins at Bowden Bridge car park, on a minor road about 1 mile (1.6 km) east of Hayfield, signposted for a campsite. The car park fills up quickly on summer weekends, but early arrivals should have no problem.

The high plateau surrounding Kinder Scout supports typical upland bog vegetation including the bog-mosses which decay, very slowly, to form peat. This area is one of the best stretches of blanket bog in Britain, though many parts of it are suffering badly from overgrazing and excessive trampling. The heather moorland provides cover and food for red grouse, and upland-breeding birds such as curlews, dunlins and golden plovers are here in spring and summer.

Nearby sites: The vast area of moorland around Kinder Scout offers many miles of footpaths, including the *Pennine Way* and the *Snake Path,* both sufficiently well trodden and signposted to be followed easily. Depending on the time of year, they offer good views of moorland birds and wild flowers. They can become busy during summer weekends, and are probably best visited in late spring and early summer.

Common mouse-ear

---

great deal to the early pioneers who fought hard for access to the countryside. This walk starts at the site of the famous mass trespass of 24 April 1932, when an army of walkers marched across the moors to Kinder Scout in protest against the landowners who denied ramblers access to the moors. Largely as a result of their actions, arrangements were made to open up footpaths and allow more free access to the countryside. In 1951, the Peak became Britain's first National Park. On the wall of the small quarry now used as the car park is a plaque describing the mass trespass. The quarry itself provides an opportunity to study the Millstone Grit – the characteristic rock type of this part of the Peak District, which is known as the Dark Peak, in contrast to the limestone country of the White Peak, further south.

RED GROUSE

One of the reasons why the early walkers were barred from the moors was that the land was the exclusive preserve of the grouse-shooting fraternity. From 12 August, when the season opened, shoots would take place through the autumn and the grouse would be driven to the guns in their hundreds, so walkers would be most unwelcome, and also in some danger. For the remainder of the year walkers were excluded to prevent disturbance to nesting birds.

Grouse feed on the growing shoots of heather and, in order to maximise a moor's potential, small areas are burnt from time to time to stimulate the heather into new growth. Many years of this practice has produced a patchwork of different ages of heather on the moorland, providing food and shelter for the grouse as well as a host of other moorland birds, mammals and insects. Today walkers are asked to keep to paths and to keep dogs on the lead; sections of moor may be closed when shooting is taking place.

The Kestrel

The kestrel, or windhover, is our most familiar and widespread bird of prey. As the alternative name suggests, these birds frequently hover, riding updraughts of air from ridges and hillsides, while they locate their prey.

Kestrels nest in old trees and cliffs, or sometimes on ledges of buildings. Females have spotted brown plumage while males have a chestnut back, a grey head and a grey tail with a black terminal band. When alarmed, they utter a loud 'kee-kee-kee' call.

THE *WALK*

1 From the quarry, cross Bowden Bridge and walk along the minor road beside the River Sett, going on to a track past Tunstead House which leads to Tunstead Clough Farm. Follow the signs giving directions round the farm buildings. The farm was once a staging post on the packhorse route across the Pennines. Grey wagtails feed along the river and opposite-leaved golden saxifrage grows in damp patches on the river bank, while the riverside trees attract feeding woodland birds.

2 Follow the farm track uphill, negotiating a kissing wicket and stiles and bearing right where Kinderlow is signposted. After another sign for Kinderlow End, cross the next wall and follow it uphill over two more stiles. The path then goes straight ahead towards the Three Knolls, contouring below Kinderlow End. In wet flushes, the tiny white flowers of ivy-leaved crowfoot, a member of the buttercup family, can be seen and the vegetation begins to change to a more typical moorland flora.

3 From the Three Knolls, the path makes for Cluther Rocks and then Red Brook, where it joins the old route of the Pennine Way and continues to Kinder Downfall. Here and there lie a few long-abandoned millstones. Bilberry, crowberry and other moorland plants grow among the ling (or heather), the food-plant of the red grouse. These birds make their loud 'go back, go back' call when disturbed, and often allow a very close approach before flying off. Kestrels may be watched hunting here and a mountain hare could be seen – usually if it is disturbed by an uncontrolled dog.

Kinder Downfall is the highest waterfall in the Peak District, at nearly 100ft (30m). During dry summers there may be very little water running over it, but after rain it is a very dramatic sight; the effect is heightened if there is a sudden gust of wind, causing the water to blow back to the summit and over the top, drenching over-eager observers. Westerly gales create a permanent spray at the top of the waterfall. In winter, when it is draped in icicles and the surrounding moors have a powdering of snow, it is a spectacular sight and well worth braving the cold to get here.

4 From Kinder Downfall continue along the edge to Sandy Heys and eventually join the Snake Path at Ashop Head. The Millstone Grit exposed here was once a marine sandbank which then became covered by the Coal Measures. About 290 million years ago, tremendous movements of the earth's crust raised the area to form the Pennines. Erosion removed the softer rocks of the Coal Measures, leaving the gritstone exposed, so the present rock surfaces would have been uncovered about 220 million years ago.

Listen for the bubbling call of the curlew, and the mournful-sounding cry of the golden plover. Ring ouzels may be seen on the rockier parts, and wheatears are present in summer.

5 Where a finger-post shows 'Hayfield 3m', follow the Snake Path down William Clough towards the Kinder Reservoir. Meadow pipits and lapwings inhabit the moors here and the vegetation becomes more varied, with tormentil and milkwort growing among the grasses. Patches of moss show where tiny springs emerge from the ground. The bright green moss is sphagnum, the main type responsible for peat formation. It absorbs large quantities of water and can be wrung out like a sponge. Never step on it, as it often grows over deep water.

6 At the reservoir, either take the path through the enclosure, or follow the Snake Path and then take the path by a wall which zig-zags down to the water company's plant. Cross the river by a footbridge. A path beside the River Kinder leads back to the road, which in turn leads to Bowden Bridge. The mixed oak woodland is a good area for woodpeckers, nuthatches, redstarts and spotted flycatchers.

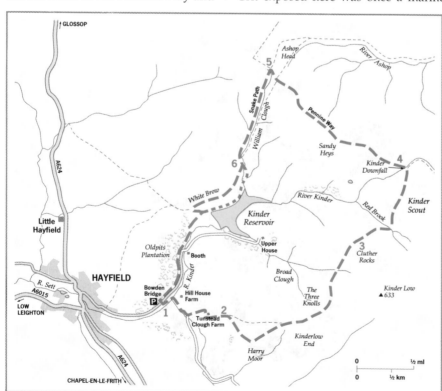

A golden plover settles on its eggs. A close-up view in sunshine leaves no doubt as to how this handsome bird got its name

FLOWING THROUGH A STEEP-SIDED VALLEY IN AN AREA OF HIGH RAINFALL, THE RIVER DERWENT WAS A NATURAL CHOICE TO BE DAMMED TO SUPPLY DRINKING WATER TO THE NORTH MIDLANDS. ACCESS TO ITS THREE RESERVOIRS IS NOW EASIER THAN EVER BEFORE, AND THE WATER AND ITS WOODED SURROUNDINGS ATTRACT A WIDE RANGE OF BIRDS AND ANIMALS.

THE ORIGINS OF THE RESERVOIRS

The industrial towns and cities of the Midlands have long looked to the Peak District for their water, and many attempts were made in the past to tap the water supply of this area of high rainfall. The River Derwent was eventually dammed in three places in the valley to form the Ladybower Reservoir, Derwent Reservoir and Howden Reservoir. In order to protect the watershed, the water boards acquired large areas of the surrounding land and created extensive conifer plantations. At one time the public had very limited access, but now the lakes are surrounded by a network of paths and longer routes.

A MAN-MADE HABITAT

The reservoirs themselves attract their share of wildlife, and many birds which would not normally be found in these upland valleys are now regularly seen here. Several species of wildfowl nest or overwinter on the lakes, although the numbers are never very high because marginal plants, which are a source of food, cannot grow on the steep banks. Stocking with fish for anglers has encouraged fish-eating birds like herons and goosanders to visit, while feeder streams are home to dippers and grey wagtails, which mostly shun the open water.

The forests on the shores attract woodland birds which would be quite unable to live on open, windswept moorland. Robins, thrushes, chaffinches and crossbills are resident, and in spring willow warblers and chiffchaffs arrive, soon to be followed by cuckoos.

WILDLIFE OF THE MOORS

The surrounding moors still have their own birdlife, and walkers who make the ascent to one of the high tops will be rewarded with sightings of upland birds like red grouse and, in the breeding season, golden plovers, curlews, redshanks, snipe, ring ouzels and wheatears. Mountain hares are easy to spot in winter when they moult

Derwent &Howden Reservoirs

Derbyshire
Grid ref. SK 174 894

Approx. 10 miles (16 km). Easy walking, mostly on fairly level footpaths and moorland roads. Weather conditions can deteriorate rapidly, however.

The reservoirs lie to the north of the A57 Sheffield–Glossop road (Snake Pass). The walk begins at Fairholme car park, on the minor road that runs along the western shore of the reservoirs.

The Derwent and Howden Reservoirs are set in attractive scenery surrounded by high moorland. Although the tops of the moors may be bleak in winter, there is always plenty of wildlife interest on the reservoirs and in the surrounding woods, making the walk interesting at any time of year.

Nearby sites: *Birchen Clough* – forest trail through a mature conifer plantation; Peak National Park Information Centres at *Castleton* and *Edale*.

The coot builds its nest of reeds

into their white coats before the first snowfall; for most of the year they are a brownish-buff colour and blend well with the dried grasses and heather. Foxes are much more elusive and wary of people, but the diminutive weasel may more easily be seen hunting for mice along drystone walls.

In late summer, when the heather blooms and the bracken starts to turn, the moors are a blaze of colour; as autumn advances and the first frosts start to bite, the larch and birch trees in the forests turn golden yellow and enliven the otherwise gloomy conifers. Through the winter there is little to brighten the buffs and browns of the dried grasses and heathers, but spring brings more splashes of colour as woodland flowers begin to bloom.

SHEEP AND SHEPHERDS

The moorland sheep are left out on the hills for most of the year, surviving severe weather conditions in winter. They are very thinly spread in some parts of the moors because there is very little good grazing for them; the moors simply cannot provide sufficient food for more than one sheep to one or two acres (0.4 – 0.8 hectare). Dog-owners are asked to keep their dogs on a lead at all times when in sheep country, as great damage can be done if sheep are panicked into running over difficult ground when they are carrying or rearing lambs. When the hill shepherds gather their sheep for shearing in the summer there is a good opportunity to watch the way their well-trained dogs gather up sheep over a vast area with the minimum of commands from the shepherd.

The mountain hare is unmistakable in its thick white winter coat

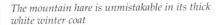

THE *Walk*

1 From the Fairholme car park take the track which runs north from the toilet block towards the Derwent Dam alongside the upper reaches of Ladybower Reservoir. A few mallards usually swim close to the shore here, hoping for food from picnickers. Moorhens search for scraps along the banks, and the resident robins and chaffinches have become very tame. The mature conifers are good feeding sites for crossbills, which use their strange, twisted bills to extract seeds from pine cones. The sound of pine cones dropping from the tree-tops and the high 'cheep' call are good clues to their whereabouts.

2 Follow the minor road over the bridge and take the footpath rising through the trees which leads to the east side of Derwent Reservoir. The path now runs alongside Derwent Reservoir for the whole of its length, continuing beside Howden Reservoir. This makes very pleasant walking, with only a few very slight inclines. Along the route are many delightful views of the reservoirs through the trees, and plenty of opportunities to see woodland birds. A thin, high-pitched 'zi-zi-zi' call is given by goldcrests, which are common in mature conifers. A sweeter note is given by the slightly larger coal tit, also very much at home here.

3 Keeping to the stony track and ignoring paths branching down to the left, continue to Slippery Stones, north of Howden Reservoir. Cross the River Derwent by the reconstructed packhorse bridge. The path now turns south and follows the west bank of Howden Reservoir back towards the Fairholme car park. The bridge once stood further down the now-flooded valley, at Derwent village. The river, seen here in its natural state as a fast-flowing moorland stream, is home to dippers, unusual birds able to walk and swim with ease under water and catch tiny insects out of reach of other small birds. They are often seen living up to their name, standing on stones in the

Ladybower, the largest Derwent valley reservoir

river and bobbing up and down. Grey wagtails run along the banks of the river searching for insects above the water and are more easily seen in summer. In late summer the colours of the surrounding moorlands are spectacular, with the purple heather mingling with the golden bracken and the ripening rowan berries.

4 At Linch Clough, stepping stones cross the stream and the track joins the forest road at the King's Tree parking place. Woodland birds may be encountered all along the route; in winter small feeding flocks of tits and finches can be located by their medley of calls. Early in the year goshawks, magnificent birds of prey, may sometimes be seen displaying over the woods. Males soar out on outstretched wings and circle over the woods in order to claim a territory. The smaller kestrel may also be seen as it hovers on rapidly beating wings in search of small voles.

5 The route now follows the road back to the start. In the busy holiday season the road is closed to traffic and makes a pleasant walkers' route. The detour around the Westend inlet adds nearly 2 miles (3.2 km) to the route, but it does give the chance to look for wildfowl sheltering in the calmer waters at the head of the inlet. In winter goosanders and goldeneyes – diving ducks which breed in harsher climates further north – can be seen alongside the resident mallards and tufted ducks.

6 The road passes the Howden Dam and runs alongside Derwent Reservoir. These reservoirs were used as training areas in World War II when the 'bouncing bomb' used by the so-called Dambusters was being developed. The mixed woodland here is home to many migrant birds such as chiffchaffs and willow warblers in summer, and their arrival is heralded by rich birdsong in May and June. In the dense woodland few flowers can

grow, as very little light reaches the woodland floor and the carpet of pine needles chokes tiny seedlings, but along the woodland edges and beneath the broadleaved trees grows a colourful display of tormentil, milkwort, red campion, foxgloves and hawkbit. Grey squirrels seem now to have replaced the red squirrels which once lived in these woods.

7 The route passes the Derwent Dam. Here there is a display board outlining the history and building of the reservoirs.

The Fairholme car park is reached by turning off the minor road to Derwent.

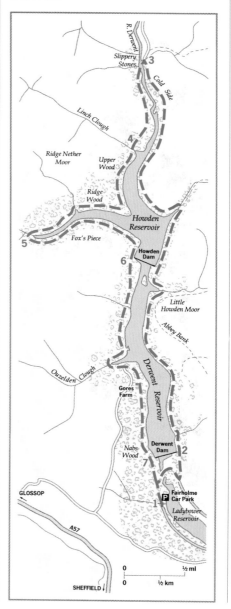

STANDING IN THE HEART OF EPPING FOREST, IT CAN BE HARD TO BELIEVE THAT YOU ARE CLOSE TO BUSY ROADS AND TOWNS, LET ALONE WITHIN 25 MILES (40 KM) OF THE CENTRE OF LONDON. ALTHOUGH THE FOREST'S MANY VISITORS HAVE EFFECTIVELY EXCLUDED THE DEER WHICH ONCE ROAMED HERE, MOST OF THE LESS RETIRING WOODLAND CREATURES CAN BE SEEN WITH EASE.

A HISTORIC FOREST

At one time, Epping Forest was part of the much larger Waltham Forest which stretched across a large area of Essex. Ancient common rights existed before the woodland became established as a royal hunting forest, and they persisted thereafter. However, the Forest was gradually reduced in area and degraded in quality: turf and brush were removed in an uncontrolled manner, gravel was extracted, deer were poached and inclosures began to encroach. The 9000 acres (3640 hectares) that existed in 1793 had dwindled by more than one-third by the mid 19th century.

The Epping Forest Act was passed in 1878, safeguarding the remaining area, which is greater today (6000 acres/2430 hectares) than when the Act was passed. The land is owned and managed by the Corporation of London. Access is free to the public.

ANCIENT POLLARDS

Although Epping Forest comprises a mosaic of different tree species of varying ages, it is for its ancient pollards that it is best known. Oak,

Centuries of woodland management have left the Forest glades rich in old pollards. Now long neglected, however, these trees are shading out many of the woodland flowers

Epping Forest

Essex
Grid ref. TQ 417 982

Corporation of London
Approx. 3 miles (4.8 km). Easy walking, though the ground may be muddy in winter and some parts are rather steep.

Epping Forest lies north-west of Loughton. The car park is to the south-east of the A11. If it is full, there is a smaller car park approximately 200 yds (180 m) south on the same side of the road or another, larger one 300 yds (275 m) north on the west side of the A11.

Epping Forest comprises some fine, ancient woodland with many superb pollarded trees. Birdlife in spring is abundant and the autumn colours and fungi are not to be missed in September and October. The walk passes through Great Monk Wood – one of the best wooded parts of Epping Forest – but elsewhere in the Forest there are areas of grassy heath. The Conservation Centre at High Beach provides information about the Forest.

Nearby sites: *Hatfield Forest* – hornbeam woodland and fresh water, good for woodland birds and flowers; *Rye House Marsh* – freshwater habitats, good for breeding wetland birds and migrants.

Top: *Wood warbler – a harbinger of spring*

beech and, in particular, hornbeam were managed in this way by cutting the trunk at a height of about 6ft (2m). This produced clusters of radiating side shoots which were used for firewood. The practice – carried out by those with lopping rights – went on until about 1870 and since it stopped the trees have gradually acquired a more mature and stately appearance. The trunks of these pollarded trees were of no use for timber, because they became unevenly swollen and hollow. However, this did benefit many of the woodland birds by providing redstarts, blue tits, tawny owls and woodpeckers with ample nesting sites.

THE WOODLAND BIRDS

Epping Forest boasts almost all the bird species that one could hope to see in a southern English woodland. Among the smaller resident species, blue tits, great tits and coal tits are always in evidence. They are easily seen in the spring, when their strident songs attract attention. In winter, they often roam around in mixed flocks which may also include goldcrests and long-tailed tits. Robins are common year-round woodland residents, but in the summer months they are joined by redstarts – easily recognised by their red tails – which still breed in Epping Forest in small numbers. Being a hole-nesting species, the redstart benefits from the abundance of holes in dead branches and ancient pollards. The nightingale can be heard in early summer in dense undergrowth.

Woodpeckers have also benefited from the many holes in trees, and the dead and dying timber supports the insect larvae that make up much of their diet. All three British species are found here, but the great spotted and green are more often seen than the smaller and more secretive lesser spotted woodpecker.

The Wood Mouse

The wood mouse is one of our commonest small mammals. It has a yellowish-brown coat with white underparts, but lacks the yellow collar of its larger relative, the yellow-necked mouse.

Wood mice forage on the forest floor, searching for fallen seeds and nuts. They are also skilled climbers and will search for ripe berries. Although they are mainly nocturnal, wood mice are often seen scurrying across the leaf litter or among piles of fallen branches where they build their nests.

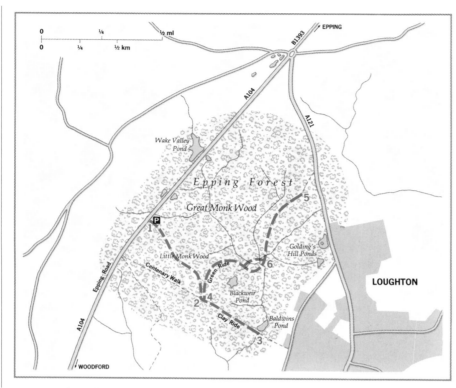

3 In the valley bottom is a small pond on the left-hand side of the path. In summer, it is covered with water-lilies and fringed with reedmace. Whirligig beetles dot the water's surface and dragonflies and damselflies can be abundant. The pond is popular at weekends and during holidays, but in quieter moments may attract a kingfisher. Search the scrub around the pond for warblers and parties of long-tailed tits.

Retrace your steps up the hill.

4 When you reach the junction in the wide, grassy clearing, turn right along the sandy track, ignoring the fork to the left. The path passes through an area of Great Monk Wood which has some magnificent pollarded trees. Beech leaves and fallen mast cover the woodland floor, and cushions of the attractive moss *Leucobryum glaucum* can be seen. This area is excellent in autumn for a variety of fungi.

The path bends to the right and descends rather steeply. Fleabane, great willowherb, greater birdsfoot trefoil and wood melick grow beside the path. Patches of nectar-rich marsh thistle are irresistible to insects.

The path crosses a stream – dry in summer – and bends to the left. It then crosses another stream and continues up a steep hill.

5 Towards the summit of the hill is one of the most attractive areas of pollarded trees in the whole Forest. This is a favourite place for woodpeckers and nuthatches, and the woodland floor is good for wolf spiders and fungi in autumn.

Follow the same path back down the hill again.

6 Having crossed the first stream, take the narrow path to the right which passes over a culvert and then bears almost immediately left over a small bridge. Explore the woodland, climbing up the track towards the hilltop, then in the open area near the summit turn left down the steep slope to the stream. Cross the small wooden bridge and climb to reach the main path again.** This slight detour allows you to walk among the ancient beeches and to marvel at their often contorted shapes.

Having rejoined the main track, continue up the hill and turn right to retrace your steps to the car park. Look for birch polypore, a bracket fungus, growing on some of the older birch trees.

1 Take the sandy track that heads south-east from the south side of the car park. This area is heavily wooded with oak, beech, birch and the occasional hornbeam. Sallows and willows grow as an understorey, and bracken adds a further splash of colour in the autumn. Small flocks of redpolls can sometimes be seen feeding in the birch trees and occasionally a hawfinch is seen in the hornbeams. These rather secretive birds possess huge, powerful bills which they use to crack the hard seeds of hornbeam. Few other species can do this, so hornbeam seeds are almost exclusively the preserve of this attractive bird. In flight, the hawfinch shows a lot of white on the wings and rump.

The sallows and willows along the ride provide food for the caterpillars of puss moths and eyed hawk-moths. Both species are boldly marked when seen away from their food-plant, but superbly camouflaged when at rest among the leaves. The thistles that border the track are favoured by butterflies such as small copper and meadow brown, as well as numerous hover-flies and other insects. Some of the ancient pollards have been blown over in recent gales, and woodpeckers – both green and great spotted – favour this area.

2 At a T-junction, turn right to reach a wide grassy area. Turn left here along a wide ride which gradually winds its way downhill. Mature oaks and beeches line the ride, and gorse and stunted holly bushes can also be seen. Woodland birds including nuthatch, treecreeper, great tit, blue tit, coal tit and robin can be found here, and chaffinches often feed on the fallen beech-mast under the trees in winter. A careful search of these flocks may even reveal a brambling. This winter visitor is similar to the chaffinch in size and shape, but is more elegantly marked, with a white rump in flight.

Birch polypore or razor-strop fungus is a widespread bracket fungus on birch trees

Newmarket Heath's former sheepwalks are now a training ground for top racehorses

RISING ABOVE THE CAMBRIDGESHIRE LANDSCAPE, THE DEVIL'S DYKE GIVES VIEWS OVER BRITAIN'S MOST FERTILE FARMLAND, THE UNIQUE NEWMARKET STUDS AND NEWMARKET RACECOURSE. BENEATH YOUR FEET AS YOU WALK ALONG THE DYKE IS SOME OF THE BEST CHALK GRASSLAND IN THE COUNTRY – A BLAZE OF COLOUR IN THE SPRING AND SUMMER MONTHS, AND THE HAUNT OF NUMEROUS BUTTERFLIES.

STRUCTURE AND SOIL

The Devil's Dyke consists of a high bank with a deep defensive ditch on the outside. It reaches 96ft (30m) wide and 60ft (18m) high. It was built in about the 7th century, to defend the Fens from invaders. Connecting clay soils at either end, it crosses the chalk of Newmarket Heath. Excavation has shown the dyke to be a long bank of soil, covered by chalk rocks and boulders. Almost pure chalk at the surface has given rise to a herb-rich grassland. Where scrub and woodland have become established over the centuries, a deeper, more nutrient-rich soil occurs, with a different range of flowers.

FLORA AND FAUNA

One of the rarest and richest floras in the region survives on the Devil's Dyke. Its herb-rich chalk grassland boasts harebells, rest-harrow, rock-rose, bellflowers, sainfoin, vetches, Pasque flower and many other attractive plants. It is at its most colourful in May, June and July, but there is something of interest to be seen all year round. The vegetation changes throughout the walk.

The wide range of plants attracts an

Devil's Dyke

Cambridgeshire
Grid ref. TL 656 581

Cambridgeshire County Council/ Bedfordshire and Cambridgeshire Wildlife Trust (part)
Approx. 15 miles (24 km) (7½ miles/12 km each way). For a shorter walk, leave a car at each end. The chalk path is uneven and may be slippery in wet weather. Please keep to the footpath along the top of the Dyke, and do not stray down the banks. Keep dogs on leads.

The Devil's Dyke lies south and west of Newmarket. Park at Ditton Green on the verge of the road from Stetchworth to Cheveley, near the water tower (please do not block accesses).

Built of chalk, this man-made linear earthwork boasts fine, herb-rich grassland and several nationally rare wild flowers. Additional habitats include chalk scrub and woodland.

Nearby site: *Stow Cum Quy Fen* – chalky pasture, pools.

Tree sparrow – a bird of woods and farmland. Unlike the house sparrow, it has black cheek patches

equally interesting variety of insects. More than 12 different species of butterfly, including the chalkhill blue, visit regularly. Other insects include colourful beetles, bees, and also dragonflies.

Most of the birds to be seen or heard are the common ones of grassland and scrub – finches, warblers and so on. At dusk owls may be seen hunting along the grassy banks, and in winter fieldfares gather in large numbers. Kestrels and other falcons can regularly be observed.

Part of the Dyke is a reserve of the Bedfordshire and Cambridgeshire Wildlife Trust, and is used by Cambridge University as a long-term research area to follow the establishment of chalk grassland.

THE RETURN OF GRAZING

A project at Ditch Farm (between points 5 and 6 on the walk) to reintroduce sheep to the Dyke will have a number of beneficial effects. Sheepgrazing was the traditional form of management: it keeps the grassland short, which favours the flowers, and prevents scrub growth.

Apart from benefiting the grassland, it is hoped that grazing will entice barn owls back to the Dyke. Barn owls need rough grassland in which to hunt for small mammals; they disappeared from the area when arable farming became so dominant. Modern agriculture is no friend to this beautiful bird, already on the edge of its European range in Britain. Barn owls have lost not only large areas of terrain suitable for hunting, but also many nest sites, as hedgerow trees have been felled and farm buildings pulled down or converted.

THE *WALK*

The Pasque Flower

The Pasque flower is one of our earliest spring flowers, often blooming in late April; the English name is derived from 'paschal', meaning Easter. The Pasque flower is one of our rarest species, found in the wild on only about 30 sites, and it is protected by law. It grows only on chalk grassland, doing especially well where rabbits and sheep have nibbled the turf to a close sward. Pasque flowers like south- or south-west-facing slopes and their purple, anemone-like flowers are a beautiful sight.

Pasque flower – quite a rarity in the wild

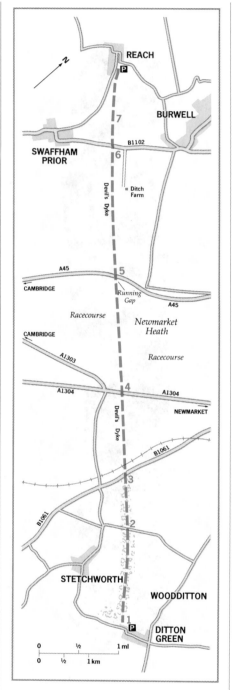

1 The footpath from Ditton Green to the Devil's Dyke is signposted to Newmarket and Reach, between houses on the north side of the road. (There is a proposal to divert this path, so watch for an alternative route which will be signposted nearby.) Follow the path across a field towards the wood; the Devil's Dyke can be seen stretching into the distance. Where the path meets the wood, follow the field edge. After a few yards (metres) this path takes you up a slope on to the Devil's Dyke. Note the profile of the raised Dyke, with the ditch to your left. The natural woodland of this area is oak, ash, field maple and hazel. Much of the ash and hazel has been coppiced (cut at the base), while some of the ash has been pollarded (cut at about head height), probably to mark out land ownership. Under the trees are nettle-leaved bellflower and clustered bellflower. In open areas knapweed, field scabious and bloody cranesbill are common. The evergreen shrub is box.
Walk north-west along the Dyke.

2 Go down the bank and cross a minor road diagonally before continuing along the Dyke. The hedge to the left has been planted along the field edge to help prevent crop sprays drifting on to the grassland.

3 The path comes off the Dyke steeply and crosses the B1061, continuing on the other side over a footbridge. Walk on for about 160yds (150m) to a stile and railway line. Take care crossing the line, and continue along the Dyke. Bloody cranesbill, rock-roses, harebells and the attractive quaking-grass make a fine summer display in this area. The ditch is clear on the left, as it would have been centuries ago. The vegetation becomes quite dense towards the end of this section, with a large open area before the road.
Follow the straight line of the Dyke across this glade.

4 Cross the A1304, Newmarket Road, and walk along the access road to the racecourse. Going through the wooden gate, you will see the Dyke on your right-hand side. Follow the path up on to the Dyke and along the top. Most of this stretch is over grassland with rest-harrow, sainfoin, horseshoe vetch and salad burnet. Pasque flowers grow in profusion. On both sides lies Newmarket racecourse. Newmarket Heath occupies the surrounding land, a small remnant of once extensive sheepwalks. There are several gaps in this section of the Dyke.

5 On race days check that this track is not being used before crossing! Cross the track, go over the stile and cross the A45 via the footbridge. Dense hawthorn scrub dominates the beginning of this section. Notice the deeper and less chalky soil; the ditch has also been filled in. Further on, you can see the beneficial effects of sheep grazing on the grassland. The ditch has re-appeared by the northern end of this section, and alder buckthorn, a local rarity, survives here.

6 The Dyke tapers to ground level at the next road junction. Cross the B1102, Burwell Road, and climb to the top of the Dyke on the far side. The thick scrub soon thins out to show grassland again.

7 After 800yds (750m), the path veers to the left down some steps. This cutting is the course of a dismantled railway. Cross it and follow the path up the far side. Steps are provided on the path to the far left if required. Follow the path through the scrub until it comes out on the green at Reach. If you have not left a vehicle here, retrace your steps along the Dyke to Ditton Green.

Wicken Fen

*One of Wicken's reed-lined dykes. The windpump, once used for drainage, now pumps water
into the fen to keep it wet*

The fen in early summer. This is the time to see the plant life and birds at their best

THE FENMAN, IT WAS SAID, SURVIVED THE EVILS OF THE MARSHES BY DRINKING OPIUM TEA. AN EVENING AT WICKEN, OUT OF SIGHT OF THE SURROUNDING WHEAT AND SUGAR-BEET FIELDS, CAN CONJURE AN IMPRESSION OF A PAGAN WILDER-NESS, A LAND DESCRIBED IN ST GUTHLAC'S TIME AS 'A MOST TERRIBLE FEN OF IMMENSE SIZE... SOMETIMES IN BLACK OOZES SWIRLING WITH MIST'.

THE SHRINKING WETLANDS

In fact the evolution of the primeval marshes of East Anglia's Great Fen from what had been a vast wetland to what is now uniform, arable farmland, is almost complete; there are the merest fragments left – places forgotten and swept aside in the race to exploit some of the richest soils in Europe. As the marshes were drained and the peat dried to dust, so the relic fens were protected by dykes and drains, and by lodes or waterways. The rest of the land shrank. St Guthlac had sought a refuge on higher ground from the phantoms of the marshes. It is ironic that, over 1000 years later, the raised sanctuaries are now the few fens that remain.

REED, SEDGE AND CARR

Unlike acid upland mires, fens are fertile and the peat is often rich in calcium, washed out of the underlying chalk. Plants grow quickly. In swamps of shallow standing water, beds of reed (*Phragmites*) develop. As the ground

---

Wicken Fen

Cambridgeshire
Grid ref. TL 563 706

National Trust
Approx. 4 miles (6.4 km). Easy walking.

The reserve is 6 miles (10 km) south of Ely, off the A1123 between Stretham and Soham. Admission charge. Parking is available at the reserve entrance.

Managed as a nature reserve, Wicken Fen has a variety of fen habitats – sedge and 'litter' fields, areas of reed, waterways and a mere. Two-thirds of the reserve is covered by scrub or carr woodland.

This walk is definitely one for late spring or early summer, when the flowers and birds are at their best. Indeed, the northern part of the walk, on wetter ground, may be closed at other times of the year – and certainly will be in winter. The boardwalk is always open.

Nearby sites: *Woodwalton Fen* (permit only) – fenland and carr woodland; *Fowlmere RSPB Reserve* – reed-beds and pools, excellent for water birds and meadow flowers.

Yellow flag is among the showiest of our common wetland plants

dries, swathes of saw sedge (*Cladium*) take their place. These are natural stages in a succession that should end with oak woodland. However, fens have a long history of controlled interference. Since medieval times, when peat-digging created many of the swamps, Fenmen have harvested the reed and sedge for use as roofing thatch. The land was intensively worked, yet rich in wetland wildlife.

When the country crafts diminished,

---

towards the end of the last century, the cutting ceased and nature was allowed to complete its work, transforming the fields of reed and sedge into 'carr' or damp woodland. Traditional sedge fens quickly disappeared under thickets of alder buckthorn and sallow. Only in the last few years has management been re-established at such places as Woodwalton Fen, the Bure Marshes and Wicken. Insects and plants are reappearing that have not been seen for decades.

A HISTORIC RESERVE

Wicken Fen has always been a famous place. In the 19th century, the discovery of many rare insects turned it into a mecca for collectors. It was largely through their efforts that it became a nature reserve; bit by bit the fen was acquired by the National Trust. Adventurer's Fen, a neigh-bouring wilderness of reeds, was drained in the early 1940s, but part of this has been added to the reserve and is now wetland again.

The main reserve, the Sedge Fen, covers an area of about 330 acres (130 hectares). Most of this is composed of carr, either the early scrub phase of alder buckthorn, or combinations of guelder rose and sallow, purging buckthorn and hawthorn. Marsh fern flourishes in the shade, as do some notable twilight birds – woodcock, long-eared owl and nightingale.

The rest of the fen is made up of either sedge, cut on a four-year rotation and sold for thatching, or 'litter' – a more varied community of plants harvested like a hay crop. The extensive litter fields are the most attractive wildlife habitat. In the summer they are full of ragged robin, purple loosestrife, meadowsweet and a host of less common flowers such as marsh pea, angelica and milk parsley. Butterflies abound; unfortunately Wicken's most famous jewel, the swallowtail, became extinct here in about 1950. Improved management may allow it to return.

FENLAND TRACKWAYS

Trackways criss-cross the fen, following drains or lodes. These provide access to most of the reserve, though some are closed at times in wet weather or to let the vegetation recover from trampling. To walk into the heart of the Fenman's world along a willow-lined drove is a satisfying experience. Evening can be the best time: reed warblers and cuckoos fall silent, woodcock begin their roding flights and moths such as reed leopards and marsh daggers take to the wing. So, of course, do the mosquitoes!

THE *Walk*

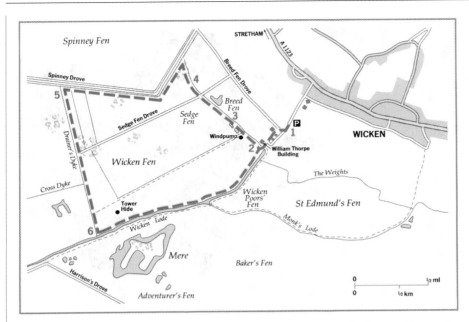

Flowers of the Ditches and Lodes

Aquatic plants have suffered more than most from the effects of modern farming. Even the still waters of the fen are affected by pollution as fertilisers and other chemicals drain off the surrounding fields, but in most respects the ditches and lodes of Wicken are a pleasure to the eye.

Many water plants such as hornwort and milfoil root in the mud and send up long shoots and narrow leaves which remain submerged. Others, such as pondweeds and water crowfoots, have both narrow submerged leaves and broader floating leaves. Crowfoots, closely related to buttercups, have shiny white flowers which grow in clusters, like drifts of confetti on the surface of the water.

The most dramatic water plants at Wicken are the water-lilies, of two species, yellow and white. These have impressively large flowers and round leaves which look as if they are free-floating. In fact the water-lilies are also rooted in the mud on the bottom and have stems up to 10ft (3m) long to get them to the surface. Wicken is also one of the few places to see the water violet, a delicate mauve-flowered relative of the primrose.

Floating plants, those which have no fixed roots, include frogbit and three sorts of duckweed. These sometimes cover the surface of the drains during the summer, but in the autumn they sink to the bottom to protect themselves from frost (the Fens are noted for some savage winters). Perhaps the most unusual of all the aquatic plants at Wicken is bladderwort. During June its flowers stand out above the surface like yellow snapdragons on spiky stems but, down below, the plant has an armoury of silvery bladders which trap and kill insects. The submerged world of the fen is as rich and gloomy as a jungle.

1 **From the car park, walk down the gravelled road past some modern houses, then right across a bridge.** The wide canal is Wicken Lode – a waterway built to channel water into the main rivers and to carry local produce to towns further down the Cam and the Ouse. The Sedge Fen on the north (right) bank of the lode is several feet higher than the arable fields and Adventurer's Fen on the south (left) side. Water levels in the nature reserve cannot be controlled with any accuracy, but work has recently been carried out to seal the banks and so reduce seepage.

The hexagonal building close to the bridge contains displays about the fen. This is where you should pay to enter the reserve.

2 **From here, walk towards the open fen and across a little bridge, then turn right along a boardwalk beside a reed-lined dyke.** The wide expanse of litter fields is impressive, particularly when the marshland flowers are out and brimstone butterflies are visiting marsh thistles or clumps of ragged robin on the dyke verges.

The boardwalk leads past a windpump, like a miniature windmill. This one was built to help drain the fields of Adventurer's Fen and was reconstructed here in 1956 to reverse the process and help keep the water in. **Just after the windpump, the boardwalk crosses a dyke and leads past some small open pools.** Several species of dragonfly and damselfly can be seen here (18 occur on the reserve),

and this is a good place to listen for marshland birds – sedge, reed and grasshopper warblers, perhaps even a bearded tit or the rare Cetti's and Savi's warblers, which are occasional visitors to the reserve and have bred here.

The route leaves the boardwalk as this bears left at a young oak tree, continuing along a grassy track or drove. To the right is the main dyke still covered in pondweed which often shows the paddleways of water voles. The banks are lined with comfrey and other taller herbs. Beyond the cut fields of litter and sedge are impenetrable tangles of sallow, perfect for woodland warblers. This is the most beautiful and varied section of the walk; dappled sunlight plays through the willows on to the fen vegetation, on to stands of early marsh orchid and yellow loosestrife, and invites you to slow down or stop for a few moments. A bridge over the dyke to the right seems to have been placed there for the sole purpose of letting you lean on the rail.

3 **Continue along the drove to a crossroads with Sedge Fen Drove, one of the oldest trackways through the fen.** This trackway is usually closed because the ground is very peaty and is often waterlogged. The tall willow trees, crack and white willows, were planted earlier this

The best chance of a daylight sighting of the usually nocturnal long-eared owl is in winter when the bird is roosting in leafless trees. Its 'ears' are really tufts of feathers

century and are now over-mature. Willow wood on the fen provides a high-fibre diet for several beautiful beetles, including the rare longhorn *Oberia oculata*, and for the larvae of some interesting moths such as the goat moth and the lunar hornet clearwing.

4 After crossing Sedge Fen Drove the route continues to the edge of the reserve, following the grassy track as it turns sharp left. The bank beyond the fence has recently been rebuilt and sealed, and this has certainly kept in most of the water. The track becomes damper underfoot; in wet weather, and in winter, this northern part of the reserve will be closed.

The walk along the northern boundary of the reserve is between the outer retaining bank and the carr or damp woodland that has colonised the fen over the past century. More than anything else, this section of the walk emphasises the contrast between the 'timeless' fen and the outside world, the flat arable farmland that now makes up what we still call Fenland.

5 Eventually the track turns left, following a dyke southwards. This is called Drainer's Dyke and is one of the oldest water-channels on the fen, dating back to the 17th century when Dutch drainage experts such as Cornelius Vermuyden were brought in by local land barons ('Adventurers') to oversee the drainage of the Great Fen. Clearings in the alder buckthorn scrub on the left as you walk along the trackway south are the result of ecological experiments and efforts to re-establish sedge fields.

The long straight track crosses Sedge Fen Drove and soon has better views of the open fens as it approaches a bridge across Drainer's Dyke; the route of the walk can be extended by taking this track right, beside Cross Dyke then cutting south to Wicken Lode.

6 The main route of the walk continues south, veering left at the end of Drainer's Dyke and meeting Wicken Lode. This is the southern boundary of the Sedge Fen. The lode has a fine fringe of swamp plants such as yellow flag and great water dock and is also good for water-lilies. Beyond the lode lie Adventurer's Fen and the mere.

Walk a little way eastward beside the lode and you come to a thatched observation tower among the carr woodland, from where the mere can be seen more clearly – but at too great a distance to make out anything much smaller than a Canada goose.

Walk eastwards along the track beside Wicken Lode. There are extensive vistas now across the open fen to the left. The sedge fields are harvested on a four-year rotation to encourage the growth of saw sedge, which is cut in the late summer. Litter fields are harvested more frequently and have much better shows of flowers. They are also ideal hunting and roosting places for hen harriers, which winter here. Further down the track is the confluence of Wicken Lode and Monk's Lode, above which neither is navigable.

The last stretch of the walk, from the meeting of the lodes to the reserve building where the old staithes used to be, is completed in the green shade of carr woodland.

Much of the Sedge Fen is covered with carr – damp woodland and scrub which choked the reed-beds when regular cutting ceased. This is now a fine habitat for many of the reserve's breeding birds, and for insect life

Bradfield Woods

*Along Front Ride. This old trackway was trodden by many generations of woodmen in the days
when Bradfield Woods was a bustling place of work*

BRIGHT SUNSHINE AND LENGTHEN-ING DAYS BRING LIFE AND COLOUR BACK TO WINTER WOODLAND. THE SEA OF BLOWN LEAVES, PICKED OVER BY ROBINS AND WRENS, DISAPPEARS BENEATH A WAVE OF SPRING FLOWERS. FOR TWO MONTHS, BEFORE THE FOREST TREES BREAK BUD, THESE PERENNIAL HERBS MUST TAKE THEIR CHANCE, USING ENERGY FROM THE LIGHT TO FLOWER AND SEED.

BRITAIN'S WORKING WOODLANDS

For many centuries the way woods were managed benefited spring flowers. Working woods never needed to be replanted; their main crop was not mature timber but the poles that grew from the stools or bases of previously felled trees. When these poles were harvested – perhaps after eight years for thatching spars (the pegs used to fix the straw) or hurdles (woven fencing panels), and maybe 15 years for fence-posts – others sprang from the stools and the process began again. This was called coppicing. It kept the woods free from dense tangles and decaying boles, and encouraged flowers that relied on an occasional break in the woodland canopy, such as primroses, wood anemones, bluebells and violets.

In many coppiced woods a scatter of saplings, usually oak, was encouraged to grow into trees or standards. Their growth did not interfere with the cut stools, as they were cut after the second or third coppice cycle, at 40 or 60 years of age, when they were of a manageable size for conversion into single beams. This system was known as 'coppice with standards' and represented an effective, sustainable production system.

Eventually, woodland crafts dimini-shed and there was a dwindling market for hurdles and thatching spars. The coppices began to fall derelict. Many woods were grubbed up or replanted with conifers, with scarcely a thought for the woodland flowers, butterflies and birds that were lost with the trees.

COPPICING REDISCOVERED

In recent years there have been efforts to re-create working woods, establish-ing new coppices and re-awakening interest in the few ancient woods that had escaped the ravages of clear-felling and neglect. Now claimed as priceless relics, these ancient woodlands are both unique wildlife habitats and wonderful examples of living history.

Bradfield Woods

Suffolk
Grid ref. TL 936 581

Suffolk Wildlife Trust
Approx. 3 miles (4.8 km). Level terrain; clear route. Please keep to marked paths.

The woods lie about 7 miles (11 km) south-east of Bury St Edmunds, off the unclassified road between Bradfield St George and Felsham. The car park is situated on the northern edge of the woods.

This fragment of ancient coppiced woodland has a mosaic of clearings which guarantees colourful flushes of spring flowers, including the rare oxlip. The different plots, varying in age, also create a contrast in wildflower communities. The wood-land population of birds and mammals includes nightingale and dormouse. Bradfield Woods demon-strate how traditional management benefits wildlife, and provide an interesting comparison both with modern plantation methods and with 'wilderness' woods.

Nearby sites: *Weeting Heath* and *Cavenham Heath* – excellent examples of Breckland habitat. Species include stone curlew, Breckland mug-wort, Breckland catchfly and Breckland, three-fingered and spiked speedwells.

Woodpigeon – a handsome bird, but one with few friends

Bradfield Woods, one of these priceless relics, originally comprised two large blocks of woodland, Monk's Park and Felsham Hall Wood. In the late 1960s, when most of Monk's Park was being grubbed up for farmland, local villagers stopped the destruction and helped the Royal Society for Nature Conservation to buy the 161

acres (64 hectares) that remained. The woods are now managed by the Suffolk Wildlife Trust. Their full-time warden is both woodman and naturalist, helping to ensure that the woodlands continue to benefit plants, animals and man.

Documents for Bradfield Woods survive from as far back as 1252, when coppicing was carried out under the direction of monks from the Abbey of Bury St Edmunds, who also kept a herd of fallow deer here. The coppiced woodland was separated into 'fells' or sections, within which smaller areas called 'panels' or 'coupes' were marked out and coppiced on a rotation of up to 20 years. In each acre (0.4 hectare) of coppice up to 15 standards were allowed to grow, and were felled at various ages as required.

WORKING FOR WILDLIFE

The system operated in Bradfield Woods today is virtually identical. Two coppice rotations are used, one of eight to ten years to supply thatching spars and the other, more extensive, of 20 years or more to supply bean poles, pea sticks, rustic poles and firewood. A nearby rake factory also takes some of the crop. The 'maiden' or standard trees are usually oak or ash, while the coppice stools may be of almost any species, depending on the soil. Some of the stools are many hundreds of years old and two or three yards (metres) across. They may be among the oldest living things in Britain. When an area is coppiced it takes two years for the spring flowers to respond fully to the increase in available light. They may then form dense carpets, the flowers crowded so close that hardly anything else is visible. Among the more common species such as dog's mercury, primrose and wood anemone there are patches of early purple orchid and herb Paris – one of the most famous 'indicators' of ancient wood-land. Bradfield is also a stronghold for the oxlip, a rare primula only found on clay soils of old East Anglian woods.

In all, at least 350 species of flower-ing plant have been found in Bradfield Woods, making it one of the richest sites in Britain. With such a ground and shrub flora it is hardly surprising that the air is often full of birdsong: nightingales, blackcaps and garden warblers are here in spring and summer, as well as the more usual woodland birds. Bradfield boasts a full complement of rare mice – yellow-necked, harvest and dormouse. These should never be anticipated, but dormice have sometimes been seen at dusk, scampering among frayed honeysuckle stems to gather nesting material. You may be lucky!

THE *Walk*

Sunlight fills a recently coppiced area of the woods

···· 1 From the car park, enclosed by trees, take the track south. It is easy to imagine you are already in a fragment of ancient 'wildwood' but this is not the case; the block of trees to the left is of very recent origin. It is sometimes difficult to tell the difference. Ancient woodland, which has never been clear-felled, may have a continuous history of tree cover going back at least 7000 years. By contrast, 'secondary' woodland, which may have grown from bare ground in less than 50 years, tends to be less interesting, being of an even age structure and containing fewer species. The species composition of the woodland gives a clue to its real age: in recent woodland you will not find small-leaved lime, field maple or hawthorn. These 'indicator' trees are common in older parts of Bradfield Woods. Similarly there are several flowers of the woodland floor which disappear when a wood is first grubbed up and never return, no matter how carefully secondary woodland is encouraged to develop.

The track leads through a gate and enters Felsham Hall Wood, then continues to a crossroads, with a little clearing to the left. You are now in the old part of Bradfield Woods and have turned back the pages of history. Ahead lies Shady Ride, one of the oldest tracks into the wood, used to extract the coppice poles and timber. Access rides were carefully maintained, with drainage ditches on either side and a camber to ensure that carts did not get stuck in waterlogged clay. Shady Ride became so rutted and muddy that it had to be reshaped a few years ago.

Clearings are important to woodland wildlife, particularly butterflies which enjoy the sunny spaces and flowers. After their hibernation, peacock, small tortoiseshell and brimstone butterflies make special use of the sallow catkins. Later in the spring, bugle is the most attractive nectar source, followed by brambles and thistles.

···· 2 Turn sharp left at the little clearing and go along a narrow winding path through the trees. This area is called Front Fell. The path passes through panels of coppice, among which can be found small-leaved lime, probably the dominant tree over most of the wood in prehistoric times.

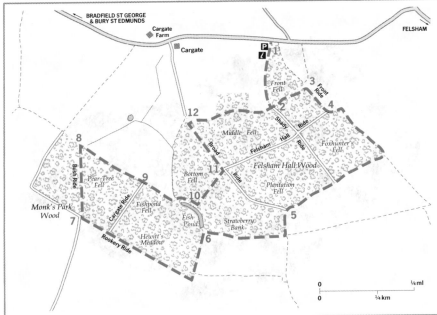

Coppicing in progress. All the resulting wood finds a use, from poles to pea-sticks

further to the south-west, but Rookery Ride now marks the boundary and the view to the left is of arable fields. There are several panels of coppice through the trees to the right, and a path to a wide clearing called Hewitt's Meadow. This was maintained by the monks as a grazing area for the deer and is quite unlike more temporary woodland glades and coupes. At its north-west corner there is a pond – a good place in the spring to look for frogs, newts and grass snakes.

Back on Rookery Ride, the path continues beside some young willow pollards marking the new boundary. Aspen and cricket-bat willow appear on the right. Very few trees have ever had to be planted in Bradfield Woods, but the willows were a speculative venture to extend the range of wood products in the 1950s.

Past Cargate Ride the wood changes character: the soil is dry and more acid, and bracken is dominant on the woodland floor.

7 **Turn right along the next ride at a crossroads where a tree-lined track leads left to a farm. The ride bears north through areas of birch coppice.**

8 **At the end of this ride, turn sharp right at the wood edge and continue along a meandering path beside Pear-Tree Fell.** This is a particularly attractive part of the wood and has some fine hazel stools as well as wild cherry, ash and some tall maiden oaks.

9 **The path leads out on to Cargate Ride, at which turn left, then right on to another path which winds along the northern edge of Fishpond Fell and leads past the opposite end of the fish pond.** Bur-reed and other emergent plant species now obscure the banks and basin of the pond, and it is unlikely ever to be reclaimed. The maintenance must have kept the abbey estate workers busy for years.

10 **Turn left along the trackway of Felsham Hall Ride.** This leads to a major crossroads where a clearing is specially managed as a butterfly corner.

11 **From here turn left, along Broad Ride to the northern edge of the wood.** Cornfields drift off into the distance beyond the bank.

12 **Turn right and continue along another winding path until it leads out opposite the first clearing beside Front Fell. From here turn left, back to the car park.**

3 **The path meets a much broader track, at which turn right.** This is Front Ride, one of the original trackways, of great antiquity and with some tall standard oaks to add their monolithic grace to the setting. The verges of the ride are enlivened by tussocks of pendulous sedge.

4 **At the end of Front Ride the route forks; bear left. The path leads through an area of blackthorn and sallow to the edge of the wood, with a footpath sign to Felsham. Stay inside the wood and bear right. The path follows the wood edge.** The boundary bank is in good condition here; there is a deep ditch on the outside, then a broad bank marked by pollarded trees. Some of these pollards are at least 300 years old. The process of keeping the branches lopped extends the life of trees considerably (most of Britain's most venerable oaks are old pollards) and, in time, often enhances their appearance. The monks established these boundary markers to keep farm stock out of the coppices.

The vegetation alongside the path includes spindle and old man's beard, plants associated with chalky soils.

Keep on the wood-edge path for some distance, around Foxhunter's Fell and past the end of Shady Ride, then beside Plantation Fell to the end of Broad Ride.

5 **Bear left at Broad Ride, staying with the wood edge. The main path bears right at a small wooden hide.** This overlooks a medieval fish pond (monks kept carp as well as deer). Although successive dry summers have reduced its volume, the pond is still a magnet for the woodland birds.

6 **Turn sharp left here to cross the boundary bank, then continue on the outside edge of the wood.** The deep ditch is full of sedges and the bank has a good mix of climbing and straggling plants. The elegant leaves of both black and white bryony are easy to pick out.

The path turns sharp right, back into the wood to continue along the wood edge. This is Rookery Ride, through the ancient deer park. Until 1966-70 the wood extended much

Walberswick

*A ruined windpump stands as a gaunt reminder of long-abandoned
attempts to drain Walberswick's vast reed-beds*

ANCIENT OAK WOODLAND, PINE PLANTATIONS, CARR, DRY AND WET HEATHLAND, MARSHES, MUDFLATS, SHINGLE, AND THE MOST EXTENSIVE REED-BED IN BRITAIN MAKE WALBERSWICK ONE OF THE TOP WILDLIFE SITES, IDEAL FOR A DAY OR A WEEKEND VISIT AT ANY TIME OF YEAR.

RETURNED TO NATURE

The great reed-beds north and south of the village of Dunwich on the Suffolk coast owe their existence to Hitler's threat to invade England. Land that had been reclaimed before the war was deliberately flooded again to hamper the Panzer columns. When peace came, there was no money left to repair the pumps and sluices, and the whole place was left to nature. Thus the RSPB was able to acquire a showpiece reserve at Minsmere, while the larger Walberswick estate remained in private ownership but is now managed as a National Nature Reserve. Walberswick has long been in Minsmere's shadow, but the two reserves can best be thought of as a single 3000-acre (1200-hectare) site.

THE HAND OF MAN

East Anglia is a dry region, so it is hardly surprising that its famous wetlands, such as the Broads and the north Norfolk marshes, owe their existence to human enterprise, or that heathland was once more extensive. The original tree cover of East Anglia was easily cleared in prehistoric times, to be replaced by farmland. However, because of the thin soil, extreme climate and bad farming practices, the heartland of the region reverted to heath. Recently the Suffolk heaths, both the Brecks and the Sandlings towards the coast, have been reclaimed again and are afforested, with pine and other conifers.

The countryside between Dunwich and the Blythe estuary reflects all these historical elements of land use, as a result of which the wildlife habitats come together in an exciting way, a stone's throw from the east coast, with good access from footpaths.

WESTWOOD MARSHES

At dusk, the Westwood Marshes, beneath the Westwood Lodge road, can be a dream world of silver mists and golden *Phragmites* reeds. Wildfowl fly in and out, and vast numbers of swallows or starlings (depending on the time of year) gather to roost. Birds of prey sometimes have to compete for air-space; in winter there may be

Marsh harrier

Walberswick

Suffolk
Grid ref. TM 479 707

Nature Conservancy Council (part) Approx. 7 miles (11 km). Easy walking.

Dunwich, at the start of the walk, lies 4 miles (6.4 km) south of Southwold on the Suffolk coast. Park in the large car park at the northern edge of the village, behind the shingle ridge of the sea wall.

This is one of the best birdwatching sites in Britain because of its location and the variety of habitats. The walk leads through farmland, forest, heath, marsh, reed-beds, salt-marsh and shingle. In summer the reed-beds hold breeding marsh harriers, bitterns and bearded tits, and there is often the occasional rarity about, such as a purple heron or a spoonbill. Walberswick is excellent at any time of the year; mid-winter is usually good for birds of prey.

Nearby site: *Minsmere RSPB Reserve* – similar to Walberswick, with a good system of hides which allows close observation of the marshes. (A permit is necessary for parts of the reserve.)

---

several hen harriers and merlins, and perhaps a goshawk or a rough-legged buzzard, all quartering the same stretch of woods or shadowing the network of dykes and earthworks that criss-crosses the marsh. In summer these birds will be replaced by marsh harriers, with perhaps a red-footed falcon, osprey or honey buzzard if you have chosen a particularly good day.

Some of the reed-beds are harvested for thatching, and this encourages a thicker growth of seed-heads. Bearded

tits (now also known as bearded reedlings) benefit from this. Over 100 pairs nest on the Westwood Marshes, making it one of the most important breeding sites for this species. There are also large numbers of sedge and reed warblers, among which there may sometimes be a pair of Savi's warblers. The cut beds attract snipe, lapwings and other waders. Until the mid 1980s these reed-beds were the home of the coypu, a big South American rodent which had become naturalised following its escape from fur-farms. Whether the coypu really damages crops and river banks as has been claimed is uncertain, but it became the subject of an eradication programme and is now considered extinct in Britain.

Essex skipper. Black-tipped antennae help distinguish it from the similar small skipper

THE SANDLINGS

The marshland of Walberswick is bounded to the west by woods and heaths, and to the east by a shingle ridge and the North Sea. The heath of the Sandlings – a ridge of thin acid soil backing the Suffolk coast – has always been outstanding for classic heathland birds. Sadly, the red-backed shrike has disappeared from Britain in the last 20 years, but in winter Walberswick is one of the most likely spots to see a great grey shrike, and the scrubby heather- and gorse-clad ground still holds good numbers of nightjars, stonechats, lesser whitethroats and nightingales. Deer are numerous – red, roe, fallow, muntjac and an occasional sika, and reptiles (adder, common lizard, slow-worm) are quite common.

WADERS AND SEABIRDS

The shingle ridge, which was repaired after the great flood of 1933 and now prevents the Westwood Marshes from turning brackish, is backed by pools and marshy fields, good for wading birds. In winter twites and snow buntings join the skylarks and finches searching for seeds above high water, and in the late summer, terns and skuas, the fishermen and pirates of the east coast, are never far from the shore.

THE *Walk*

The western part of the reserve is a fragment of the Suffolk Sandlings. More than nine-tenths of this once extensive tract of heathland has been destroyed in the past 200 years

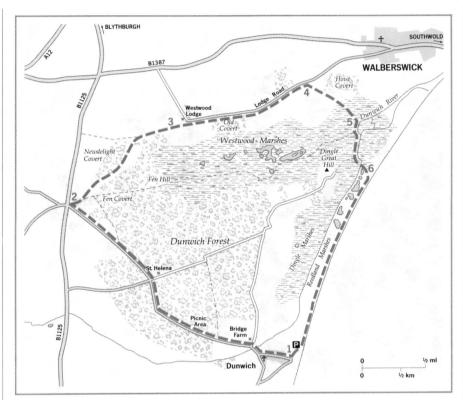

1 From the car park, walk back along the main street of Dunwich village and past the Ship Inn, then past a terrace of cottages and some attractive gardens. The hedgerows are lined with Alexanders – a yellow-flowered umbellifer with celery-like leaves and stem. Its blanched lower stem was once used as a winter vegetable and it is thought to have been introduced here from the Mediterranean, perhaps by the Romans. Behind the banks of Alexanders, and a thick elm hedge, there is marshland and scrub where grasshopper warblers sometimes sing.

The road continues, passing a church on the left and the turning for Minsmere. **Bear right with the road, across a stream and past Bridge Farm to the right. For the next mile (1.6 km), follow the road.** This is far from being a tedious section of the walk; the road passes through Dunwich Forest – a Forestry Commission plantation with verges of birch and oak, and bramble and gorse thickets which are alive with small birds such as whitethroats and willow warblers in spring and summer. Many acres of the plantation have been storm-damaged in recent years and there are now even more clearings. The pines sometimes contain crossbills, and this is also a locality for the pine hawk-moth, the adult of which can be found at rest on pine trunks in June and July.

Keeping to the road, go straight on at a little crossroads (signed as a 'No Through Road' to the right), after which the woodland soon ends and the road descends, with heathland of bracken and hawthorn scrub to left and right. Nightingales and tree pipits are to be found here in summer.

2 Just before another crossroads, where the Dunwich road meets the B1125 (Blythburgh) road, turn sharp right along a wide track to enter the National Nature Reserve. Continue north-east along the broad sandy path (not the grassy path to the right). The dry heathland here is good for solitary bees and wasps, such as the black and red sand wasp *Ammophila*, which finds the sand easy to dig into for nest building. Birds of this habitat include stonechats, lesser whitethroats and nightjars.

The track bears right, up and out of the trees and through an area of bracken with a fence to the right, then past a little cottage and a mature block of woodland called Newdelight Covert. Redstarts, nuthatches and all three species of woodpecker are found here, and this is also a good place for butterflies including holly blues, commas and Essex skippers.

3 Continue along the track, past Westwood Lodge, the large house to the left. Past an old quarry on the right there are now excellent views to the south and south-east across Westwood Marshes. This is the best place in winter to watch for birds of prey – almost certainly hen harriers, but anything can turn up: rough-legged buzzards, peregrines, even a red kite!

The track becomes a metalled road, called Lodge Road. Follow this past an oakwood on the right (called Old Covert) and through farmland. Walberswick church can be seen on the skyline ahead as the road winds downhill.

4 Turn right, off the road and along a bridleway which leads between scrub-covered hillocks. After about 100yds (90m) bear right along a sandy path, with a fence to the right and Hoist Covert, another block of woodland, across the heath and reed area to the left. Continue through an area of mixed woodland. Mainly blackthorn, sallow and oak, this wood-land is a good area for butterflies, including both green and purple hairstreaks.

At the end of the woodland,

through a clearing where cut reed is **often loaded, the path leads straight on, and out on to the marsh.** Marsh sow-thistle, a rare yellow-flowered plant which can reach 10ft (3m) in height, grows here. Soon the path along the old dyke carries you into a quite different world of open skies and whispering reeds. In the distance ahead lies the sea wall, but the most imposing feature is the remains of a windpump which once worked to drain the marshes.

Reed-beds stretch away in all directions, with Westwood Marsh (the best place to look for marsh harriers) to the west. Sounds carry a long way, particularly the calls of cuckoos, which lay their eggs in reed warblers' nests. Pig-like squeals will reveal the presence of water rails, while metallic 'ping, ping' calls will tell you that a party of bearded tits is close by.

5 **The path passes close to the windpump, then bears left towards the sea wall.** Two gorse-covered hills rise out of the marsh to the right, of which the bigger one is Great Dingle Hill, the site of a bird-ringing station.

6 **Continue to the sea wall.** The shingle ridge can be climbed for a view of the sea. Although this stretch of coast is not very good for seabirds, there are usually some to be seen – little terns in summer, and perhaps a diver or a grebe in winter. To the north is Walberswick village, to the south you can see the coastguard cottages at Minsmere and the brooding monster of Sizewell Nuclear Power Station. The shingle ridge is colonised by a surprising number of plants, among which sea pea, yellow horned poppy and sea kale are the most notable. There is usually some sea holly too.

Turn right (south), either along the top of the shingle ridge or at its base. Take care not to disturb nesting waders, such as ringed plovers or oystercatchers, which will let you know if they think you are getting too close. There are good views still of the reed-beds, of Dingle and Dunwich Marshes. The shallow, sometimes smelly pools just inland from the sea wall are caused by seepage and are slightly salty or brackish. They may not look very exciting but waders find them irresistible because of the little crustaceans and worms that they contain, and there are always several species about, especially in late summer and early autumn. Avocets, spotted redshanks, curlew sandpipers and little stints are often present, and recent rarities have included white-rumped and buff-breasted sandpipers.

If it is late in the day, this may be a good place to pause and listen to the sounds of evening. Bitterns may be booming, and nightjars may begin their churring flights over the heath.

The route follows the sea wall back to the car park.

Reed-beds, water and heath: Walberswick's variety of habitats guarantees plenty to see, whatever the time of year

Deeply divided leaves help distinguish the musk mallow from its many relatives

THE BRECKS, A UNIQUE AREA OF DRY EAST ANGLIAN HEATHLAND, IS EASIER TO FIND IN BOOKS THAN IN THE PRESENT LANDSCAPE. FORESTRY COMMISSION PLANTATIONS AND AMERICAN AIR BASES HAVE BECOME THE TRADE-MARK OF THE THETFORD AREA, TRANSFORMING A BLEAK AND WINDSWEPT, TREELESS LANDSCAPE INTO A SINISTER LAND OF SHADOWS. EAST WRETHAM (PRONOUNCED 'RET-TAM') HEATH IS A TINY SCRAP OF A PLACE WHERE ALL THE HISTORY OF BRECKLAND COMBINES WITH PERCEPTIVE SITE-MANAGEMENT UNDERTAKEN BY THE NORFOLK NATURALISTS TRUST. ALTHOUGH THE WALK IS SHORT IT IS PACKED WITH GOOD THINGS.

BRECKLAND IN HISTORY

The story of the Brecks began to unfold many thousands of years ago when Neolithic settlers cleared the virgin wildwood and established fields and farmsteads. Because the light soil was so easy to work, even with primitive tools, the land was quickly turned to cultivation. However, the thin, free-draining soils were almost as quickly exhausted, so the farmers began to open up new areas and move their crops and livestock from place to place. Eventually over 300 square miles (680 sq.km) of steppe were created through transient farming. The introduction of rabbits by the Normans gave the Brecks area another useful lease of economic life; warrens were easy to establish and about 10 per cent of the heathland was set aside for their management. For the rest, a shifting system of sheep-grazing and arable cultivation kept the land poor.

East Wretham Heath

Norfolk
Grid ref. TL 913 886

Norfolk Naturalists Trust (*permit required* – available at reserve. See below.)

Approx. 2¼ miles (3.6 km). Easy walking.

The reserve is closed all day on Tuesdays.

The car park is next to the Warden's House, close to Langmere on the A1075 road north of Thetford.

All visitors to the reserve must have a permit. These are available, free of charge, from the reserve shop on Sundays, or on weekdays, except Tuesdays, from the warden at 10am or 2pm daily (ring the bell in the car park for attention).

This small but very varied nature reserve comprises woodland, open water and grassland. The mere is especially fascinating, and the grassland is being managed to recreate Breckland conditions, favoured by a unique fauna and flora adapted to dry 'steppe' conditions.

Nearby sites: *Knettishall Heath* – Breck heath, calcareous grassland, fen and woodland with nightjars and green woodpeckers, also good for insects and spiders; *Santon Downham Bird Trail* – Breckland and woodland populated by woodlarks, woodpeckers, woodcocks, nightjars and nightingales.

Heath speedwell, also known as common speedwell, can form carpets of pale violet-blue flowers on dry heathland and grassland

Dry grassland backed by hawthorn and broom scrub – the old airfield at East Wretham

THE 20TH CENTURY

The beauty of the Brecks was of an uncompromising sort, and it had few friends. However, when war broke out in 1939 it became apparent that the flat East Anglian countryside would make an ideal base for Allied bombers. Airfields sprang up all over the place, and some of the biggest were on the Brecks. After the war the strategic importance of East Anglia had been established and the air bases grew, rather than diminished, in size. Also, the Forestry Commission had been charged with increasing timber production, so vast areas of the Breck country were turned conifer-green.

BRECKLAND RESTORED

East Wretham demonstrates, in microcosm, all that has befallen the Brecks. A stone's throw away are 30 square miles (78 sq.km) of virgin heath, owned by the Ministry of Defence, out of bounds but safe. Beyond that stretch mile upon mile of conifer plantations and a few cornfields. East Wretham Heath itself comprises less than 400 acres (162 hectares), of which a large slice is open grassland once overgrown, but now cut down and grazed again. The rabbit population is thriving, having built up some immunity to myxomatosis, the sheep are back and there is every hope of attracting stone curlews to nest here.

Breckland flowers are a complex mixture of rarities associated with dunes, cropped turf or disturbed ground. The rare fingered speedwell (*Veronica triphyllos*) and Breckland speedwell (*V. praecox*) are to be found in spring, and there are also unrivalled shows of more common plants such as viper's bugloss and musk mallow.

WALK 67

i

THE *Walk*

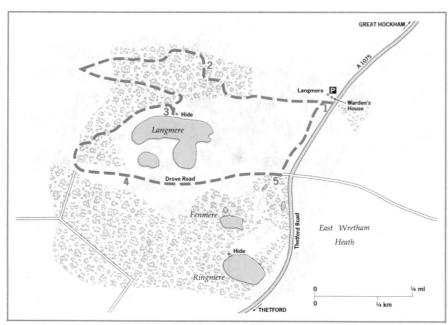

Pine trees lining the old pathway

harmless) and the pine hawk-moth.

After the pines the track crosses open grassland and bears left into a wood. Turn left along a wooded path, which meanders through bracken before leading out into an area of scrub. When the path meets a wide metalled section of runway, walk along this to a junction with another spur of the runway, at which turn left along it. The route continues through an area of open scrub, then woodland again to pass a short section of hand-rail which forms part of the reserve's excellent trail for visually handicapped visitors. From here head straight on, along another old metalled track then right along a grassy track. The reflection of light on the surface of one of the meres should now be visible through the trees, and a short detour will take you to a hide on its north bank. This is Langmere, the most attractive of East Wretham's family of lakes. There are groups of meres right across the Brecks, like pearls stitched into an old blanket. When the Brecks were an open desert the meres were green oases, used as gathering places for drovers to water stock and idle a few hours before travelling on. The water level of Langmere fluctuates, not according to recent rainfall but because of an eccentric upwelling of groundwater through the underlying chalk.

1 A fenced track leads from the car park to a gate. Go through this, heading west on a clear track. Only a few years ago the close-cropped sward here had disappeared along with the rabbits, in the wake of myxomatosis, and there were extensive beds of rosebay willowherb and other taller herbs and grasses. Better management, a return to grazing by sheep and a recovery in rabbit numbers has brought back the Breckland vegetation, and there is now a chance of finding one of the rarer speedwells.

Continue along the track towards the wood, passing some old pines before reaching a stile and gate. Go through this and bear right, beginning on a grassy track but continuing on a metalled surface – a remnant of the wartime air base. Where the track forks bear left (away from the fence). The tall scrub, of hawthorn, broom, ash and oak, has grown up since the 1940s and is ideal for insectivorous birds.

2 The route bears right, then off the metalled surface left, wandering along a grassy track before heading left beside a line of old pines. Crossbills nest here in varying numbers, boosted by influxes of immigrants every few years. The Breckland pines attract some impressive insects too, including the great horntail wasp (fearsome-looking but

3 Back on the main track, continue south-west with woodland (including some more tall pines) and the mere to the left. The track passes the trail for the visually handicapped again, at which bear left, then turn left again to meet a wide drove road. Turn left down this. It is impossible to tell how old this trackway really is; certainly it must be pre-Roman and it is quite possible that it dates back to Neolithic times. It is still a right of way, so that when the rest of the reserve is closed it is possible to take an evening walk from the main road.

4 Continue along the drove road, passing a spur of Langmere (probably dry), and eventually reaching a stile and gate on the left. The vegetation of the wide droveway begins as hair-grass but there is heather too, especially to the right where it grades into bracken and mixed woodland.

5 Cross the stile and walk back to the car park over grassland, rather than going along the road just to the right.

The flooded Washes in winter. The clump of trees is the old duck decoy

---

FENLAND IS NO LONGER AN APPROPRIATE NAME FOR THE SWEEP OF INTENSIVE ARABLE FARMLAND AROUND WISBECH AND ELY IN CAMBRIDGESHIRE, BUT SEVERAL HUNDRED YEARS AGO THIS WAS AN INHOSPITABLE DISTRICT OF PEAT SWAMPS. RAIN THAT FELL IN THE EAST MIDLANDS REACHED THE WASH VIA SLOW-FLOWING RIVERS SUCH AS THE WELLAND, THE NENE AND THE OUSE. INEVITABLY, THERE WAS EXTENSIVE FLOODING EVERY WINTER.

THE LOST WETLANDS

Early attempts to change the course of the rivers, or to build drainage channels, were of very limited success and it was left to a group of 17th-century entrepreneurs to tame the Fens by implementing ambitious and expensive engineering schemes. When these were successful, the local population of wildfowlers and eel-catchers tried to sabotage the operation and there began a long and bitter struggle between the 'Adventurers' and the 'Fen Tigers'. Of course, progress, and agricultural improvement, was inevitable and has continued to the point where virtually all the wetlands have been removed, even Whittlesey Mere which defied all such attempts until 1851 and was one of the last strongholds of the large copper butterfly.

A WILDFOWL HAVEN

Apart from a few scraps of land, the only parts of the Fens not under

---

Nene Washes

Cambridgeshire
Grid ref. TF 397 025

Approx. 15 miles (24 km) (see below for a shorter walk). Level walking.

Ring's End lies 4 miles (6.4 km) north of March on the A141. Park near the Fisherman's Haunt inn, or at Guyhirn. It is probably best to find a car space opposite the Fisherman's Haunt, below the arches of the railway line. For a shorter walk, park near Bassenhally Farm and walk to Eldernell and back.

An area of 'washland' or rough pasture which often floods during winter, this is an internationally important site for winter wildfowl. It is good in summer for wading birds and has some interesting flowers. When the Washes are flooded, avoid causing disturbance on top of the bank. Keep dogs on leads.

Nearby sites: *Ouse Washes (Manea and Welney)* – breeding waders, wintering swans and ducks; *Nene Washes RSPB Reserve* – hay meadows good for summer flowers and wintering swans and ducks (access by written permit only).

The short-eared owl usually hunts in daylight

---

intensive cultivation are the corridors of 'washland' intended to carry away occasional winter floodwater when the rivers cannot cope. The Ouse Washes, a ribbon of grazing land between the Old and New Bedford Rivers from Earith to Denver Sluice, are the more famous, but the Nene Washes are recognised as of comparable value for wildlife, particularly since they are now better managed and are liable to flood in most winters. The effect of flooding is, of course, to attract wildfowl by the thousand, including large numbers of Bewick's swans, pintails and wigeon. The rough banks and the abundance of wild grass seeds encourage finches and small mammals, which in turn attract birds of prey. During the summer the Washes provide breeding sites for black-tailed godwits and ruffs – two rare wading birds with only a very few breeding sites in Britain. Both birds have startlingly colourful spring plumage. The male ruff grows an elaborate ruff and indulges in 'leks' to attract a mate. The smaller female ruff is called a reeve, and is often mistaken for a different species.

ALONG MORTON'S LEAM

The Nene Washes lie between Peterborough and Ring's End, near Guyhirn. Here the present course of the River Nene (diverted in 1728) shadows a 15th-century drainage channel called Morton's Leam. It is possible to walk along the high dyke or retaining bank of Morton's Leam, with the washlands to the north and fields of wheat and sugar beet to the south. The landscape is as flat as a pancake and there are only a few willow trees and gateways to break the horizon, but in winter the stark simplicity of the place, and the piercing cold, can take your breath away.

The Bewick's Swan

The distant sound of wild swans, and the sight of a family of these great white birds beating their way over the marshes to the open water, is one of the most magical experiences of winter. Numbers of year-round resident mute swans are augmented by two migratory species that come from the Arctic. The whooper swan, which is the bigger of the two, has a prominent yellow patch on its beak and breeds in Iceland while the smaller Bewick's swan breeds around the Yamal peninsula in north Russia and shows a smaller patch of yellow on the beak. The Bewick's swan, in particular, used to be quite rare in this country, but in recent years more and more are overwintering here. Of a total European population of about 16,000 well over 4000 are to be seen around the Nene and Ouse Washes.

THE *Walk*

1 To the right of the inn is a track and a space for fishermen to park; walk along this track, through a gate and up a bank. From the top it will be apparent straight-away if the distant Washes are flooded. If there is no standing water then do not despair: look for birds of prey rather than wild swans. In winter, up to 25 short-eared owls, six hen harriers and occasional peregrines and merlins hunt along the banks. This is the narrowest point of the Washes, between Morton's Leam and Nene Bank, and the fields here do not usually flood. They are covered with tussocky grass and thorn scrub – ideal for flocks of finches and buntings which can no longer scratch a living from the arable farmland.

Walk along the path to the top of the bank. The ploughed 'black fen' is rich and dark because of its peat content. But as it dries, peat shrinks, and the level of the fields to the left of the bank is much lower than the washlands to the north of Morton's Leam. Past Guyhirn Corner there is a narrow strip of grassland and a thorn hedge to the left of the bank which is often patrolled by short-eared owls. These are diurnal hunters, feeding almost exclusively on field voles. They have a unique moth-like flight which makes them easy to identify, even from a considerable distance.

The Washes open out to the right as the two banks diverge; the fields undulate slightly and this allows pools of water to accumulate and stand well into the spring. These are the conditions favoured by breeding and passage waders.

Male pintail – sure to be seen here in winter

2 Continue along the path, crossing several fences, until a farm is passed. In winter, the arable fields are used by herds of Bewick's swans which sometimes get weighed down by mud on their feet and may then fly into overhead cables. Up to 1000 of these birds regularly use the Nene Washes. Over 3000 pintails, 5000 wigeon, 2000 teal, 1000 golden plovers and 800 snipe are some of the winter figures. Numbers increase dramatically after the end of January when the shooting season ends and the area is safe.

The central section of the Washes is constricted by recent embankments enclosing new farmland, but the Nature Conservancy Council is negotiating management agreements with landowners to try to avoid such problems in the future.

3 The route continues past a triangulation column and on to Eldernell, where it crosses a track by a sluice but then keeps to the top of the bank again. The clump of crack willows out in the Washes is the remains of a duck decoy – a circle of trees hiding a pool into which ducks were once lured. There were dozens of decoys in East Anglia in the 18th and 19th centuries. Today the old decoy pool has been colonised by thorn bushes and is a haunt of woodcock and long-eared owls.

Past Eldernell Farm the Washes are a little shallower and there is a small area of osier and fen. Close to the bank is an alder grove in which herons nest, and just after this is the start of the RSPB Nene Washes reserve. This can be visited only by written application to the warden (access is from the B1040 north of Whittlesey), but part of the reserve can be seen from the public footpath here. Management for wildlife has brought about a transformation here to varied fields attracting a wide range of birds. The drains are more likely to hold aquatic plants too, such as frogbit and flowering rush.

4 The Delph Dike at Whittlesey marks the effective end of the Nene Washes, and Bassenhally Farm is a convenient stopping point for the walk. The return walk is along the same route, back to the Fisherman's Haunt.

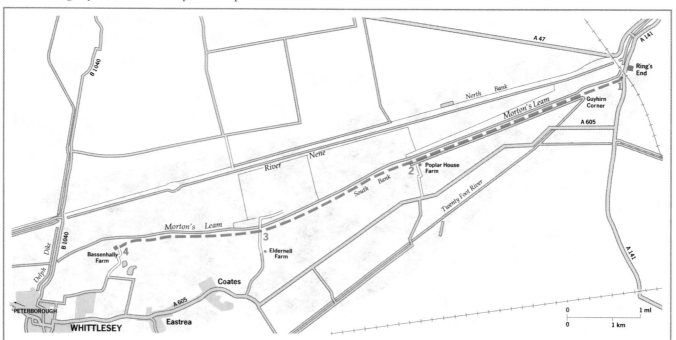

Sea asters can tolerate a salty environment because the fleshy leaves retain fresh water

'BREYDON' DERIVES FROM THE DANISH WORD MEANING THE BROADENING OF A RIVER. IT IS AN APT NAME FOR THIS ESTUARY, WHERE THREE RIVERS – WAVENEY, YARE AND BURE – MEET BEFORE THEIR WATERS POUR JOINTLY INTO THE SEA THROUGH YARMOUTH HARBOUR. IT REMAINS A REMOTE, WILD PLACE, DESPITE ITS PROXIMITY TO THE BUSTLING PORT AND HOLIDAY RESORT OF GREAT YARMOUTH. THIS IS A LANDSCAPE OF HUGE SKIES, LONELY GRAZING LEVELS AND MUDFLATS – THE HAUNT OF WILDFOWL, PARTICULARLY IN WINTER.

DRAINAGE OF THE MARSHES

Changing water levels are the key to understanding this land and its wildlife: both tides and man-made drainage systems play an important role. Once the estuary of Breydon was unconfined by walls; extensive saltings graded into freshwater marshes. During the 18th and 19th centuries these marshes were progressively drained with a network of drainage ditches, and sea walls were strengthened. Water was pumped from the marsh dykes into Breydon by a series of windpumps. The Berney Arms Mill remains as a reminder of these times. The 20th century saw the use of steam-powered pumps, which were later succeeded by electric pumps. These proved even more effective and winter flooding became a rarity.

Breydon Water & Berney Marshes

Norfolk

Grid ref. TG 460 053

Royal Society for the Protection of Birds/Great Yarmouth Borough Council

Approx. 5 miles (8 km). Easy walking, but very exposed in winter.

Breydon Water lies immediately west of Great Yarmouth. The walk involves a short train journey to avoid retracing the route: park at Great Yarmouth station and catch the train to the remote station at Berney Arms on the Norwich – Yarmouth line. Trains stop here only by request, so please notify the guard before the train leaves Yarmouth. The journey takes about 9 minutes.

This large estuary and its associated marshes are good in winter for birds, especially wildfowl and waders. In summer the saltings and grazing marshes are studded with wild flowers. These habitats contrast with those elsewhere in Broadland.

Nearby sites: *Strumpshaw Fen* – broadland freshwater marshes, good dykes and plant life, with a fair chance of seeing Cetti's warbler and water rail; *Upton Broad* – broadland fen, nature trail; *Ranworth Broad* – nature trail, interpretative centre and boardwalk through broadland.

Wood sandpiper, seen on the east coast in spring and autumn. These birds breed in northern Europe and overwinter in Africa

FARMING AND CONSERVATION

Until the late 19th century Breydon supported a hardy breed of men who lived by catching eels and shooting wildfowl from punt and shore. While the marshes were poorly drained, these men were able to make a precarious living out of the thousands of wildfowl which congregated on Breydon. During this period Breydon developed a reputation for being a favoured locality for rare birds. However, increasing concern about declining bird numbers led to the passing, in 1880, of a Wild Birds Protection Act covering Breydon – a forerunner of modern Bird Protection Acts.

Continuing improvements in the drainage of the grazing levels after World War II led to a heightening interest among farmers in converting these rough pastures, traditionally used for grazing, to arable land. These conversions led to confrontations between conservationists and farmers in the late 1970s and early 1980s, which were finally resolved when the Government agreed to compensate farmers for not ploughing pasture. For arable farming to succeed, the water levels in the dykes had to be kept low, creating unfavourable conditions for both summer breeding birds like redshanks and winter visitors like wild Bewick's swans. Now, with changing attitudes and the purchase of land by the RSPB, some of the grazing marshes are being managed with higher summer levels in the dykes and winter flooding of the grasslands. Already the benefits of this are being seen. Increasing numbers of wildfowl are returning to the grazing levels in winter, and redshanks and lapwings nest in summer.

Unlike the North Norfolk coast, Breydon Water has only a very small fringing salt-marsh except at the Yarmouth end, so that as the tide comes in many birds have to move off the estuary. This means that for bird-watching, most birds are concentrated at high tide.

The Black Tern

Although they do not breed in Britain, black terns are regular passage migrants to Britain in spring and autumn. Their nearest breeding colonies are in Holland so, not surprisingly, British sightings are most frequently recorded along the east coast of England; Breydon Water is a particularly good spot.

This is a comparatively small tern, with a buoyant and graceful flight. Unlike other terns, black terns do not dive in the water but instead catch insects on the wing or pick them from the surface of the water. In breeding plumage, the black tern is unmistakable, with a black body, dark upperwings and pale underwings. Outside the breeding season, its plumage is rather mottled.

THE *Walk*

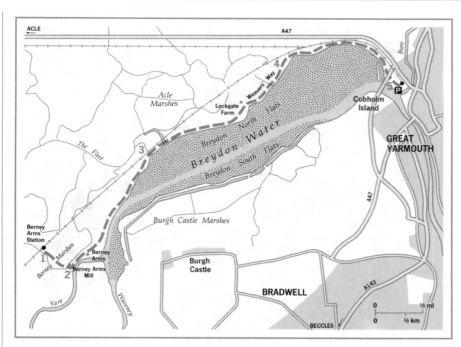
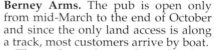

1 After alighting at Berney Arms station, cross the railway line and go through a gate. Follow the signs to the windmill, passing the RSPB reserve notice. On either side of the track are the Berney Marshes, part of an extensive area of grazing marshes drained by an intricate dyke system. The dykes are mostly fringed with reed. Look for scattered plants of the handsome pink-flowered marsh mallow which has distinctive soft grey leaves, and which prefers to grow in marshes close to the sea. The common buttercup in this area is the hairy buttercup, a characteristic species of pastures near the sea.

Winter is the time for wildfowl; numbers vary according to the amount of flooding and the severity of the weather. There is a good chance of seeing Bewick's swans, wigeon, pintails, teal and sometimes white-fronted or other geese. In some winters, the day-flying short-eared owl is not uncommon on these marshes. In spring, the damp grassland is ideal for nesting redshanks, lapwings, mallards, shovelers and gadwalls.

2 The footpath goes to the right of Berney Arms Mill and then on to the river bank. Turn left, to follow the river bank, then the sea wall, for the rest of the walk. The windmill is open in summer and is worth a visit. There are displays on the history of the mill and the surrounding marshes, while the views across the marshes are superb.

Continue along the bank, with the River Yare on your right, past the Berney Arms. The pub is open only from mid-March to the end of October and since the only land access is along a track, most customers arrive by boat.

The path continues along the river bank past the point where the Rivers Yare and Waveney enter Breydon Water. The increasing influence of the sea is noticeable: the base of the wall is covered in the brown seaweed, bladder wrack. A few salt-marsh plants appear, including sea aster and grass-leaved orache. On the landward side, look out for the tall spikes of marsh sow-thistle, once a rare plant largely confined to this part of Broadland, but now a familiar feature in late summer along Broadland rivers. Cormorants and oystercatchers are a sign of the start of the estuary.

3 The path leaves the Berney Marshes RSPB reserve where the Halvergate Fleet drain discharges into the estuary. Here there is a fragment of salt-marsh with sea aster, marsh arrowgrass and sea plantain. At low tide, extensive mudflats appear, providing a rich feeding ground for thousands of waders, particularly in the winter months. Waders and wildfowl that frequent these mudflats include dunlins, curlews, black-tailed and bar-tailed godwits, knots, curlew sandpipers, grey plovers, goldeneyes and red-breasted mergansers. There is always the chance of a rarity. In summer, great crested grebes often congregate in the estuary during their moult.

4 The path continues along the bank until it comes very close to the railway. From this point the saltings become more extensive, and are particularly attractive in summer when they are coloured purple with common sea-lavender. Look out also for glasswort or marsh samphire, which forms a narrow fringe along the edge of the salt-marsh in summer. There are two hides along this stretch, which give good views over the saltings and mudflats. The first is owned by the RSPB and the second by Great Yarmouth Borough Council. The RSPB hide overlooks platforms which have been built to provide nesting places for common terns.

5 The path continues under the new Breydon road bridge and finishes at a large supermarket car park close to the railway station.

Breydon Water in winter – the best time to see birds, but go prepared for east winds

THE *W*ALK

Clear and still: sea-light at dusk on the creek, with Cley village and windmill beyond

••••1 At the western side of The Eye car park, above the road-end, is a grassy bank with a path along the top of it. This is the West Bank, separating the reclaimed marsh from the saltings. Turn left along the path and follow it towards Cley village. The well-preserved windmill is Cley's most distinctive feature. The muddy creeks of the salt-marsh are hidden beneath a quilt of sea purslane. This stretches as far as the eye can see to the west, framed on one side by the wooded rise around Blakeney church and on the other by the long shingle ridge of Blakeney Point. The building just visible along the Point is called the Watch House, but is known to most birdwatchers as Half-way House.

Continue along the West Bank. The mournful cries of wading birds such as redshanks, greenshanks, curlews and grey plovers ring around the marshes all the time. Waders evolved these contact-calls to carry across open spaces, and the sounds resonate wonderfully.

The West Bank follows the road, with a narrow ribbon of reeds between the two. Opposite the small pool and sluice-gate it is a good idea to descend and follow the road, but if you have boots you can carry on a little further, until the bank angles westwards, then drop down to the road. The pool sometimes carries a few ducks, and the bushes beside it always seem to attract one or two autumn migrants such as barred and icterine warblers.

••••2 The beach road meets the main coast road, at which turn left, away from the village. Cars are not usually travelling fast, but take care and try to keep on the grass verge. It is easy to be distracted by birds over the marshes to your left, but the views are poor at first because the road is barely higher than the reeds.

A path above a car park on the right leads up to the Norfolk Naturalists Trust visitor centre, from where a permit may be bought to use the hides dotted around the marsh. Although not essential, it is worth visiting the hides, either in the course of the walk or as part of an evening car tour. Some birds, such as passage warblers, crakes and rails, and the nesting avocets, are only seen properly by entering the reserve.

Continue along the roadside. Off the road are several public hides

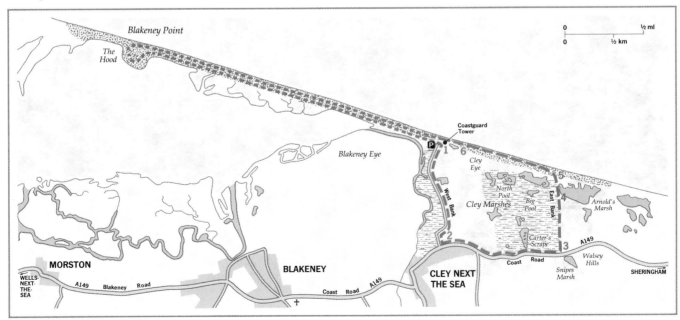

Whimbrels are unusual visitors to Britain. They are most likely to be seen in the spring

which give better views over the marshes. Carter's Scrape is one of the larger areas of mud and open water which is good for passage waders (ruffs, greenshanks etc.) and marsh terns if there are any about. After ³/₄ mile (1.2 km) of road-walking you approach a scrub-covered hillside (Walsey Hills) with a reed-fringed pool (Snipes Marsh) on the right. For many years Walsey has been the site of a bird-ringing station and observatory (a hut), now run by the Norfolk Ornithological Association.

3 There is a small car park on the left side of the road, just before Snipes Marsh, and next to it is another grassy bank leading towards the sea. This is the East Bank – one of the best-known birdwatching spots in Britain. Walk along the path on the top of the bank. To the right are grazing marshes, to the left is the Naturalists Trust reserve, of reed-beds and associated drains and channels. Many people walk straight along the East Bank, to reach either the reserve hides or the sea wall, but one of the most successful strategies can be to sit for a while in the grass and wait for birds to fly over. They always do; anything from bitterns to black terns, depending on the time of year. Mid-summer is perhaps the least interesting time, but even then there are bearded

tits, bitterns and harriers in the reed-beds. Drinker-moth caterpillars, cinnabar and burnet moths may share the grassy bank with you.

4 Towards the end of the East Bank pass Arnold's Marsh, on the right. This National Trust property used to be one of the best bird-watching places before the creation of all the other lagoons and scrapes, and it still attracts good numbers of wildfowl and waders.

5 At the end of the East Bank turn left and walk either along the top of the sea wall or at its base. The sea is sometimes worth watching (for shearwaters, skuas etc.), but if there is little coastal movement it is less tiring to walk close to the marsh where the shingle is firmer underfoot.

6 Continue along the sea wall, towards the coastguard tower, passing a stile to the Naturalists Trust hide and a small brackish pool with a wartime pillbox beside it. This unattractive little pool has provided a haven for phalaropes and other storm-driven vagrants, and there are often one or two gulls, terns and plovers around it.

Return to The Eye car park.

7 The second, optional part of the walk now leads west along Blakeney Point. To walk the 8 miles (13 km) to the end of the Point and

back needs considerable time and energy and is only recommended if you are fit and motivated. (A 1¹/₂–2 hour boat trip from Blakeney or Morston Quay is an enjoyable alternative in the summer, to see the tern colonies and the seals.) The Hood – about half-way along the Point – is as far as you really need to go unless there has been an exceptional fall of migrants. The shingle ridge, colonised by yellow horned poppy, sea kale and spurrey, is the first landfall for birds on the move. When the winds have been in the east but the weather has deteriorated, thousands of migrants reach the beach in an exhausted state. Long-eared owls, woodcocks, wrynecks and a variety of other species can then be found here, drugged by tiredness and reluctant to fly. The scraps of cover sometimes carry hundreds of black-caps, robins, goldcrests or redwings. In the winter there are usually a few snow buntings, shore larks or Lapland buntings about.

Return from The Hood along the landward side of the ridge; a path between the shingle and the mud offers an easier return route back to The Eye. The seablite bushes are worth careful consideration in the autumn, when they may contain skulking rarities such as bluethroats and red-breasted flycatchers. In summer the salt-marsh is a mass of sea-lavender and marsh samphire – still sold locally as a speciality salad vegetable.

SHIFTING SAND MAKES A HARSH ENVIRONMENT FOR PLANTS AND ANIMALS. DUNES ARE CREATED BY THE POWERFUL FORCES OF THE SEA AND THE WIND. EVEN WHEN MARRAM GRASS HAS FIXED THEM INTO SHAPE, THEY ARE STILL VULNERABLE TO HIGH TIDES AND BLOW-OUTS. FOR WILDLIFE, AN EXTENSIVE DUNE SYSTEM SUCH AS AINSDALE IS A CHALLENGING WORLD.

A HOSTILE ENVIRONMENT

Sandy ridges alternate with depressions or 'slacks', some of which are dry while others are wet and marshy for most of the year. Dune plants cope with the problems of well-drained soils and drying winds in a variety of ways. Many flower early and have finished their yearly cycle by midsummer. Others have succulent stems or leaves to store water, thick outer skins and curled leaves to reduce transpiration, or deep root systems to reach down to the water table below.

THE SEASIDE TRADITION

As well as being a fascinating wildlife habitat, dunes are often associated with traditional seaside pleasures; with memories of sunny days, ice-creams and donkey rides. It is certainly possible at Ainsdale to enjoy a dune walk with a notebook in one hand and an ice-cream in the other: the wilderness is adjacent to Southport beach, and the main car park for the nature reserve is next door to a holiday camp. The great surprise at Ainsdale is that after a few minutes everything but the dunes and their wildlife is forgotten, invisible and irrelevant.

A WORLD OF WILDLIFE

Snakes and lizards, bees, wasps and hunting spiders find conditions here very much to their liking, even – or especially – in the heat of summer. The rare sand lizard is one of the specialities of the site; the male is unmistakable in the breeding season, when his flanks are green. Sand lizards are also larger than common lizards. Natterjack toads spawn in the shallow waters of the slacks and are often overlooked because they usually come out only at night. Most visitors are impressed by the drifts of dune flowers – marsh orchids, marsh helleborines, round-leaved wintergreen and grass of Parnassus – and by the constant buzz of insects around the slacks and above the banks of sea spurge on the sandy slopes. There is

every incentive to linger in the sheltered suntraps of the dunes.

White dead-nettle

Ainsdale Dunes

Merseyside
Grid ref. SD 297 127

Nature Conservancy Council/Sefton Borough Council
Approx. 6 miles (9.5 km). Easy walking.

Ainsdale is 2 miles (3.2 km) south of Southport on the A565. Park between Pontin's Holiday Village and the Trafalgar Inn, or alternatively on the beach.

The northern part of the walk area is a Local Nature Reserve owned and managed by Sefton Borough Council; the southern part is a National Nature Reserve. Both reserves have extensive dune systems with ponds or slacks. Insects, plants, reptiles and amphibians are the main wildlife interest, so this is definitely a walk for a summer's day.

Nearby sites: *Sands Club Lake* – sand-dune flora and fresh water; *Seaforth Coastal Nature Reserve* – pools and marshes, good for migrant seabirds and shore birds; *Ribble Marshes* salt-marsh and estuary with large numbers of waders and wildfowl in winter and migration periods.

The damp, lime-rich sand of some of Ainsdale's dune slacks provides ideal conditions for early marsh orchids, which bloom in abundance

Bees and Wasps – Creatures of the Dunes

Bumble bees are peculiarly British creatures – their 'fur coats' and social habit suit them to our climate. However, most other bees and wasps do better on the Continent where the weather is more reliable. They need warmth, and for this reason dunes are good places to find them.

Most of the bees and wasps found at Ainsdale are solitary rather than social: each female makes her own little nest and provisions a series of cells with pollen and nectar (in the case of bees) or insect prey (in the case of wasps). Look for holes in the sand, then sit and wait to see what arrives. It may be a leaf-cutter bee, a red-bodied sand-wasp or a yellow-bodied sand-wasp. It may even be a spider-hunting wasp – a small but fierce creature which fills its nest cells with spiders. These have to be paralysed and dragged back to the burrow, often several yards (metres) away over the shifting desert.

THE *WALK*

Natterjack toad – more often heard than seen

1 Take the dune path, which starts close to the perimeter wall of Pontin's Holiday Village. After about 50yds (45m) take the left fork (signed 'Pinfold Path') and continue along the sandy path, at first beside the perimeter wall, then bearing right to follow the marker posts. There is some sea buckthorn, specially planted to reinforce the marram and lyme-grass in the battle against the shifting dunes. In the more marshy hollows there are patches of meadowsweet and creeping willow. An abundant shrub here, this looks quite unlike other willows and has distinctive 'cottonball' seeds. The small red blisters on the leaves are galls made by sawflies.

2 At a junction, turn right along the Dune Trail. This leads to a wet slack, covered with horsetail, bogbean and marsh pennywort – a good place for dragonflies. This path then continues with a dune ridge to the right, a bank of windswept and friable sand colonised by clumps of rest-harrow and sea spurge – a very local and exotic-looking plant. Solitary wasps and robber-flies are especially numerous here.

Soon, **turn left and cross a boardwalk.** Here there is another good view of a wet slack with a boggy area of cotton-grass and, at the right time of year, patches of the brick-red flower spikes of early marsh orchid.

3 Turn right, back on to the Pinfold Path, and follow the posts of this waymarked path to the boundary of the National Nature Reserve. Again, there are some good wildlife sites along the way. Many of the flowers, such as storksbill, milkwort and hawkweed, are small and brightly coloured – another response to climate. Butterflies appear in good numbers too; they include the dark

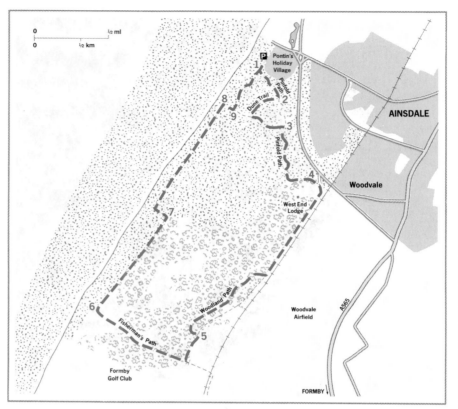

green fritillary as well as the more usual grassland species such as common blue, large skipper, meadow brown and small heath.

Continue into the National Nature Reserve along the Pinfold Path. There are more slacks beside the path, which passes through scrubland of birch, hawthorn and dog rose and then grey and black poplars (look for puss moth caterpillars on the lower leaves). The path then leads through pine and sycamore woodland, planted to anchor the mature dunes.

4 When the path meets a metalled track, turn right along this and head straight on, with trees to the right and the railway and Woodvale Airfield to the left, for about ½ mile (800m). After this, turn right along a sandy path, signed 'Woodland Path'. This winds its way through an attractive pinewood with birch clearings.

5 Eventually the Woodland Path meets a gravelled track. This is the main track again. Turn right on to it, past a golf club to the left and through more open woodland before turning right again along the Fisherman's Path. This leads to the coast and a ridge of windswept sand,

the first stage in the dune-creation process.

6 Turn right before the dune ridge where there is a clear path. This is a good area for flowers, with numerous orchids. Sea holly grows in the dunes. The small water-filled slacks may have natterjack tadpoles; this is where the toads come to breed each spring.

7 At the National Nature Reserve/Sefton Borough Council boundary turn left to reach the beach by the vehicle barrier and walk along the high-tide mark until you are past the second barrier. The beach here was once separated into fishing 'stalls', which were leased by the Lord of the Manor for the stake-netting of cod and whiting.

8 Turn right by the public toilets, along the Dune Trail, following the marker posts. The trail leads to an area of slacks with more natterjack toad breeding ponds, and drifts of orchids.

9 Turn left, parallel with the coast, and follow the posts back to the starting point of the walk and your car.

MAPS OF THE SPURN PENINSULA FROM CENTURIES AGO SHOW QUITE A DIFFERENT STRUCTURE FROM WHAT WE SEE TODAY; THE NORTH SEA HAS MOVED THE WHOLE PENINSULA BODILY, AND TODAY ELABORATE SEA DEFENCES ARE NECESSARY TO PREVENT IT FROM DISAPPEARING ALTOGETHER.

PROTECTING THE SPURN PENINSULA

Erosion of the Holderness coastline further north has provided the sand and shingle that have been deposited at the mouth of the Humber estuary to form the long ridge of Spurn. The building of sea walls and groynes has slowed down the process of erosion further up the coast, so the supply of building material has been reduced and the peninsula has become narrow and dangerously low in places. Severe storms could now breach the peninsula in some places; if this happened, the consequences for the sheltered mudflats of the estuary would be very serious. For this reason the beach is protected by groynes and other sea defences to help keep it in place. This is not a new phenomenon; there are records of the spit being washed away following a breach in 1608, and a series of breaches in the 1840s and 1850s reduced the peninsula to a chain of little islands.

BIRDS AT SPURN

Throughout the winter, wildfowl, especially brent geese, shelducks and mallards, feed on the mudflats. During migration periods they are joined by many waders, including dunlins, oystercatchers, knots, turnstones, curlews and redshanks. Several species of tern pass through in late summer, and sometimes an arctic skua causes panic as it chases them, hoping to make them drop their food.

The dominant shrub in the sandier areas is sea buckthorn, an attractive plant with silvery-grey leaves and clusters of orange berries. It is important as a stabilising plant on sand dunes, although in some places it is considered too invasive and is strictly controlled. Here it is a useful food- and shelter plant for birds, and in autumn pied and spotted flycatchers, redstarts, whinchats and wheatears may all be found here. Winter brings hungry flocks of starlings, redwings and fieldfares which devour the berries after their crossing of the North Sea, while the resident robins, dunnocks and blackbirds live secretive lives deep in

Waxy leaves help sea holly to conserve water

Spurn Head

North Humberside
Grid ref. TA 417 151

Yorkshire Wildlife Trust
Approx. 5^1/$_2$ miles (8.8 km). Level walking, but very exposed. Walking on loose sand can be difficult in places. No dogs allowed. No access to surroundings of coastguard station at Point.

Spurn Head lies at the mouth of the Humber estuary, about 22 miles (35km) south-east of Hull. There is parking at the entrance to the nature reserve, on a minor road south-east of Kilnsea.

This long and narrow ridge of sand and shingle protects the mouth of the Humber estuary from the North Sea and is one of the best places in Britain for seeing migrant birds. Extensive tidal flats inside the ridge are rich feeding grounds for waders, gulls and wildfowl.

Nearby site: *Blacktoft Sands* – lagoons and reed-fringed ditches overlooked by hides which offer close views of estuary and marsh birds.

Sand martin – sometimes seen here

---

buckthorn thickets. A great number of bird species is recorded annually at Spurn, but sometimes the numbers of one individual species are amazing; on one occasion a 'fall' of 6000 blackbirds was recorded in a single day.

The whole peninsula is very well watched by birdwatchers and in addition to the more regular species seen in large numbers each year, some rarities turn up which should not be there at all; they are often species which should be much further east and have been blown across the North Sea by storms, making Spurn their first landfall. Bird traps and mist nets are used to capture birds which can then be weighed, measured and ringed before being released perfectly unharmed.

PLANT AND INSECT LIFE

The sand dunes have an interesting flora dominated by marram grass on the seaward side and sea buckthorn in the more stable area, but attractive plants like sea holly, sea bindweed and spring beauty also grow here, and a number of chalk-loving species can be found in sheltered spots. Restharrow, storksbill, ploughman's spikenard, pyramidal orchid and yellowwort may all be here as a result of the chalk and various building materials brought in to strengthen the ridge. The mudflats are being colonised by cordgrass which helps to stabilise the mud, but it does reduce the available feeding areas for birds.

Insect life is also abundant on Spurn, with several species of butterfly, moth and beetle found here but not elsewhere in Humberside or Yorkshire. Small tortoiseshell, wall brown, red admiral and painted lady are regularly seen and the six-spot burnet moth is an attractive day-flying moth which lays its eggs on clovers and vetches. The beach is often littered with algae, seamats, cuttlebones and shells after a storm, and offers good pickings for beachcombers.

THE *W*ALK

1 From the entrance gate to the nature reserve walk down the road. After a short distance, stop and scan the bushes through binoculars for migrant birds. Spring and autumn are best, and calm days after stormy weather may produce the highest numbers. Check for butterflies on bramble and ragwort flowers.

2 Continue down the road. Scan the mudflats with binoculars, or preferably a telescope. A rising tide is best as this will push the birds towards the shore, and mornings are better than afternoons, as the sun will be behind you. Check the small area of salt-marsh immediately next to the shore, as larks, pipits, wheatears and buntings may be feeding here at various times of year.

3 From the raised sections of road, scan out to sea for passing seabirds. In summer and early autumn auks from the Bempton Cliffs colonies may be seen far off shore, and gannets

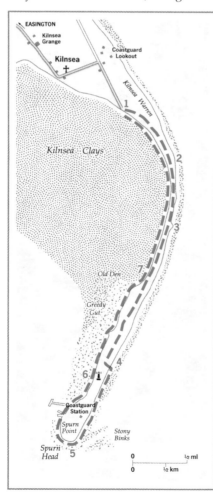

Grass and scrub anchor the sand of the dunes, but Spurn Head's vulnerable beach has to be stabilised to protect it from storms

and divers move through later in the season. Sometimes a predatory skua chases other seabirds; the great skua is larger and more bulky, and may chase kittiwakes or gulls, but the more agile arctic skua usually chases terns.

4 Check the sea buckthorn bushes carefully for migrant birds. Look for sea holly in the more open, sandy areas, and watch for migrant butterflies, such as painted ladies, feeding on it. The presence of rabbits may be detected by their droppings; foxes and weasels, though resident, will be much more difficult to see.

5 Continue around the Head on the shore. Do not enter the gardens or the surroundings of the buildings near the Point. Look along the strand line for shells and other debris. The pebbles themselves are interesting, as some may have drifted here from a great distance away. Among them are always a few fossils from further up the Yorkshire coast. Terns fish off shore in summer, and in

autumn red-throated divers pass through. Gulls are nearly always present, following fishing boats and larger vessels in and out of the estuary. Whatever the time of year, there will always be some bird movement here. Common seals are sometimes seen off shore or hauled out on sandbanks, and occasionally porpoises are seen by birdwatchers with telescopes trained on the sea.

6 Follow the shore around the western side of the peninsula and head back towards the road. Look at the surface of the sand for signs of marine life below the surface. Lugworms and tellin shells, both important food species for fish and birds, leave their characteristic marks at the surface; the worms leave casts and holes and the tellins leave tiny depressions.

7 Return to the start along the inner shore. Check carefully for small birds along the strand line. The seeds of some of the dune and salt-marsh plants collect here and are a useful source of food for birds. A kestrel sometimes hunts in this area, hoping to take an unwary bird by surprise.

Bird cherry blooms well before the ash trees come into leaf. Limestone pavements like this support a unique and very rich flora

ONE OF ONLY A HANDFUL OF NATURAL LAKES IN YORKSHIRE, MALHAM TARN IS SURROUNDED BY SOME OF BRITAIN'S FINEST LIMESTONE SCENERY – AN AREA OF GREAT BEAUTY AND OUTSTANDING INTEREST, ESPECIALLY TO NATURALISTS AND GEOLOGISTS.

GEOLOGY OF THE DALES

The main rock type in the Dales is Carboniferous Limestone, a tough white rock which forms impressive crags, limestone pavements and deep gorges; hidden from view is an extensive cave system and a network of underground streams. In places the limestone is overlaid by other rock types. The Yoredale Series consists of many layers of limestone, shale and sandstone; these wear away at different rates, giving a tiered effect to slopes, with a series of small but steep cliffs interspersed with gentler slopes such as on Ingleborough. Millstone Grit occurs in some places, giving rise to boggy, acidic conditions where cotton-grass and sphagnum moss can flourish.

The landscape of the Dales has

Malham Tarn

North Yorkshire
Grid ref. SD 882 672

National Trust

Approx. 4½ miles (7.2 km). Mostly easy walking along good tracks, but may be muddy after heavy rain. No shelter from rough weather on some sections. This is sheep-farming country, so dogs should be kept under strict control, or preferably not taken on to the hills during the lambing season.

Malham Tarn lies off minor roads about 2½ miles (4 km) north of Malham village, east of Settle. The walk begins at the car park below Chapel Fell, to the west of the Tarn, 200 yds (180m) past the start of Home Farm Lane.

Malham Tarn is an unusual lime-rich upland lake set amid a variety of habitats. Parts of the lake have silted up and a species-rich fen has developed, while the surrounding grassland is noted for its limestone flora. A nature trail runs through the woodlands on the northern shore, and there is a Field Studies Centre in Malham Tarn House.

Nearby sites: *Malham Cove* – a natural amphitheatre carved out of the limestone; *Gordale Scar* – a spectacular limestone gorge, with outstanding examples of limestone pavement on the plateau above it and many lime-loving plants in the woodlands and in crevices in the limestone pavements.

Amphibious bistort

undergone many changes. Glaciation smoothed the hilltops and carved broad valleys through which the rivers now flow. When the glaciers retreated, the rivers, swollen with melt-water, further deepened valleys and deposited fertile silt on flood plains.

Rainwater, naturally slightly acidic, dissolved the rock to form fissures and eventually large caves. Streams often disappear below ground to run along subterranean passages, reappearing, equally suddenly, some distance further down the dale.

MAN'S IMPACT ON THE LANDSCAPE

Man's influence on the Dales has been just as dramatic; the construction of mile after mile of drystone walling was a major achievement. Huge quantities of stone were moved off the slopes and piled up to produce one of the most characteristic features of the Dales: the network of criss-crossing stone walls contrasting with the bright green grass makes for a most attractive landscape. Dotted about in the fields are numerous stone barns built to store winter feed for cattle; several of these would have served one farm. The long, low farmhouses are also characteristic of the area.

The early farmers had a major impact on the ecology of the Dales by removing much of the natural tree cover. The bare hilltops will always have been devoid of trees and the limestone pavements can never have supported large areas of woodland, but the more sheltered slopes and valley bottoms would have been filled with open mixed ash, woodland, interspersed with hazel, bird cherry and many unusual understorey shrubs like baneberry. Alder and birch flourished on more acid soils and along riversides. Now only on the steepest slopes and in the most inaccessible places is there any tree cover remaining. Heavy grazing by sheep maintains a close-cropped grassland; in a few places it is rich in herbs, and some of the wetter riverside meadows are wonderfully colourful in early summer before the hay is cut.

ROADS AND PATHS IN THE DALES

The Yorkshire Dales National Park offers some excellent walking on paths and tracks which are mostly well defined and easy to follow. Many of them are very old, created by some of the first inhabitants of the Dales, and some were constructed by the miners who worked to exploit lead, copper, iron and zinc in the past. Some, like the Monk's Road used in this walk, had religious significance, although they may have been in existence long before monks used them. Present-day walkers are catered for by a network of waymarked footpaths, including the long-distance Pennine Way, which runs through the National Park.

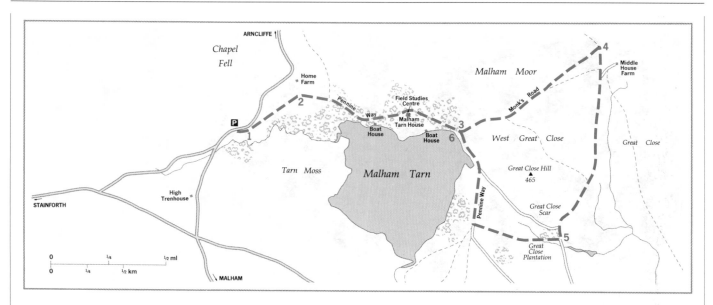

1 **From the Chapel Fell car park, take the track towards Home Farm on the east side of the road.** Tarn Moss lies to the south-east of the path and forms part of a large nature reserve around Malham Tarn, owned by the National Trust. Although it is set in a limestone area, an acid-loving flora has developed in parts, where a thick blanket of sphagnum mosses covers the peat below. Lime-loving plants grow here as well, and there are many species of sedge as well as horsetails, broad-leaved cotton-grass, marsh marigolds and marsh valerian to be found.

2 **Turn right on to the lane leading to the Field Studies Centre. This soon enters a wood, where it is joined by the Pennine Way.** A little way into the wood a bird hide has been provided overlooking the Tarn, where coots and great crested grebes can usually be seen.

Follow the Pennine Way past the Field Studies Centre. The woodlands have a rich limestone flora and abundant birdlife, and will repay several visits. Spring and early summer will probably be the most rewarding time. Native trees like ash and bird cherry grow alongside introduced species in the wood, but the ground flora is a colourful mixture of native spring woodland flowers.

3 **Where the path leaves the wood, turn left uphill beside the wall and right at a signpost to follow the Monk's Road towards Middle House Farm.** Ravens may fly over, often giving away their presence by their characteristic calls. Wheatears, skylarks and meadow pipits are common in summer. The grassland is heavily grazed and the flora less interesting here, but check damp hollows and small patches protected by stones for limestone grassland plants.

4 **Where the Monk's Road swings away to the north, take the rough track to the right which soon joins a crumbling tarmac road heading south towards Great Close Plantation.** Several species of wading bird, some more normally associated with water, may be seen here in the breeding season and on migration: lapwings nest on open grassland and

Bleak limestone scars overlook Malham Tarn, one of Yorkshire's few natural lakes

golden plovers, snipe, curlews and redshanks pass through, a few individuals nesting in some years. If a lapwing dives repeatedly, making plaintive squealing calls, it may be trying to lead you away from its nest, so try not to disturb it.

5 **At Great Close Plantation, take the path heading west below the plantation and Great Close Scar back towards Malham Tarn, keeping to the wall on the right. This joins the Pennine Way again and follows the eastern shore of the tarn back to the woods in the direction of the boat-house.** The grassland is dotted with flowers and the scree slopes beneath the scar conceal many more plants, including ferns which need some shelter. Swifts are often seen, feeding in large numbers over the Tarn.

6 **From the edge of the woods, follow the outward path back to the car park.** Check the tarn for birds; in busy holiday periods very few birds will be feeding along the shore, but when it is quiet common sandpipers, redshanks and herons may be found here, and wildfowl feed further out away from the edge. Black-headed gulls and the occasional lesser black-backed gull are likely to be visitors from breeding colonies on more isolated lakes and tarns. In summer, many species of aquatic insect complete their life-cycles and emerge from the water as adults; several species of caddis fly and mayfly can be seen over the water and on the bankside vegetation.

Ingleborough

Limestone pavement at Souther Scales. Rainwater has gradually deepened the gullies or 'grikes', enabling ferns and many other plants to find welcome shelter on this exposed hillside below Ingleborough's summit

THE LANDSCAPE OF THE YORKSHIRE DALES IS JUSTLY FAMOUS. FOR THOSE BROUGHT UP ON THE SOFT LIME-STONE COUNTRY OF SOUTHERN ENGLAND, THE SEVERE WHITE ROCK OF THE DALES IS A REVELATION. ANYONE WHO HAS HEARD OF HARD-ROW FORCE, GAPING GILL, GORDALE SCAR AND THE THREE PEAKS WILL HAVE A VISION OF CAVING AND CLIMBING COUNTRY, OF PICTURE-POSTCARD VIEWS AND BIG WALKS. BUT THERE ARE ALSO SOME MAGICAL PLACES FOR WILDLIFE.

The walk described here is one of several dramatic routes starting from Horton in Ribblesdale. It combines classic landscape features and wildlife habitats in a long day's journey based on the Ingleborough Massif, a great triangular block of land between Ribblesdale, Chapel-le-Dale and the A65 cross-Pennine trunk route.

THE GREAT SCAR

All the important rocks of the Dales belong to the Carboniferous period, dating back about 300 million years. A huge slab of hard limestone, called The Great Scar, forms the foundation of the visible landscape and it is through this that the main valleys are cut. The upper layers of this 800ft (260m) block produce scars or cliffs along the sides of the valleys, topped by benches of flat, bare limestone. These 'pavements' are very special indeed, and provide the greatest wildlife interest.

The Great Scar limestone is hard and pure; it was formed as a sediment of compacted shells beneath tropical lagoons. Above The Great Scar lies a more varied series of sediments called the Yoredale rocks ('Yoredale' is the old name for Wensleydale).

In the southern half of the Dales this rock is mostly limestone again with just a few bands of shale and sand-

---

Ingleborough

North Yorkshire

Grid ref. SD 807 726

Nature Conservancy Council/Yorkshire Wildlife Trust (parts) Approx. 13 miles (20 km). Challenging, with a long climb and, in places, a very steep and stony descent.

Horton in Ribblesdale is 6 miles (9.7 km) north of Settle on the B6479. The village car park lies off this road, east of the River Ribble, but is often full; many people park beside the straight road just west of the river.

A long walk up one of the 'Three Peaks', with stunning views and classic limestone scenery. Features of geological interest along the way include erratics, drumlins, large areas of limestone pavement and a possible detour to Alum Pot. The chief wildlife highlights are the plant communities of the limestone pavements, and there are also hay meadows full of summer flowers. Upland breeding birds such as curlews and golden plovers may be seen, and the range of insect life includes some nationally rare species.

Nearby sites: *Swaledale Meadow* – classic meadow flora; *Pen-y-ghent* – classic limestone uplands.

The magpie's dashing plumage makes it unmistakable

Brittle bladder fern favours rock crevices

stone. In many places it has been worn away, but it forms the steep cones of the Three Peaks which, capped by a thin layer of Millstone Grit, rise to over 2000ft (660m) above sea level. Ingleborough is the stiffest to climb, but provides the best views.

LIMESTONE AND WEATHER

Limestone is partly soluble in rain-water, which is slightly acidic, so exposed rock surfaces are very gradually etched and eroded. Water sometimes collects in hollows in the rock, but most of it disappears on impact, running into pre-worn channels and gathering into subterranean rivers. Thus Ingleborough is a honeycomb of potholes and caves, some famous and worth visiting for their stalactites. Meanwhile the surface of the ground soon becomes parched – creating what is known as a 'karst' landscape, and the vegetation takes on a fugitive existence, thriving wherever roots can reach moisture.

WILDLIFE OF THE DALES

The mix of plants is surprising, and the associated insects often unexpected. Nationally rare sawflies, beetles and bees have been found here, and there are certainly other species waiting to be identified.

The open hills and the wide expanses of the Dales attract a few wading birds that seek out these loneliest of places in which to rear their young. Curlews, lapwings, redshanks, golden plovers and a few pairs of dunlins nest on the moors. Otherwise the skies are often empty and the only birdsong is that of meadow pipits and skylarks.

This is a landscape to be savoured for its great horizons. For the naturalist, however, the greatest treasures are likely to be at your feet.

1 After parking, walk westwards along a straight road until it turns sharp right to head up the valley. The steep private drive straight ahead is a public footpath, signed Crummock Dale. Go up this and cross the railway line. This is the famous Settle to Carlisle line, built in the 1870s. Horton in Ribblesdale station is a beautifully kept little piece of Victoriana, with a spotless booking hall and signal box and well-tended flower-beds.

After crossing the railway a path leads uphill. The banks of wild flowers beside the path include great burnet, knapweed and rosebay willow-herb, the 'fireweed' which tracked across England in the wake of steam trains.

Go through a wicket-gate and across open grassland. To the right is a field barn, one of thousands in the Dales, built to store the hay crop harvested from individual fields. Many of the Dales barns are still in use, but many more are decaying, their stone-slabbed roofs collapsing and nettles crowding the doorways. There are simply too many barns to conserve.

The view ahead and to the left is soon dominated by Horton Quarry. Limestone has been quarried on the site for many years, initially perhaps for building stone, then for slaked lime to make mortar and fertiliser. The quarry now produces roadstone.

Cross the field and go through a gate, then bear right and follow a grassy path, with Beecroft Hall Farm down to the left. Continue across several fields. Above you now are bands of the Great Scar limestone. Across the other side of Ribblesdale stands Pen-y-ghent. The green slopes of Ribblesdale contrast with the dry limestone plateaux, and have been farmed for thousands of years. Medieval field systems or terraces can be seen above Harber, the farm on the far side of the river.

Follow a series of yellow-topped posts, bearing left opposite a corner in a wall and striking uphill on a stony path. You are soon walking over limestone pavement, but not very deeply sculpted and without much vegetation. Sheep, Swaledale and Dalesbred, have grazed the sward for centuries.

The path is indistinct over stony ground, but cairns (piles of stones) mark the route. Cross a ladder-stile over a drystone wall and follow the path across a grassy plateau broken by blocks of limestone pavement. Ahead now lies Ingleborough – not at

its most impressive from this direction. To the right of it, in the foreground, is Simon Fell.

Eventually the path crosses another ladder-stile, then follows a wall on the right, heading west-north-west. There are now some much better stretches of pavement on the left. The grikes or clefts are much deeper, and there are interesting plants – sanicle, dog's mercury, herb Robert and wood sage. Away to the right, beyond the wall, the pavement stretches much further. The large boulder towards the edge of the scar is an erratic – a big

A limestone pavement ashwood, typical of those found in the Dales

rock dumped by the ice sheets when they retreated about 14,000 years ago.

2 The path follows a cleft in the pavement called Sulber Nick. Continue, with the wall to your right, crossing a little stream to a derelict shooting hut. Bear left here on to the shoulder of Simon Fell. The soil is much less shallow here and holds some water, so there is more vegetation in the form of rushes and fescue grassland. Golden plovers nest on these great expanses. Their call, a far-carrying 'tlu-i', is an appropriately mournful sound. (Keep dogs on leads.)

3 The path up Simon Fell is steep, but eases off a little after a ladder-stile. Follow the path up to the right of the summit ridge. A steep pull brings you on to a shoulder of the mountain. Views to the north suddenly open out into a sweep of limestone scenery unrivalled anywhere else in Britain, with a broad shelf of white pavement stretching for miles above the valley of the Chapel and Winterscales Becks. Beyond this is Whernside, the highest of the Three Peaks at 2416ft (786m). Further round to the north lies Ribblehead and the famous viaduct.

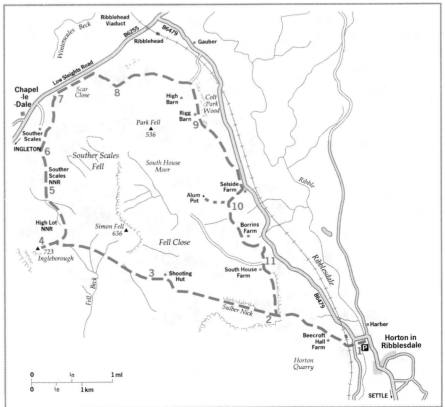

4 Continue left up to the summit of Ingleborough for a splendid panoramic view of North Yorkshire. It was probably not very different when Venutius, leader of the Brigantes – the most warlike of the Iron Age tribes – looked out for signs of the advancing Romans.

Retrace your path downhill, forking left where the ascent route leads down to the right, and head downhill. There is a short scramble down the shoulder of limestone, after which bear left into a National Nature Reserve enclosure called High Lot. Head downhill, fence to your left, taking the very steep path of stone steps and picking your way with great care from rock to rock. There are moments when this seems a near-vertical descent; take it very slowly, with side-footing in places. Plant life among the boulders may attract your attention. There are some rarities such as brittle bladder fern, but most noticeable is the abundance of limestone bedstraw. Overhead you may see a peregrine sailing on the updraughts of air around the cliffs and screes.

5 The path levels off and the ground becomes grassy with some marshy areas. Ahead is Whernside. Cross a stile into Souther Scales Nature Reserve and continue between two impressive blocks of limestone pavement. These have a light covering of scrub including ash, hawthorn and sycamore. The deep grikes contain hazel, dog's mercury, herb Robert and a rich variety of fern species. More localised plants include baneberry, green spleenwort and herb Paris. Souther Scales is managed by the Yorkshire Wildlife Trust and is the most attractive of the limestone pavement reserves.

6 Downhill again, the route bears right, beneath the scar. To avoid further erosion, keep to the right of way which continues northward. Whernside lies ahead; behind you is an impressive view of Ingleborough.

7 Leaving the reserve, the public footpath leads out on to the B6255, called Low Sleights Road, at which turn right. Scar Close Wood lies above you on the right – another broad stretch of limestone pavement, with much denser scrub. It is a National Nature Reserve and may not be entered without a special permit.

Just after the scar ends, turn right off the road, on a footpath signed Selside. Continue on a track to its end; over the wall are views of Scar Close.

Stone walls, meadows and barns in Ribblesdale

8 At the end of the wall, at a nature reserve sign, turn left round the edge of an area of pavement with a wall to your right. After several hundred yards (metres) cross a ladder-stile over the wall and bear half-left over a grazed section of pavement, then cross another ladder-stile. Before you lies a sea of grass. The path is obscure, but continue straight ahead, angling gradually right, around the foot of the great grassy dome of Park Fell. In the distance to your left is Ribblehead Viaduct.

Eventually a farmhouse comes into view, with Pen-y-ghent visible in the distance behind. Make for the farm, crossing an area of grass-covered pavement, then bearing right through a gate and past the farm buildings. Continue through another gate and past a big barn, then along the upper side of several hayfields. Many of these have escaped agricultural 'improvement' and still contain a beautiful array of wild flowers.

9 Continue past Rigg Barn, then bear left into the far corner of the next field and down a path between two sections of woodland. This is Colt Park Wood, another limestone pavement nature reserve, this time of particular interest because it is dominated by ash woodland, virtually unaltered for thousands of years and with a ground flora of both woodland and subalpine plants.

The path bears left, but immediately the wall ends turn sharp right and cross the pasture to a ladder-stile over the wall. After this cross two more fields; there is no obvious path, but head in the general direction of Pen-y-ghent. This leads you to a road, at which turn right. When the road

bends to the left, at Selside Farm, take the stony track right. Continue all the way along this track. At the end, a green track bears left. (Ahead is a detour to Alum Pot. To visit it there is a small charge; pay at the farm.)

10 Take the green track, then cross a stile and cross the fields, heading to the right of two farms. After passing the second of these, Borrins, by crossing a stile uphill of the buildings, continue beside a wall, then bear left with the wall and follow a track downhill. At first this is indistinct, but Pen-y-ghent is again a useful feature ahead.

Continue downhill on the track as far as the farm entrance, then turn sharp right over the field. There is no obvious path, but this is a right of way. There is an attractive view north-east across Ribblesdale, another landscape of barns and meadows and with an impressive cluster of drumlins – oval hillocks made up of glacial debris.

11 Over the brow, join a metalled track and continue to South House Farm. The footpath bears to the left of the main house, through stock yards. Go through a gate at the end of the yard and cross a track to a step-stile in a wall. After this, continue straight ahead up to the stony brow of the ridge, with a wall to your right. Beyond the brow keep to the level, grassy shelf between limestone shelves to left and right. Continue straight ahead on this contour. The view to the left is of Pen-y-ghent, and a geometric pattern of drystone walls.

Eventually, reach the gap in the scars that marks the outward route. Turn left here and follow the path down to Horton.

SWEEPING VIEWS OF MORECAMBE BAY AND THE LAKE DISTRICT FELLS ARE A MEMORABLE FEATURE OF ARNSIDE KNOTT. THE LIMESTONE PROMONTORY IS A NATURALIST'S PARADISE, WITH OVER 200 WILD FLOWER SPECIES AND A WIDE RANGE OF BIRDLIFE.

GEOLOGY AND GLACIATION

A prominent landmark on the edge of the River Kent estuary, Arnside Knott is a limestone hill reaching 521ft (159m) in height. Its slopes are wooded, but there are some open grassy areas and slopes of limestone scree. The Carboniferous Limestone of which the hill is composed is rich in the fossils of various species of coral and shellfish. It is not too difficult to find the large cockle-like shells of ancient bivalves. The effects of glaciation can be seen in some parts of the Knott where slabs of rock show 'scratch' marks, made by a glacier slowly grinding over them. There are also boulders of limestone breccia, formed where the action of slightly acidic water has 'cemented' fragments of limestone together. Glacial erratics are also found; these are large boulders of a completely different rock type transported over great distances by a glacier. A large block of andesite was transported from the Lake District in this way.

WOODLAND, GRASSLAND AND COAST

The plant life of the whole area is of great interest. On the gentler slopes a varied and interesting woodland has developed and a large number of native tree species can be found, many of them becoming scarce elsewhere: wych elm, yew and juniper are fairly low-growing trees, but larch and Scots pine reach a larger size. The woodlands have a colourful ground flora, including the rare herb Paris.

More open areas of the Knott have a rich limestone grassland flora dominated in places by the rare blue moorgrass. There is an abundance of orchids, most notably the dark red helleborine and fly orchid, but several other more common species like the broad-leaved helleborine may be found. Thyme forms large patches and is popular with bees and butterflies. The wild violets are food-plants for fritillary butterflies, and the rare high brown fritillary is one of the many species that occur.

Crevices in the limestone offer shelter for plants like hart's tongue and other ferns. Snails and other invertebrates live here in relative

Early purple orchid

Arnside Knott

Cumbria
Grid ref. SD 455 787

National Trust (part)
Approx. 4½ miles (7 km) or 7 miles (11 km). Some steep ascents on stony tracks, but mostly of only moderate difficulty.

Arnside lies 3 miles (4.8 km) south-west of Milnthorpe on the B5282. Arnside Knott is just to the south of the village. Park along the promenade in Arnside.

Arnside Knott is a Site of Special Scientific Interest, with many plant species, both rare and common, growing in the woodlands and limestone grassland. For the birdwatcher there are birds of prey, numerous woodland birds, and the waders and wildfowl of the estuary.

Nearby site: *Leighton Moss* – a wetland reserve with meres surrounded by reed-beds, rich in wildlife, especially rare birds like the bittern, and a good place for seeing otters.

safety, protected from the drying effects of wind and sun, and safe from predators like thrushes.

The rocks nearest the sea and the coastal marshes have a variety of maritime plants including rock samphire, scurvy-grass, thrift, sea campion and sea aster, and a salt-marsh has developed in sheltered parts of the estuary.

BIRDLIFE

Woodland birds are common on the Knott and nest boxes have been erected to help species like the tits. The summit is a good spot for watching birds of prey including sparrowhawks and kestrels. The vast, sandy estuary is very important for birds and many species of wader, gull and wildfowl are found on it. Great flocks of curlews, dunlins, oystercatchers, redshanks, grey plovers and knots feed here, and sea ducks and grey geese arrive in strength in the winter.

MAMMALS

Not many visitors to Arnside Knott are lucky enough to see an otter, but those who sit quietly by the shore early in the morning may just catch a glimpse. Red squirrels in the woodland may be easier to see, but they, too, are more active in the mornings, especially in warm weather. Larger mammals like red and roe deer also occur, and quiet observers may be lucky enough to see them. Stoats and weasels hunt the mice and rabbits, and bats are also present: pipistrelle and noctule are the most frequently seen.

The high brown fritillary, now rare in Britain

THE *WALK*

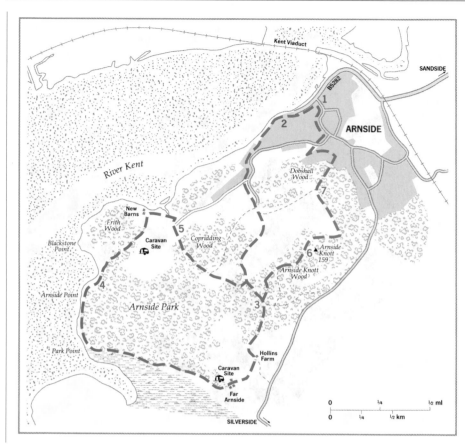

the mud for otter tracks, but do not try walking on it.

5 At a left-hand bend in the track, go through a gate on the right and cross the field to a stile on the far side. The path then leads through a wood and across a number of side-paths, bearing left alongside a ruined wall to the signpost for White Creek, where the outward route is rejoined. Go right to where the tracks cross and turn left up to the summit of Arnside Knott. Check for woodland birds and red squirrels, and look for deer tracks and droppings. The holly blue butterfly may be seen here.

6 From the summit follow the path to the east. Go straight ahead where a stile crosses the wall on the left, down through the wood and turn left at the bottom. Cross a ladder-stile and, with the wall on the right, go to the far bottom corner of the field. The views are splendid from here and in fine weather a vast area of the Lake District and Morecambe Bay may be seen.

Avoid walking on the limestone screes and always stick to well-worn paths. Apart from the danger of slipping, the scree is a valuable habitat for limestone plants like bloody cranesbill, spring sandwort and rue-leaved saxifrage.

7 Cross the stile to join the woodland path and follow it down the hill. After the kissing-gate turn left, then right at the T-junction, following the road back into Arnside.

1 From Arnside village, walk south-west along the foreshore (left as you face the estuary). Go up and continue along the concrete terrace just above the foreshore to a sign reading 'HM Coastguard – Rescue Equipment'. Bear left into the lane signposted Knott Road. Check the Kent channel at low tide for gulls and ducks, and look for waders like oystercatchers and curlews on the exposed sandbanks.

2 Go up the lane and turn right on to the road, then fork left after about 300yds (270m) to follow the road up the hill. Go through a gateway where there is a National Trust notice, and continue on the road uphill. At the top, the road becomes a track and bears left past a car park and straight on where a sign shows White Creek to the right. The limestone grassland here is rich in flowers in spring and summer, and is an excellent area for butterflies and bees. Green tiger beetles live on the slopes and the green hairstreak butterfly flies in early summer. In summer, small scabious is a speciality here, and autumn gentians flower in open areas later in the year.

3 Where the tracks cross, the shorter version of the walk turns left, then follows the instructions from number 6. To continue with the full walk, turn right through a gate and follow the track signposted Far Arnside. This leads to a road through a caravan site, following signs for Arnside Point. Fork left at the end of the site on to the cliff-top path going west then north to Arnside Point. Bear left at a fork where a signpost points back to Far Arnside. The estuary below is excellent for waders and wildfowl, although at low tide they may be far out across the sands; viewing them on a rising tide is best, when they will gradually be driven to the shore. The woods on the hillside are good for woodland birds and spring flowers, and there are several quiet spots that will repay a few minutes' pause.

4 At a fork in the path where a signpost shows White Creek and Arnside to the left, take the right fork through a caravan site and on to a concrete track which turns right at New Barns Farm. Look for salt-marsh plants, including scurvy-grass, and for waders feeding in the creeks. Check

Far-reaching views and big skies form the backdrop to this remarkable wildlife haven

Wasdale

A classic Lakeland view: Wast Water, the deepest lake in England, backed by some of the highest and most spectacular fells, including Great Gable. The edge of the Screes can just be seen on the right.

Though common in the south, the gatekeeper is near the northern edge of its range here

THE LAKE DISTRICT WAS A WORKING LANDSCAPE LONG BEFORE IT WAS DISCOVERED BY WORDSWORTH AND RUSKIN, AND IT BEARS MANY SCARS. HOWEVER, AN ACCIDENT OF GEOLOGY AND GEOGRAPHY HAS ENSURED THAT THE SOUTH-WEST CORNER OF WHAT IS NOW A BUSY NATIONAL PARK IS STILL LARGELY UNTOUCHED. BELOW SCAFELL PIKE AND GREAT GABLE LIES WAST WATER, THE DEEPEST, CLEAREST LAKE IN ENGLAND.

MAN AND NATURE

Not everywhere in Britain would be green and verdant if left to nature, and some of the most inspiring landscapes have been as much of a challenge to plants and animals as they have to farmers. The great mountains that rise to the north and east of Wast Water are all composed of hard volcanic rock. The ample rainwater that cascades down their steep slopes arrives at the lake virtually free of dissolved minerals, and any soils are thin and poor. Only at the head and foot of Wast Water are there pastures and fields, and Wasdale Head is so jostled by Lingmell, Kirk Fell and Yewbarrow that its scattered farms, built on the sites of Viking settlements, are no bigger now than they were a thousand years ago. The human population is almost certainly smaller.

THE WAST WATER SCREES

Along the south flank of the lake beneath Illgill Head, instead of sheepwalks and sweeps of bracken there is a spectacular curtain of scree, a succession of great fans of rocks and pebbles separated by deep gullies beneath vertical cliffs. Every few years there is an avalanche. Hundreds of tons of this rock debris or talus fall into the lake, and the path above the shore has to be redefined across a new boulder field. Not surprisingly the 'live' screes bear few plants, but where they have consolidated, and in the rock chasms and gullies, there are mountain flowers such as purple saxifrage, mountain sorrel and lesser meadow-rue, and a total of at least 22 species of fern. The screes are unique, magical and dangerous; apart from the marked path there is no safe way across them. Even the sure-footed Herdwick sheep keep their distance.

Ravens and peregrines are to be seen above their nesting sites, on crags and unreachable cliffs. The lake itself is used by a very few black-headed gulls and red-breasted mergansers; these only seem to emphasise the vastness of the place and the harsh conditions.

A RURAL IDYLL?

The approach to Wast Water is through Nether Wasdale, a tiny hamlet close to the foot of the lake where the River Irt (a famous salmon river) begins its winding course, through some of the greenest, softest countryside, to reach the Irish Sea between Drigg and Ravenglass, to the south-west. The farmland between Nether Wasdale and the lake is of another age, as close to the vision of a rural idyll as it is possible to achieve. The meadows and pastures, hedgerows and copses beside the Irt are as ageless as the distant mountains. Walking through Easthwaite Farm, past an old hogg house, byre, stable and barns with chickens, ducks, cats and collie dogs all around your feet, is a rare experience. The grassy paths are lined with harebells and speedwells, and the old sod-cast dykes are topped by thick hedges of hawthorn, rowan and bird cherry. Gatekeeper butterflies skip among the brambles. Blackcaps and wood warblers sing from the oakwoods.

Today, most of Wasdale is owned by the National Trust. Agriculture could certainly no longer survive here without heavy support. Even this forgotten corner of Lakeland cannot exist in isolation; it is a piece of a national jigsaw which must also embrace the less charming aspects of the 20th century. For example, some of the water from the lake is pumped down to the British Nuclear Fuels works at Sellafield, only a few miles away as the gull flies. It is hard to escape economic reality, even here.

The great pleasure of Wasdale, still, is to see the breathtaking beauty of the wilderness enhanced by a farming tradition that has encouraged the diversity of wildlife, the whole landscape managed with sensitivity. It is necessary to appreciate the bargain struck, over the centuries, between people and nature, in order to become attuned to the unique spirit of Wasdale.

Wasdale

Cumbria
Grid ref. NY 128 038

National Trust (part)
Approx. 4 miles (6.4 km). Easy walking.

The walk begins from Forest Bridge, on a minor road ½ mile (800m) south-east of Nether Wasdale. It is possible to park close by on the grassy verges of the wooded triangle of land just north of the bridge.

Setting off through green meadows, pastures and old woodland, this walk leads out on to the shores of one of the deepest and most barren lakes in Europe. There is an opportunity to walk along the Wast Water Screes, famous for mountain flowers, but most of the main route follows a gentler, more pastoral course. In the distance are the Goliaths of the Lake District. Buzzards and ravens fly overhead, wood warblers and redstarts sing from the woodland. Choose a dry day, if possible!

Nearby sites: *Eskdale and the Duddon Valley* – wooded valleys leading to fells; *coast near Ravenglass* – dune flora, wintering wildfowl.

Marsh marigold can bloom as early as March

1 Cross to the south side of Forest Bridge, over the River Irt. The river is shallow and stony, the riverside vegetation dominated by sycamore and Japanese knot-grass – both species introduced into Britain in previous centuries by adventurous gardeners. Neither is appreciated by modern naturalists, least of all in such a rural setting.

Just beyond the bridge, before Flass House, turn left up a gated track signed 'Public footpath Lake Foot'. To the left of the track there is a scatter of pine trees, probably the remains of an old plantation rather than natural regeneration, though they have grown up with plenty of light and have lent a parkland atmosphere to the place. Beyond, on the slopes of Latterbarrow, is a more recent, more regimented conifer plantation of 1982, while further along the track there are oaks descended from the original inhabitants of the valley. Buzzards find the mix of trees and crags to their liking and their mewing calls, uttered as they wheel in the air currents higher and higher above the hills, carry for miles across the valley.

Continue along the track to Easthwaite Farm. New silage pits and the rendered farmhouse contrast with the old rubble walls of the cart shed and other buildings; Easthwaite is a working farm, no matter how traditional its setting, but it simply cannot hide its roots, and is a joy to behold. The fields around the farmhouse usually hold cattle or ewes and lambs; the traditional breed is the Herdwick (white woolly face; no horns) but in recent years the Swaledale (black face with white muzzle; horns) has become more pervasive.

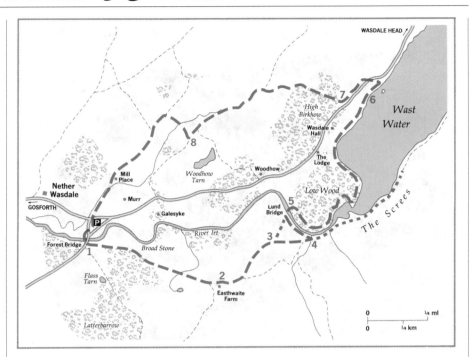

Look for alpine lady's mantle on the Screes

2 Go through a gate. After the farmhouse, bear left through another gate and along a track, taking the left fork where the path divides. After the next gate it is worth stopping for a moment to look at the field boundaries, a mixture of hedges, fences and walls. The hay meadows to the left were originally bounded by sod-cast dykes – low walls topped by earth with a low hedge along the top. There is also a traditional hedge of hawthorn, invaded by elder, dog rose and bird cherry, while to the right are the more austere walls built at the time of the enclosures in the early 19th century. Post-and-wire fences complete the picture for a fleeting decade or two.

3 The track leads to two gates; to the left is a more grassy short cut down to Lund Bridge, while to the right is the main gravel track to the lake foot. Unless you are very short of time or the weather has deteriorated, bear right along the main track. This leads through an old hazel coppice, with the River Irt to your left, through a gate to the pebble-lined shore of Wast Water. There is a little boat-house and a stone-clad pumping station which extracts water for use at Sellafield.

4 An optional detour then leads along a path on to the Screes, which now dominate the foreground. This path is clear to begin with and provides an excellent opportunity to see the commoner montane plants such as clubmoss, alpine lady's mantle, parsley fern and yellow saxifrage. There are rarities too, but do not be tempted on to the unstable ground.

You can walk along the scree path as far as you wish – even to Wasdale Head – but the path deteriorates and the terrain is tiring; better to sample the habitat and then turn back, retracing your steps to rejoin the main route just past the gate.

Follow a path alongside the River Irt. In summer, the start of the path is marked by a show of deep pink flowers from the downy rose – one of the most beautiful of wild roses – beneath which will be patches of germander speedwell and enchanter's nightshade. Little black moths may be disturbed from the grassy verges; these are chimney sweepers, which lay their eggs on pignut flowers. The riverside path passes some fine sessile oak trees, covered in lichens and polypody fern, and some alders and sallow bushes.

5 The path bears right to cross the river by a stone packhorse bridge, Lund Bridge, then turns right, off the track and through a wicket-gate into a wood (signed as a footpath around the lake-shore and to the YHA). The river is now to your right, while to the left is Low Wood, a block of very mixed woodland, much of it

The Screes, wild and grand, seen across the lake

planted as part of the estate associated with Wasdale Hall. Because sheep are excluded, the woodland floor is rich in flowers – bluebells and wood anemones followed by yellow pimpernel and wood avens. There are fungi too: the stinkhorn reveals its presence in early summer by its nasty smell and is followed by such species as the blusher and fly agaric.

After passing behind the boathouse the path bears left, through rhododendrons and along the riverside as it broadens into the lake. On the far side are the impressive, frightening screes.

The path becomes wide and gravelled, with excellent views now up the lake, then comes out of the woodland to pass beneath Wasdale Hall. This imposing building has been transformed into a youth hostel. Soon after it there is a seat beside the path, from where one of the most famous Lakeland views opens out. Framed by oak branches, the head of Wast Water

is visible in the distance; beyond this rises Great Gable, with Yewbarrow to its left and the shoulder of Lingmell (leading to Scafell) to its right. Spectacular, beautiful, but barren – these fells are as empty of wildlife as anywhere south of the Arctic Circle.

6 Continue along the lakeshore, past a little island on which black-headed gulls often nest. The path rises to a ladder-stile: cross this and turn left up to a road. This is the main access route to Wasdale Head and provides more good views of the Screes and lakeside.

Turn left and walk along the road, first over a cattle grid, then with woodland on either side.

7 Turn right up a broad track through the woodland, with the old walled garden of Wasdale Hall on your right. The crags to the north are called Buckbarrow; ideal country for peregrines. Beyond, the ground rises to Seatallan.

At the end of the walled track, cross

a stile and bear left over open ground, following a rough track as this bears right, around a rocky outcrop and over rough moorland inhabited by lapwings and wheatears. Follow the track straight on until, over a stile, enclosed pastureland is reached, passing a rocky knoll and a footpath sign.

8 After the next fence and gate, turn right over a stile by a gate and continue along a track between a fence and a dyke, through a gate and on to meet a bridleway. Turn left along this, through more gates to cross a stream. In summer the stream is lined with hemlock water dropwort – one of the most poisonous of plants, even to cattle.

The track is now easy to follow, through the yard of Mill Place, with the ruined mill building to the left, and along a pretty walled lane with a stream, or beck, on your right. The track leads to a road; turn right then left along it to reach the starting point.

WALK 79

Rook – seldom alone

BORROWDALE WAS ONCE A SCATTERED COMMUNITY OF MINERS AND QUARRYMEN, FARMERS, CHARCOAL-BURNERS AND BOBBIN-MAKERS. THIS WORKING WORLD HAS LONG SINCE PASSED AWAY, BUT ENOUGH REMAINS IN THE FABRIC OF THE LAND TO MAKE A WALK NEAR THE TOURIST 'HONEY-POT' OF KESWICK A LESSON IN HOW THE RAW MATERIALS OF NATURE WERE CROPPED, MANAGED AND SUSTAINED.

FELLS AND VALLEYS

Herdwick sheep, the hardy, wire-fleeced breed reputed to have been introduced by the Vikings, are often blamed for turning the upper Lakeland fells into a barren land of mat-grass and scree. Over-stocking of sheep has certainly had a disastrous effect on mountain grassland, but other factors have also contributed to the general lack of wildlife at high altitudes. The rocks of the northern Lake District, Skiddaw slates, are infertile and any nutrients that are released into the soil are quickly washed away in torrents of rain. Thus the high fells are more popular with adventure-seekers than they are with people interested in fauna and flora. However, on the lower slopes and in the wide Lakeland valleys it is a

Autumn in Borrowdale. Birch trees often grow with sessile oaks here. They are very hardy, and thrive even in poor, acid soils

Borrowdale

Cumbria
Grid ref. NY 266 229

National Trust (part)
Approx. 4 miles (6.4 km). Moderately easy walking, but steep in parts.

The walk starts from the car park reached by driving out of Keswick on Borrowdale Road (the B5289), then turning right towards Derwent Water.

The Borrowdale oakwoods, south of Keswick on the eastern shore of Derwent Water, have been heavily managed for centuries and are an example of how social history, and wildlife, can sometimes benefit from what may be thought of as exploitation. The walk links five woods just south of Keswick, of which Castlehead is probably the most outstanding.

Nearby site: *Johnny Wood* (at the southern end of Borrowdale) – rich in ferns, lichens and other characteristic plants of wet Atlantic woodland.

different story: lakes and marshes, meadows and oakwoods are a legacy of a managed, productive landscape, rich and varied and steeped in the magic of Beatrix Potter and Arthur Ransome.

BORROWDALE'S WOODLANDS

With a wall of mountains all around and Derwent Water as its centrepiece, Borrowdale is dramatic and imposing. The cloak of woodland draped across almost every slope, shore and island makes the place even more exciting. There are some Victorian plantations of larch and pine, often on headlands or knolls where their impact is greatest, and some recent plantings of ornamental trees and conifers, but in Borrowdale most of the woods are dominated by sessile oak, the tree that belongs here. Clad in ferns and lichens, these trees sweep down to the lake-shore, providing a home for pied flycatchers, wood warblers and red-starts, badgers and red squirrels.

Epiphytic plants

In many parts of northern and western Britain, the high rainfall and clean air encourage a rich growth of lichens, mosses and ferns in our native woodlands. Some of these plants actually grow on the trunks and branches of the trees; these are called *epiphytic* plants.

THE $\mathcal{W}$ALK

1 From the back corner of the lakeside car park a path leads into Cockshot Wood, to the right. Take this path and turn left, with the wood edge to your left.

2 After several hundred yards (metres), take a path out of the wood to the left, between two meadows. Ahead now is the dome of Castlehead Wood. The path meets a road; cross this and go up the steps into the wood, then follow a path left which soon bears right, parallel with the wood edge, and runs quite steeply uphill. There are good views to the left, out of the wood and over Keswick to Skiddaw and Blencathra.

It is possible to make a detour off the path to the right to reach the rocky summit of Castlehead. The hilltop offers one of the best views over Derwent Water and southwards to the jaws of Borrowdale.

3 The main path soon drops downhill. Note the mature beeches and oaks, with a good spring flora where the light strikes through the canopy.

At the bottom, reaching the wood edge and continuing straight on, go through a gate out of the wood and between two small fields to reach a road with houses along it. Turn right along this road. The houses to the left bear such names as Broadoaks, Woodside and Greenacres, while the hedge to the right is varied in composition, and has dog's mercury growing beneath it. These clues suggest that the hedge was once a wood edge, and that Castlehead may have been joined to Springs Wood until quite recently.

The road leads to a farm; go straight on, over a bridge across a stream, then between a slate-built stable and a hay-shed, through a gate and into Springs Wood. This is an old hazel coppice with more mature trees on the slopes of the boulder-strewn Brockle Beck ('brock' = badger).

4 Before a bridge over the stream to the left, turn right, on a path signed to Rakefoot Farm. Continue along this as it bears left uphill to follow the wood edge, past a radar mast. Before the next gate and stile, turn right along a grassy path, signed Great Wood, beside a wall and with fine views over Derwent Water and Cat Bells. Cross a stile into Great Wood. The path descends through mixed woodland, mainly larch at first but with tell-tale oak stumps.

Ignore the side-path down to the right and continue along what is now a foresters' track, losing height gradually. The track-side is good for flowers during the summer; foxgloves are abundant, as they are everywhere on the acid Lakeland soils, but there is also herb Robert, wild strawberry and heath speedwell. Clearings to the left provide a view of Walla Crag, and there is a good chance of seeing peregrines, kestrels, buzzards and sparrowhawks.

Eventually the track meets a junction, at which turn right down to a car park. The woodland around the car park is excellent for summer songbirds, most notably wood warblers and pied flycatchers.

5 On the car park road turn left, down to join the main road. Cross this and go through a gateway (signed Calfclose Bay). Go down the track to the lake-shore. Like all the larger lakes, Derwent Water is comparatively infertile and birdlife is not prolific, though there are usually a few feral greylag geese and mallards about. The wooded islands opposite Calfclose Bay are Rampsholme and, further away, St Herbert's Island (featured in Beatrix Potter's *The Tale of Squirrel Nutkin*).

6 Turn right along the lakeshore, around several bays and wooded headlands. Just off shore now is Lord's Island, once the home of the Earl of Derwentwater, who was executed for his part in the Jacobite rebellion of 1715.

Bear right before Stable Hills to join a metalled track to the right of the buildings. Follow this track, with marshy woodland to the left, but turn left off the track and into the wood at a gate and wicket. Follow the broad track through the wood. This is The Ings, a fine example of carr woodland with mature alders and willows and an excellent fen flora.

7 After The Ings the path passes Strandshag Bay, with Lord's Island close by to the left, then continues to Friar's Crag. This wooded dolerite headland is another famous beauty spot.

Continue, meet a road, and follow it past the landing stages and back to the car park.

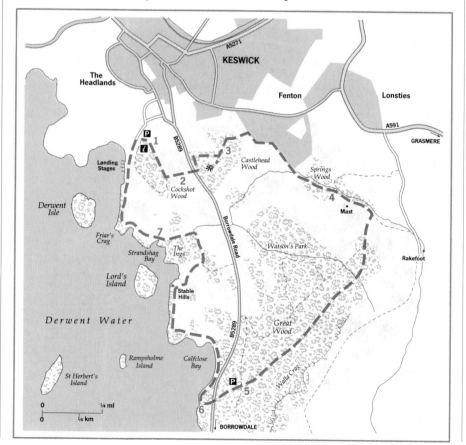

Unimproved pastures like these are a last refuge for many once-common grassland plants

DRAMATIC ROLLING MOORLAND, CUT BY THE RIVER TEES, EDGED BY PASTURES AND TRADITIONAL MEADOWS AND TOPPED BY OUTCROPS OF ROCK SUPPORTING SUCH JEWELS AS THE SPRING GENTIAN AND TEESDALE VIOLET, MAKE TEESDALE A WONDERFUL PLACE. THIS WALK ALONG THE RIVER IS MADE MORE SPECTACULAR BY A SERIES OF WATERFALLS, CULMINATING IN HIGH FORCE.

The Tees and the Whin Sill at High Force

TEESDALE: A SPECIAL PLACE

Sometimes it is impossible to tell why one place is better for wildlife than another. If soil and climate are the same, why do different plants grow in different places? For many years nobody had satisfactorily explained why sites like Ben Lawers and upper Teesdale were so fabulously rich in rare flowers, and why unrelated species from all sorts of habitats cropped up together in such places. Then, in 1949, Sir Harry Goodwin put the clues together (in particular, the analysis of pollen grains in peat, which gave a series of dates for plant communities) and suggested that these

High Force
County Durham
Grid ref. NY 906 281

Nature Conservancy Council (part) Approx. 7½ miles (12 km). Easy walking.

Park in the roadside lay-by at Bowlees, on the B6277 3 miles (4.8 km) north-west of Middleton-in-Teesdale. If this is full, there is a car park and a picnic site a little further down the road, beyond the Bow Lee Beck.

The highlight of the walk is the series of spectacular views of the 70ft (21m) waterfall of High Force. The fells to the south and west form part of an extensive National Nature Reserve; they are dangerous and difficult of access, and the wildlife habitats are sensitive. This riverside walk, which follows the route of the Pennine Way, is safe and easy underfoot yet still allows you to see many of the special Teesdale flowers (birdseye primrose, globeflower, shrubby cinquefoil and many more) and characteristic upland birds (ring ouzel, golden plover, wheatear etc).

Nearby site: *Cow Green Reservoir* – Nature Conservancy Council nature trail, along a metalled track but with views of the 'sugar limestone'.

Spring gentian – a rare flower of the fells

sites had remained unaltered since post-glacial times; that when trees covered virtually all of Britain there were still pockets of tundra vegetation left, and that thousands of years of farming, which has eliminated most of the woodland, have still not removed these links with a prehistoric past.

This theory, supported by subsequent research, is now accepted as fact, and there seems little doubt that Teesdale is assured of celebrity status and special protection. However, the building of a reservoir, which flooded part of the site in the 1960s and brought the issue of wildlife protection into sharp public focus, has left a permanent reminder that very little is sacred. Perhaps it is the fragility of Teesdale that will be its greatest strength in years to come.

THE WHIN SILL

The Durham moors are wild and windswept, covered with blanket bog or heath. But through the acid sandstone and shale runs a ribbon of dolerite, a hard crystalline rock which was pushed up through a crack in the earth's crust nearly 300 million years ago. It now forms the famous Whin Sill, which runs beside this section of the Pennine Way and continues as a ridge, scarp or cliff all the way to the Farne Islands.

CRAGS, RIVER AND MEADOWS

Teesdale remains a very special place, and this walk is as good an introduction to its wildlife as any. Ring ouzels and wheatears haunt the crags and dolerite cliffs; sandpipers, dippers and wagtails are to be seen on the riverside boulders. And everywhere there are flowers. The only drawback with Teesdale is that it is usually raining!

1 From Bowlees, cross the B6277 to a stile. Cross it and head southwards through two fields to a wall-stile, then down through woodland following a clear path to a bridge. In the spring the wood is good for bluebells and anemones, followed by red campion and ramsons as the season progresses. Wood warblers, chiffchaffs and willow warblers are common, and there are also blackcaps, redstarts and a few pied flycatchers.

2 Cross Wynch Bridge. This footbridge is safer than it looks; it was built in 1830 to replace a less secure lead-miners' bridge. After the bridge there are excellent views of the Tees as it negotiates a series of whinstone steps called Low Force.

Follow the path as it bears right, in the shade of wych elms, ashes and oaks, and follows the river. It is possible to get down on to the boulders and look at the flowers growing in the clefts, in the mineral-rich pockets of soil and gravel and on the grassy shelves washed by winter floods. Here you can find a wide range of Teesdale rarities. At the right time of year (late June is probably the best for the greatest number of species) you are almost certain to see birdseye primrose, mountain pansy, wood cranesbill and globeflower, and there is a chance of a spring gentian (though this is more at home on the 'sugar limestone' of Widdybank and Cronkley Fells).

Continue along the Pennine Way, with the river to your right and meadows and pastures to your left. Some of the Teesdale hay meadows are so full of marsh marigolds that it is difficult to believe that they are not the intended crop. Among the marigolds (known also by such names as May blobs or molly blobs) will be meadow saxifrage, globeflower and 20 or 30 other species. Lapwings and snipe, redshanks, oystercatchers and curlews nest in the fields and bring their young down to the river here.

3 Eventually the route passes Holwick Head Bridge and climbs to a stile, where a notice indicates the start of the National Nature Reserve. After crossing the stile, continue along the path through an area of dense juniper scrub. Juniper is another relict species – a low-growing conifer and a pioneer when tundra still dominated the land, but soon edged out by pine, hazel and oak when the climate improved. It grows here as it has grown for 9000 years.

4 Soon, breaks in the junipers to the right frame views of a deep gorge, and High Force comes into view. Go through a gate and approach the top of the waterfall. The peaty water cascades over a band of hard dolerite above a bed of shale on limestone, and falls 70ft (21m) to a plunge pool in the gorge below. As you approach, the noise becomes deafening, but it is quickly lost as you follow the path onwards.

Continue along the Pennine Way, still with the river to your right. From here the Tees is a much gentler spirit; dippers and grey wagtails are more numerous. On the far bank, opposite Bleabeck Force (the small shoot of water on the left), is a massive whinstone quarry, extracting dolerite for roadstone. The scale of the operation is daunting but quarrying, like mining, has a long tradition here and is important to the local economy. Beside the quarry is Dine Holm Scar, a multi-tiered face of whinstone and a typical habitat for ring ouzels.

5 The path rises again up Bracken Rigg, on which is another scatter of ancient juniper. From the crest of the ridge there are views to the south of Cronkley Fell and, to the north, of Forest-in-Teesdale, with its white-walled farmhouses.

6 Head along the top of the hillcrest, still following the Pennine Way, which descends towards a fence but then veers right to meet a wall. Continue, with a wall to your right, to a stile, then down a cleft, with rowans and other trees growing among the rocky outcrops, to Cronkley Farm. The path bears to the left of the buildings to meet a track. Follow this across level pastureland.

7 Eventually the Pennine Way crosses a bridge. This is a good place to end the walk. There are usually redshanks, sandpipers and other wading birds about and the meadows are beautiful.

As with many riverside walks, the best return route is back the way you have come. (Should you wish to accept the challenge, the Pennine Way continues along the far bank to re-cross the Tees at Saur Hill. As far as Widdy Bank Farm, Falcon Clints and Cauldron Snout the route is still quite easy – an extra 8 miles (13 km), there and back; beyond this you should only go if thoroughly prepared.)

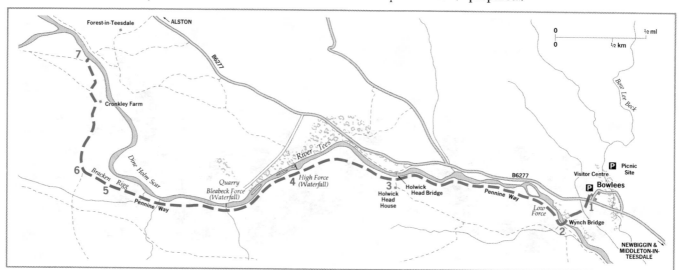

AN 18TH-CENTURY MAP OF YORK-SHIRE NAMES THE ROUNDED HILL OF KISDON AS 'KISDON ISLAND'. IT IS CERTAINLY A CONSPICUOUS HILL, AND FROM ITS SLOPES THERE ARE EXTENSIVE VIEWS OF THE SURROUNDING FELLS, THE SWALE GORGE AND THE ABANDONED LEAD MINES AND RUINS OF CRACKPOT HALL.

HOW KISDON WAS FORMED

The striking shape of Kisdon may be due to the fact that the original course of the River Swale lay to the west of the hill in what is now a relatively 'dry' valley; the beck called Skeb Skeugh and the B6270 now run through it. At the end of the last Ice Age the valley became blocked with glacial debris, so the only way out for the melt-waters of the glaciers was through the narrow valley to the east of Kisdon. The river was able to join its original course at what is now Muker, making a turn to the east and continuing down Swaledale along an increasingly broad dale.

On its way down its new course, the River Swale carved itself a deep gorge; some beautiful waterfalls were formed and the Kisdon Gorge is a fine example of a wooded dale with unspoilt limestone scenery on every side. The limestone is present in separate beds, with different rock types, such as shale, between them. These erode at different rates, giving the waterfalls a stepped effect. For several thousand years the waterfalls have been retreating towards the head of the valley, cutting themselves deeply into the gorge. Even the tiny streams joining the main valley have impressive waterfalls, and the sound of running water is a pleasing accompaniment to walks through Swaledale.

MINING IN SWALEDALE

Valuable minerals are present beneath the surface of Swaledale, the most important in the past being lead. Evidence of lead mining can be seen on the slopes of Beldi Hill; old shafts, spoil tips and 'levels' are now slowly being colonised by plants, but their presence is easily detected, especially in winter when the bracken has died down. One of the ways in which galena, the ore which yields lead, was extracted was by 'hushing'. Streams were dammed and then a great flood of water was released, sweeping down a hillside and removing the surface vegetation and soil. The heavy, ore-bearing rocks would be left behind and could then easily be removed. This

Kisdon

North Yorkshire
Grid ref. SD 910 978

Approx. 5 miles (8 km). Some steep ascents and descents, and some sections can be muddy after rain, but mostly of only moderate difficulty.

Kisdon lies to the north of Muker, a village in Upper Swaledale on the B6270 Richmond – Kirkby Stephen road. The walk starts in Muker, where there is a car park at the eastern end of the village.

Kisdon is a rounded fell, 1637ft (499m) high, lying at the heart of Upper Swaledale, and conveniently encircled by footpaths. This circular walk leads across an open hillside, through woodlands, along a gorge and across flower-filled meadows, before returning to Muker.

Nearby sites: *Tan Hill* – a moorland hilltop which offers good bird-watching from the road or from footpaths (red and black grouse, curlews, golden plovers, lapwings, common sandpipers, ring ouzels and wheatears in summer), also good expanses of heather and sphagnum bogs; *Semer Water* – the largest natural lake in the area, and a favourite site for overwintering birds, with an interesting summer flora (including orchids) on the limestone banks.

Marsh thistles grow in damp woods and meadows

Hay meadows like this one near Muker were common in Britain until the last few decades

has left a landscape of deep gullies and loose spoil tips which are slowly blending in with the landscape. Plants are sometimes slow to colonise these mining remains because of the presence of poisonous metals in the rocks; a few specialised plants like spring sandwort are able to cope with this and are sometimes the only species present, even a century after the tip was abandoned.

HAY MEADOWS

Flower-filled meadows are another characteristic feature of the Dales. Cut for hay in the summer, they provide ideal growing conditions for species that can tolerate high water-levels in winter and grazing later in the year. The summer cutting does not damage the wild flowers, for most of them will have set seed by the time the hay is ready, and the light grazing in the winter helps to prevent competition from more aggressive species. Changes in farming practices, including plough-ing and re-seeding of old meadows, have destroyed many of the best hay meadows in much of the country, so those that remain in Swaledale are especially valuable: some are now being managed in the traditional way as nature reserves. As well as being valuable reserves for meadow flowers, they are important feeding areas for birds and insects.

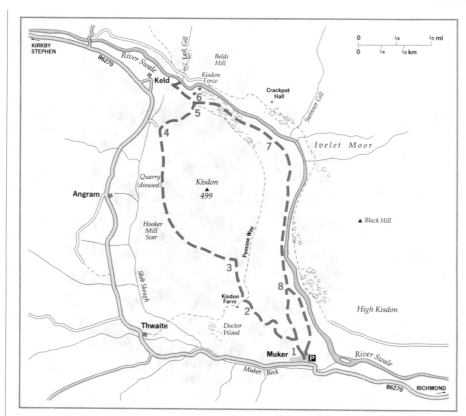

adults can be found. Dippers and grey wagtails frequent this stretch of the river, feeding on the abundant aquatic insects.

6 Having admired the view from the footbridge, return up the slope for a short distance to find the path which leads back to the village of Muker on the west side of the gorge.

At a fork, a signpost indicates Kisdon Force. This offers a short diversion to an overlook which gives a view of the falls, but an unofficial path has been made across a steep slope (not recommended in wet weather or for those who are not sure-footed) to see the falls from a better vantage point. In spring, the mixed woodlands are carpeted with wild flowers, such as primroses and wood anemones, and filled with birdsong; resident chaffinches and blackbirds compete with migrant willow warblers and blackcaps, and many other species of woodland bird are also present; it is always worth pausing for a few minutes where there is a good view, to see what birds pass by.

7 Return to the main path and follow it south. Opposite Swinner Gill the path drops down to the lush waterside meadows and swings closer to the river. The meadows are filled with wild flowers in summer and attract many insects, including butterflies. Look for giant bellflower, marsh marigolds and cranesbills.

8 At a barn just before the footbridge the path forks. Take either path, both branches return to Muker. The left fork continues through the meadows and the right fork crosses the hillside, joining the Kisdon Farm lane and returning to the starting point of the walk in Muker village.

1 From Muker take the road up past the old Literary Institute, go left behind the post office, and follow the lane signposted Keld up the steep hill towards Kisdon Farm. Keep to the metalled surface and close all gates behind you. Look at the old walls, which have an interesting covering of lichens, mosses, ferns and wild flowers in places.

2 The lane goes up, between walls, to join the Pennine Way briefly before Kisdon Farm, then turns right at the Kisdon signpost up the steep hillside, again between walls. The view opens up, with the great expanse of Thwaite Common and Great Shunner Fell appearing to the south-west. Check for hovering kestrels overhead.

3 After emerging from the walled lane, keep on uphill alongside the stone wall on the right, bearing left with it near the top. After a gate, the path levels out along the west flanks of Kisdon. This is the old Corpse Road along which bodies were carried to be buried in Muker. Several upland species of bird can be seen here, although they may not all be resident. Lapwings and golden plovers are summer visitors which feed and

nest out in the open. They are joined by ring ouzels and wheatears, which nest in crevices in rocks and old stone walls. Meadow pipits and skylarks are more difficult to spot, but are also present; the skylark's song is a characteristic sound of a spring day on the hills.

4 Follow the path, gradually descending along the hillside towards Keld but, 50yds (45m) before the bottom of the final steep descent, turn right through a gate into a walled lane. Continue around the hillside past an old building, between walls again, until the lane ends. Keep to the wall on the left down a short, steep descent, turn left through a squeeze-stile, keep ahead to another, and go on to the corner of the next field.

5 A gate gives access to the Pennine Way once more. Follow the Way down to the foot-bridge over the river in the Swale gorge. Take care near the water's edge, as the stones are sometimes very slippery. East Gill flows down over a series of falls to join the Swale here. Mayflies, stoneflies and caddis flies thrive in this type of river; both the aquatic larvae and the free-flying

A lapwing on its well-camouflaged eggs

THE ROLLING PURPLE MOORLANDS AND DRAMATIC NORTH SEA COAST OF THE NORTH YORK MOORS NATIONAL PARK ARE WELL KNOWN, BUT THIS RELATIVELY ISOLATED AREA OF UPLAND COUNTRY ALSO OFFERS SOME GENTLER LANDSCAPES IN SHELTERED VALLEYS WHICH REPAY FURTHER EXPLORATION.

WILD DAFFODILS

In mid April, Farndale's meadows offer an unforgettable display. For 7 miles (11 km) the banks of the River Dove are lined with wild daffodils, which spill over into the meadows and many of the nearby woods as well. Thousands of visitors come to see these famous flowers, and to many people this is the only reason for visiting Farndale, yet there is a wealth of other wildlife to be found here. Conditions suitable for vast numbers of daffodils are also good for other wild flowers, and something of interest can be found through the summer months. Other meadow flowers grow alongside the river, although the variety is not as great as in limestone valleys. In order to protect the daffodils and other wildlife, the area was designated a Local Nature Reserve in 1955 and the wild flowers are now strictly protected; it is an offence to pick, uproot or in any way damage them.

Many people imagine that the reason for the abundance of daffodils is that they were planted here long ago – there is a popular notion that the monks of Rievaulx Abbey may have been responsible in the Middle Ages. The name 'Farndale' appears in a charter of 1154 granting the monks a clearing in the dale, but in fact the daffodils would already have been here long before the monks appeared in the valley. Daffodils are native wild flowers in Britain and occur in many other parts of the Yorkshire Moors and

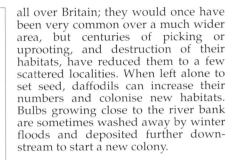

Farndale

North Yorkshire
Grid ref. SE 673 953

Approx. 3 miles (4.8 km). Mostly easy walking on riverside and meadow paths. Some sections may be muddy after rain and waterproof footwear is needed. The valley is farmed and dogs should be kept under strict control, especially during lambing time. Try to avoid taking them into fields, even on the lead, if sheep with lambs or cows with calves are present.

Farndale lies in the North York Moors, north of Kirkbymoorside. The walk begins at Low Mill, where there is a designated car park.

Farndale is an outstanding site for wild daffodils, which carpet the riverside meadows and woods in spring when most visitors see the reserve. It has a great deal of other interesting wildlife, however, and is worth visiting at any time of the year.

Nearby sites: *Sutton Bank* – a steep limestone cliff with a nature trail and varied habitats including woodland, calcareous grassland, scrub and a lake; *Ashberry Wood* – species-rich mixed woodland.

Wild daffodil

all over Britain; they would once have been very common over a much wider area, but centuries of picking or uprooting, and destruction of their habitats, have reduced them to a few scattered localities. When left alone to set seed, daffodils can increase their numbers and colonise new habitats. Bulbs growing close to the river bank are sometimes washed away by winter floods and deposited further downstream to start a new colony.

ANIMALS OF FARNDALE

The alder trees on the river bank attract feeding flocks of siskins and redpolls, and the riverside woods are home to many woodland birds such as tits, woodpeckers and treecreepers. Dippers can often be seen on the river. On the surrounding moors, whinchats and stonechats breed and ring ouzels nest in rocky places, while in winter, flocks of redwings and fieldfares fly in from across the North Sea to feed on berries in the hedgerows. The moors are managed for red grouse and are purple with heather in late summer. Adders and lizards bask on sunny rocks but are not often seen, as they usually disappear at the first sign of disturbance.

Mammals are also difficult to see, most of them being nocturnal; roe deer live here, but are seen much less often than their tracks and droppings. Foxes and badgers are also present, but are very secretive. Rabbits are much easier to see, and smaller mammals like shrews may betray their whereabouts by their shrill squeaking in the undergrowth. Water voles live along the River Dove and may be spotted by a quiet observer; tell-tale 'vole gardens', where shoots have been nibbled down outside their burrows, show where to watch for them.

The wild tops of the North York Moors cradle the gentler farming countryside of remote and unspoilt Farndale

THE *WALK*

1 From the corner of the car park, follow the signposted path down the slope to the bridge. Cross the bridge, turn left and follow the path along the river bank as far as High Mill. The River Dove flows down off the moors and its clear water is ideal for aquatic insects like stone-flies and caddis flies. Dippers live on the river and may be seen by quiet observers; look for stones in the river splashed with white droppings to find their favourite perches. Check the river bank for signs of water voles.

2 At High Mill, follow the path between the houses and keep on it as far as Church Houses. Daffodils are abundant on this section, growing in profusion on the river bank and out in the meadow. The damp soil suits them very well, and the light shade enables them to flower and set seed successfully.

3 Return from Church Houses towards High Mill on the same route. The daffodils grow in large numbers in the fields here, and are especially numerous in damp hollows which were once part of the river bed. Look for chaffinches and grey wagtails near the river. A flowering plant with soft, fern-like leaves and umbels of white flowers is sweet cicely; its leaves have a pleasant scent reminiscent of and are sometimes used as a culinary herb.

4 A slight detour can be made on the return from Church Houses to High Mill: cross the river by the footbridge. Here you can view the daffodils from a different angle, and take a closer look at the river. Damselflies may be present in summer, and brown trout can be seen rising for small flies in still pools.
Rejoin the main path and continue back past High Mill to the wood.

5 When the path enters the wood, take the higher path on the left which starts at a bridlegate. Cross the field diagonally left, making for the next bridlegate. Check the woodland edge for great spotted woodpeckers and treecreepers, which are easier to see from here.

6 Continue uphill, keeping the wall on the right and the farm on the left. Pass between two big oak trees and continue across the fields towards the track below Cote Hill. There are good views of the surrounding moors from here; check the skyline

Foxes are common, but can be wary of man

for birds of prey including buzzards and kestrels. Stonechats and whinchats pass through on their way to nesting sites on the moors, and ring ouzels may turn up in the fields. Curlews nesting on the moors fly over in spring and early summer, and are easily detected by their beautiful bubbling calls.

7 Follow the track downhill, keeping the hedge on the left. Go through a gate and turn left through another gate into an enclosed lane leading to High Wold House farm. Check the hedgerows for thrushes, especially redwings and fieldfares in winter.

8 At the farm, go into the farmyard, following the signs, and leave it by a field gate on the right. Follow the path downhill, with the wall on the right, cross the stile, then the bridge over the stream and take the paved track back to Low Mill. Golden saxifrage, primroses and red campion grow in the damp places and mosses, liverworts and ferns are abundant in shadier spots. In early summer a strong smell of garlic is present; this comes from the spear-shaped, shiny leaves of ramsons, which produce rounded heads of white flowers. Wrens and dunnocks nest in the ivy, and may be seen feeding on the ground and on mossy tree-trunks.

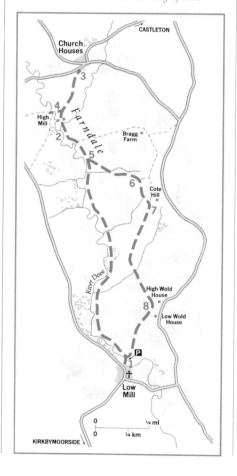

Inaccessible to man, but packed with ledges suitable for nesting, Bempton Cliffs are the summer home of tens of thousands of seabirds

THIS IS ONE OF THE BEST PLACES IN MAINLAND BRITAIN TO GET CLOSE TO A THRIVING SEABIRD COLONY. THE VIEWS OF THE COASTLINE ARE OUTSTANDING, BUT ADD TO THIS THE SIGHTS, SMELLS AND SOUNDS OF THOUSANDS OF SEABIRDS AND A VISIT TO BEMPTON CLIFFS WILL BE VERY MEMORABLE.

CHALK CLIFFS

Bempton Cliffs are composed of chalk with flints and capped with a layer of boulder clay. The upper layer of chalk is very flinty and erodes easily, providing a great range of nesting sites for seabirds. The Dane's Dyke earthwork, of uncertain origin but thought to be pre-Bronze Age, runs to the edge of the cliffs at Dyke's End. The 400ft (125m) cliffs are some of the highest chalk cliffs in England and are home to the southernmost seabird colonies on the East Coast. Every available ledge and crevice is used in the breeding season, and the air is filled with the cries of the birds for several months in spring and summer.

GANNETS AND AUKS

England's only mainland colony of gannets is here; more than 1000 pairs nest in most years. These magnificent birds have a 6ft (1.8m) wingspan and dive dramatically to catch large fish like mackerel and herring. From the cliff-top they can be glimpsed on their nests, but even more exciting is the sight of a flock of gannets plunge-diving into the water among a shoal of fish.

The auks are much smaller than gannets, but far more numerous. Guillemots line rock ledges in their hundreds, looking like miniature penguins, and large numbers of razorbills huddle in narrow crevices. Puffins nest in crevices and burrows near the top of the cliffs and on loose scree slopes. All these species spend a lot of time on the water, the guillemots in long lines and puffins and razorbills in small flocks, rolling and preening and sometimes riding out a rough sea. As the breeding season progresses, the adults start bringing in fish for their young and the activity becomes more frenzied still. Unlike gulls, which glide and sail through the air, the auks fly on whirring wings, throwing themselves into the air and returning arrow-like to their nests.

OTHER BIRDS OF THE CLIFFS

A staggering 65,000 pairs of kittiwakes are estimated to nest on Bempton Cliffs; these small gulls have dainty grey wings with pure black wing-tips, and short black legs. They constantly call their name. Other, larger gulls also breed on the cliffs, but their numbers are almost insignificant compared with those of the gannets, auks and kittiwakes. Smaller numbers of fulmars and shags nest here, and cormorants are also present occasionally.

Several other species nest on the cliffs, and jackdaws, feral pigeons and rock pipits also make use of holes and crevices. During migration times large flocks of terns (perhaps being chased by skuas), shearwaters, scoters, waders and divers, can be seen flying past. In winter, flocks of redwings and field-fares cross the North Sea and the occasional shore lark and snow bunting may be seen.

OTHER WILDLIFE

The cliff-faces support an interesting mixture of chalk and maritime plants, and there are impressive displays of red campion in deeper soils on the cliff-top in summer. The 15 species of butterfly recorded include migrants like the red admiral and painted lady, and attractive residents such as common blue and small copper. The trees and shrubs of Dane's Dyke and the hedgerows inland from the cliffs provide cover for small songbirds like tree sparrows, corn buntings and yellowhammers. At migration times whitethroats, willow warblers, chiffchaffs and other small birds are seen here.

Bempton Cliffs

Humberside
Grid ref. TA 197 738

Royal Society for the Protection of Birds
Approx. 5 miles (8 km). Mostly on level ground, but with some muddy sections and some sections very close to the edge of high cliffs so take care, especially in windy weather.

Bempton Cliffs stretch for several miles along the coast some 4 miles (6.4 km) north of Bridlington. The walk starts from the RSPB car park and information centre, on a minor road leading north from Bempton village. (From the B1229 near the north end of the village, follow School Lane and the RSPB signpost at the next junction.) There is a car parking charge for non-members of the RSPB.

Many thousands of seabirds breed on this precipitous stretch of the North Sea coast, making Bempton Cliffs an unmissable site for bird-watchers. It is the only gannetry on the English mainland, and other numerous species include kittiwakes, guillemots, razorbills and puffins.

Nearby site: *Hornsea Mere* – the largest natural freshwater lake in Yorkshire, close to the sea and with many birds, aquatic invertebrates, and abundant moths and butterflies in the surrounding scrub and woodland.

Fulmar – here nearly all year

THE *WALK*

1 From the car park and information centre walk down the track towards the cliff. Check the hedgerow for buntings, and look for migrants in spring and autumn.

2 At the cliff-top path, turn right and follow the path towards Dane's Dyke. Take great care here, and along the whole length of the cliffs, as they are very high. Make use of the observation areas and overlooks provided by the RSPB. Seabirds to be seen on this section include puffins, guillemots and razorbills. Red campion blooms on the cliff-top.

3 The prehistoric ditch, Dane's Dyke, runs south right across Flamborough Head. The tree and shrub cover here is a good area for migrant songbirds in spring and autumn. Butterflies bask and feed in sunny and more sheltered spots. Look for tree sparrows, recognisable by their brown crowns. Jackdaws nest in crevices just below the cliff-top, but often feed on the fields inland.

Return westwards along the cliff path.

4 Pass the track down from the RSPB centre and continue north-westwards towards Buckton Cliffs. Here there are good views of guillemots, razorbills and puffins.

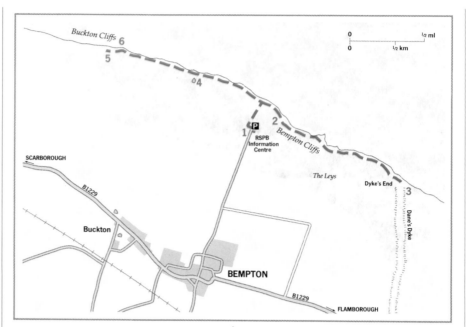

Herring gulls nest here and great black-backed gulls are also present in smaller numbers. Fulmars also nest on the cliffs. They look gull-like at first, but their strange beaks and lack of black on the wing-tips make them easy to identify. They perform outstanding aerobatics, using the updraughts from

The chalk of the Yorkshire Wolds meets the North Sea here, with spectacular results

the cliffs to glide and wheel around with the minimum of effort. Their feet are used to help them steer, and when necessary they can drop easily down on to their nesting ledges, which always seem to be over a sheer drop.

5 After passing a finger-post showing paths to Buckton, Speeton and Bempton, stop at the next stile and take in the view. The most outstanding species of this section is the gannet, which nests on narrow ledges. Gannets collect their nesting material from the sea; traditionally they have used seaweed and other plant debris drifting near the surface, but in recent times they have taken to collecting nylon fishing line and fragments of nets; these can be seen clearly through binoculars if a nest is examined carefully. The RSPB arranges a clean-up of the nests each year at the start of the breeding season to remove any dangerous materials.

6 Return to the start by walking back along the cliffs on the same path. Kestrels hunt in this area, but at migration times the dashing merlin, our smallest falcon, may also be present. Keen birdwatchers should scan the cliffs and fields here very carefully as almost anything can turn up: there is as good a chance of seeing a bluethroat or a wryneck here as at any other good birdwatching spot in Britain. Birds often arrive during the night, so an early morning visit, before there has been too much disturbance, can be profitable.

The great sweep of Robin Hood's Bay, seen from Ravenscar, with the village in the distance. The Cleveland Way footpath follows the coast, which is full of geological interest

ROBIN HOOD'S BAY IS ONE OF THE MOST ATTRACTIVE SEASIDE VILLAGES IN ENGLAND, LOOKING OUT OVER A BAY CUT DEEP INTO THE NORTH YORK MOORS COASTLINE BY THE NORTH SEA. THE SEA CONTINUES TO BATTER THE COAST, WEARING IT AWAY AT AN ESTIMATED RATE OF 2 INCHES (5CM) PER YEAR.

A MECCA FOR GEOLOGISTS

The coastline around Robin Hood's Bay displays many interesting geological features in a relatively small area. There is a classic wave-cut platform and cliffs of glacial till. The main cliffs have been eroded by the sea to reveal a section through rocks of the Jurassic period from 160 million years ago, and a vast number of ammonites and other fossils have been found here.

Ravenscar has a geological trail which explores various rock types and the old alum quarries. The limestone beds overlie the shales and have been eroded by the sea on the foreshore to form striking mushroom-shaped 'mermaid's tables'. In the beds of sandstone there are fossilised 'ripple marks', formed when the rocks were on the bed of a shallow sea. Dinosaur footprints can be traced, although no skeletons have been found, and there are good specimens of ancient horse-

tails. The beds of shales are a good source of ammonites, belemnites and oysters.

Coastal erosion is still causing problems in this area, and several houses have fallen into the sea. Extensive coastal defences have been constructed in order to combat this.

ALUM QUARRIES

Alum was an important chemical in the tanning and dyeing industries, and is still used as a colour fixative in dyed cloths. Huge quantities of shale were removed from the cliffs around Ravenscar in order to extract alum. In the process of quarrying, many fossil ichthyosaurs were uncovered and several museums obtained good specimens. Most of the alum was loaded on to ships from a jetty in Robin Hood's Bay. The remains of the jetty can still be traced today. When the railway came in 1885, the industry was already declining, so even though the line passed through the quarries it was never used to transport the alum. The National Trust, which owns the main works site at Low Peak, is consolidating the remaining structures and carrying out archaeological investigations.

SEASHORE LIFE

The submerged rock ledges stretching far out into the bay offer excellent hiding places for marine organisms and at low tide it is possible to explore them and discover something of the life below the high-tide line. Several species of brown seaweed grow on the shore, including bladder wrack, with its gas-filled flotation bladders, and serrated wrack, with its saw-tooth edge. Beneath them live many creatures which shelter from predators or the heat of the sun when the tide is low. Gulls and wading birds visit the shore to forage among the seaweeds for small prey like tiny shrimps and crabs. Near the low-water mark are the large kelps, rarely uncovered by the tide; cormorants may be seen here when the tide is in, trying to catch some of the many fish which shelter under the seaweed. Storms throw large quantities of seaweed and other debris on to the strand line, where it begins to decompose. Kelp flies lay their eggs in it and these produce tiny larvae which feed on the decaying seaweed. These are an important source of food for turnstones and land birds like rock pipits and pied wagtails. Twice a day the tide rises and falls, bringing a fresh supply of food to the seashore creatures and depositing more material on the high-tide line, so this is one of the richest of wildlife habitats.

Robin Hood's Bay

North Yorkshire
Grid ref. NZ 980 016

National Trust (part)
Approx. 7½ miles (12 km). Mostly easy walking, with some sections near cliffs. Can be muddy in winter.

Robin Hood's Bay lies on the coast about 5 miles (8 km) south-east of Whitby. The walk begins some 3 miles (4.8 km) down the coast at Ravenscar. Park on the demarcated roadside verge approaching the Raven Hall Hotel.

This walk combines plants and birds of the coastline with moorland and woodland species, and is worth while at any time of year. The area is renowned for its fossils and is of great interest to geologists.

Nearby site: *The Cleveland Way* – 93 miles (150km) of superb walking with coastal, woodland and moorland views.

Turnstone – aptly named

THE *Walk*

1 Take the path signposted 'Cleveland Way' leading past the National Trust Coastal Centre, then turn left by a sign indicating a geological trail to reach the abandoned railway track. The sides of the railway track have become colonised by an interesting range of wild flowers, trees and shrubs. Plants like hemp agrimony and fleabane attract butterflies in summer, and bramble and gorse patches are good places to look for other insects like hoverflies, bumble bees and beetles.

2 Follow the railway track for 3 miles (4.8 km), descending to cross roads in two places where the original railway bridges are missing. The mixture of woodland, scrub and open fields provides excellent opportunities for birdwatching, and several species of songbird can be seen along the route. Small mammals are abundant here, although not often seen; the tiniest of all, the pygmy shrew, sometimes betrays its presence by the shrill squeaking noise it makes when it meets another shrew. Foxes may be glimpsed early or late in the day.

3 When a caravan site on the left is reached, climb over the ladder-stile on the right where there is a public footpath sign. Cross the field diagonally left to a gate in the far corner, then follow the path alongside the hedge to Robin Hood's Bay. Herring gulls are common here, but the bay may have more unusual species sheltering in it or roosting on exposed rocks at low tide. Look for turnstones, purple sandpipers, oyster-catchers and redshanks on the rocks, and rock pipits on the upper shore.

4 At low tide it is possible to walk along the shore for ½ mile (800m) as far as Boggle Hole Youth Hostel. The Cleveland Way can be joined here, or you can walk along the beach for a further 500yds (450m) or so to the next tiny inlet, where a footbridge crosses a stream. Join the main cliff path (Cleveland Way) here. The gently shelving rocky shore is an excellent habitat for marine life and is worth exploring at low tide. The brown seaweeds, or wracks, hide delicate creatures like beadlet anemones beneath them and periwinkles, topshells, dogwhelks, limpets and shore crabs can all be found here. The strand line is a good place to look for empty shells and interesting seaweeds washed up from deeper water. After winter storms, many fossils will be found among the beach pebbles. (Do not hammer fossils out of the rocks and cliff-faces.

5 At high tide do not go on to the foreshore; take the stone steps to the right at the end of the road in the village and follow the signs marked 'Cliff Path'. The path crosses the Mill Beck below the Youth Hostel and the Stoupe Beck by footbridges. With binoculars, it should be possible to watch seabirds from breeding colonies further down the coast as they fly by to feed. Small numbers of gulls and fulmars breed here, but many of the cliffs are too unstable to provide safe nesting sites. Cormorants sometimes fish close to the shore at high tide. Patches of gorse and bramble on the cliff-top provide nesting sites for stonechats and the less conspicuous whinchat, and rock pipits breed here and there below the cliff-edge.

6 The Cleveland Way leads back to Ravenscar, running along the cliffs as far as High Scar, then turning inland in the direction of some abandoned quarries. Wheatears may be seen in more open places, especially in early summer.

7 Fork right by the signpost before the golf course and continue to the abandoned railway line and the start of the walk in Ravenscar. Green woodpeckers occasionally feed on the golf course, and kestrels are frequent visitors.

The whinchat's white eye-stripe distinguishes it from the similar female stonechat

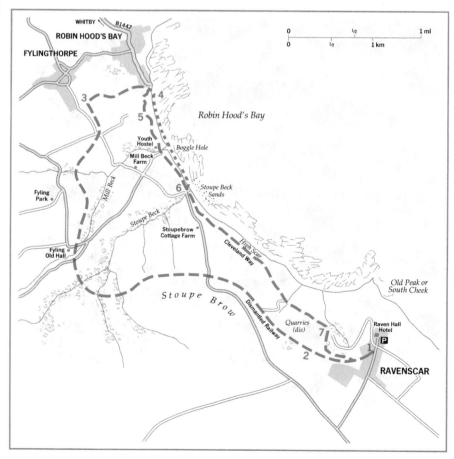

THE DEEPLY CUT VALLEY OF THE CASTLE EDEN BURN OFFERS SHELTER TO A HOST OF WILDLIFE. ANIMALS FROM ROE DEER TO RED SQUIRRELS FIND PLENTY OF GOOD HIDING PLACES IN THE DENSE WOODLAND, WHICH IS ALSO A NATURAL HAVEN FOR BIRDS INCLUDING MIGRANTS NEWLY ARRIVED ACROSS THE NORTH SEA.

HOW THE DENE WAS FORMED

The rich wildlife of the Dene is due in part to its variety of rock types. In Permian times, approximately 200 million years ago, Magnesian Limestone was laid down, and eventually lifted, by movements in the earth's crust, to form the coastal plateau of what is now Durham. During the Ice Ages the Dene was carved out of this plateau by a torrential river. Later, the Dene became buried beneath silt and rock fragments left behind by glaciers; this material formed a clay which the present river is still cutting through. The head of the Dene is cut into this clay, but lower down, the Castle Eden Burn has exploited a fault in the limestone and rushes through a narrow ravine. Nearer the sea, the river flows through a wider valley with a clay flood plain, and the limestone reappears as sea cliffs.

PLANT LIFE IN THE DENE

The natural vegetation for the Dene would be mixed woodland of oak, ash and yew, but over the centuries other tree species have been introduced. Pine was planted for timber, and there are larch plantations on flatter ground. Sycamore, beech, horse chestnut and sweet chestnut are all growing well since their introduction, and in places rhododendrons are doing too well, forming dense, dark thickets which shade out the native ground flora. The wetter valley bottom suits alder and bird cherry, and there is a luxuriant understorey of hazel, rowan, dogwood, spindle, holly, elder and blackthorn on the slopes.

The ground flora is spectacular in spring, with great drifts of wood anemones and ramsons, especially in less shady areas where a tree has fallen or clearance has taken place. Dog's mercury forms a carpet in places and primroses, bluebells and violets add colour. Later in the year, wood, meadow and bloody cranesbills flower and the smaller herb Robert, with its unpleasantly smelling leaves, blooms in shady spots. The curious birdsnest orchid, which has no green leaves and is common in woods on the Downs of the south, has a northern outpost here, along with the fly orchid. Other scarce plants include lily of the valley, herb Paris, columbine and round-leaved wintergreen. Giant bellflower and foxglove are both present, and are more readily noticed by casual observers.

Lower down the slopes, in wetter places, there are colourful displays of marsh marigold and opposite-leaved golden saxifrage, with dame's violet growing along the river bank. Lush green tufts of male fern, hart's tongue and hard fern grow among fallen branches and at the base of damp rocks.

Autumn brings a colourful display of fungi. Some persist through the winter, and even in spring the scarlet elf cup produces its bright red cups on dead twigs.

ANIMALS AND BIRDS

Roe deer inhabit the woods, and badgers and foxes live out their nocturnal lives largely unnoticed by most visitors. Several small mammals, from pygmy shrews to wood mice, live in the understorey and red squirrels in the canopy. Birdlife is very varied and several woodland species occur. The nuthatch is at its northern limit as a regular breeding bird here and treecreeper, green and great spotted woodpeckers are also found. Sparrowhawks and kestrels hunt in the Dene by day, and tawny owls at night. The thick understorey attracts warblers such as blackcaps and willow warblers and the canopy provides food for bullfinches, chaffinches and tits. Being close to the sea, the Dene woods are a good feeding place for migrants, and there is a good chance of finding bramblings, siskins, waxwings or sometimes a great grey shrike. Insects are abundant; over 3000 species have been identified in the area, including the unique Castle Eden argus butterfly (a form of the northern brown argus) and a number of unusual moths such as Blomer's rivulet and the barred carpet.

Poisonous herb Paris grows in damp woodland on lime-rich soils. It is slow to colonise new ground, so is found only in very old woods

---

Castle Eden Dene

County Durham
Grid ref. NZ 428 393

Nature Conservancy Council
Approx. 3 miles (4.8 km). Some steep sections, which may be muddy after rain, but paths mostly firm underfoot and waymarked. Some sections of path near steep cliff-edge with 100ft (30m) drop.

The reserve lies just south of Peterlee. Park at the reserve centre at Oakerside Dene Lodge, Stanhope Chase, which is signposted off Durham Way in Peterlee.

Castle Eden Dene is a deep, densely wooded valley which cuts through a coastal plateau to the sea. A river runs the length of the valley and there is a network of paths. The woods have an exceptionally fine spring flora, and are rich in birds and insects.

Nearby sites: *Hawthorn Dene* – a similar valley to Castle Eden Dene, with some introduced trees adding variety to its rich flora and fauna; *Wingate Quarry* – Magnesian Limestone flora on old spoil tips, scree slopes and hollows, and interesting plants on the rock faces and ledges.

Dusk is the most likely time to see a woodcock

THE *W*ALK

1 Go through the gate from the car park and down the steep track to a more level area where the tree canopy is more open. The track is marked by red markers. This is the Arboretum, where many introduced tree species grow – a good area to start looking for woodland birds.

2 Follow the red markers, turning left at the open area surrounded by tall spruce trees and right at the bottom of the slope just before the bridge. Follow the path parallel with the river. The path leads through an area of coppiced hazel. The ground flora is excellent in newly coppiced areas, and when the bushes become denser they provide good nesting sites for warblers. The area with many yew trees has a sparse ground flora and is less suitable for birds and insects, but it is one of the unique features of the Dene.

3 Cross the river by the plank bridge. Look at the limestone cliffs covered in ivy. Wrens and robins feed here and mosses and ferns are abundant, especially hart's tongue fern. Opposite-leaved golden saxifrage grows in very damp places and flowers in spring.

4 At a junction where the red arrows point sharply left, go straight ahead and cross the river again. The path climbs steeply from the bridge and at the top merges with another path joining from the right. Fork left at the next junction and bear

Wood anemone is one of several plants that thrive because they flower before the trees come into leaf, shading the woodland floor

right, when Gunner's Pool Bridge comes into view, to follow a path along the north side of the Dene indicated by brown arrows. Take care, as there is a drop of about 100ft (30m) on the left. Ignoring the bridges where two rivers meet, keep on upstream, still following the brown arrows. The path passes through several areas where hazel and ash have been coppiced, and other, contrasting sections with dense thickets of yew. The ground flora in the coppiced areas in spring is a complete carpet of ramsons and wood anemones.

5 Where the brown arrows point both ahead and left, bear

left. Cross the river and follow the path across the small meadow. Rock-rose grows here, and several species of butterfly, including orange-tip, meadow brown and large skipper, can be found. The meadow is mown regularly to prevent scrub from encroaching. The river is too badly polluted for freshwater life, but deer tracks may be seen in the mud beside it.

6 The path leads to the head of the Dene. Turn left here, over the river, and left again to return along the south side of the Dene.

7 The path passes through an area of sycamore and pine which is far less rich in wildlife than other areas of the Dene that support native species of trees and shrubs; the alien species here are gradually being replaced by more valuable native trees.

8 After descending back to the valley floor, cross the two bridges at the confluence of the rivers and climb the slope, bearing left where the path divides. The rhododendrons here are destroying the native shrub species by shading the woodland floor and releasing poisons from their leaves. They are gradually being removed, but recolonisation is very slow.

9 At Gunner's Pool Bridge, pause to look down into the gorge and scan through binoculars for woodland birds. Do not cross the bridge, but continue along the south side of the Dene to rejoin the path indicated by red markers. The tall beech trees were planted in the 1860s.

10 Cross the Dene by Castle Bridge to return to Oakerside Dene Lodge.

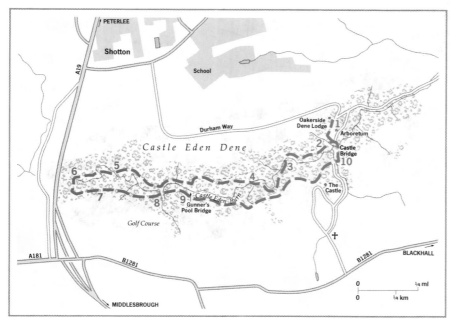

AN EXCURSION TO THE FARNE ISLANDS IS LIKELY TO INVOLVE LITTLE ACTUAL WALKING. THE ISLANDS TAKE ONLY HALF AN HOUR TO REACH BY BOAT, AND EVEN LESS TIME IS NEEDED TO WALK ROUND IF YOU ARE IN A HURRY; BUT THE EXPERIENCE ADDS UP TO MORE THAN THE SUM OF ITS PARTS. AS A WILDLIFE SPECTACLE A VISIT TO THE FARNES HAS FEW EQUALS.

THE INNER AND OUTER ISLANDS

There are 15 proper islands in the group; others come and go with the tide. There can be up to 30, separated into two groups. One is dominated by Inner Farne, the major island, while the more scattered outer group includes Staple Island, Brownsman and Longstone.

A LONG TRADITION OF WILDLIFE

St Cuthbert, the charismatic Bishop of Lindisfarne, appreciated the Farne Islands' wildlife as early as the 7th century when he retired to Inner Farne and befriended the birds and animals – so much so that when he went to bathe, wild otters were reputed to have dried his feet by rubbing themselves against him. He was particularly fond of eider ducks, which nested all around his stone shelter, and in Northumberland they are still called St Cuthbert's or Cuddy ducks in his honour. Today about 1000 pairs of eiders still nest on Inner Farne, using any available shelter (beneath the walls of the present lighthouse and the chapel, for example).

BREEDING SEABIRDS

Inner Farne and Brownsman are the best islands for terns: about 4000 pairs

Right and below: Guillemots sit shoulder to shoulder on the tops of The Pinnacles, inaccessible rock stacks off Staple Island. Neighbouring shags are by nature less gregarious

Arctic tern

Farne Islands

Northumberland
Grid ref. NU 220 323
(Seahouses harbour)

National Trust
Mainly a boat trip, but walks of a few hundred yards (metres) are possible on Staple Island and Inner Farne.

The Farne Islands lie about 2 miles (3.2 km) off the Northumberland coast. Boats leave from Seahouses, on the B1340 coast road between Bamburgh and Beadnell. Several companies run boat trips to the Farne Islands in spring and summer. Some boats land on Inner Farne, others on Staple Island. Other islands can be seen from the boat. All voyages do a circuit of the islands, though the exact itinerary and route varies with tide, time of day and weather conditions. For details, contact the Tourist Information Centre in Seahouses. The National Trust makes a charge for landing on the islands.

The Farnes are bird islands without equal in the opportunity they provide for close views of seabirds, particularly eiders, terns, shags, auks and kittiwakes. The islands are at their best from late May to early July; any later than this and some of the birds (auks and eiders, for example) will already have left. Grey seals may often be seen from the boat.

Nearby sites: *Chillingham Park* – ancient deer park with fallow deer and famous white cattle; *Low Newton* – dunes and fresh water, good for migrant birds.

---

of arctic terns, 3000 of Sandwich terns, 200 of common terns and a sprinkling of roseate terns. Being dive-bombed by irate and persistent arctic terns is one of the most memorable experiences of a Farne visit in summer (it is well worth taking a hat).

Staple Island is the other major bird island – the best place for guillemots (which crowd the famous Pinnacles), puffins and shags. Kittiwakes are everywhere, and there are significant numbers of fulmars, cormorants and razorbills. Compared with spectacular islands far off the Scottish coast the seabird populations on the Farnes are small, but the nesting birds are so approachable that it is possible to take full-frame photographs without telephoto lenses. To be close enough to an eider duck to touch it, or to a shag to see the vivid green of its eyes, is something magical – a legacy, perhaps, of St Cuthbert.

The Puffin

The puffin is one of our most engaging seabirds. It has a brightly coloured bill and black-and-white plumage. Markings on the head give it a shaven-headed appearance which is reflected in its scientific name *Fratercula arctica* – 'little monk of the Arctic'. It spends most of its life at sea, coming to land only to breed.

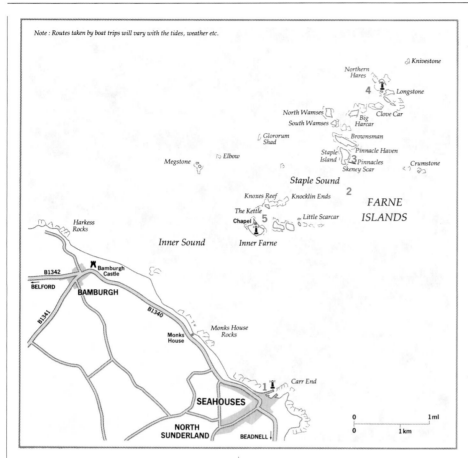

Note : Routes taken by boat trips will vary with the tides, weather etc.

1 The boat leaves from Sea-houses harbour. Seahouses is a busy and interesting place with a motley assortment of fishing craft. In winter there are sometimes glaucous and Iceland gulls about.

The first impression after leaving the mainland is of the small size of both the boats (despite the fact that they carry between 40 and 80 people) and the islands themselves. Inner Farne dominates, partly because its cliffs and lighthouse now face you; the rest are smaller and lower in the water. Look back for good views of the mainland. Bamburgh Castle stands out, north-west along the coast, and between it and Seahouses is Monks House, once the embarkation point of St Aidan and St Cuthbert on their trips to the Farnes.

As the boat approaches the islands, you begin to see auks (guillemots and puffins) in the water or flying to and from the islands. This stretch of water in winter is favoured by long-tailed ducks, scoters, divers and grebes.

2 The boat crosses Staple Sound (between the inner and outer island groups). Crumstone is the isolated island to the east. Approach-ing Staple Island, the Pinnacles come into view. These tall, dark needles of whinstone (dolerite) are capped like Christmas cakes with white guano and topped by a shoulder-to-shoulder assembly of guillemots.

3 On trips that stop at Staple Island, the boat pulls into Pinnacle Haven where passengers can clamber out for a short walk around the island. Although only a tiny island of bare, fissured rock, with a five-minute circuit around it, Staple Island has excellent seabird colonies and you will soon be engrossed. It is possible to approach quite closely large numbers of nesting shags, kittiwakes and puffins. Roped-off areas mark where you should not go – for your own safety and that of the birds. The best views are on the south-east side of the island, looking over the Pinnacles and Kittiwake Gully.

Just to the north of Staple Island is Brownsman – separated by a narrow channel or 'gut', uncovered at low tide. Large numbers of terns nest on Brownsman. The stone tower is the remains of an early lighthouse, built in 1810 and abandoned in 1826 because it did more harm than good.

4 From Staple Island the boat will probably head around Longstone. The dramatic red and white lighthouse was built to replace the Brownsman light. Near by are the rocks called the Northern Hares – one of the most important nurseries for grey seals. The young seals are born in November, but there are usually a few adults hauled out, looking as if they haven't a care in the world. In fact they do have enemies, notably humans (the colony has to be culled from time to time) and killer whales, which visit the Farnes occasionally.

The South Wamses, mid-way between Longstone and Staple Island, still carry some wreckage of the *Spica*, which sank in 1916, and Big Harcar, close by, was the place where the *Forfarshire* went down in 1838. Five of the crew were rescued by the lighthouse keeper, William Darling, and his daughter Grace, who became a national celebrity (much against her will) as a result.

5 After passing the Wamses and crossing Staple Sound the boat puts into St Cuthbert's Cove at Inner Farne. This island has much more vegetation than the others, mainly sea campion with a few gnarled bushes of elder, planted by the lighthousemen many years ago. There are ruins, a chapel (St Cuthbert's, of course) and a small visitor centre, which provides some shelter if the weather has turned against you. Terns nest among the vegetation, as do the eiders. It is these two species that attract the most attention – in the terns' case chiefly because of their dive-bombing on-slaughts on visitors – but the cliffs also have nesting kittiwakes and guille-mots, while the grassy cliff-tops are home to burrow-nesting puffins. Tired songbirds occasionally litter the island after hitting bad weather while crossing from Scandinavia on their way south.

There has been a lighthouse on Inner Farne since 1809 and its whitewashed walls now provide a focal point for a short walk around the island.

The boat returns across the Inner Sound. It is worth looking into the sea as you approach shallower water; the north-east coast is famous for its marine wildlife and the water is remarkably clear. The trip from Inner Farne to Seahouses usually takes about 20 minutes, though it can be very much longer if there is a heavy swell – by no means uncommon.

Holy Island

Visible from all over the island, Lindisfarne Castle was built in 1550 to protect Holy Island's harbour

THE LINDISFARNE GOSPEL, ST CUTH-BERT, A RUINED PRIORY, THE WHIFF OF VIKING RAIDERS; ADD TO THESE A FAIRY-TALE CASTLE AND A LITTLE HARBOUR LINED WITH LOBSTER-POTS AND IT IS NOT SURPRISING THAT THE CAR PARK ON HOLY ISLAND IS BUSY FROM WHITSUN TO SEPTEMBER. BUT WINTER – SHORT DAYS, COLD WINDS – IS A DIFFERENT MATTER.

SUMMER AND WINTER

Lindisfarne National Nature Reserve harbours wonderful summer dune flowers and contains some rare plants such as coralroot orchid and dune helleborine. For the birdwatcher, however, it is from early October to March that Holy Island comes into its own, outstanding for birds migrating south from the Arctic and sub-Arctic. Only the hardiest naturalists see Holy Island at its best for birds: bleak and lonely, and cut off from the Northumberland mainland by a sweep of the cold North Sea. Twice a day the water recedes for about five hours to reveal extensive sand- and mudflats, ideal for wildfowl and waders, and to allow access to and from the island.

AN ISLAND APART

It is far nicer to be on Holy Island when it really is an island, for seven hours as the tides swirl in and out, but this is not always possible in daylight. Fortunately Holy Island has a village, with shops and pubs, if the weather deteriorates.

The island is about 3 miles (4.8 km) long, but most of this is made up of a panhandle of dunes (The Snook) along its north shore; the core of Holy Island is a square mile (2.6 sq.km) of farmland with the village and priory ruins on its south-west corner. The only high ground is a dyke of black dolerite (the same volcanic rock as the Whin Sill of the Farne Islands and Teesdale, but pushed up vertically). This outcrops in two places: The Heugh, on the south-west corner, where it is topped by storm beacons and an old coastguard station, and on Beblowe Hill on the south-east corner where it has been used as the foundation for Beblowe Castle (now generally known as Lindisfarne Castle).

WADERS AND WILDFOWL

The Lindisfarne sand- and mudflats, which stretch from Goswick to Fenham Flats and beyond, are the only significant feeding ground for wildfowl and waders between the

---

Holy Island

Northumberland
Grid ref. NU 127 421

Nature Conservancy Council (part) Approx. 4 miles (6.5 km). Easy walking.

Holy Island is accessible by vehicle at low tide via a causeway near the village of Beal, reached by turning east off the A1 at West Mains. Safe crossing times need to be checked carefully before leaving the mainland. (There are some stopping places along the causeway, the best of which is a parking area just before the main channel. There is an escape tower here for stranded motorists. Every few years someone gets caught out and has to wait for the tide to recede from their stalled and half-submerged car.) The walk starts from the village car park, on the south side of the island.

Holy Island is popular with tourists and summer is not the best time to visit. Winter is excellent for seabirds, wildfowl and waders. Migration time, particularly October, always brings rarities. Early summer is good for dune flowers. The northern part of the island (mainly comprising dunes) and the mud- and sandflats form the Lindisfarne National Nature Reserve.

Nearby site: *Budle Bay* – mudflats, waders, wildfowl.

Goldfinch – a seed-eater

Firth of Forth and the Humber estuary and are of international importance. Crossing the causeway between Beal and The Snook when the tide is fully out and birds are widely dispersed, it is difficult to imagine that tens of thousands of wigeon, knots and dunlins winter here. However, when the tide is nearly full, pushing birds on to the higher flats closer to the causeway, it is impossible not to be impressed by the numbers and the variety of species. Bar-tailed godwits and curlews, oystercatchers and grey plovers are always in evidence. In the creeks and channels there are usually a few sea ducks: red-breasted merganser, goldeneye or scaup. There is also the only British flock of light-bellied brent geese, a subspecies of the goose which breeds in Spitzbergen and overwinters here. Numbers at Lindisfarne vary according to the weather, two or three hundred in a mild winter but up to 3000 when there is a long cold spell.

BIRDS OF LAND AND SEA

The sea around Holy Island is especially good for ducks, divers and grebes, which fish the rich coastal waters towards the Farne Islands and Ross Back Sands. There are always large numbers of eider ducks which harvest the submerged mussel-beds, but in winter these are augmented by rafts of scoters and long-tailed ducks, and by good numbers of shags and red-throated divers. Slavonian and red-necked grebes are regular, and there are sometimes black-necked grebes about.

Most of the sea-watching on Holy Island is done from Emmanuel Head, where a beacon set on the north-east corner of the island provides a convenient back-rest. The nearby dunes and slacks that form most of the northern end of the island can be intimidating when a biting east wind is blowing, but these are the conditions that can bring in snow buntings, Lapland buntings and shore larks. In October there is a good chance, too, of a Siberian vagrant, a Radde's warbler or Pallas's warbler perhaps, in addition to the more regular yellow-browed warblers and red-breasted flycatchers that turn up in gardens.

As Holy Island has become better known among competent observers, so more and more is being discovered or seen. Even so, a lot escapes attention. This applies particularly to rare winter birds but is also true of plants, insects and mammals. A summer visit may turn up something quite unexpected in the quiet dunelands away from the tourist route. However, anyone who has visited Holy Island on a midwinter morning will have seen it at its best.

THE *W*ALK

The dunes backing the north shore are worth exploring for orchids and other flowers

1 Turn right at the main car park entrance and walk along the road past the Lindisfarne Hotel. The little gardens here and round the corner are worth checking in the late autumn when east winds might have brought in migrant songbirds. These will usually be such birds as blackcaps or redstarts, but there is a good chance of a Siberian vagrant.

At the road junction turn left, then right along the main street and past the Castle Hotel and post office. At the road end turn left and continue past a row of houses, then past a church on the left. The little town was once notoriously rough and lawless, but considering the island's history there has been little violence. Jacobites, in the shape of two local characters, once captured the castle because most of the garrison were away for the day. The recapture was equally bloodless. Even when the Vikings attacked the Benedictine priory in 875 they found

the monks had already left for the mainland (taking St Cuthbert's preserved body with them). However, the Vikings burned down the wooden priory. The stone ruin on the site today, on the other side of St Mary's Church, is the remains of a much grander effort of 1093. It is now in the care of English Heritage and is open to visitors (there is a fee, payable at the excellent visitor centre).

2 From the side of the church follow the road downhill as it becomes a track, leading to a boulder-strewn shore. The little island to the left is called St Cuthbert's Isle. Cuthbert was prior and bishop of Lindisfarne in the late 7th century before moving to nearby Inner Farne. He was very fond of birds and animals (he had no other company for most of his life) and is said to have been particularly fond of eider ducks. Locally, eiders are still known as 'cuddy-ducks', cuddy being the widespread diminutive for Cuthbert. There are sure to be eiders about, either loafing on the island or swimming in the offshore channel.

3 It is possible to walk across to St Cuthbert's Isle at low tide, or to beachcomb among the slippery boulders. Otherwise, turn left (east) along a path as the track bears right to the old lifeboat house. The path climbs to the top of a ridge and passes a coastguard station and a war memorial cross. The ridge is called The Heugh (pronounced 'He-uff'), a

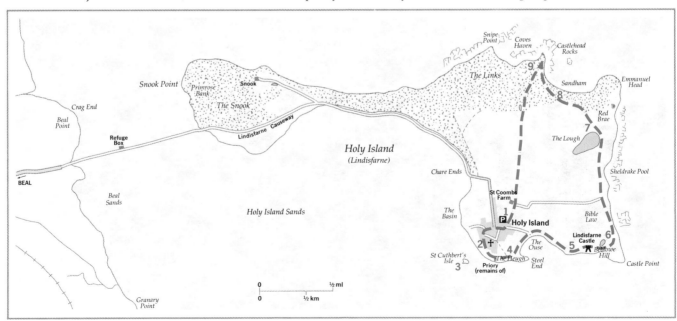

volcanic dyke intruded into the existing sediments and base-rich, therefore good for wild flowers. Exploring the rocky columns of this black, fine-grained dolerite should produce typical species like sea campion and sea plantain.

This is the best vantage point on the island. There are excellent views, west to the mainland and the Cheviots, east to the harbour and castle, north over the town and priory, south across the sea to the Farne Islands and Bamburgh. The two needles, built on the point of Ross Back Sands, were built as navigation aids to align fishing boats coming into harbour.

4 **Walk along The Heugh to its northern end. The path then descends to the left, past a gate to the priory and on to the crab-sheds and upturned boats on the south side of the harbour.** There are lobster pots, crates, barrels, torn nets and upturned fishing boats turned into sheds. In fact it is over a century since the island's fishing fleet was viable; what remains is small-scale despite all the debris. The harbour is called The Ouse. A white-billed diver was seen here a few years ago, and great northerns are regular. Bear left past the boats and continue around the harbour, following the road towards the castle.

Clearly, Beblowe Hill, on which the castle sits, is another piece of the dyke. Fulmars are usually in evidence, sitting on available crags from the late winter onwards, often not even attempting to nest. They are beautiful birds and have a gentle expression, caused in part by sooty eye-shadow, and an abashed manner, which belies their habit of squirting foul-smelling oil at anyone who approaches too close. . .

5 **Bear right at the castle, and the smaller outcrop of rock beyond it, then cross a grassy area to a group of limekilns.** These were in use a century ago to burn lime quarried from a limestone outcrop on the north shore of the island. Coal was brought from Dundee for the purpose, the resulting slaked lime forming the return cargo.

From the kilns continue eastwards to the shore, by Castle Point. This is a broad spit of boulders and pebbles on the south-east corner of the island and is a good place to stop for a look at the open sea and the Farne Islands.

6 **Turn north along the shore, picking up a grassy path above the boulder-beach and following this between a fence to the left and the cliff-top of boulder clay to the right.** Along the high-tide mark dead birds

may be seen, either oiled or storm-blown. Many of the winter corpses are of guillemots, but after strong northerly gales there may also be little auks and puffins.

The path passes a shallow lake to the left, called Holy Island Lough (pronounced 'loff'). In early summer the water is covered with bogbean flowers and there is a noisy colony of black-headed gulls. In the winter it attracts mallards and teal and families of whooper swans.

7 **Continue past the lake to a stile, then bear left on a grassy ridge (the remains of an old wagon-way used to transport limestone to the kilns). Go through a wicket-gate, then bear right to Emmanuel Head, the north-east corner of the island and the best vantage point to stop for a sustained look at the sea.** The dazzlingly white pyramid makes a good windbreak and place to sit, though in easterly gales (the best conditions to bring seabirds close inshore) it is exposed and desolate and comes into its own as a beacon. Holding a telescope steady is impossible in a gale, which is perhaps why identification can be so difficult. Skuas, auks, shearwaters, divers, grebes and a host of waders and ducks can all pass by without being positively identified. If the sea proves to be too frustrating it is worth looking over the dune slacks and heathland; this is as reliable a spot for merlin as it is possible to find, and there are always finches and buntings about.

The causeway and mudflats are uncovered for several hours when the tide is out, attracting thousands of wildfowl and waders in winter

8 **A path westwards around the headland leads you to a beautiful sandy bay, perfect for beachcombing and attractive to a variety of wading birds.** Although the bay never seems to hold large numbers of any species there is always a good variety, including bar-tailed godwit, sanderling, turnstone and redshank. Castlehead Rocks usually hide a few purple sandpipers.

9 **After walking around the bay to the limestone headland, look for a path leading south through the dunes.** Explore the dunes in spring and summer for flowers such as grass of Parnassus, marsh helleborine, the naturalised pirri-pirri bur and marsh orchids, and for butterflies including dark green fritillary.

Return to the path and follow this to the edge of the dune grassland where there is a National Nature Reserve sign. Beyond the sign is a walled track, called the Straight Lonnen ('lonnen' = lane). Walk down this track, with open fields to the left. Again, this is good merlin country, with a chance of seeing a sparrowhawk or a peregrine. Wind-swept hawthorns along the side of the ancient track sometimes hold flocks of redwings and fieldfares.

The track leads straight back towards the town, past St Coombs Farm and to the car park.

Mudflats seldom look the same twice. Constantly changing light lends them a unique appeal

A DARKENING OF THE SKY HERALDS THE ANNUAL ARRIVAL OF THE BARNACLE GEESE AT CAERLAVEROCK. IN A BREATHTAKING SPECTACLE, AN ARCTIC ISLAND'S ENTIRE POPULA-TION OF THESE GEESE FLIES IN TO WINTER ON THE SOLWAY SALT-MARSH, WHICH OFFERS WINTER FEEDING TO MANY OTHER SPECIES OF WILDFOWL AND WADER. WOODS, FIELDS, RIVER AND SEA COMPLEMENT THE MARSH, MAKING CAERLAVEROCK AN ALL-YEAR WILDLIFE HAVEN.

BARNACLE GEESE AND CAERLAVEROCK

Every autumn, as the Arctic winter deepens, up to 12,000 barnacle geese from the northerly island of Spits-bergen fly some 2000 miles (3200km) south to the shores of the Solway Firth around Caerlaverock. Up to 1000 of the birds may die on the two-day flight, but against this loss must be set the fact that in 1945 the total number of wintering barnacle geese on the Solway had dwindled to a mere 400. Since then, shrewd land management and cooperation between farmers and conservationists at Caerlaverock have helped the barnacle goose population rally dramatically to its present figure.

THE MERSE

It is the salt-marsh (or merse, as it is known locally) – one of Scotland's last stretches of natural tide-washed grass-land – that brings the barnacle geese to Caerlaverock. The merse has a natural mix of grasses which, unimproved for farmstock, forms a high-energy diet for the geese. To ensure that the salt-marsh provides top-quality nutrition for the grazing geese, the land is used in summer for cattle. They crop the grass, preventing it from growing too long to be of benefit to the geese. This arrangement is one aspect of the agreements reached between farmers and the conservation groups which manage the merse.

Caerlaverock is not merely good feeding territory for Spitsbergen's geese. It is vital to their survival. They must be ready, when they return home, to breed immediately after the sapping journey. They must be in peak condition, and it is the sea-washed grass of the Caerlaverock merse which helps to ensure that they are. There are few other areas left where they can feed in peace.

The world population of these beautiful birds is around 100,000. They do not yet face the danger of global extinction. But the 12,000 Spitsbergen birds are so delicately balanced with their environment that it would take only a bad winter to tip the balance against them.

CAERLAVEROCK'S OTHER BIRDS

Although the barnacle geese are perhaps the jewel in Caerlaverock's crown, other waterfowl also benefit from the preservation of the merse. Whooper and Bewick's swans, greylag and pink-footed geese and wigeon all winter on the salt-marsh. The mudflats between sea and merse provide ideal feeding for oystercatchers, curlews, knots, redshanks and golden plovers, while mallards, teal, pintails, golden-eyes and mergansers feed in the estuary of the River Nith.

The woods and fields backing the merse attract birds of prey. Sparrow-hawks and kestrels find food here, as do buzzards and the occasional merlin. Hen harriers and, in winter, short-eared owls hunt over the merse itself. Caerlaverock is also home to a night-flier now sadly under threat. The barn owl has, through persecution and loss of habitat, become increasingly rare throughout Britain. But south-west Scotland, although experiencing some decline in its 'barnie' population, still has relatively large numbers of this beautiful, ghostly bird.

A HAVEN FOR WILDLIFE

Caerlaverock is more than a bird sanctuary. The nocturnal natterjack toad – one of Britain's rarest amphibians – has its main Scottish stronghold at Caerlaverock. The secluded nature of the site allows otters to go almost unnoticed in the many narrow channels that traverse the merse. Other mammals making their home on the reserve include foxes, roe deer and badgers, for which Castle Wood provides dense cover.

Caerlaverock

Dumfries & Galloway
Grid ref. NY 018 653

Nature Conservancy Council
Approx. 2½ miles (4 km). Level walking, but may be wet underfoot in places. Some gullies to cross.

Caerlaverock lies some 7 miles (11 km) south of Dumfries, off the B725. The Castle Corner car park is on a right-angled bend in the road, 3 miles (4.8 km) south of Glencaple.

One of Britain's finest coastal grass-lands, the salt-marsh around Caer-laverock sustains the entire barnacle goose population of the Arctic island of Spitsbergen throughout the winter. As well as hosting this annual influx of some 12,000 geese, Caerlaverock is a stronghold for the disappearing barn owl and holds Britain's northernmost colony of natterjack toads. It is also a haven for otters and badgers, and provides winter feeding for a variety of birds.

Nearby sites: *Wildfowl and Wetlands Centre, Caerlaverock* – excellent views from hides and observatory over the coastal marshes where waders and wildfowl feed in winter; *Dalbeattie Forest* – natural deciduous trees, conifer plantations, ornamental trees and shrubs with residents including sparrowhawk, buzzard, little owl, willow tit.

Barnacle geese

THE *W*ALK

1 From the car park follow the B725 north-eastwards for about ³/₄ mile (1.2km) as far as a right turn signposted to Caerlaverock Castle. Hedges along the road are home to chaffinches, while the road itself provides insects for pied wagtails, recognisable by their short, dipping flight and cock-tailed gait as they scurry across the ground in short bursts. At dusk, little owls and barn owls hunt across the fields.

2 Turn right at the sign for Caerlaverock Castle and follow the road through the gate. The three-cornered castle, dating back to the 13th century, is ringed by a moat. The tall reeds around the castle provide cover in summer for sedge warblers, spotted flycatchers and whitethroats.

3 Take the road to the left of the moat. This soon narrows to a woodland path. A dense wood of oak, rowan, silver birch and larch hides badgers, foxes and roe deer. Jays, heard chattering in the trees, may sometimes be seen. Two species of woodpecker are found here: the green, or yaffle, and the great spotted. This differs from the lesser spotted not only in size, but also in having a plain black back and a scarlet flash under the tail.

4 The path continues to a five-bar gate opening on to fields

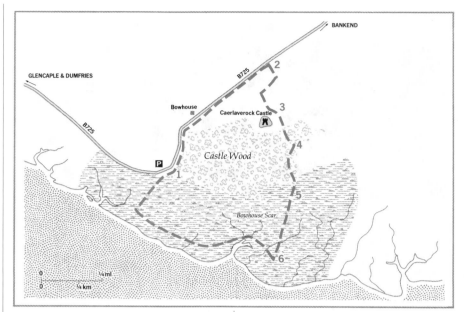

and offering a fine view of the Lake District across the Solway. The path veers right past a tea-garden (summer only) and over a small footbridge back into the wood. After about 50yds (45m), the path emerges in a clearing surrounded by conifers. Continue through this screen of trees

Deep tidal creeks break up the western fringes of the merse, which look across the Nith estuary to the slopes of Criffel beyond

to a stile on the seaward side of the wood. Where the wood opens out, gorse and foxgloves grow, attracting a number of bees, butterflies and moths. The striking six-spot burnet moth is often seen.

5 Cross the stile, passing a nature reserve information board on your right. Cross another stile and follow the fence towards the sea. High tides occasionally swamp this area, but it is possible to return to the car park by walking westwards close to the trees. Spring evenings here are filled with the sound of the natterjacks, while winter days resound with the yelping of the barnacle geese. Most of the wintering birds feed on the Wildfowl and Wetlands Trust refuge, to the east of here, but many can be seen on the 600 acres (240 hectares) of land that the Trust shares with the Nature Conservancy Council.

6 Turn right and walk westwards, parallel with the shore, for about ³/₄ mile (1.2km). This area is criss-crossed by narrow gullies, so must be taken carefully. Where the view to the landward side opens out into rising fields, turn right and walk back to the road and the car park. The estuary is fished by red-breasted mergansers and cormorants, while oystercatchers and knots dominate the mudflats. Inland, the fields alongside the B725 are visited in winter by flocks of fieldfares and redwings keen to raid the hawthorn hedges. Summer dusk may offer a sighting of the elusive barn owl, beating its way across the fields.

A wooded gorge, rich in wildlife, frames the River Clyde at spectacular Corra Linn

Falls of Clyde

Strathclyde

Grid ref. NS 882 425

Scottish Wildlife Trust
Approx. 1½ miles (2.4 km). Relatively easy walking, with some steps.

The reserve is just outside New Lanark, immediately south of Lanark. Park above New Lanark village near the visitor centre.

The River Clyde, with its spectacular and famous falls, is the highlight of the walk, but the woodland of the gorge supports a rich wildlife, from fungi, ferns and mosses to woodland birds and red squirrels.

Nearby sites: *Braehead Moss* – raised and blanket bog; *Clyde Valley Woods* (Cleghorn Glen) – ancient gorge woodland; *Barons Haugh* – riverside habitats, good for breeding water birds and warblers, and wintering wildfowl.

Ragged robin is not yet a rarity, but its distinctive flowers have become much less widespread because of wetland drainage

FAMED IN POETRY, PROSE AND PAINTING, THE FALLS OF CLYDE WERE AN OBLIGATORY STOP ON THE TOURS OF SCOTLAND WHICH WERE SO POPULAR IN THE LATE 18TH AND EARLY 19TH CENTURIES. COLERIDGE, WORDSWORTH AND TURNER WERE AMONG THOSE INSPIRED BY THE FALLS, WHICH REMAIN A WELL-KNOWN AND POPULAR ATTRACTION TODAY AS PART OF A RESERVE OF THE SCOTTISH WILDLIFE TRUST.

THE CLYDE AND ITS WILDLIFE

Encompassing both banks of the Clyde Gorge, the reserve takes its name from the Clyde's three large waterfalls – Bonnington Linn, Corra Linn and Dundaff Linn. Stretching from the historic village of New Lanark southwards to Bonnington Weir, the reserve includes some fine old mixed oak woodland.

A 160ft (50m) drop in the river bed here led to the opening of a hydro-electric power station in 1927. The production of electricity removes water from the river, unfortunately reducing the spectacle of the falls, but the Scottish Wildlife Trust now has a special arrangement with Scottish Power which enables visitors to see the falls in full flow on certain days of the year. Despite these unnatural fluctuations in water-level, this stretch of river supports several pairs of breeding dippers and grey wagtails. Signs of otters are also now regularly found. Water quality in the Clyde has

Alpine lady's mantle, a plant of the uplands

The Red Squirrel

The red squirrel is our only native species of squirrel – its grey cousin was introduced from North America. It is easily recognised by its orange-red fur, bushy tail and prominent ear-tufts; in some places, it becomes quite accustomed to man's presence and these features are easy to observe. Sadly, recent decades have seen a dramatic decline in the numbers and range of the red squirrel. Once widespread in Britain, it is now only locally common in Scotland and northern England, being restricted to a few isolated spots in the south. Red squirrels prefer coniferous woodland, although they are by no means restricted to this habitat. The chewed remains of pine cones are often a good clue as to their presence.

improved greatly recently, allowing salmon and sea trout to migrate up the river to breed – though not as far as the Falls of Clyde, as falls further downstream impede their progress.

RETURN OF THE OAK

Fringing both sides of the gorge is a mosaic of woodland, partly natural and partly planted. The steepest sides of the gorge have never been cleared of trees, and what is left is the remnant of an ancient oakwood which covered a much larger area. Perhaps the greatest change in land use in the whole history of the area was the felling of much of this woodland in the 1940s and subsequent replanting with conifers around 1960. The Trust has embarked on an ambitious programme of restoring the majestic oak woodland to its proper home along the banks of the Clyde. The damp, shady floor of the wood is ideal for mosses and ferns, and over 340 species of fungi have been recorded. Resident woodland birdlife includes woodcock, sparrow-hawk and great spotted woodpecker. The summer months bring willow and wood warblers, blackcaps and spotted flycatchers.

Where the vertical sandstone walls of the gorge are too steep to support trees, a number of interesting plants grow, notably purple saxifrage, found nowhere else in Lanarkshire. Interesting man-made structures also occur alongside the falls; the ruins of Corra Castle now provide a summer roost for a colony of Natterer's bats.

THE *Walk*

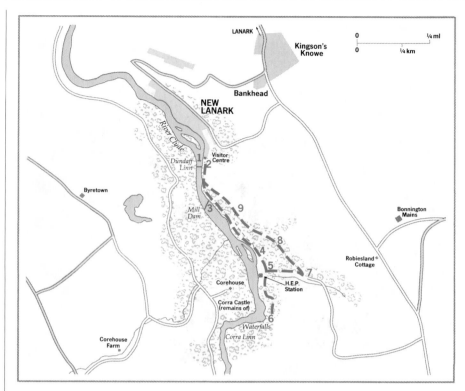

1 The Dye Works of New Lanark, now sympathetically converted into a visitor centre, is the starting point for the walk. This attractive building commands a stunning position overlooking the River Clyde and the first of the falls, Dundaff Linn. It is an excellent vantage point to look for riverine birds.

Droppings on the rocks in the river are likely to be those of a dipper searching for food among the stones on the river bed, and frequently submerging to pick up insects from the bottom. Common sandpipers also breed on the Clyde. This small brown and white wader has a distinctive continuous bobbing motion. The grey wagtail completes the trio, flitting along the river banks and rocks, showing flashes of brilliant yellow.

2 Climb the steps opposite the centre, turning right at the top through the arch, and follow the riverside path. Few shrubs and woodland plants can grow under the dense shade of the conifers above the path. Plans are in hand to gradually restore oak woodland to these areas and many other parts of the reserve. The rich mixture of trees, shrubs and woodland flowers can be seen along the river bank remnant, with oak, hazel, rowan, birch, blaeberry (bilberry) and woodrush.

3 Continue on the lower path past Mill Dam. Here woodland springs bubble to the surface. Conifers have already been removed, leaving the tall ash trees to develop without restriction. The wetter ground supports a specialised and colourful combination of marsh marigolds, valerian, angelica and meadowsweet.

4 Bear right on joining the upper path. The small rock face to your left provides an appropriate niche for the common polypody, one of a number of different species of fern found on the reserve.

5 Passing close to the hydro-electric power station, take the lower track and walk up the hill. This section includes a number of exotic trees and shrubs including rhododendron. To compensate for the lack of old trees in the reserve, a number of bird- and bat-boxes have been attached to the trees. This is the most likely area to catch a glimpse of the bushy tail of a red squirrel as it leaps from branch to branch in a tall Scots pine. Look for gnawed cones on the side of the path – evidence of the red squirrel's presence.

6 As you approach the water pipes again, climb up the flight of steps to the viewpoint. This overlooks the most impressive of all the falls, Corra Linn – most spectacular during the winter, or when the reserve has 'full-flow' days. Above the view-point is a derelict building known as the Hall of Mirrors where a more arresting view was once had of the falls. Erected by Sir James Carmichael in 1708, the pavilion had a mirror on its back wall to create the illusion of being surrounded by water.

Retrace your steps to point 5 on the walk and turn right on to the tarmac road. The cutting back of scrub underneath the power lines is for safety reasons, but it has the benefit of diversifying woodland structure. Acting as a substitute for a woodland ride, the cleared area is a favoured haunt of feeding butterflies. Woodcock also inhabit this part of the reserve. Because of their excellent camouflage, they are unlikely to be seen during the day unless flushed from cover, but on fine spring evenings their roding flights and strange whistling calls are unmistakable.

Cross the cattle-grid and continue up the road to the pond. Here a pond-dipping platform has been constructed to enable children to get 'hands-on' experience of pond life. The marshland opposite the pond holds a good variety of wetland plants with ragged robin, greater birdsfoot trefoil and the greater tussock sedge, not at all common in Scotland.

7 Go through the gate next to the pond and turn left along the woodland path. Oaks have been planted to replace cleared areas of conifers, and are attracting a wider range of woodland birds and insects. Gradual thinning of the remaining conifers is continuing. White foxgloves are common throughout this area.

8 A short flight of steps on the left leads down to a viewing platform overlooking an active badger sett. At dusk, badgers can be seen emerging from their underground tunnels and chambers, oblivious (if you keep quiet and still) of their onlookers above. Spring and summer are the best time, when the badgers are more active and cubs may be playing outside the sett. Badger-watches are a feature of the reserve's busy wildlife calendar; details can be found in the visitor centre.

9 On joining the main track, turn right and make your way back towards New Lanark, crossing the stile on your left back down to Mill Dam and the riverside path.

THE 'PRECIPITOUS CITY', AS ROBERT LOUIS STEVENSON DESCRIBED EDINBURGH, IS ONE OF THE MOST ATTRACTIVE IN THE WORLD. IT IS ONE OF THE FEW TO HAVE ITS OWN MOUNTAIN AND VOLCANO, ALBEIT EXTINCT, WITHIN THE CITY BOUND-ARIES. AT 822FT (251M), ARTHUR'S SEAT IS THE HIGHEST OF THE SEVEN HILLS ON WHICH EDINBURGH WAS BUILT.

HOLYROOD PARK

The lion-shaped profile of Arthur's Seat dominates the Royal Park of Holyrood, created in the 12th century by King David I, who founded Holyrood Abbey, and gave to it all the land around the crag of Arthur's Seat.

There is still great debate over the origins of the name of Edinburgh's mountain. Some say it comes from the Gaelic *Ard-na-said* meaning 'the height of arrows', while others prefer to link it to King Arthur. What is fact is that Arthur's Seat has a long, intriguing and remarkable history, with evidence of early settlements and associated defensive ramparts, medieval cultiva-tion terraces and tombs. In 1645, with Edinburgh in the grasp of the Great Plague, Holyrood Park was used as an isolation area for the infected, and a graveyard for those who did not recover.

A RICH AND VARIED FLORA

The small, composite volcano of Arthur's Seat (other remnants of the volcano are Castle Rock and Calton Hill) is one of the most studied ancient volcanoes in the world. The complex geology of this area is reflected in the richness of its flora. Much of Holyrood

---

Arthur's Seat

Lothian
Grid ref. NT 270 737

Approx. 3¼ miles (5.2 km). Easy walking apart from the climb to the summit, which is strenuous. Near the summit, the ground is bare, with loose stones.

Arthur's Seat is situated at the eastern end of Edinburgh's Royal Mile, adjoining the Palace of Holyroodhouse. The walk starts from the Holyrood Park Visitor Centre. The main car park is near by.

Arthur's Seat is the dominant feature of Holyrood Park, a large area of unimproved grassland and scrub with freshwater lochs, rock crags and cliffs. The park is home to a surprisingly wide range of wildlife.

Nearby sites: *Pentlands Regional Park* – heather moorland, reservoirs and peat bog; *Aberlady Bay* – exceptional for coastal birds including waders, divers and sea ducks, also good maritime flora; *Musselburgh Lagoons* – man-made lagoons now infilled with waste ash, but still used by roosting gulls and waders. Sea ducks are seen off shore in winter.

Harebell

Views of the city, the Firth of Forth and distant Fife make the summit worth reaching

Park is covered in unimproved grassland and can be acid, neutral or calcareous in character, depending on the underlying rock type. The richer plant communities occur where the mineral content of the rocks changes to form a more base-rich substrate. Bloody cranesbill, rock-rose, maiden pink, purple milk-vetch and dropwort are found in these areas.

Gorse scrub, marsh and three fresh-water lochs add to the complex of habitats, leading to an exceptional diversity of plants. The only natural loch, Duddingston, with its associated woodland and reed-beds, is an important habitat in its own right. In the 1970s this loch provided an attractive and safe roosting area of open water for up to 6000 pochards, which used to feed in the Firth of Forth in the vicinity of Edinburgh's sewage outfalls.

CHANGING TIMES

While walking in some parts of Holyrood Park, it is easy to imagine oneself in some secluded Scottish glen, and not within a short distance of the hustle and bustle of city life. However, recent decades have seen an increase in the use of the park by dog-walkers and cars, so sheep can no longer graze here. Having been part of the Royal Park since the 16th century, the sheep and their shepherd have not been seen here since 1979. The gorse has flourished since the removal of the sheep, and now threatens the very plants that were previously being overgrazed. Who knows, perhaps the shepherd and his flock will return to the mountain one day.

THE *WALK*

1 Leaving the visitor centre, turn left past the main car park, continuing on the pavement on the opposite side of the road. The visitor centre is well worth a visit for its displays on the history, geology and wildlife of Arthur's Seat and the park.

2 Pass St Margaret's Well, in a grotto on your right, and continue to the near shore of St Margaret's Loch. This shallow artificial loch is home to coots, mallards, tufted ducks, mute swans and gulls, which all enjoy visitors' offerings of stale bread. Pochards visit the loch in winter, and the park's feral greylag geese swell the numbers of native species. Wild greylags are normally only seen in large flocks in the winter, and then only in the distance or overhead. The current flock of 150 or so are the descendants of 13 birds introduced on to Duddingston Loch in 1961.

3 Turn away from the road with the loch on your left, and climb the path in front of you, keeping St Anthony's Chapel above and to the left. A broad valley called Dry Dam appears, with the summit of Arthur's Seat ahead. The rough grassland typical of the park covers much of Dry Dam, providing nesting cover for meadow pipits and skylarks. The

slopes of Whinny Hill are ablaze with gorse in May, filling the valley with a heavy scent. Linnets, gregarious throughout the year, fly among the gorse, attracting attention with their twittering flight, while meadow brown butterflies flutter on summer breezes through the tall grasses, wood sage and lady's bedstraw.

4 Continue into Dry Dam and take the higher path to your right, which climbs towards Arthur's Seat. (This section is very steep so stay on the lower path if you do not feel attracted to the summit or your footwear is unsuitable, and rejoin the walk at Dunsapie Loch.) On the way to the Seat, look out for kestrels, which breed on the crags and can be readily distinguished by their characteristic hovering flight. In spring, wheatears and the occasional ring ouzel stop to rest and feed on Arthur's Seat before making their way further north.

5 The view from the summit is one of the most spectacular in Britain. Look northwards to the Firth of Forth, important for its waders and breeding terns. To the south-west are the heather-clad slopes of the Pentland Hills, and to the north-east the East Lothian coast and the Bass Rock, home of a famous gannet colony.

From the summit, follow the main

route down to Dunsapie Loch. Also man-made, this attracts similar birds to those seen on St Margaret's Loch.

6 Cross the road, turn right on to the pavement and continue along the Queen's Drive. If you look back towards Arthur's Seat you may see the impressions of cultivation terraces, roughly following the contours of the hill. They are thought to date back as far as the Bronze Age.

7 Further along, the Queen's Drive looks down over Duddingston Loch, the only natural loch in the park. Water rails, tawny owls and sedge warblers nest here, and the number of nesting herons has increased recently to around 10 pairs. The reed-bed, the largest in the Lothians, was once harvested for thatching reeds. These were also woven into a coarse fabric known as 'Duddingston hardings' and sold in Edinburgh's markets.

8 As you continue along the pavement, the cliffs drop down more sharply on your right. This area is more lime-rich and is consequently one of the best and most colourful plant areas of the park with rock-rose, viper's bugloss, rest-harrow, knapweed and many other species, both rare and common. Sparrowhawks are sometimes seen flying over this area or over Duddingston Loch.

9 Cross the road before the roundabout to the path between Arthur's Seat and Salisbury Crags. The valley to the north is still known as Hunter's Bog, but is now much drier as a result of drainage work.

10 Retrace your steps, then take the broad track below Salisbury Crags, known as the Radical Road. There are several quarries along here, the first being one of the most famous geological sites in Scotland.

11 Continue along the Radical Road. The impressive skyline of Edinburgh appears again, and another of the seven hills – Castle Rock, topped by Edinburgh Castle – comes into view. Fulmars nest on the crags above you, breeding among the harebells in this unusual site. Gull-like in colouring, they belong to the petrel group of seabirds.

Cross the road to the car park or retrace your steps to the park entrance and visitor centre.

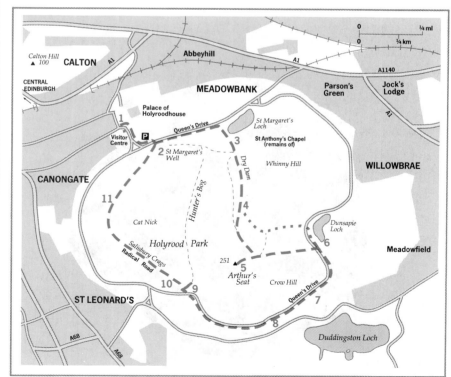

CLIFF-NESTING COLONIES OF SEA-BIRDS PRESENT ONE OF THE MOST EXCITING SPECTACLES IN EUROPEAN WILDLIFE. THE MOST IMPRESSIVE SITES ARE USUALLY ON REMOTE ISLANDS, BUT THERE ARE SEVERAL EXCELLENT MAINLAND SITES WHICH GIVE A GOOD IMPRESSION OF THE CHAOS AND FRENZIED ACTIVITY OF BIG SEABIRD CONGREGATIONS. OF THESE REMARKABLE PLACES, ST ABB'S HEAD IS THE BEST.

THE ST ABB'S AREA

The waters off St Abb's have been designated a Voluntary Marine Reserve; the mix of currents brings in a unique undersea flora and fauna which can only be guessed at from the cliff-tops. The village of St Abbs, with its little harbour, is always busy with scuba-geared amateur divers and local fishermen, and is worth a visit. The Head lies north of the village. The reason it is so good for seabirds is that it is composed of volcanic rock which is hard, slow to erode, and forms sheer cliffs. The volcanic rock is separated from older sediments by a fault line, marked by a dip now filled by Mire Loch which gives the higher, more rugged headland every appearance of being an island. St Aebbe, daughter of King Edilfred (a 7th-century King of Northumbria) founded a nunnery on the highest point of the Head, Kirk Hill, and so lent her name to the area.

PLANTS AND BIRDS

There are some interesting plants on the grassy slopes of the cliff-tops:

St Abb's Head

Borders
Grid ref. NT 913 674

National Trust for Scotland/Scottish Wildlife Trust
Approx. 3¼ miles (5.2 km). Steep in places; great care needed on cliff path.

The Reserve car park is off the B6438 at Northfield, 5 miles (8 km) north-west of Eyemouth, and ½ mile (800m) west of St Abbs village.

This National Nature Reserve offers fine coastal scenery and spectacular views of cliff-nesting seabirds as well as sightings of migrants passing off shore.

Nearby sites: *North Berwick* – departure point for island boat trips to the *Bass Rock,* for gannets, and *Craigleith,* for breeding puffins and other seabirds; *Dunbar* – kittiwake colony on castle ruins beside harbour.

Scurvy-grass, found all round Britain's coast

Salt-tolerant lichens bring splashes of colour to the rocks close to the tide-line

purple milk-vetch and Scots lovage as well as the more usual scurvy-grass and thrift. However, it is the birds that make St Abb's special, and from Easter to mid July they will make the walk to Nunnery Point a memorable experience. The numbers are staggering: in 1990 some 68,000 seabirds nested on the headland. The majority are kittiwakes and guillemots but there are good numbers of razorbills, a scattering of fulmars and shags, and even a few puffins. Out to sea there are always flights of gannets heading to and from the Bass Rock, and in the late summer and autumn there will be shearwaters and skuas.

To look down towards the deep shadowy waters from the cliffs north-west of St Abb's lighthouse and try to make sense of the swirling avian activity induces a mixture of elation and vertigo. In a few short weeks the kittiwakes will fly from their nests and the young guillemots and razorbills, incapable of flight, will launch themselves and tumble down into the waves to be carried by the currents to their true home, the open sea.

A guillemot with its precariously perched egg

THE *W*ALK

Before leaving the National Nature Reserve car park, it is worth looking among the trees and bushes for migrant warblers, chats and thrushes. Spend a few minutes, too, in the visitor centre, to find out what is about (whales perhaps, or peregrines).

1 From the visitor centre, walk downhill beside the farm building and cross a stile at the side of the road. Turn right to follow the wall, with a fenced field on your left and the road to your right. At the end of the field turn sharp left at a nature reserve sign, away from the road and with a high wall to your right. Follow the track through two wicket-gates. Ahead now lies Starney Bay, where a seat on a grassy knoll commands a view of both the bay and White Heugh – the cliff-face to the north. The colour of the rock, and therefore its name, is mainly the result of whitewashing by kittiwakes, for this is the first of the major seabird colonies. Their urgent cries (of 'kittiwake', or something similar) echo across the bay. From this distance the delicate sea-going gulls look like wind-blown confetti. Starney Bay is composed of softer rock than the cliffs to the north, and in spring the grassy slopes carry flowers such as primroses.

2 A winding path leads down to the pebble beach of the bay if you wish to explore. Otherwise, keep to the main cliff-top path which bears left (clockwise above the bay), and rises as it heads north. From here there are much better views of the kittiwakes of White Heugh. Banks of gorse rise above the fence, and looking back there are good views of St Abbs and the coastline to the south.

The path drops down and the main headland appears for the first time. The steep-sided hill ahead, beyond Horsecastle Bay, is Kirk Hill, the site of St Aebbe's nunnery which was destroyed by Vikings at the end of the 9th century. To the left of Kirk Hill is the Mire Loch, nestling in a broad trench scoured out by Ice Age glaciers which followed the fault line between the volcanic rock of the Head and the adjacent sediments.

3 The path angles down to Horsecastle Bay where access is again possible to the shore, but this is boulder-strewn and uninviting. Most of the rocks are of a characteristic red colour.

The path now bears left, uphill again and beside a fence, leading to the left of Kirk Hill and away from the sea. Follow the path as it heads north-westwards with the Mire Loch to your left. The loch is an artificial lake, dammed at its southern end. It is a popular bathing place for kittiwakes, which enjoy fresh water for this purpose, and is the home of dabchicks and tufted ducks. The bushes along the shore sometimes hold large numbers of migrant thrushes making a landfall from Scandinavia. To the right of the path the steep dry slopes of Kirk Hill are cropped short by rabbits, but provide good stony nesting sites for wheatears. The fence keeps out sheep in order to encourage the growth of rock-rose, the food-plant of the rare northern brown argus butterfly.

4 At the end of Kirk Hill the path meets the coast again but is less distinct as it continues north, away from the cliff-top, over springy, close-cropped grass and thrift, towards the lighthouse. Make for the left side of the lighthouse, with views of the old walled lighthouse garden and the loch away to the left. There is usually a strong scent of gorse here, drifting eastwards from the banks above the loch.

5 The path drops down to a surfaced road and a small car park. Beyond this are the main cliff-faces with deep chasms and knife-edged ridges. These carry the most important seabird colonies.

Continue along the cliff-tops, on level, grassy ground, to view Nunnery Point and the other dramatic breeding sites. Tier upon tier of guillemots, clefts full of razorbills, open rock-faces stacked with kittiwake nests, add up to a marvellous spectacle.

There are usually a few puffins about (they nest in cliff-top burrows and do not find this site so suitable) and there is a chance of seeing a peregrine.

6 After spending some time around Nunnery Point and Headland Hill, join the road and follow this down to Pettico Wick, the little bay at the north side of the valley containing Mire Loch.

7 When you are ready to return to the nature reserve car park, follow the road, which rises quite steeply then heads south through farmland.

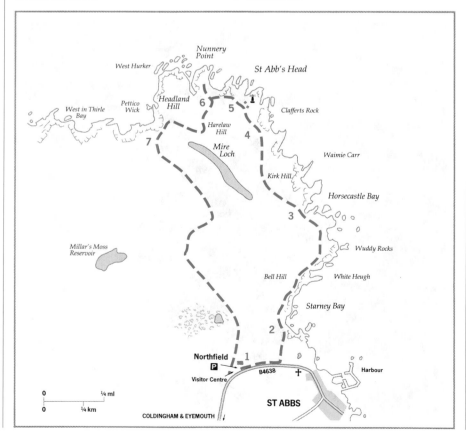

Rothiemurchus

Lochan Mor, its surface studded with water-lilies, is backed by the less hospitable-looking terrain of the Cairngorms in Britain's largest nature reserve

GLIMPSES OF BRITAIN WITHOUT THE STAMP OF MAN ARE ELUSIVE: EVEN THE MOST REMOTE HILLS AND FORESTS HAVE BEEN EXPLOITED AT ONE TIME OR ANOTHER. MOST EXPERIENCED WALKERS WOULD DESCRIBE THE CAIRNGORMS AS THE CLOSEST THING TO WILDERNESS IN BRITAIN – A SEEMINGLY LIMITLESS WORLD OF SNOW-COVERED MOUNTAINS LINKED BY STRETCHES OF MOORLAND, LOCHS AND PINE FORESTS.

A DELICATE BALANCE

The Cairngorms can certainly be both beautiful and frightening, offering enough to satisfy anyone's taste for adventure. Yet this is a managed landscape where deer husbandry, forestry and tourism are big business. It is also the most extensive National Nature Reserve in Britain. Habitat conservation is an important consideration in any land management agreements, so although there are some obvious conflicts (the opening of ski-lifts or the overstocking of deer, for example) there is also a clear impression of harmony on the hills. Thus any imprint by farmers or foresters is light and it is possible to accept their influence as part of a natural system. The perfect balance has yet to be struck, but in the meantime a day at Rothiemurchus will give as good an impression of primeval Scotland as it is possible to get.

CONIFERS OLD AND NEW

Naturalists tend to dislike conifer plantations. Spruce, in particular, is associated with dark and dreary plantations, yet it is not the trees themselves, but the way they are grown, that causes the real problem – they are planted too close together and are block-felled after 30 or 40 years. If they were allowed to reach full maturity in a more open canopy they would look quite different, and if they were harvested individually then the forest would take on a continuous life of its own, able to sustain other plants and animals. Unfortunately spruce can never be fully accepted because it is an alien; although Norway spruce grew here before the last Ice Age it failed to cross the European land-bridge afterwards. Hence there was no gradual establishment of natural spruce woodland, with all its associated wildlife.

In the south of England it is quite possible to lump all coniferous trees together in the same dismissive way, but in the north this would be to deny

the supreme importance of the Scots pine, the tree that once clothed much of upland Britain and still occurs in relict forests across the north and east of Scotland. These 'Caledonian' pinewoods are unique; the trees are not the usual Scots pine but a special Scottish subspecies. Given time and space they take on a range of shapes and forms, culminating in gnarled monoliths. Enclaves of the old forest are to be found at such places as the Black Wood of Rannoch (on the shores of Loch Rannoch) and Glen Tanar (south

---

Rothiemurchus

Highland
Grid ref. NH 915 108

Approx. 6 miles (9.5 km). Level terrain; clear route.

The walk begins at Coylumbridge, a mile (1.2 km) south-east of Aviemore on the B970. Park in the wide lay-by on the B970, just before a caravan site with holiday cabins.

The Cairngorms, comprising a wilderness of mountains and ancient pine forests, are designated as a National Nature Reserve but much of the land is privately owned. The Rothiemurchus Estate is one of the major fragments of Caledonian forest; the RSPB also has extensive landholding in the area. The pinewoods, with an understorey of juniper and other shrubs, are beautiful and full of interesting plants and insects, though it is the birds that attract the most attention – notably the unique Scottish crossbill, the crested tit and the osprey.

Nearby sites: *Rannoch Moor* – bog and marsh flora including Rannoch rush; *Cairn gorm summit* – mountain birds and flowers (take the ski-lift up and walk down); *Vane Farm* – wintering wildfowl on the shores of Loch Leven.

Adult osprey

---

of the Dee) but the most extensive and most famous Caledonian pinewoods are those of Strathspey, on the northern slopes of the Cairngorms.

WILDLIFE OF THE CAIRNGORMS

Rothiemurchus, a private estate with open access along clear footpaths, extends to almost 25,000 acres (10,000 hectares). Near by are the Queen's Forest (owned by the Forestry Commission) and Abernethy (now owned by the RSPB). Together they form one of the most important wildlife sites in Europe. At Rothiemurchus the pines are often widely spaced, particularly as they climb the foothills southwards, but around Coylumbridge and Loch an Eilein there are some quite dense stands of even-aged timber and some more open 'parkland' areas with over-mature trees up to 300 years old, decaying into graceful skeletons. The variety or mix of ages is important to the associated fauna and flora. In some places there are dense patches of heather, bilberry and crowberry, with bushes of juniper and holly. The ground flora here includes such specialities as creeping lady's tresses orchid and one-flowered wintergreen. Elsewhere there are moss carpets, bogs and lochans where drifts of cranberry and sundews cover the sphagnum, and rocky outcrops where alpine flowers make an appearance.

There are many insects associated with the Caledonian forests, particularly beetles such as the spectacular wood-boring longhorns. There are also some very obscure species, including the little beetle *Cis dentatus* which lives in fungi on pine trees and is only known from Rothiemurchus. Birchwoods in the area are the headquarters of the Kentish glory and Rannoch sprawler – two notoriously rare moths – and wet flushes and pools are the home of the northern Coenagrion damselfly. Lucky visitors may even see a blue Aeshna dragonfly.

Of course, it is the birds that attract most naturalists to Strathspey. A short walk should produce crested tits and perhaps siskins and Scottish crossbills. The most elusive forest bird of Rothiemurchus is one of the biggest – the capercaillie, which is the size of a turkey but still manages to evade most birdwatchers.

When visiting the Cairngorms, most birdwatchers include trips to lochs and mountain tops – the former for nesting goldeneyes, Slavonian grebes and ospreys, the latter for eagles, ptarmigan and dotterels. The pinewoods span the middle ground. Although they are the most exploited of the region's habitats, they offer the greatest rewards to the naturalist.

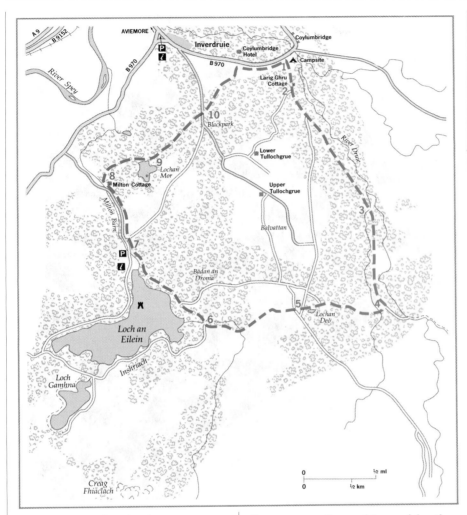

the path narrows. Although there are still some big pines here (look for crossbills, which like to sit on the very tops) there are also considerable areas of young trees or seedlings, the product of natural regeneration. As the views open out, across heather moorland, the granite domes of Cairn Gorm lie ahead, probably covered with snow and shrouded in cloud.

···· 4 **The path eventually leads through a wicket-gate, beside a big gate through a tall deer-proof fence.** The fence is intended to keep red deer out of regenerating woodland. Deer are the bane of forest management but bring in money in the form of fees for deer-stalking.

The track continues south-east, following the Larig Ghru, but soon meets another track on the right. (If you are feeling fit and are enjoying the day it is possible to follow the Larig Ghru a little further but you will then need to turn back, for the turn on the right offers the only circular route back to Coylumbridge.) Taking this right turn, the track heads westwards through open moorland. The sparse tree cover in this area is the result of wartime extraction and forest fires. Red and black grouse occur here, though the latter has decreased in recent years, like the capercaillie. Sphagnum bogs lie to the left and right – interesting places for plants, and the habitat of the large heath butterfly. The raised track allows you to look closely and still keep your boots dry.

···· 1 **From the lay-by a narrow path, signed 'Public footpath to Braemar by the Larig Ghru' leads south, with the cabins and camp site to the left.** As soon as you leave the road you are in the midst of magnificent pines, broad-limbed and festooned with lichens. Birch and juniper make up the low canopy, beneath which is a dwarf shrub layer of heather and bilberry. Lest you should be tempted to consider the Larig Ghru as an afternoon stroll, it should be pointed out that this is one of the classic, most dramatic and most strenuous routes across the Cairngorm massif. The walk shares its path to begin with, so for a mile or so you walk in the footsteps of heroes.

···· 2 **The path soon forks, at which bear left to keep parallel with the little River Bennie.** There are some clearings where it is possible to stand back and appreciate the various shapes of the pines, and to look at the ground flora among the cushions of heather. The commonest flowers are likely to be tormentil, cow-wheat and chickweed wintergreen, but it is worth looking carefully for more local plants such as frog orchid, lesser twayblade and serrated wintergreen. The most obvious insects of the pinewoods are wood ants, which will probably come to your attention when you brush past foliage or sit down. However, the wood ant here might well be the rare *Formica aquilonia* rather than the more widespread northern wood ant *Formica lugubris*. A less combative insect to look out for, in the grassy clearings, is the Scotch argus butterfly – a member of the *Erebia* genus of brown butterflies that also includes the mountain ringlet.

···· 3 **Continue along the path, which is wide and stony, through a gate, over a stile and across a little side-stream. Pass a National Nature Reserve sign, beyond which**

The aptly named hoof fungus is characteristic of Scottish woodland

Further on is a lochan or small lake, called Lochan Deò. Again there are fine views of the mountains to the south and south-east. The weather may be pleasant here (certainly this part of Scotland enjoys a more continental climate) but over on the hills things may be very different. The Cairngorms claim lives every year through cold, fatigue and exposure.

5 **The stony track continues westwards to a crossroads, at which go straight on.** Small streams cross the track, draining the slopes of Creag Dhubh. The rolling heather, broken by pine stumps and clumps of juniper, rises steadily to the south-west. In the distance, high on the flanks of Creag Fhiaclach, are some scattered pines growing at 2080ft (640m) and marking the highest natural tree-line in Britain.

6 **At a T-junction bear right, over a bridge, still on a wide stony track.** Tantalising glimpses of blue water will appear through mature pines on the left as the track picks up part of a circular route around Loch an Eilein. Turning left for a longer route around the loch would take you past the smaller Loch Gamhna, the Loch of Stirks, an ancient watering place for stolen cattle on the 'Thieves' Road'.

The track right leads through a wicket-gate, then past Lorimer Cottage (a little stone cottage with a corrugated iron roof) and finally passes the foot of Loch an Eilein to the left. This is the best place to detour left for the classic view of the lake. Loch an Eilein is best known for its romantic 'castle on an island', the ruins of a hall house probably built in the 13th century, and at one time connected by a causeway to the loch shore. In the 19th century it was also famous as Britain's last breeding site for ospreys, which nested on the ruins. Fortunately, after a long absence from Britain, ospreys now breed again in Strathspey, though not on Loch an Eilein. The lake sometimes carries a few wildfowl such as goldeneyes and whooper swans; otherwise it is a picturesque and silent sheet of water.

7 **Back on the track, the route heads north-west to meet a road, at which turn right along the road.** To the left is a pretty stream, the Milton Burn, lined with alders which may harbour willow warblers and redstarts. Beyond the stream is a beautiful bank of birch trees. They look as if a fall of snow or a winter gale would see them away, but birch arrived in this area at least as long ago as pine – in the boreal period between 8000 and 9000 years ago – and birch

Scots pines – mature and young, planted and self-sown – on the shores of Loch an Eilein

trees are much more hardy than they look. On the right of the road is an enclosure containing red deer, farmed by the estate.

8 **Past Milton Cottage, and before a bridge over the Milton Burn, turn right through a gate and along a track. This descends to another little cottage, then continues through rolling open country, with birch dells and stands of pine, to a lake-shore.** This is Lochan Mor, quite unlike Loch an Eilein because the water is richer in nutrients and therefore in associated plant life. Marsh pennywort, lesser spearwort and a host of sedges and rushes line the shore and there are floating islands of white water lilies. Dragonflies and damselflies patrol the shallows. Lochan Mor began as a natural pool but has been enlarged and stocked with brown trout. For this reason it is on the fishing circuit of ospreys and is as good a place as any (apart from the fish farm loch) to wait in hope of seeing one of these famous birds. The backdrop of mountains and pine forests makes a nice setting for a long vigil. Alternatively, and more sensibly perhaps, continue on your way and

keep a visit to Loch Garten for another day.

9 **The track heads north-east, past some majestic and lonely pines.** There are also a few alien conifers, planted, perhaps, by wealthy landowners who were inclined to experiment with park trees or potential money-spinners. Although the pine-woods have been exploited for centuries, to produce timber for everything from ships' masts to domestic furniture, estate owners over the past 200 years have been keen to try out imports which might grow more quickly or at a better stocking density. Scotland was particularly favoured with such experiments. Fortunately, whilst other trees came and went, the pine remained.

10 **The path forks, at which bear right to a road. Cross this on to a track, leading through more grassy heathland with pines, then across open moorland to a road. This is the B970, at which turn right towards Coylumbridge.**

OSPREYS MADE LOCH GARTEN FAMOUS, BUT THERE IS MORE TO THE FORESTS AND LOCHS OF STRATHSPEY THAN A SINGLE PAIR OF CELEBRITY BIRDS. THE PINEWOODS ON THE LOWER SLOPES OF THE CAIRNGORMS ARE IMMENSELY BEAUTIFUL AND CONTAIN A LOT OF INTERESTING BIRDS AND MAMMALS. SOME OF THESE, SUCH AS THE CRESTED TIT AND THE RED SQUIRREL, ARE QUITE EASY TO SEE. OTHERS, LIKE THE CAPERCAILLIE AND THE PINE MARTEN, ARE ELUSIVE UNLESS YOU KNOW EXACTLY WHERE AND HOW TO LOOK.

THE CALEDONIAN PINEWOODS

The pines of ancient Caledonian forests are quite different from the tall plantation trees of southern Britain. The supporting plant life is unique too, often comprising a shrub layer of juniper, heather and bilberry, together with rare herbs including creeping lady's tresses orchid, twinflower and several species of wintergreen.

Some of Scotland's great pines were reaching maturity before Bonnie Prince Charlie was born, but the Speyside forests have long been exploited for their timber and on many estates these venerable trees, known to foresters as 'granny pines', were left

Pinewoods like these ones by Loch Mallachie attract crested tits and Scottish crossbills

Goldeneye (male)

Loch Garten

Highland
Grid ref. NH 972 185

Royal Society for the Protection of Birds
Approx. 3½ miles (5.6 km). Mainly level walking.

The loch lies off a minor road 1½ miles (2.4 km) east of Boat of Garten. There is a car park on the south side of the road from East Croftmore to Loch Garten. An alternative car park can be found near the osprey hide on Loch Garten's north-east shore. There is an admission charge for visits to the hide for non-members of the RSPB.

The nature reserve consists mainly of old pinewoods with some recent pine plantations. Lochs, streams and moorland add to the habitat range.

Nearby site: *Inish Marshes* – breeding wetland birds and good marsh flora.

---

because they were badly formed and were not worth cutting down. The pinewoods have therefore become a scattered collection of gnarled leviathans in a sea of their straight-grained descendants. There are some recent plantations, otherwise most of the regeneration is natural. Walking through one of the Garten woods for an hour sharpens the senses; the smell of resin and the whisper of the wind through the needles is soon taken for granted, but you still find yourself walking on tiptoe, careful not to tread on a fallen branch, and easily startled by the crash of a cone, dropped by a crossbill or a red squirrel. You are very aware that you share the forest with its inhabitants. This sort of harmony is noticeable in many tracts of ancient woodland but is especially strong here.

BIRDS OF THE LOCHS

The many lochs that lie hidden in the forests of Strathspey are invariably beautiful but are often acidic and poor in nutrients. However, several carry nesting pairs of goldeneyes, and of course, they are the haunt of ospreys.

The Loch Garten ospreys usually arrive at their eyrie in early April and the young are fledged by mid July. This has to be the season to visit Strathspey. Although there are now several dozen other pairs of ospreys nesting in Scotland, there is something very special about the Garten site, where the birds' well-known success story began in 1954.

THE *Walk*

1 From the car park a track leads southwards, beyond a gate and information board, through mature pine woodland. Some of the trees are tall and straight, others thick-set and heavily branched. The Garten woods show considerable evidence of having been selectively felled on several occasions. Having been taken out, the valuable timber was transported to the Spey from where it was floated downstream to sawmills on the coast. The bushes beneath the canopy have survived the comings and goings of the trees and some of the individual juniper and heather clumps are impressively well-formed.

When the track forks, bear right – the temptation is to turn left to the loch shore, but there are better access points a little further along. Continue for several hundred yards (metres), past a low wooded knoll which obscures the loch for a few minutes. The pattern of old and new management varies as you walk south; there is a mosaic of growth with patches of 100-year-old trees and some areas of self-sown regeneration. Dead or dying pines are now left by the RSPB to provide nest-holes for crested tits and redstarts; old stumps stand alongside some recent planting.

2 After the knoll there are views again of the loch, and access to the sedge-lined shore. It is possible to walk along the shore, around several inlets and gravel spurs, and regain the track further south. The loch is wide, and in an east wind this is not a place to linger. The water is stained brown from the peat and there are submerged tree-roots in the shallows. Garten itself does not attract many birds. Greylag geese and occasional family parties of whooper swans are to be seen early in the spring, with congregations of sand martins and swallows a little later, but during the summer there are only black-headed gulls and an occasional mallard or goldeneye to divert your attention from the forest. The ospreys feed on Loch Garten only in certain conditions: the murky water makes it hard for the birds to see the many pike that live in the loch.

3 A path bears right, away from the loch to rejoin the main track. Follow the track as it bears south-west, meandering through pine and juniper and eventually dropping down on to a gravel promontory on the shores of Loch Mallachie. This is a more attractive stretch of water for

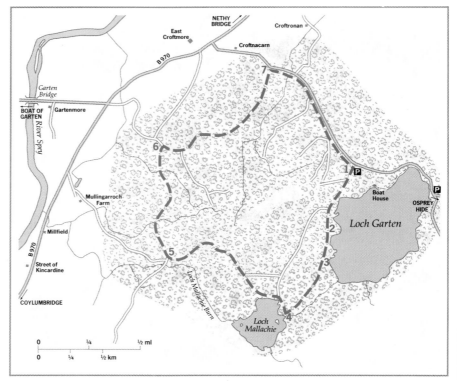

most birds, including ospreys. The water level has been raised recently, restoring the loch to its former level. The boggy shore is worth exploring and there are several good plants to be found, including marsh cinquefoil, heath spotted orchid and bog asphodel. There are bushes of bog myrtle and juniper too; both are aromatic and refreshing to smell – particularly the latter which was once used to flavour gin.

4 Follow the track right, above the loch shore, until there is a fork in the track. Bear left (i.e. straight on, not turning left to keep with the shore). The track bends to the right now, past some good stands of older pines and clearings of saplings. Go through this; the track is now grassy and the clearings have opened out into expanses of moorland. This is black grouse habitat and there is some birch scrub. Tiger beetles and northern eggar moth caterpillars may be sunning themselves along the verge if it is a warm day.

5 At a crossroads, with a bridge to the left, turn right on to a gravel track and continue along this, past recently managed plantations of young pines. There are grassy rides, marshes and ponds to add interest to

this part of the walk. The ponds contain whirligig beetles and palmate newts, and are the home of several northern dragonflies such as the black sympetrum.

6 Eventually the track meets a T-junction, at which turn right, heading east. The plantation is drier here, and there are granite boulders showing through the drifts of glacial gravels. The Cairngorms, which are now behind you, are composed almost exclusively of this hard volcanic rock.

7 After another long walk in a north-easterly direction, the track leads to a T-junction, with a road ahead. Turn right on a track beside the fence and head south-east, past a large pond and on, with the road to your left, until the ground rises and the trees become tall and graceful, back in the older part of the wood. A track then bears right to the car park.

To visit Loch Garten's famous ospreys' eyrie, before or after the walk (a 'must' during the breeding season), walk or drive eastwards along the road that runs along Loch Garten's northern shore. The large wooden hide (charge payable) is on the north-eastern side of the loch and is reached by a short walk from the RSPB's roadside car park.

Otter cubs. Declining in most of Britain, otters still thrive in western Scotland

EIGG IS THE CINDERELLA OF THE INNER HEBRIDES, OVERSHADOWED BY THE SIZE AND REPUTATION OF SOME OF ITS NEIGHBOURS, BUT ONE OF THE MOST BEAUTIFUL. THE 'SMALL ISLES' – THE GROUP TO WHICH EIGG BELONGS – CONSISTS OF A QUARTET OF ISLANDS ALSO INCLUDING CANNA, MUCK AND RHUM.

THE FERRY CROSSING

The journey to the island takes you through some of the most breathtaking scenery in Britain, and the waters around Eigg are feeding grounds for many seabirds, notably guillemots, razorbills and everyone's favourite – puffins. They can often appear clumsy in flight, frantically flapping their wings to get airborne when disturbed on the surface of the sea. The more relaxed individuals wait until the ferry gets that wee bit closer before diving into the safe depths of the Atlantic.

The Manx shearwater is another bird likely to be seen on the crossing. It breeds in burrows in huge numbers on the nearby island of Rhum, although around 100 pairs breed on the cliffs above Cleadale on Eigg. Named from the Isle of Man, where it was recorded breeding in the 11th century, it is most at home on the wing, being extremely clumsy on land. The nearest gannetries are off the Outer Hebrides and off the Ayrshire coast on Ailsa Craig, but gannets are regularly seen from the ferry, diving spectacularly from great heights into the sea for their food.

On the journey to Eigg it is always worth keeping an eye out for the much

Eigg
Inner Hebrides
Grid ref. NM 485 838

Scottish Wildlife Trust (part)
Approx. 4 miles (6.4 km). Relatively easy walking, mostly on tarmac road, with a small incline at Druim an Aoinidh over rocky slopes.

Eigg lies to the south of Skye and about 8 miles (13 km) off the Scottish mainland. Passenger ferries run from Arisaig and Mallaig to Galmisdale, in the south-east corner of Eigg, where the walk begins.

Eigg has a rich and varied wildlife ranging from breeding seabirds to bluebell woods. Habitats include croftland, sheep-grazed pasture, uplands with alpine plants, hazelwood on steep coastal cliffs, mixed woodland, lochans and bogs.

Nearby sites: *Rhum* – National Nature Reserve with red deer, white-tailed eagles, seabird colonies; *Canna* – rocky shore, cliffs, croftland, with seabirds, corncrake; *Ardnamurchan* – attractive sea cliffs with interesting maritime flora and seabirds seen off shore.

Chough

smaller storm petrel, the size of a swift, all black with a square tail and prominent white rump. Somewhat larger is the minke whale, between 23ft (7m) and 36ft (11m) in length and up to 10 tons (10 tonnes) in weight. It is regularly seen in these waters and fortunately for 'whale-watchers' it can be very inquisitive, giving ferry passengers some excellent close views. As you get nearer the island, make a point of scouring the skyline above the dramatic Struidh cliffs of Eigg (to your right) where golden eagles are occasionally seen soaring.

AN SGURR

Eigg is dominated by that remarkable landmark An Sgurr, rising over 1280ft (393m) above sea-level, and standing proud and defiant even when shrouded in mist. An Sgurr is a reminder of the time when powerful volcanic activity created this massive pitchstone lava ridge – one of the most easily identifiable and famous landmarks in the whole of the Hebrides. The spectacular views from the summit take in the three peaks of Rhum, the jagged ridge of Skye's Cuillins and Torridon to the north, Coll, Tiree, Muck, Mull and Ardnamurchan to the south, and even the distant profile of the Outer Hebrides on bright, clear days.

WILDLIFE ON THE ISLAND

Although Eigg is one of the smaller isles of the Hebrides, it has a surprisingly varied landscape. Its wildlife ranges from tiny arctic-alpine plants to majestic golden eagles. The call of the coast is never far away: otters, seals and seabirds may all be seen. To the south of the harbour lies the small, uninhabited Eilean Chathastail or Castle Island. Herring, common, greater and lesser black-backed gulls all breed here, together with greylag geese. These keep guard over the grave of one of the island's previous owners, who chose to be buried on Castle Island in 1913.

Unlike most of the rest of Eigg, the sheltered south-east corner is wooded. A mixture of conifers and broadleaves, planted around a century ago, provides much-needed shelter for birds in one of the most windswept parts of Britain. Not all the woodland is planted, however. Dense stands of hazel scrub hug the slopes below the island's basalt escarpments; some of the hazel stools are of great antiquity and a very rich lichen flora grows on their trunks and branches.

THE *Walk*

1 There are few roads or vehicles on Eigg, but take care. Follow the lower tarmac road which hugs the sheltered Galmisdale Bay. Eider ducks and ducklings swim and feed amongst the seaweed in the bay, fringed by stands of yellow iris, a typical shore plant of western Scotland. The shallow and rapid wing-beat of the common sandpiper is a familiar sight along the bays.

2 Pass the cottage on your left and follow the road up the hill, leaving the bay. Superb views can be had towards An Sgurr. Buzzards circling above add to the dramatic effect.

3 Continue on the tarmac road past the post-boxes. Pause before you reach the moorland to listen for wood warblers in Manse Wood. The damp, heathy ground alongside the road is rich in both plants and insects in summer. The insectivorous pale butterwort and sundew share a place with both four-spotted chaser and golden-ringed dragonflies.

Pass the church, with the hill of An Cruachan facing you in the distance. Birds of open moorland come into their own now – cuckoo, meadow pipit and skylark.

4 Turn right just before the school and make your way back towards the coast. The drumming of snipe is a familiar sound above these boggy pastures. Look out also for twites, the northern equivalent of linnets. Twites are uncommon throughout Europe, but Britain holds a strong population.

5 As you drop down to Kildonnan Bay, take the path to your right at the foot of the hazel-covered cliffs of Druim an Aoinidh. Bluebells and wild garlic flourish under the hazel coppice and aspen. This is another sheltered part of the island – a favourite sunning and feeding slope for small pearl-bordered fritillary, common blue and speckled wood butterflies.

Make your way carefully along the boulder-strewn slopes to the top of the cliff.

An eagle's-eye view of Eigg, showing Kildonnan and the road to Cleadale

6 Pass through a gap in the fence and turn left, following the cliff-top into a grazed sedge pasture. An Sgurr appears again, sharing the stage on this occasion with lovely views to the mainland with the white sands of Morar, and Kildonnan Bay itself. The rocks in the bay are a regular haul-out site for common seals, which can easily be seen sun-bathing.

Carry on down towards Galmisdale Bay, passing through a derelict wall and across a football pitch. Arctic terns occasionally breed on the small headland, Eilean Feòir, so please do not approach this area too closely or the birds may leave their nests, and their young or eggs could be taken by gulls or crows. Remarkable for its long-distance migration, the arctic tern is Britain's most numerous nesting tern, breeding in small (or, in a few instances, very large) colonies mostly around northern coasts.

7 Cross the burn. This is a favourite freshwater bathing site for gulls and kittiwakes, with large numbers of the latter gathering here after breeding.

Take the lower of the two tracks, past Clanranald Pier (built in 1790), back to the jetty. Before boarding the ferry, look out for black guillemots – commonly seen between the pier and Castle Island. This beautiful black seabird, with its red feet, is frequently called by the Old Norse name of tystie. It is the least common of all the auks, breeding among the boulders and crevices of Eigg's coastline. Black guillemots are one of the most sedentary of all our seabirds, and generally stay very close inshore.

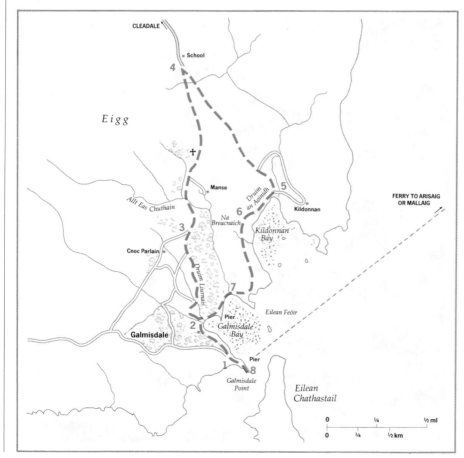

The Quiraing

*The Quiraing's forbidding landforms are like no others in Britain – an unlikely haven for the tiny
plants that gain a foothold in pockets in the basalt*

SKYE IS A SPIRITUAL HOME FOR MANY TRAVELLERS. THE NAME CONJURES A VIVID IMAGE OF TOWERING MOUNTAINS AND ROCKY COASTS, OF SWIRLING CLOUDS AND A JADE OR COBALT SEA. WITH AN AVERAGE RAINFALL AS HIGH AS SKYE'S, A SUNNY DAY IS A PRECIOUS GIFT, BUT ANY VISITOR SHOULD GIVE THE PLACE A SECOND AND THIRD CHANCE. AN EVENING OF BLANKET MISTS AND DRIZZLE IS QUITE LIKELY TO BE FOLLOWED BY A MORNING OF CRYSTAL SKIES AND BREATHTAKING VIEWS.

CUILLINS AND COAST

The most dramatic and dominating mountain blocks of south Skye are the Red Cuillin and the Black Cuillin; they lie adjacent to each other but are quite different, the former made up of domes of granite and the latter a much higher and even more spectacular collection of ridges and craggy peaks of gabbro. The Cuillins provide some of the fiercest and most dangerous walking routes in Britain and should be avoided by all but the fittest. The rewards and the risks are equally great.

Going north past the Red Cuillin, the road skirts the coast, which is typically rocky with small beaches of shell-sand and low headlands. The sea is always interesting: the floating fronds from submerged forests of kelp may hide a seal or even an otter, and seabirds such as gannets and auks fish the Inner Sound in some numbers. North again, with the island of Raasay close inshore to the east, the road follows Glen Varragill down into the town of Portree. Pastures and meadows crowd the fertile valleys and there is some woodland too, but the distant views now are of Trotternish, a northward-pointing peninsula with a spine of basalt dipping to the west.

THE TROTTERNISH RIDGE

Trotternish is circled by a road linking scattered settlements of brightly painted crofts and flower-rich meadows. Inland there is nothing. The black ridge linking The Storr with Beinn Edra and Meall na Suiramach is the longest inland cliff in Britain and was laid down 50 million years ago as volcanic lava. The eastern face of the ridge is sheer, broken by landslips and pinnacles of weathered basalt. The Storr, at the southern end of the ridge, is the most famous landscape feature, but the Quiraing is by far the most inspiring, and is blessed with a direct

The Quiraing

Skye (Inner Hebrides)
Grid ref. NG 440 679

Approx. 5½ miles (8.8 km). Difficult in parts.

The walk, taking in the northern point of the Trotternish ridge to the Quiraing and Sròn Vourlinn, begins from a lay-by and small car park just west of the ridge crest on a side-road above Staffin, about 20 miles (32 km) north of Portree.

Skye is worth a week or two of anyone's time; the scenery is very special. Golden eagles are almost guaranteed, otters are as numerous on the rocky shores as anywhere in Europe (look for them at low tide) and there are some interesting plant communities – particularly on Trotternish. Try to avoid high summer, because of the midges. Rain and mists are almost unavoidable.

Nearby sites: *Strathsuardel* (near Broadford) – limestone pavement and woodland, with an excellent flora; *Balranald, North Uist* – RSPB reserve with breeding waders and corncrakes.

Golden eagle – by no means unlikely here

The long and precipitous Trotternish Ridge

and comparatively easy footpath.

The Quiraing's landscape is one of decaying black columns and screes, a strange scene reminiscent, perhaps, of pictures by Arthur Rackham. Here, as elsewhere along the Trotternish ridge, there has been land-slippage as the basalt has cracked into great slabs the size of office-blocks. These have been weathered into impressive shapes, while the surface of the rock, full of bubbles and encrusted by minerals, has provided a good rooting medium for arctic-alpine plants. These occur especially in nooks and crannies where sheep cannot reach. Notable species to be found include holly fern, mossy cyphel, northern rockcress, moss campion, purple saxifrage and alpine pearlwort.

The Quiraing is also a good site for mountain birds. Trotternish 'regulars' include merlin, peregrine, ring ouzel and rock dove, but most naturalists who visit Skye are also on the lookout for eagles. Perhaps 40 pairs of golden eagles nest on the island, and Trotternish is as good a place as any. However, the birds range widely over their hunting territories and a sighting can never be guaranteed. If you see a large bird of prey it is important to look carefully to check its identity. Not only are buzzards quite common (and they can look much bigger than they really are) but there is also a real chance of seeing a white-tailed eagle. Skye was one of their strongholds in the 19th century, but their numbers dwindled and eventually they died out. Now, after 50 years' absence from Britain, white-tailed eagles have been successfully reintroduced to the island of Rhum, just off Skye's southern coast. Young birds are regular visitors to the neighbouring islands as well as Skye. Most eagle sightings are likely to be golden. However, if the bird is really huge – white-tailed eagles are sometimes likened to a barn-door in flight! – with a heavy head and a short tail, it may be one of the newcomers.

THE OUTER ISLES

Standing on the top of Sròn Vourlinn, at the extreme northerly point of the ridge beyond the Quiraing, it is possible to look out across The Minch to the islands of Harris and Lewis. If the weather has been kind and the Inner Hebrides have inspired you, then it is worth thinking of a visit to the Outer Isles – Harris, North Uist, Benbecula and South Uist. A boat leaves from Uig, a few miles across Trotternish, and a two-hour crossing will carry you to the start of another adventure. Islands can be addictive.

THE *WALK*

1 From the car park cross the road and follow a grassy path north-east, with Maoladh Mór ('the Big Bare Hill') to your left. The route is clear but the ground is marshy in places and it may be necessary to detour slightly to the right to find the best line. This will bring you closer to the edge of the steep scarp slope with spectacular views southward, over two small lochs (Loch Leum na Luirginn and Loch Cleat) and down the main ridge to Beinn Edra. If all this seems familiar then you can thank the power of advertising: the view has appeared on countless television adverts and travel brochures. These may exclude the road and the cemetery in the foreground but it is not so easy to block out the other tell-tale signs of settlement, such as sheep and the rectangular patterns of peat diggings.

The path continues north-east, crossing several clefts where the headwaters of small streams gather to flow eastwards into the River Brogaig. The first cleft, especially, needs care in clambering across. Rocky outcrops in the clefts shelter common upland plants such as wild thyme and butterwort, and the first and most universal of the mountain flowers, the alpine lady's mantle.

2 The path is quite narrow in places and crosses stony scree, so cautious footwork may sometimes be necessary. The face of the main cliff now appears on your left, and the path bears right, continuing north-east below the black cliff-face and making for a gully between two dramatic rock outcrops ahead. To the right is a wonderful view across Skye to the mainland of Wester Ross and Torridon. The landscape closer at hand resembles no other in Britain; it has more in common with Iceland. The approach to the gully or saddle between great black columns of detached rock can be unsettling, like entering a giant gateway. Bird calls echo around the basalt wall: the explosive reel of a wren, perhaps, and the dry stone-clipping call of the wheatear. Occasionally there may be a loud 'kek-kek-kek' from a peregrine flying overhead, followed by a clatter of wings as rock doves make for cover. This might be just the place for an ambush, or an avalanche. However, the only real danger is from missing your footing on the loose ground. The square block to the right, which looks like an upturned bedstead but is called The Prison, can be explored by scrambling up a narrow pathway which leads around its tall pillars to a

The spring-flowering purple saxifrage

good vantage point for views to the north and east.

On the main path, after climbing up the slope of gravel and boulders to the middle of the saddle, there is a much steeper side-path which leads up the scree to the left to a feature called The Needle. The path to it really is daunting and should only be attempted if you are as sure-footed as a goat. At the top there is a fascinating labyrinth of huge black buttresses and deep recesses that defy description. Exploring them takes only a few minutes and leaves a lasting impression. Not far away to the north is a level grassy shelf called The Table – another unique landform, of eerie stillness and some botanic interest. The name 'Quiraing' may refer to this place, and has been variously translated as 'the round cattle fold' or 'the pillared stronghold'.

3 From the saddle between The Prison and The Needle the main path turns northwards, still over weathered scree and beside crumbling rock faces. It is worth looking closely at a shard of basalt; the fine-grained volcanic rock is pock-marked and rotted. When first extruded, the molten lava was full of gas bubbles. Later, these spaces were filled with minerals called zeolites. The basic (i.e. not acidic) nature of the basalt, and the availability of the resulting minerals when weathered, have encouraged the development of an unusually rich flora.

The path crosses a fence and continues north, on the left flank of the valley with a small lochan to the right. Ahead on the skyline is another dramatic basalt outcrop, a steep ridge with buttresses and pinnacles. The

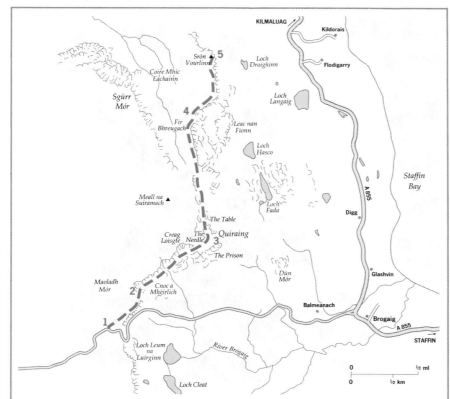

path bears to the left of this, climbing to a low saddle, through a gap in a wall. **The main rock face is still to your left. The path now drops down into a valley.** Here shattered fragments of rock have filled in the split between the ridge and the landslip blocks that now form the crest of the hill to your right. Some of the boulders carry blankets of moss or flowers such as roseroot, alpine lady's mantle and primrose (a summer flower at this latitude). Wheatears, pipits and ring ouzels are the only small birds to be seen here during the summer; ravens and hooded crows patrol the shadows in search of dead lambs or helpless nestlings.

4 In spite of the rugged scenery, the going is now easy. **At the end of the valley is a final rock wall; to the right is a level grassy area but the route instead bears left, up the side of the valley, then zig-zags up to the ridge.** The path is much less clear now as it turns right on the crest and follows the contour north-east on the steep dip slope of the ridge. The mountain to the left is Sgùrr Mór, the last peak of Trotternish; after this the ground levels to soft Jurassic sediments of sandstone and shale, grass-covered and rolling northwards to Rubha Hunish, the far point of Skye. Across the sea are Harris and Lewis, and beyond them the open Atlantic Ocean.

Follow the path as it bears north-wards, keeping well away from the edge. There are views to the south now for the first time, and it is much easier to see how the volcanic flows of lava have split and slipped down on to the underlying Jurassic beds. These are the most dramatic examples of land-slippage in Britain and their images grace many textbooks. They are both beautiful and worrying. How firm is the solid ground on which you now stand? The dark faces of the cliffs are sheer and are covered here and there by drifts of roseroot and other mountain flowers, well out of the

The Quiraing under a suitably brooding sky

reach of sheep and curious naturalists. Binoculars only increase the frustration of not being able to get close enough. To the east, a few hundred yards (metres) from the cliff face, is Loch Langaig, an interesting loch for wildlife, and beyond that is the coast and the little islands of Eilean Flodigarry and Sgeir Eirin.

5 The last point on the ridge is Sròn Vourlinn, from where you can take in a final view of the north Skye panorama before turning back and retracing your steps. Places can look very different when approached from the opposite direction and particular care should be taken not to miss the zig-zag path down into the Valley of Rocks. Otherwise the return route, along the same path, is easy and there will be time to look up to Meall na Suiramach in the hope of seeing an eagle silhouetted against the afternoon sky.

Liathach, one of Torridon's highest peaks

THE TORRIDON HILLS ARE ONE OF THE MOST RUGGED AND SPECTACULAR MOUNTAIN AREAS IN BRITAIN. THEIR LANDSCAPE SHOWS THE UNMISTAKABLE SIGNS OF PAST GLACIATION, WITH ITS 'U'-SHAPED VALLEYS, GLACIAL MORAINES, AND HIGH MOUNTAIN CORRIES CARVED OUT OF THE ANCIENT TORRIDONIAN SANDSTONE, ONE OF THE OLDEST ROCK TYPES.

THE HIGHLANDS BEFORE MAN

Some 12,000 years ago this area was in the grip of a fierce ice age. All but the highest mountains were covered by huge snow- and ice-fields, and glaciers flowed from the high corries, gouging out the valleys below. Few plants and animals could survive.

By 10,000 years ago the climate was warmer and the ice had melted. Gradually, shattered rock and debris deposited by the glaciers were colonised by low-growing lichens, mosses and liverworts, which were able to withstand the arctic conditions. Around 1000 years later the first trees, such as Scots pine, birch and willow, appeared.

The trees spread rapidly as the climate continued to warm and by 6000 years ago the 'Great Wood of Caledon', containing much Scots pine, had spread to cover about 4 million acres (1.6 million hectares). At this time, most of the now bare lower slopes of the Torridon Hills (Liathach, Beinn Eighe, Beinn Alligan and Beinn Dearg) were covered by woodland. The landscape was one of pristine mountain, forest, river and loch, inhabited by brown bear, lynx, wolf, wild boar, red deer, otter, arctic fox and golden eagle.

The Torridon Hills

Highland
Grid ref. NG 869 577

National Trust for Scotland
Approx. 6½ miles (10.5 km). An uphill walk, often on stony paths, with some boggy areas and streams to cross: strong, waterproof footwear and warm, waterproof clothing should be worn. Take food and a map. The walk should not be attempted in winter, nor in poor visibility, except by experienced hillwalkers.

The walk starts 2 miles (3.2 km) west of Torridon on the minor road to Inveralligin. Park in the car park above Torridon House.

The 16,000-acre (6500-hectare) Torridon Estate offers magnificent Highland scenery and a wealth of upland wildlife. Blanket bog and heath cover the hill slopes, supporting red deer and golden eagles as well as the more familiar birds of open country such as meadow pipits. Insectivorous plants, mosses, ferns and dragonflies are highlights of the wetter areas on the walk, while in the woodland small birds such as goldcrests, siskins and wrens enjoy the tree cover.

Nearby site: *Beinn Eighe National Nature Reserve* – ancient pinewood, scree slopes and heather moorland supporting red deer, golden eagles, ptarmigan and other upland wildlife.

Greenshank

FIRE, FARMING AND GRAZING

Neolithic man first colonised this wilderness about 5400 years ago and brought with him fire and primitive crops. Although the numbers of these pastoral nomads in the Highlands were very small, this was when the first clearance of the primeval forest began. By the early 1800s, man had transformed the landscape. The introduction of large numbers of sheep during the Highland clearances of 1810-30, the increase in native red deer populations on the great Victorian sporting estates, and regular deliberate burning of the hill vegetation to improve grazing, all further depleted the ancient forest.

A LOST WILDERNESS

Today all that remains of this once vast woodland are fragments of pine- and birchwood in the steepest valleys and on damp, shaded slopes, and the stumps of ancient trees preserved in the blanket-peat. The woodland vegetation has been replaced by acid grasslands, heaths and bogs. Many of the larger mammals are gone; the red deer, once a woodland animal, has adapted to life on the open hill. Arctic-alpine plants are confined to high pinnacles and rocky ledges where grazing deer and sheep cannot reach them.

Although today's landscape, shaped by man, is no longer a true wilderness, its mountains, bogs, lochs and rivers support characteristic animals, birds and plants, many of which are now

Bogbean – its name belies its delicacy – flourishes in acid bogs and pools, where it frequently becomes the dominant plant

THE WALK

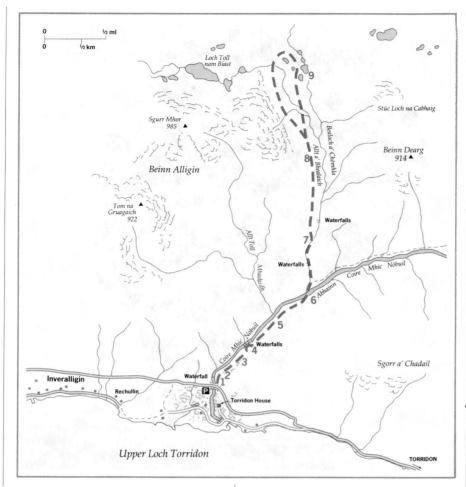

1 From the bridge, the path follows the Abhainn Coire Mhic Nòbuil up the valley. In wet weather the waterfalls fill the gorge with spray, encouraging ferns and mosses. Scots pine, oak, birch, holly, willow, aspen and rowan cling to the walls of the gorge, a vestige of the original native woodland.

2 The woodland along the path was probably planted about 100 years ago, though the trees have now seeded freely. Open ground is dominated by purple moor-grass or by heather and bell heather. In shade, the heather is replaced by blaeberry (bilberry).

3 As you leave the wood, you can see Beinn Alligin on the left, Beinn Dearg ahead and Sgorr a' Chadail, the western summit of Liathach, above on the right. The vegetation here is brightened in summer by the flowers of tormentil, bog asphodel, milkwort and, here and there, heath spotted orchids. Where water drains or lies, bog myrtle is abundant.

4 Make a detour to the footbridge and the waterfall. At the bridge, mountain catsear grows on rocks, and by the waterfall (on the right before the bridge) is a sheltered bank where angelica, honeysuckle, woodrush, golden-rod and marsh hawksbeard grow.

5 Continue along the main path. On summer days you may see the golden-ringed dragonfly, the large heath butterfly or, earlier in the season, the emperor moth. Dragonfly larvae and diving beetles live in the pools, and on damp peat you should find the insectivorous plants sundew and butterwort, and the leafy liverwort *Pleurozia purpurea*.

6 Cross the next footbridge and follow the left fork of the path up the Allt a' Bhealaich. Across the stream is a high, east-facing cliff with more trees, moss and ferns.

7 The path continues steadily uphill. At the next footbridge you will find alpine lady's mantle and lemon-scented fern (which, when bruised, in fact smells of cowslips).

Cross the bridge and follow the path northwards. Beyond the bridge, the vegetation becomes sparser and more stunted; this is the effect of altitude and exposure. In August the hillsides are yellow with deer-sedge: *bhuidhe* (yellow) is common in place-names in the hills. Dwarf juniper grows here and there, especially where the ground is stony.

8 Continue north into Bealach a' Chòmhla. The path extends further than the Ordnance Survey map shows, but becomes indistinct, though it is marked by cairns. In the shelter of the slope, the heather is tall and luxuriant, with blaeberry bushes and an interesting community of mosses and liverworts. Dwarf cornel grows in a small patch of grassy and mossy heath beside the path; look for its white flowers in June and its scarlet berries in August. Look also for the box-like evergreen leaves and black berries of crowberry.

9 After the path ends, continue, following the loop marked on the map. It is easier to proceed to the col across the damp and hummocky ground of the valley than to pick your way among the rocks at the foot of the slope. Take care crossing the streams. The ground is a mosaic of moist hollows with sphagnum moss and cotton-grass, and bare, stony hummocks with sparse, tundra-like vegetation. Notice the abundant cushions of *Racomitrium* moss, pale green when moist but woolly-white in dry weather. On the larger hummocks at the head of the *bealach* (pass) look for bearberry and alpine bearberry, and again for mountain catsear.

The view from the col is particularly fine. The three peaks of Baosbheinn lie to the north across Loch a Bhealaich, and to the east is an arc of sandstone hills, with Meall Ghiubhais beyond.

It is well worth spending an hour or so exploring the moraine and its pools. There are water plants in the larger pools (water lobelia, least bur-reed, bogbean). You will probably see a dipper, and perhaps a red-throated diver or a greenshank. There are little trout, even in some of the smallest pools, and many frogs. This is also a likely spot for seeing an eagle.

Rejoin the path and return by the same route.

SOME OF BRITAIN'S STORMIEST WATERS LIE BETWEEN CAITHNESS AND ORKNEY. THE MEETING OF SEVERAL TIDES AND CURRENTS IN THESE NARROW STRAITS NORTH OF HOLBORN HEAD LEADS TO SEVERE TURBULENCE; ADD THE STRONG WINDS WHICH SEEM TO BLOW PERMANENTLY, AND ALL THE INGREDIENTS FOR ROUGH SEAS ARE PRESENT. THE POWER OF THE SEA HAS ERODED THE ROCK TO FORM SOME DRAMATIC CLIFF SCENERY: MANY STACKS, GULLEYS, ARCHES AND CAVES ARE ARRANGED AROUND THE HEADLAND.

CAITHNESS SANDSTONE

The sandstone of Holborn Head has been quarried since the early 19th century to provide the famous Caithness flagstones; these have been exported to many parts of Britain, including London, to make paving stones. Locally they are used to make the characteristic flagstone fences; in a treeless landscape they make a cheap and efficient material for field boundaries. Where the sandstone is exposed, such as on cliffs and isolated stacks, its horizontal bedding provides superb nesting ledges for a variety of seabirds.

BIRDLIFE

Although these rough waters are a hazard to sailors, they are not as damaging to wildlife as might be expected. Ocean currents bring a constant supply of food, and these cold northern waters are a fertile feeding ground for fish, birds and sea mammals. The steep cliffs, with their multitude of nesting ledges, provide ideal conditions for seabirds, and large colonies are found along this coast.

The larger gulls and kittiwakes are present everywhere, following the fishing boats in and out of harbour and loafing in large flocks on half-tide rocks. Guillemots, razorbills and puffins crowd the rock ledges, crevices and grassy cliff-tops in early summer and fly out to the deeper waters of the Firth to feed on sand eels. Fulmars make use of the updraughts on the cliffs to glide and wheel past their nesting ledges, and the occasional great or arctic skua visits from nesting colonies on Hoy. The largest British seabird of all, the gannet, with a 6ft (1.8m) wingspan, is often seen off shore, although none nests on the mainland cliffs.

In winter a new population of birds appears and, although the nesting

---

Holborn Head
Highland
Grid ref. ND 100 702

Approx. 4½ miles (7.2 km). Mostly easy walking, but some sections are on the edge of sheer cliffs, so take care not to stray off the path, especially in windy weather.

Holborn Head lies about 2 miles (3.2 km) north-west of Thurso. The walk starts from Scrabster Harbour car park.

Holborn Head protects Thurso Bay and Scrabster Harbour from the stormy seas of the Pentland Firth and offers spectacular views of the wild Caithness coastline and the Orkney Islands. Scrabster's busy harbour is used by a fishing fleet and by car ferries to Orkney.

Nearby sites: *Dunnet Bay* – a vast sandy bay, excellent for birdwatching in winter and summer, with cliffs at either end and backed by a huge dune system of great botanical importance; *Dunnet Head* – the northernmost point on the British mainland, with nesting seabirds and flower-covered cliffs in summer, and good birdwatching at most times of the year on the moorland and lochans just inland.

White-fronted goose – seen here on migration

ledges may be deserted, the harbour and Thurso Bay will have many divers, sea ducks and gulls over-wintering. Many of these will be from the far north; Iceland gulls, which actually breed in Greenland, large, pale-winged glaucous gulls, and the tiny and very rare Ross's gull all turn up from time to time. The sandy beaches and exposed rocks are home to large numbers of waders, especially dunlins, turnstones, sanderlings and redshanks, and rock pipits and snow

---

The tiny, bright flowers of Scottish primrose grow only on the coastal turf and dunes of the far north of Scotland

buntings feed along the high-tide line. The flat Caithness landscape is fertile farming land and popular with over-wintering geese and swans; after the grain harvest the fields are visited by flocks of white-fronted geese, ducks and whooper swans. Short-eared owls and hen harriers hunt over the fields and moorlands, and the tiny merlin may also be seen chasing pipits or buntings. Many unusual species turn up here on migration, some coming from as far away as Siberia.

PLANT LIFE

The cliff-tops of Caithness are home to many attractive coastal flowers and at Holborn Head a unique plant was discovered; the Scottish primrose, *Primula scotica*, is found on the north coast and the Orkney Islands, but nowhere else in the world. It is surprisingly small, growing in very short turf near the cliff-edge, and its tiny pink flowers are very difficult to pick out among other cliff-top plants. Thrift, sea campion and scurvy-grass are more widespread coastal flowers and grow in profusion where there is only the thinnest covering of soil. Kidney vetch, birdsfoot trefoil and yellow hawkbits add more colour and attract insects, including butterflies.

THE *Walk*

Holborn Head helps to shelter Scrabster and its lighthouse from the prevailing strong winds

1 From Scrabster Harbour take the harbour road towards the lighthouse. In winter check the inner harbour for gulls, including glaucous gulls, and divers. Further along the road towards the lighthouse, scan the rocks below for waders like turnstones and look for divers and black guillemots in the bay.

2 Just before the lighthouse, take a path to the left, passing through a gate and following the path up the hill. The grassy path then leads along the cliff-top to Holborn Head, crossing two stiles on the way. Check the fields on the left for skylarks and pipits and, in winter, flocks of lapwings and golden plovers. In summer, small numbers of seabirds will be seen on the cliffs below. Kittiwakes are small, dainty gulls with black-tipped wings and a 'kitt-e wake' call. They nest in small, noisy colonies along the cliffs.

3 At the headland are the remains of an Iron Age fort, built in a strategic position overlooking sheer cliffs on one side and an easily defended narrow neck of land on the other. A wall was built across the neck of land as a further defence. From the headland it is possible to look across the Pentland Firth and see large numbers of seabirds in summer; watch fishing boats in case unusual gull species are following them. Pilot whales, white-sided dolphins and common porpoises are seen out to sea and the appearance of a large number of seabirds, especially gannets, feeding excitedly on a shoal of fish is usually a good pointer to where these small whales may appear at the surface.

4 Return to the main cliff-top path from the headland, keeping the caves on the right and the wire fence on the left. Beyond the caves, cross the fence for safety as the cliffs here are steep. Continue heading west, with the wire fence on your right. In summer check the short turf for wild flowers, but be very careful near the edge. The huge rock stack set off from the main cliff is the Clett – a superb nesting habitat for seabirds like fulmars, guillemots and puffins. They are present in summer during the breeding season, but there is so much competition for good nesting ledges that some birds, especially fulmars, visit in the winter to stake a claim to a prime nesting site.

5 Cross the stile in the stone wall and keep straight on towards the quarries; keep to the inland side of the wire fence for safety. Where it is safe to do so, scan the cliffs through binoculars to look for nesting seabirds. Check the rough ground inland on Holborn Hill for short-eared owls and flocks of waders in winter. Look out for the flagstone fences; the pure, damp air of Caithness is ideal for lichens, and many species have colonised these exposed stones.

6 On reaching the gravel road, turn right towards the old quarry; go through the gate and then turn right. This is a good place to look at the Caithness flagstone and see how it was quarried. From the edge of the quarry there is a good view of some sections of the cliff with nesting seabirds. Check the sheltered spots below the cliffs for sea ducks in winter. Take care near the cliff-edge.

7 Return to the gravel road and follow it for about a mile (1.6 km) towards Scrabster. On the right is Scrabster Loch and a number of smaller shallow pools, which may hold birds in winter and summer; try not to disturb nesting birds in the breeding season.

8 The gravel road joins a tarmac road which should be followed as far as a post-box. Turn sharp left here, then right down some steps to reach the main road which leads back to the car park at Scrabster Harbour. Gulls and waders feed along the shore towards Thurso at low tide, and divers and sea ducks may be seen in the bay.

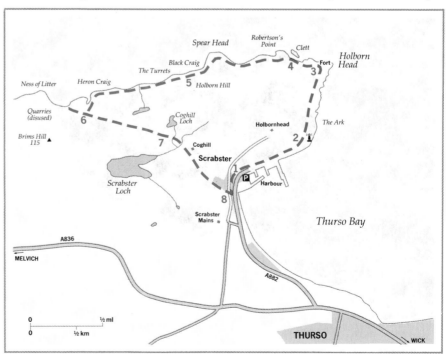

Scaled by climbers, and nested on by fulmars – the almost unbelievable Old Man of Hoy, Britain's highest sea stack

FEW PEOPLE HAVE NOT HEARD OF, OR CANNOT PICTURE, THE OLD MAN OF HOY. SET ON THE WEST COAST OF HOY, THIS DRAMATIC, ERODED PILLAR OF OLD RED SANDSTONE IS A FAMILIAR FEATURE TO ANYONE WHO HAS CAUGHT THE FERRY FROM SCRABSTER TO STROMNESS. THE OLD MAN IS ALSO SOMETIMES VISIBLE FROM THE MAINLAND.

THE SEABIRD CLIFFS

The Old Man of Hoy, a 374ft (138m) stack, is part of a dramatic cliff wall which runs for 3¾ miles (6km) along the west coast of Hoy. Rising to 1115ft (340m) at St John's Head, the area provides a stunning setting for large numbers of breeding seabirds, while inland, the moorland is home to some of Britain's most important colonies of upland breeding birds.

The puffin – our most familiar and endearing seabird – is a common sight

Berry-bearing Plants

The moorland of North Hoy comprises hardy, low-growing shrubs, many of which produce luscious-looking berries, mostly red or black, in the autumn. Species with black berries include crowberry, Alpine bearberry and bog bilberry. Cowberry produces red berries.

North Hoy

Orkney
Grid ref. ND 203 992

Royal Society for the Protection of Birds
Approx. 8½ miles (13.6 km). Rather difficult walking. Very steep in places, with precipitous and crumbly cliffs. Stout footwear and sensible wet-weather clothing essential. Be careful to keep well away from the cliff-edge.

The walk is along Orkney's most westerly coast, in north-west Hoy. A passenger ferry runs from Stromness on Orkney Mainland to Moaness on Hoy; a car ferry runs from Houton on Orkney Mainland to Lyness on Hoy. There is ample parking in Rackwick, reached by a minor road which heads west off the B9047 at Bay of Quoys.

In addition to one of Britain's most famous landmarks – the Old Man of Hoy – this walk takes in magnificent cliff scenery, and moorland rich in vegetation, with a wealth of breeding upland birds.

Nearby sites: *Birsay Moors & Cottasgarth* – heather moorland with associated breeding birds; *Marwick Head* – breeding seabirds; *Yesnaby Cliffs* – magnificent sea cliffs and Scottish primrose; *North Hill, Papa Westray* – rocky shore, coastal heath, excellent for birds in summer, Britain's largest colony of Arctic terns.

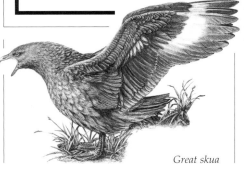

Great skua

in the breeding season along the cliffs of north Hoy. With their neat black and white plumage and colourful beaks, puffins always look faintly comical. They nest in burrows in the cliffs, and in June and July can be seen arriving with beaks full of fish to feed to their hungry offspring. Razorbills, guillemots and kittiwakes all breed on the ledges far below, and fulmars and rock doves are a familiar sight, sometimes flying by at eye level. When trying to watch seabirds on the cliffs, never attempt to look over the edge, but rather find a spot where you can scan along the cliffs with your binoculars. The worn, grassy slopes near the cliff-edge can be slippery.

Peregrines also grace the cliffs of Hoy. These dashing falcons can occasionally be seen overhead, and lucky observers may even witness a 'stoop' as the bird plunges downwards in pursuit of a rock dove. Further inland, great black-backed gulls nest in colonies, their droppings and trampling encouraging rich growths of sorrel and red campion.

MOORLAND BIRDS ON HOY

The skuas are without doubt the most characteristic of Hoy's moorland birds. Great skuas, of which over 1500 pairs breed on Hoy, are large, brown gull-like birds which are extremely aggressive to intruders. They are pirates, forcing other seabirds to disgorge their last meal, and even taking puffins and the young of other seabirds. The more elegant arctic skua is also present on the cliff-top moorland. Two colour phases are seen, one a uniform brown colour and the other with a pale breast. Red-throated divers breed on isolated moorland lochans further inland. These elegant birds fly to the sea to feed and can sometimes be seen returning, carrying fish to their youngsters. They are very susceptible to disturbance and must be left alone.

PLANTS OF THE MOORLAND

The heather and grassy moorland which cloaks north Hoy is one of the finest examples of this habitat in Britain. Typical species include ling, whose pale lilac sprays of flowers are at their best from June to August. Alpine bearberry, whose pale pink flowers produce red berries later in the season, and black bearberry are also common. The black berries of the latter species could be confused with those of crowberry, which grows in a prostrate form and has smaller leaves. Patches of dwarf willow can also be seen, and the area as a whole is renowned for the abundance and variety of lichens that it supports.

THE *W*ALK

1 **From Rackwick, walk down to the beach at Rackwick Bay.** Search the shore for marine life and scan for gulls, which also bathe and preen on a nearby pool, and waders. Towards dusk in the summer months, Manx shearwaters, which breed in burrows on north Hoy, may gather off shore in groups known as 'rafts'. They fly, with wings held stiffly, in long lines close to the water.

Return to the car park and continue up the road, turning left towards the Outdoor Centre.

2 **The path contours around the hillside (look for heath spotted orchids) and climbs steeply in places. Take great care along parts of the path, since the hillside is steep, and the track and vegetation alongside frequently wet and slippery.** Look for stonechats and the occasional small party of twites. This bird is the northern equivalent of the more familiar linnet and has a pale bill and pinkish rump, visible in flight. Continue across the open moorland, looking for plants such as ling and bearberry. You should see your first skuas on this stretch as well as great black-backed gulls around the Loch of Stourdale to your left.

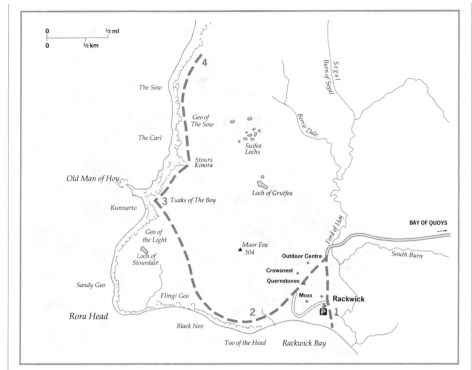

The steep cliffs of St John's Head

3 **At the Old Man of Hoy, pause to admire the impressive sandstone stack. Although you can walk right to the cliff-edge to view it, this could be dangerous. Better overall views are had a few hundred yards** (metres) further south or north, where it can be seen in relation to the cliff as a whole. Seabirds are numerous along this part of the cliff. Fulmars and kittiwakes sometimes fly by at eye level, riding the updraughts of the sheer rock face. The calls of the kittiwakes – from which the bird gets its name – echo from below. Also look for rock doves, peregrines and more distant guillemots and razorbills on the rocks below. The heather moorland in the area around the Old Man of Hoy is outstanding and full of berry-bearing dwarf shrubs and lichens.

4 **Continue along the coast, heading northwards, keeping well away from the cliff-edge and exercising extreme caution at all times.** Great skuas are commonly seen along this stretch of the walk. They nest among the moorland vegetation and are hostile to human intruders in their territory. Aerial attacks are frequent if you linger too long in the vicinity of a nest, so take heed of the bird's alarm and depart. Keep a look out for arctic skuas, which also nest on the moorland. The best views of St John's Head, often shrouded in mist, are from the area to the south of the highest point.

Retrace your steps back along the path to Rackwick. Pause at frequent intervals to admire the view, study the ground vegetation and look for birds.

The Black Guillemot

The black guillemot – a member of the auk family – is one of our most elegant seabirds. The black plumage is set off by the striking white wing panels and the orange-red feet. When the bird calls, it shows a bright red gape. Black guillemots – or tysties, as they are known in Scotland – nest under boulders. Unusually for auks, they lay two eggs and the young do not fledge until quite late in the summer. In winter plumage, the black guillemot becomes mottled grey and white in appearance but the white wing panels, contrasting with the dark wings, are still prominent.

EVEN BY SHETLAND STANDARDS, THE ISLAND OF NOSS IS REMOTE. ITS COMPARATIVE ISOLATION HAS ENABLED THE ISLAND'S OUTSTANDING SEABIRD COMMUNITIES TO THRIVE LARGELY UNAFFECTED BY THE INFLUENCE OF MAN. AT ONE TIME, IN THE NOT TOO DISTANT PAST, TRAVELLING TO NOSS WOULD HAVE REQUIRED CONSIDERABLE PLANNING AND EFFORT, BUT NOWADAYS – WEATHER PERMITTING – THE ISLAND IS EASIER TO REACH.

A UNIQUE LANDMARK

Noss is one of the most distinctive and memorable landmarks to greet the eye as you approach Lerwick by ferry from the south. In relief, the island looks like a huge wedge emerging from the sea. From close to sea-level in the west, it rises towards the east and at Noss Head the sheer cliffs drop almost 600ft (180m) straight to the sea.

THE SEABIRD COLONIES

Noss is justifiably best known for its seabirds. The range of breeding habitats encourages a wide variety of species. Their numbers are immense and almost all are indifferent to the presence of man, providing wonderful viewing and photographic opportunities.

Some 30,000 guillemots nest on rock ledges, along with about 7000 pairs of gannets and about 10,000 kittiwakes. Pairs of fulmars cackle from sheltered ledges, and razorbills emerge from nest sites in rock crevices and beneath boulders. Puffins, when not visiting their burrows, relax close to the path, eyeing visitors with apparent curiosity and disdain. Sometimes their composure is such that they even nod off to sleep in front of you. Noss is also an excellent spot to see black guillemots at close range; visitors can often see their bright red gapes as they call to one another.

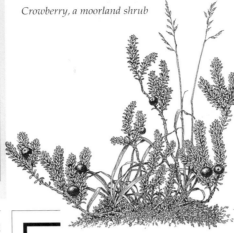

Crowberry, a moorland shrub

Noss

Shetland
Grid ref. HU 521 409

Nature Conservancy Council
Approx. 5 miles (8 km). Steep in places; stout shoes essential.

The Isle of Noss is separated by Noss Sound from Bressay, which itself lies across Bressay Sound from Mainland Shetland. There is a regular ferry service from Lerwick to Bressay, and the Nature Conservancy Council operates a small ferry from Bressay to Noss in summer, when the warden is on the island. The ferry operates at his discretion, subject to suitable tide and weather conditions, so the service can be irregular at times. Check in advance with the Shetland Tourist Office or the NCC. When you arrive on Bressay, drive across the island and park in the car park beyond Ullins Water. There is a fee for landing on Noss, and visitors must keep strictly to the designated routes to avoid disturbing nesting birds.

Noss National Nature Reserve combines superb cliff scenery with one of the most outstanding seabird colonies in Britain – great skuas, puffins, fulmars, black guillemots and many other species.

Nearby sites: *Hermaness* – northernmost point of British Isles, with magnificent views and huge seabird colonies; *Fetlar RSPB Reserve* – no access to main part of reserve during breeding season, but still a chance of seeing snowy owl and red-necked phalarope.

With this abundance of breeding birds, predators and scavengers also thrive. Great black-backed gulls and great skuas take their toll of puffins and guillemots as well as eggs and nestlings of other species, and newly fledged kittiwakes. The great skuas, known to Shetlanders as 'bonxies', also attack gannets as they fly in to their nesting ledges with fish. The skua's intention is not to kill the gannet, but rather to force it to regurgitate its last meal – an approach which rarely fails.

CREATURES OF SEA AND SHORE

Although the abundance of nesting sites on Noss is an important reason for the island's large populations of breeding seabirds, these birds would not thrive without the rich marine life in the seas around Shetland. All the birds depend on this in one way or another. Marine life around the shores is equally abundant. The rocks are cloaked in rich growths of seaweeds and, at low tide, sea anemones, barnacles, limpets, periwinkles, starfish and even sea-urchins can be found by careful searching.

Occasionally, observant visitors may find piles of broken sea-urchin shells above the tide line. This could be a sign that you are in an otter's territory. These engaging mammals are quite common here and on other islands in the Shetlands, providing regular sightings. Porpoises frequent Noss Sound, and the shore is also home to grey seals, whose moaning calls can be heard above the crashing waves.

Black guillemot or tystie – remarkably striking in its breeding plumage

1 Having reached the parking spot near Ullins Water on Bressay, walk east down the track to the departure point for the Noss ferry. While waiting for the ferry, scan Noss Sound for eiders, red-throated divers, porpoises and seals, and the shoreline for otters.

2 After the short crossing, the ferry will land you at Gungstie. Here you will be met by the NCC warden, who will collect a visitor's fee and give an introduction to the island. From the information centre, walk east, then follow the southern shores of Noss. The rest of the walk also follows the perimeter of the island and is well trodden and obvious along its length. The stone walls are covered in lichens and mosses which testify to the purity of the air. Twites sometimes perch on the walls and Shetland wrens search crevices for insects.

3 The path runs along the eastern shore of the Voe of the Mels. Look for family parties of eiders on the waters below. Fulmars nest on the cliff-faces and often ride up-draughts of wind. These masters of flight often glide past visitors at eye level. Do not stray too close to their nests, however, because both adults and young can regurgitate the contents of their crops and propel half-digested fish or evil-smelling oil to a distance of some 6ft (2m) – with considerable accuracy!

4 Continue along the Point of Hovie to the Holm of Noss (commonly known as Cradle Holm). From here on, you will begin to notice

Several thousand gannets breed in this noisy colony on the sheer cliffs at the Noup of Noss, the island's highest point

seabirds in flight and will certainly smell them. Great skuas dive-bomb visitors who stray into their nesting territory, so do not linger if the birds seem disturbed. Thrift, sea campion and spring squill grow beside the path.

5 The path climbs up the cliff-top edge of the Hill of Setter. Numerous puffins can be seen near to their burrow entrances or resting on the rocks and old stone walls. Others fly into the colonies with beaks full of

small fish for their young: great skuas and great black-backed gulls, however, are never far away and are ever-alert for a free meal.

6 Reach the Noup of Noss. Here, at the island's most dramatic and famous viewpoint, sit for a while and scan the vertical cliffs beyond. *Take great care near the cliff-edge.* Thousands of gannets nest below and are constantly coming and going with food. By August, the young birds in the nest are nearly as large as the adults. Guillemot and kittiwake breeding ledges can also be seen, together with puffins and great skuas.

7 Continue north along the cliff-top path as it descends towards The Cletters. Pause to watch seabirds at appropriate points.

8 Follow the path along the North Croo. Here, look for black guillemots standing about on the rocks. These birds nest underneath the boulders between the path and the cliff-edge, so do not stray off the path. Rock pipits share the same nesting habitat. As you pass rocky gullies on your right, look for lush growths of scurvy-grass, roseroot and Scots lovage.

9 Return to the ferry point. On the approach, look for rabbits which emerge from their burrows to feed, especially in the late afternoon.

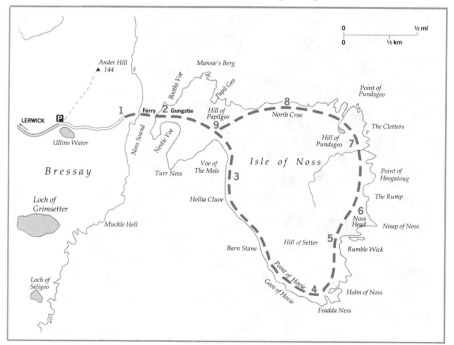

Index

Index of Sites
W: Walk

Index of Species and Habitats

W: Walk

ACKNOWLEDGEMENTS

The Automobile Association would like to thank the following photographers, libraries and associations for their assistance in the preparation of this book.

J & C BORD 47i Moel Famau

TONY HOPKINS 79i Gatekeeper, 87i Pinnacles, Farne Islands

TOM MACKIE *Cover* Country lane with bluebells

C MOLYNEUX 41ii Pen-y-Fan

NATURE CONSERVANCY COUNCIL 54i Short Wood

NATURE PHOTOGRAPHERS LTD *Cover* Kingfisher (H Clark), 1 Summer meadow (P R Sterry), 2 Waste ground flowers (D Washington), 6 Greater stitchwort (P R Sterry), 9 Golden eagle (F V Blackburn), Wood anemone (B Burbidge), 10 Puffins (P R Sterry), 11 Gt willowherb (J L Hyett), 12 Orange tip, 13 Speckled bush-cricket (P R Sterry), 14 Red deer stag (W S Paton), 1i Painted Lady, 2i Land's End (P R Sterry), 2ii Coastal heath (A J Cleave), 3ii The Lizard (P R Sterry), 4i Grey seal (D A Smith), 4ii Sandy gully, 5i Common blenny (A J Cleave), 5ii Start Point (P R Sterry), 6i, 6ii Elberry Cove, 7i Teign Valley (A J Cleave), 7ii Wood mouse, 8i Common field grasshopper (P R Sterry), 8ii Gt Haldon, 9i Exe estuary (A J Cleave), 9ii Flowering rush (J L Hyett), 10i Lundy cabbage, 10ii Thrift (A J Cleave), 11i Hartland Point (P R Sterry), 12i Sea stock (B Burbidge), 12ii Braunton Burrows (A J Cleave), 13i Common hair moss (B Burbidge), 14i Cheddar pink, 14ii Scrub & grasses (A J Cleave), 15i Marsh marigold (P R Sterry), 15ii Fritillaries (R Bush), 16i Portland (A J Cleave), 16ii Ringlet (E A Janes), 17ii Lulworth skipper (P R Sterry), 18i Dartford warbler (F V Blackburn), 18ii Studland Heath (S C Bisserott), 19i Sainfoin (C Grey-Wilson), 19ii Martin Down (P R Sterry), 20ii Gorse (B Burbidge), 20iii Large marsh grasshopper, 21i Golden samphire (P R Sterry), 21ii Old salt pans (A J Cleave), 22i Wood-sorrel (P R Sterry), 22ii Gt spotted woodpecker (M K Walker), 23i Silver-washed fritillary (F V Blackburn), 23i Yews, 23ii Wild daffodils, 24i Redshank, 24ii Mudflats (P R Sterry), 25ii Primrose (E A Janes), 26ii Common lizard (C B Carver), 27i Mandarin (R J Chandler), 27ii Virginia Water (P R Sterry), 28i Purple emperor (F V Blackburn), 29i Gt grey shrike (R Tidman), Ashdown Forest (P R Sterry), 29ii Silver-studded blue (F V Blackburn), 30ii Cuckmere River (N A Callow), 31i Rye Harbour (P R Sterry), 33i Nightingale (F V Blackburn), 33ii Broom, 34i Stodmarsh (P R Sterry), 34ii Gt Spearwort (A Wharton), 35i Skomer, 35ii Sea campion, 37i Bosherston Ponds, 37ii Kingfisher, 38i Early purple orchid, Pearl-bordered fritillary, 39i Dunes (P R Sterry), 39ii Ruddy sympetrum (K D Wilson), 40i Oak Wood, 40ii Waterfall (P R Sterry), 41i Meadow brown (N Phelps-Brown), 42iii Marsh cinquefoils, 43i English stonecrop, 43ii S Stack cliffs (P R Sterry), 44iii Moss campion (C Grey-Wilson), 45i Aber Falls (A J Cleave), 45ii Coal tit (P J Newman), 48iii Guelder rose (R Bush), 49i Oaks (E A Janes), 50i Mistletoe (F V Blackburn), 50ii Small-leaved lime (A J Cleave), 52ii Spotted flycatcher (M K Walker), 53i Gt crested grebe (C B Carver), 54ii Black hairstreak (L G Jessup), 55i Adder (C B Carver), 56i Coombes Valley (A J Cleave), 56ii Badger (O Newman), 57i Meadow cranesbill (P R Sterry), 58iv Lathkill Dale (R O Bush), 59ii Ringed plover (H Clark), 60i Kinder Scout (A J Cleave), 60ii Golden plover (P J Newman), 61i Mountain hare (H Miles), 61ii Ladybower Res. (P R Sterry), 62ii Birch polypore (E A Janes), 63ii Pasque flower, 64ii Yellow flag (P R Sterry), 64iii Long-eared owl (R Tidman), 66ii Essex skipper (P R Sterry), 67i Musk mallow (R Bush), 68ii Pintail, 69i Sea aster (P R Sterry), 70ii Swallowtail (R Bush), 71i Avocet (J F Reynolds), 71ii Titchwell (E A Janes), 72i Holkham Wells woods (A J Cleave), 72ii Hawk-moth caterpillar (R Tidman), 73i Cley mill (R Tidman), 73ii Whimbrel (P R Sterry), 74ii Natterjack toad (R Tidman), 75i Sea holly (R Bush), 75ii Spurn Head, 76i Ash wood, 76ii Malham Tarn, 77ii Brittle bladder fern, 78ii Arnside Knott (A J Cleave), 78i High brown fritillary, 79iii Alpine lady's mantle (R Bush), 80i Borrowdale (D Bonsall), 81i Spring gentian (B Burbidge), 82ii lapwing (M K Walker), 83i Farndale (A J Cleave), 83i Wild daffodil (P R Sterry), 83ii Fox (O Newman), 84i Bempton Cliffs (A J Cleave), 84ii Bempton Cliffs (E A Janes), 85i Robin Hood's Bay (A J Cleave), 85ii Whinchat (D Bonsall), 86i Herb Paris (P R Sterry), 86ii Wood anemone (A J Cleave), 90i Ragged robin, 92i St Abb's Head, guillemot, 93iii Hoof fungus (P R Sterry), 95i Otter cubs (H Miles), 95ii Eigg (C R Mylne), 96iii Purple saxifrage (R Bush), 97i Liathach (C Mylne), 97i Bog bean (B Burbidge), Greenshank (K J Carlson), 98i Scottish primrose (R Bush), 99i Old Man of Hoy, 99ii St John's Head, 100i Black guillemot, 100ii Gannet colony (P R Sterry)

NATIONAL POWER 6 Rugeley Field Study Centre, Roesel's bush cricket, 7 Hogweed, Padiham, Small tortoiseshell, Field bindweed (P R Sterry)

P RIGBY 89i & ii Caerlaverock

All remaining pictures are held in the association's library (**AA PHOTO LIBRARY**) with contributions from:

P BAKER 10 Seven Sisters, **J BEAZLEY** 8 Dowel Dale, **M BIRKITT** 63i Newmarket, **D CORRANCE** 91i Views from Arthur's Seat, **V GREAVES** 51i British Camp, 52i Wyre Forest, 53ii Keeper's Pool, 55i Sherbrook Valley, **D HARDLEY** 14 Five Sisters of Kintail, **TONY HOPKINS** 12 Lathkill, 13 Devil's Punchbowl, 1i Gt Pool, Tresco, 1ii Borough Farm, 1iii Gimble Porth, 1iv Farm fields, 3i The Horse, 17i Winspit, 17iii Dancing Ledge & Durlston Head, 17iv St Aldhelm's Head, 20i New Forest, 20iv Butts Lawn, 25i Bedham, 25iii Crimbourne Farm, 25iv Thursley Common, 26i Thursley Common, 26iii Track, Thursley Common, 26iv Marsh area, Thursley, 30i Seven Sisters, 32i Downland, 32ii Devil's Kneading Trough, 42i Cors Caron, 42iv Afon Teifi, 44i & 44iv Llyn Idwal, 48i View from Symonds Yat, 48iv Wye Gorge, 58i, 58ii, 58iii Lathkill Dale, 59i Gibraltar Point, 64i, 64ii & 64iv Wicken Fen, 65i, 65iii & 65iv Bradfield Woods, 66i Walberswick windpump, 66iii Walberswick heath, 66iv Walberswick reedbeds, 67i & 67ii E Wretham, 68i Flooded Washes, 73i, 73iii Cley Marshes, 74i Ainsdale dunes, 77i Souther Scales Scar, 77iii Ashwood, 77iv Ribblesdale, 79i Wast Water, 81i Low Force pastures, High Force, 88iii Holy Island, 88iv Lindisfarne mudflats, 93i & 93iv Rothiemurchus forest, 94i L Mallachie, 96i The Quiraing, 96ii Trotternish Ridge, 96iv The Quiraing, 98i Scrabster, **S & O MATHEWS** 13i Valley of the Rocks, 28i Box Hill, 73i Breydon Water, 70i Hickling Broad, 82i Muker, 87i Farne Islands, R Newton 46i Gt Orme, 90i Corra Linn, **T SOUTER** 11 R Ant, How Hill, **R SURMAN** 57ii Dovedale, **H WILLIAMS** 36i St David's Head